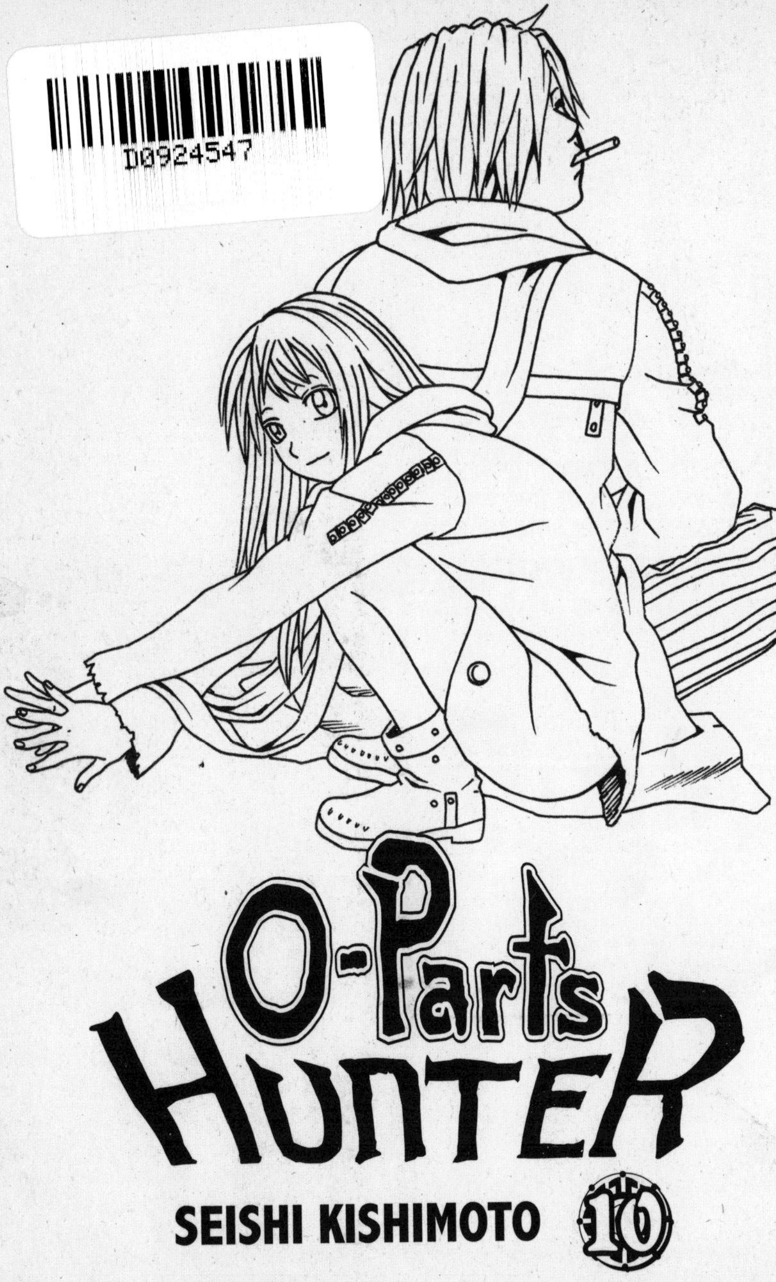

O-Parts HUNTER

SEISHI KISHIMOTO

10

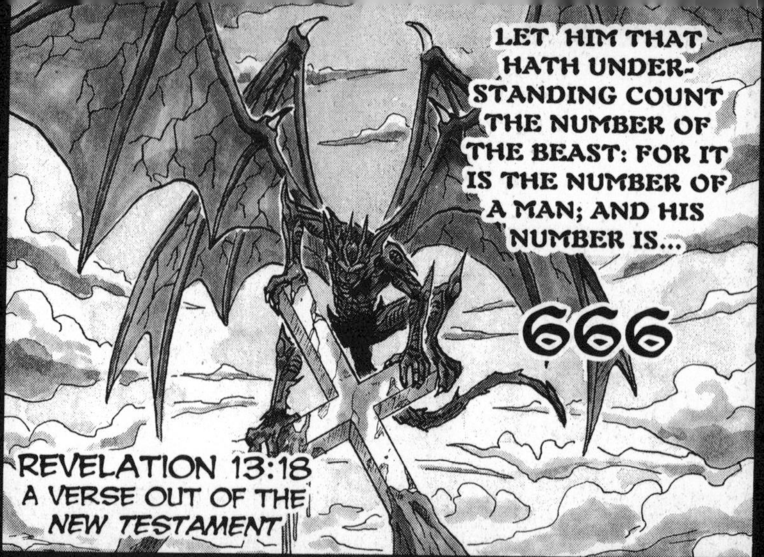
LET HIM THAT HATH UNDER-STANDING COUNT THE NUMBER OF THE BEAST: FOR IT IS THE NUMBER OF A MAN; AND HIS NUMBER IS...
666
REVELATION 13:18
A VERSE OUT OF THE *NEW TESTAMENT*

O-Parts Hunter

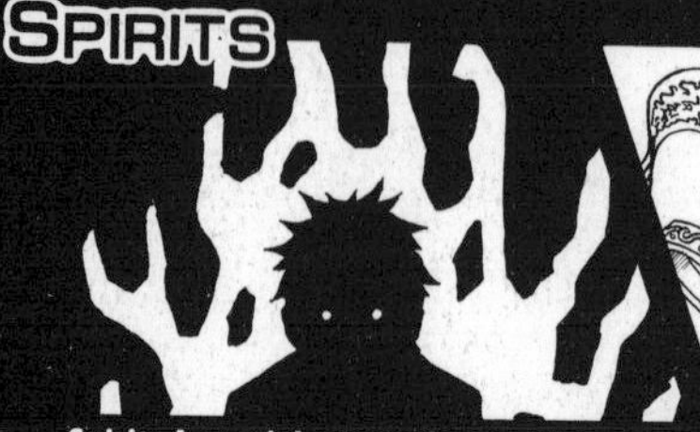
SPIRITS

Spirit: A special energy force which only the O.P.T.s have. The amount of Spirit they have within them determines how strong of an O.P.T. they are.

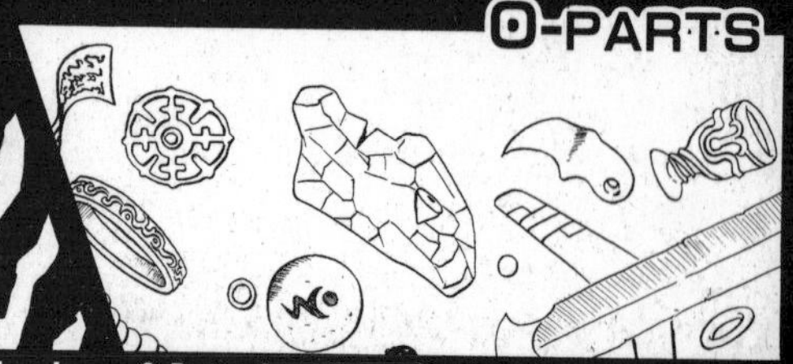
O-PARTS

O-Parts: Amazing artifacts with mystical powers left from an ancient civilization. They have been excavated from various ruins around the world. Depending on their Effects, O-Parts are given a rank from E to SS within a seven-tiered system.

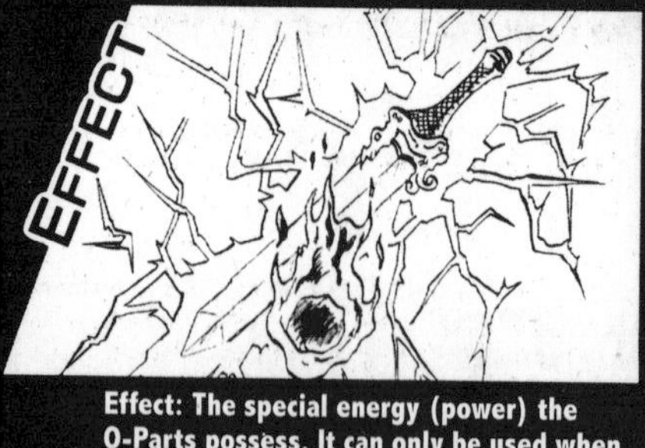
EFFECT

Effect: The special energy (power) the O-Parts possess. It can only be used when an O.P.T. sends his Spirit into an O-Part.

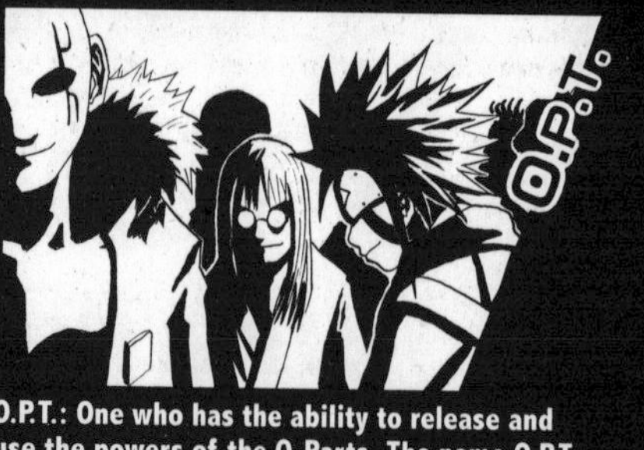
O.P.T.

O.P.T.: One who has the ability to release and use the powers of the O-Parts. The name O.P.T. is an abbreviated form of O-Part Tactician.

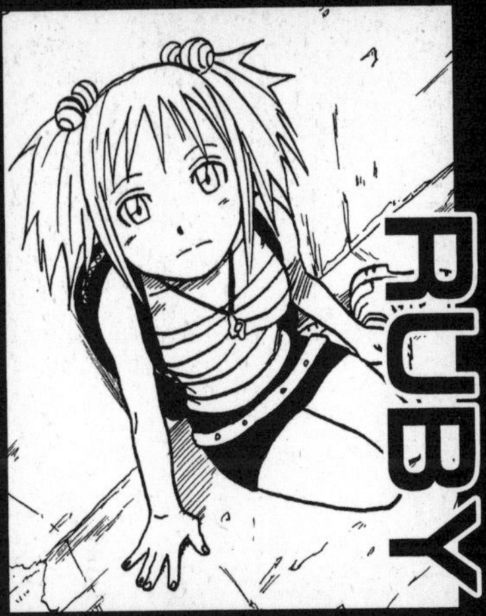
RUBY

Ruby
A treasure hunter who can decipher ancient texts. She meets Jio during her search for a legendary O-Part.

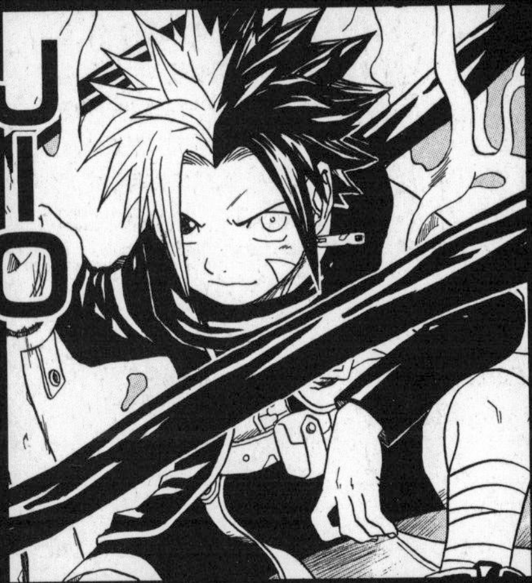
JIO

Jio Freed
A wild O.P.T. boy whose dream is world domination! He has been emotionally damaged by his experiences in the past, but is still gung-ho about his new adventures! O-Part: New Zero-shiki (Rank B)
Effect: Triple (Increasing power by a factor of three)

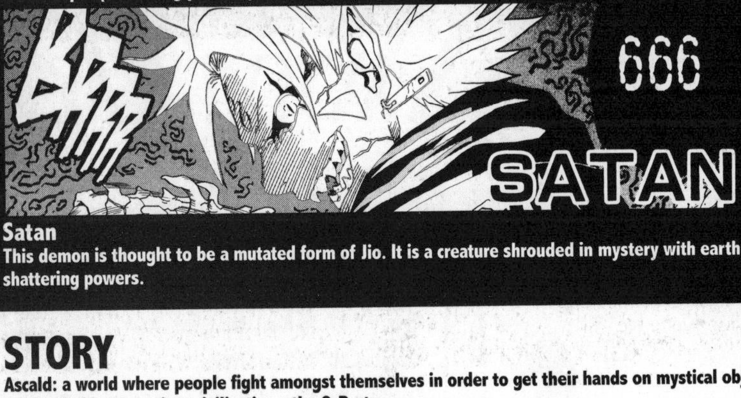
666
SATAN

Satan
This demon is thought to be a mutated form of Jio. It is a creature shrouded in mystery with earth-shattering powers.

STORY

Ascald: a world where people fight amongst themselves in order to get their hands on mystical objects left behind by an ancient civilization...the O-Parts.

In that world, a monster that strikes fear into the hearts of the strongest of men is rumored to exist. Those who have seen the monster all tell of the same thing–that the number of the beast, 666, is engraved on its forehead.

***

Jio, an O.P.T. boy who wants to rule the world, travels the globe with Ball, a novice O.P.T., Kirin, a mentor figure with a penchant for pickles, and Ruby, a girl searching for a legendary O-Part and her missing father. On a quest to find the Kabbalah before the Stea Goverment can use it for world domination, our heroes meet Cross, a young but formidable O.P.T. who has hunted Satan all his life. Cross doesn't recognize Satan in Jio, and the two part ways...but then Jio's team stumbles onto the city of Rock Bird, where Olympia, a deadly world tournament for O.P.T.s, is being held. Jio and Ball barely beat their opponents in the first round, and the worst is yet to come...

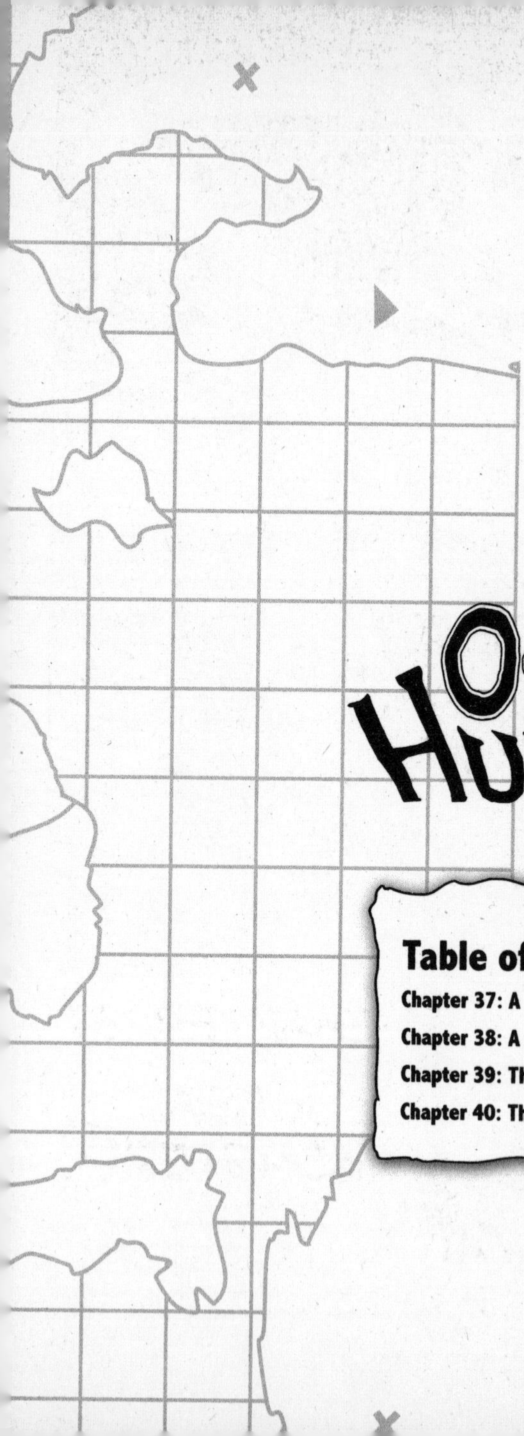

O-Parts Hunter

10

Table of Contents

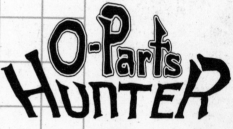

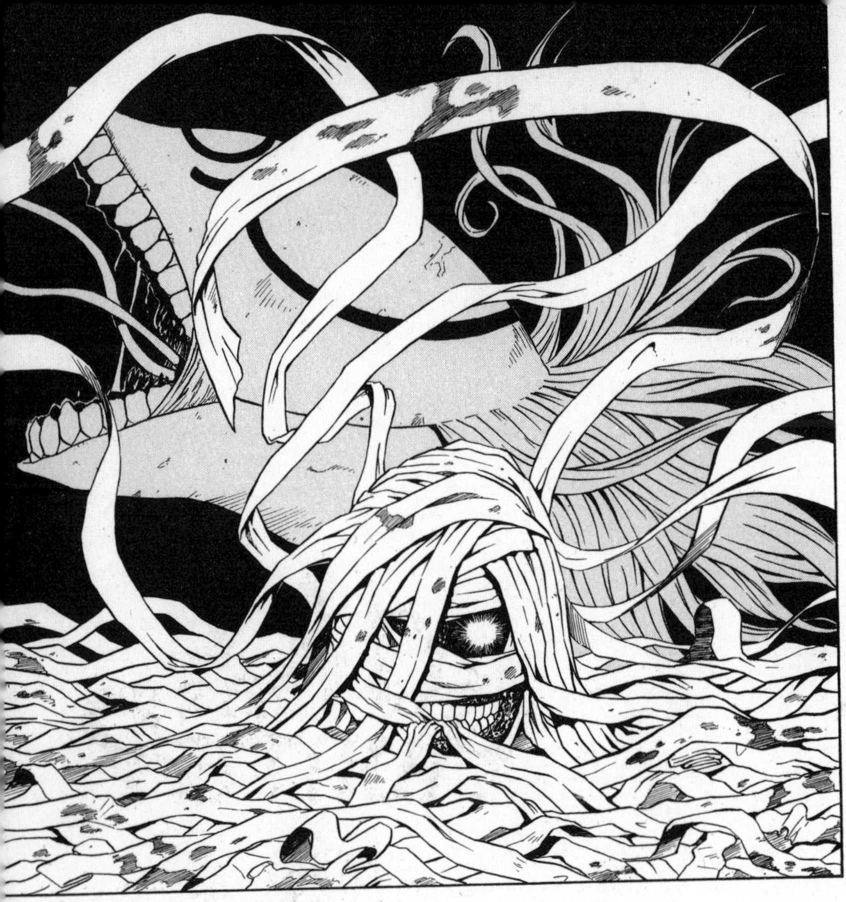

CHAPTER 37
A REAL MONSTER ①

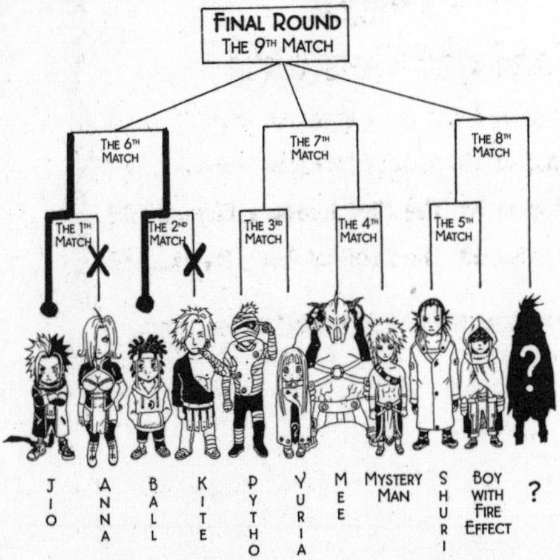
FINAL ROUND
THE 9TH MATCH
THE 6TH MATCH
THE 7TH MATCH
THE 8TH MATCH
THE 1TH MATCH
THE 2ND MATCH
THE 3RD MATCH
THE 4TH MATCH
THE 5TH MATCH
JIO
ANNA
BALL
KITE
PYTHON
YURIA
MEE
MYSTERY MAN
SHURI
BOY WITH FIRE EFFECT
?

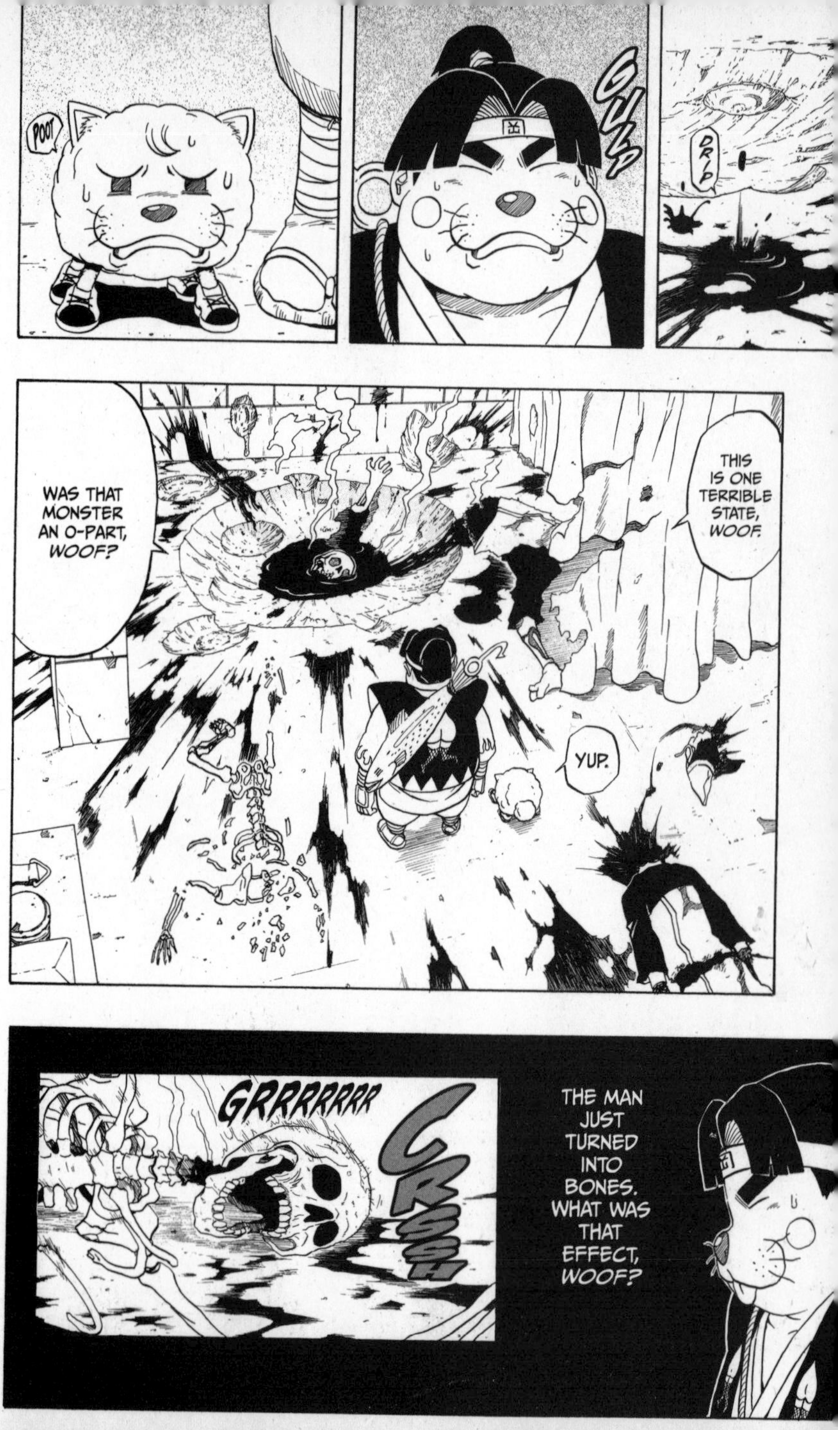
DRIP
GULP
POOT
THIS IS ONE TERRIBLE STATE, WOOF.
WAS THAT MONSTER AN O-PART, WOOF?
YUP.
THE MAN JUST TURNED INTO BONES. WHAT WAS THAT EFFECT, WOOF?
GRRRRRRR
CRSSH

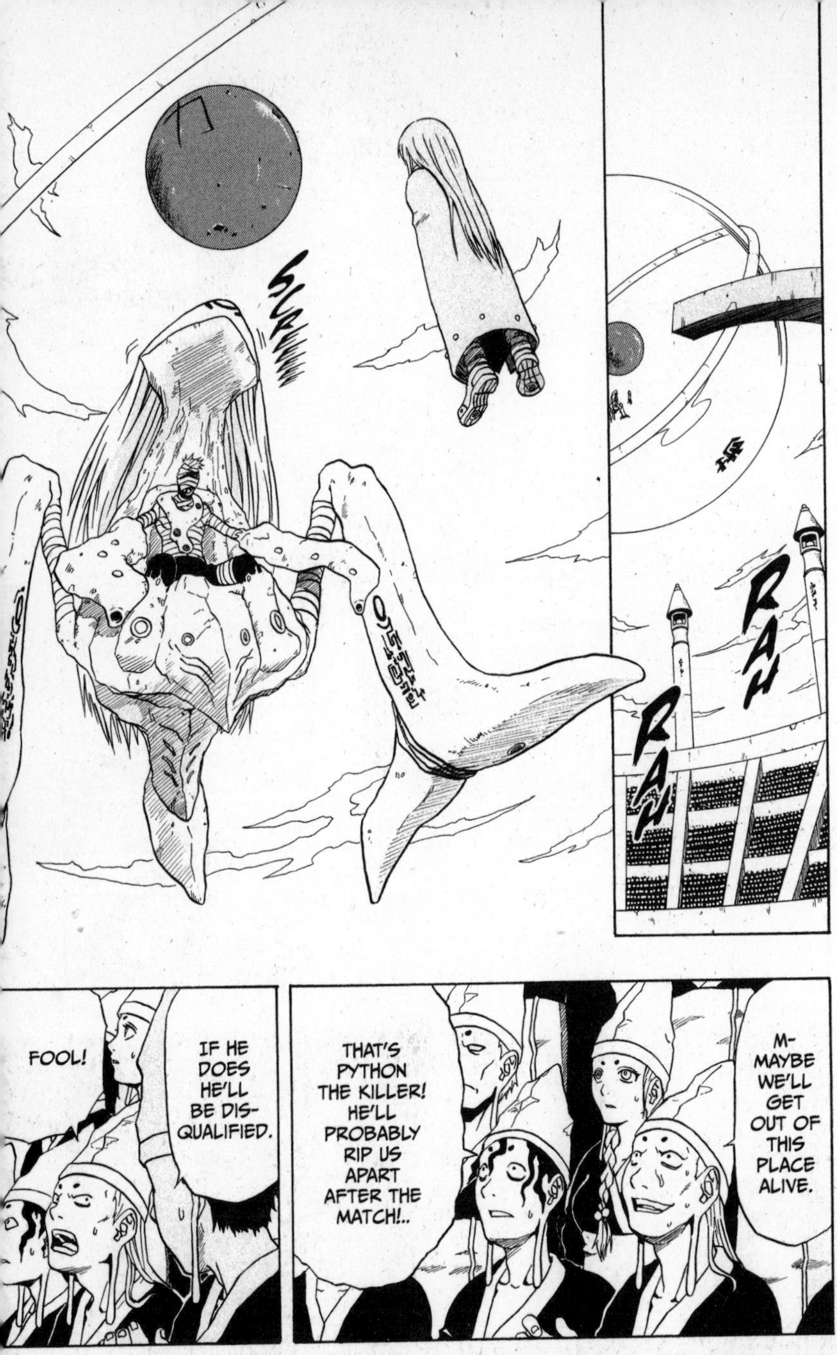
RAH
RAH
M-MAYBE WE'LL GET OUT OF THIS PLACE ALIVE.
THAT'S PYTHON THE KILLER! HE'LL PROBABLY RIP US APART AFTER THE MATCH!..
IF HE DOES HE'LL BE DIS-QUALIFIED.
FOOL!

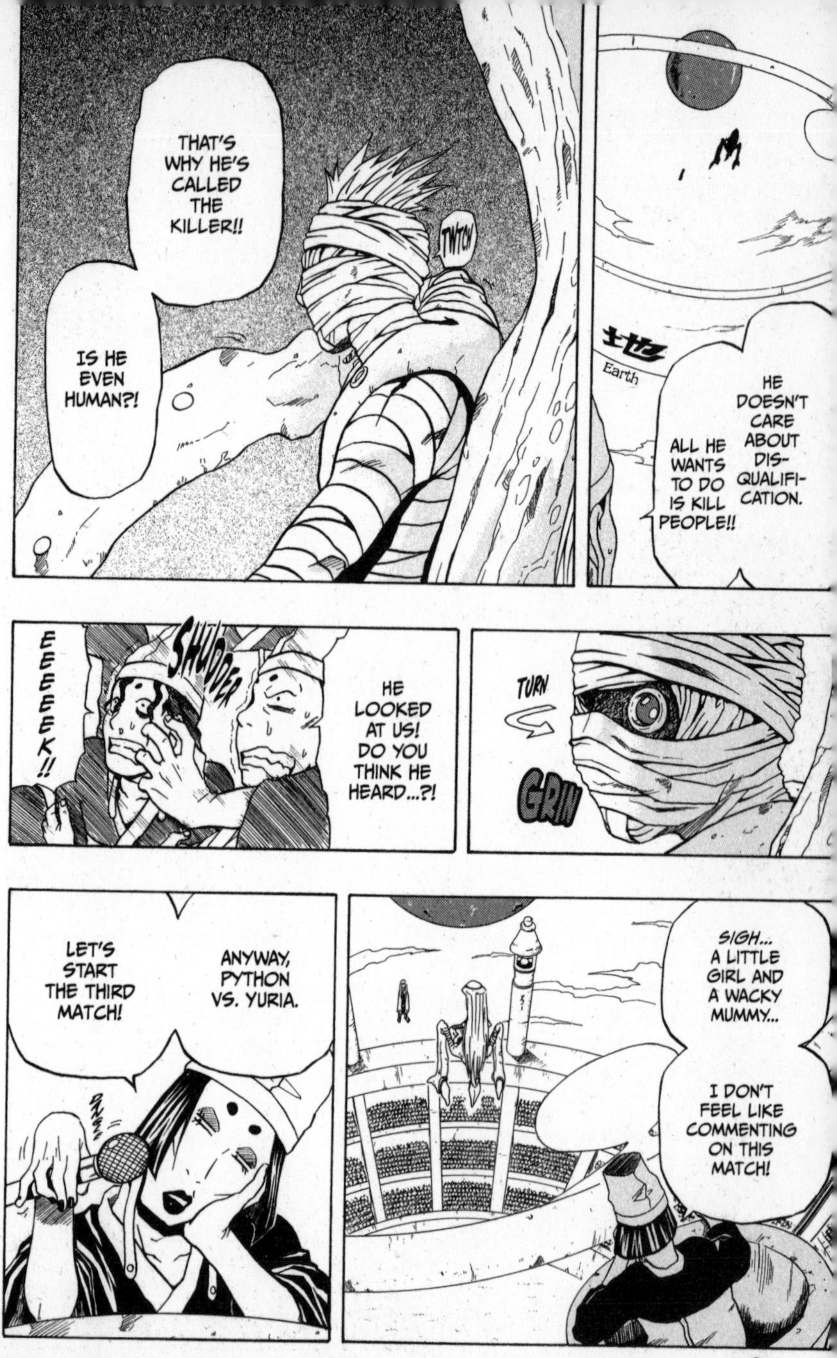
Earth
HE DOESN'T CARE ABOUT DIS-QUALIFI-CATION.
ALL HE WANTS TO DO IS KILL PEOPLE!!
THAT'S WHY HE'S CALLED THE KILLER!!
IS HE EVEN HUMAN?!
TWITCH
TURN
GRIN
SHUDDER
EEEEEEK!!
HE LOOKED AT US! DO YOU THINK HE HEARD...?!
SIGH... A LITTLE GIRL AND A WACKY MUMMY...
I DON'T FEEL LIKE COMMENTING ON THIS MATCH!
ANYWAY, PYTHON VS. YURIA.
LET'S START THE THIRD MATCH!

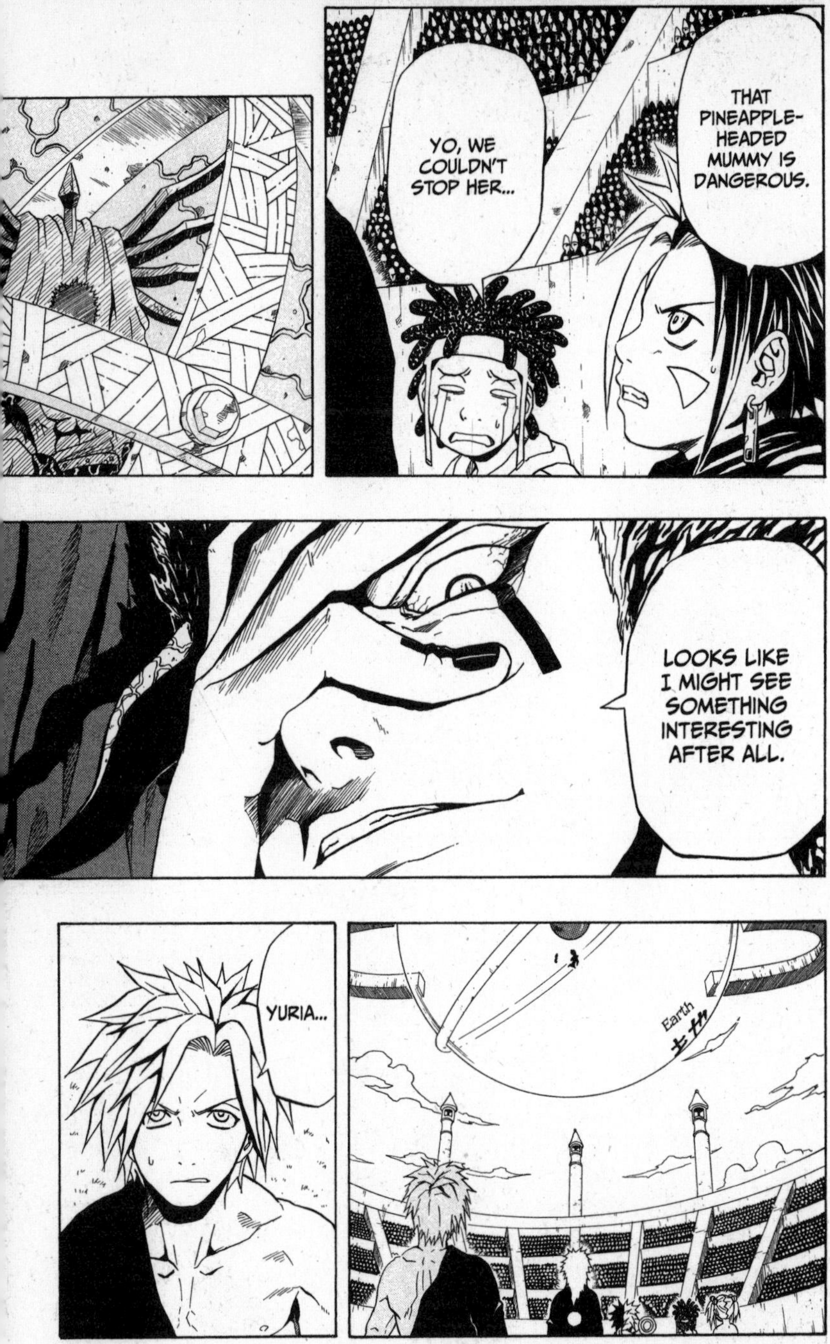
THAT PINEAPPLE-HEADED MUMMY IS DANGEROUS.
YO, WE COULDN'T STOP HER...
LOOKS LIKE I MIGHT SEE SOMETHING INTERESTING AFTER ALL.
Earth
YURIA...

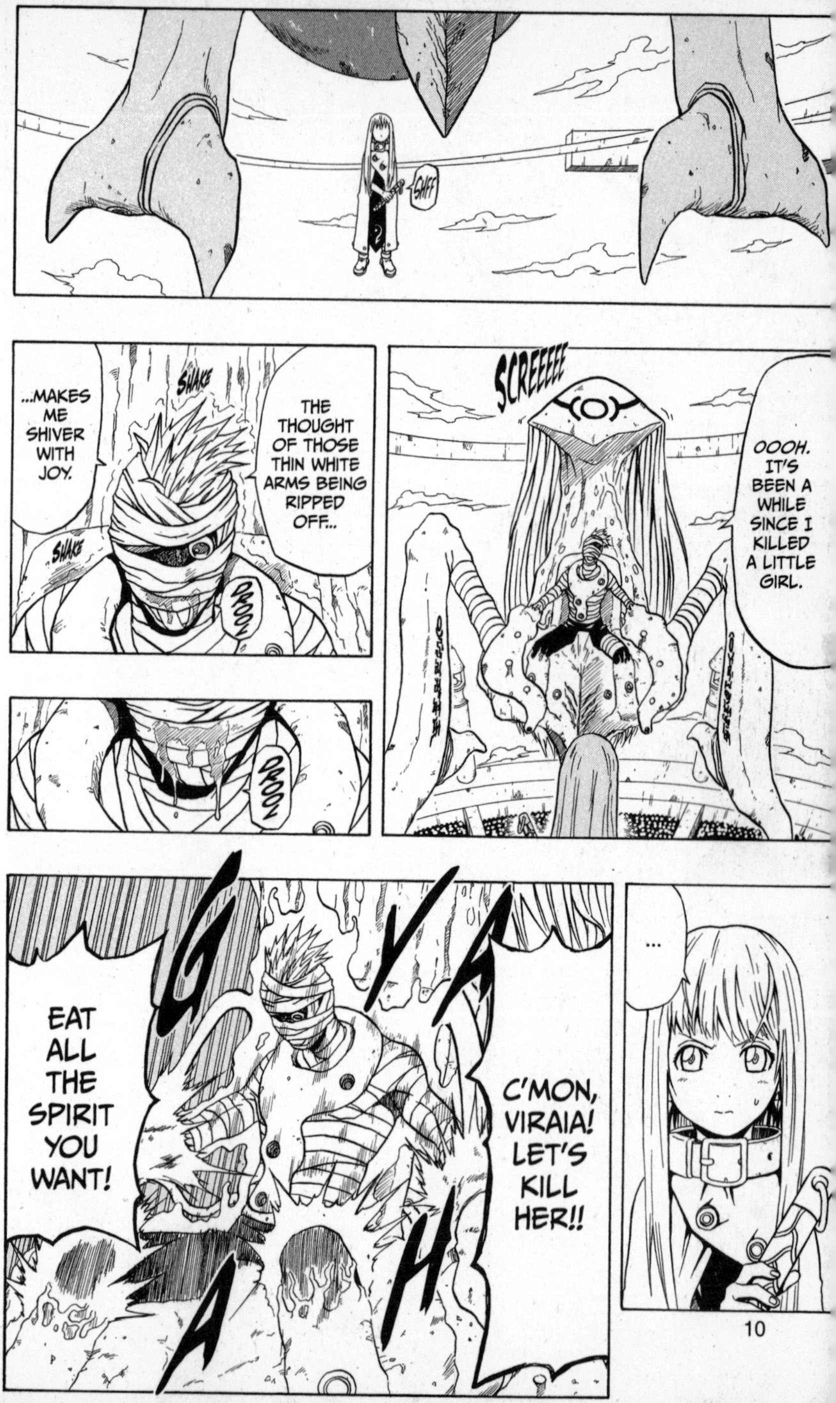
SHFF
SCREEEEE
OOOH. IT'S BEEN A WHILE SINCE I KILLED A LITTLE GIRL.
THE THOUGHT OF THOSE THIN WHITE ARMS BEING RIPPED OFF...
...MAKES ME SHIVER WITH JOY.
SHAKE
SHAKE
DROOL
DROOL
...
C'MON, VIRAIA! LET'S KILL HER!!
EAT ALL THE SPIRIT YOU WANT!
GYAAH

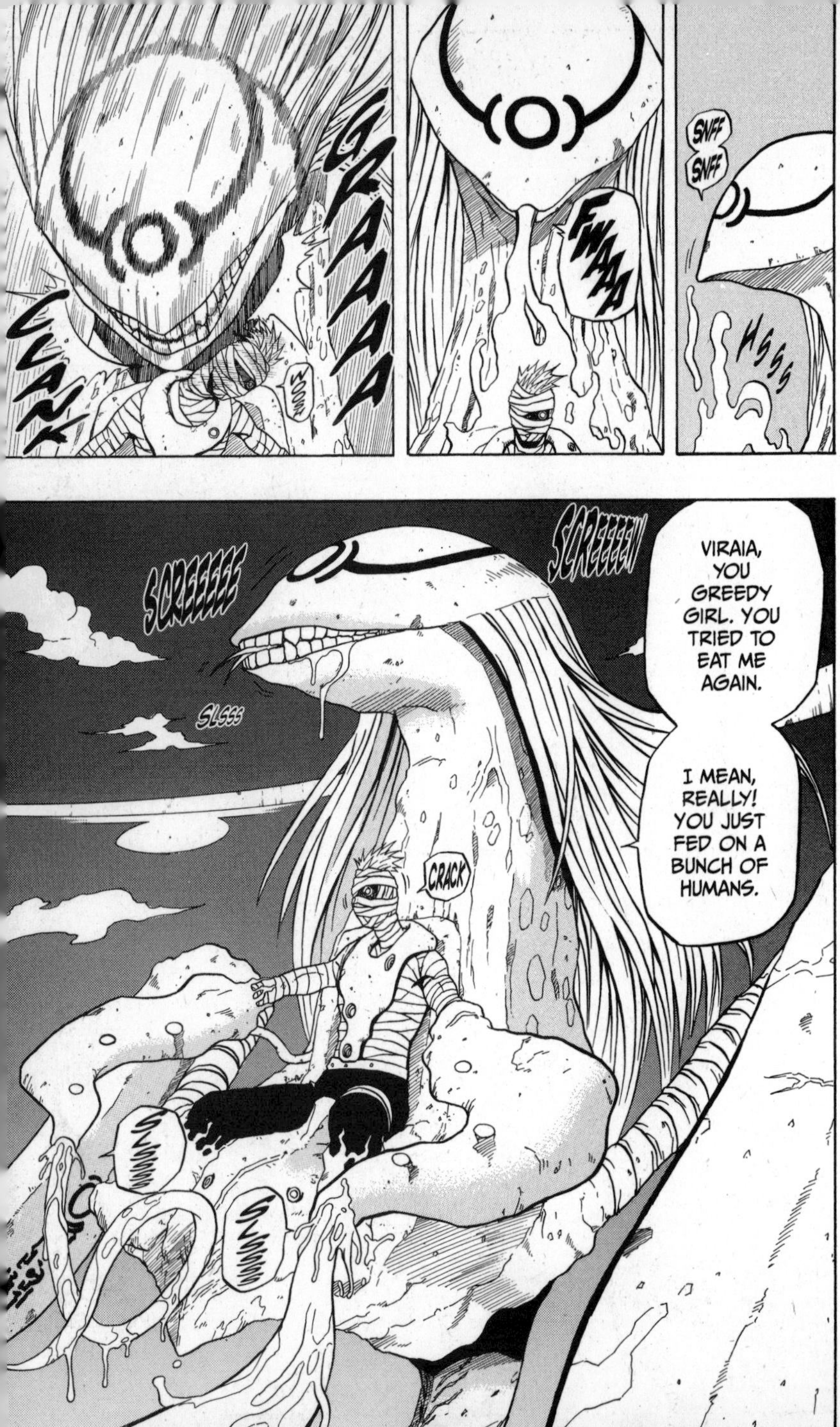
SNFF
SNFF
HSSS
FWAAAA
GRAAAAAA
WOOSH
CLANK
VIRAIA, YOU GREEDY GIRL. YOU TRIED TO EAT ME AGAIN.
I MEAN, REALLY! YOU JUST FED ON A BUNCH OF HUMANS.
SCREEEEEN
SCREEEEE
SLSSS
CRACK
SLSSSSS
SLSSSSS

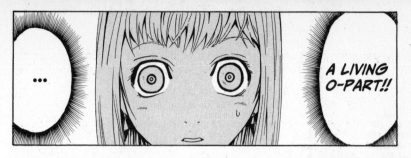

A LIVING O-PART!!
...
WHAT?! IS THAT O-PART ALIVE?!
I'VE NEVER SEEN ANYTHING LIKE IT!!
HEY, THAT O-PART IS—
I KNOW.
IT'S THE SAME TYPE OF BIOLOGICAL O-PART AS THE ONE...
...THAT WAS DUG UP FROM UNDERNEATH ENTOTSU CITY.
MOST O-PARTS ARE WEAPONS AND TOOLS...
...MADE TO FIT INTO OUR EVERYDAY LIVES.
BUT BIOLOGICAL O-PARTS ARE EXTREMELY RARE.
SINCE ANCIENT TIMES THEY'VE BEEN COVETED...
...AND TREATED AS SACRED RELICS.

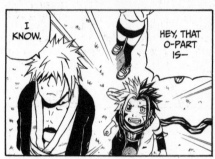

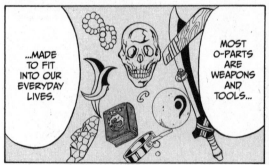

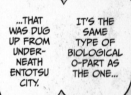

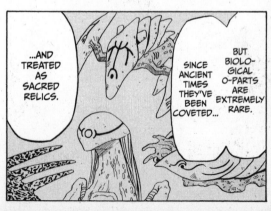

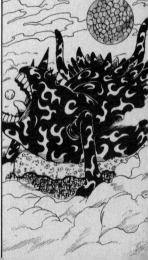

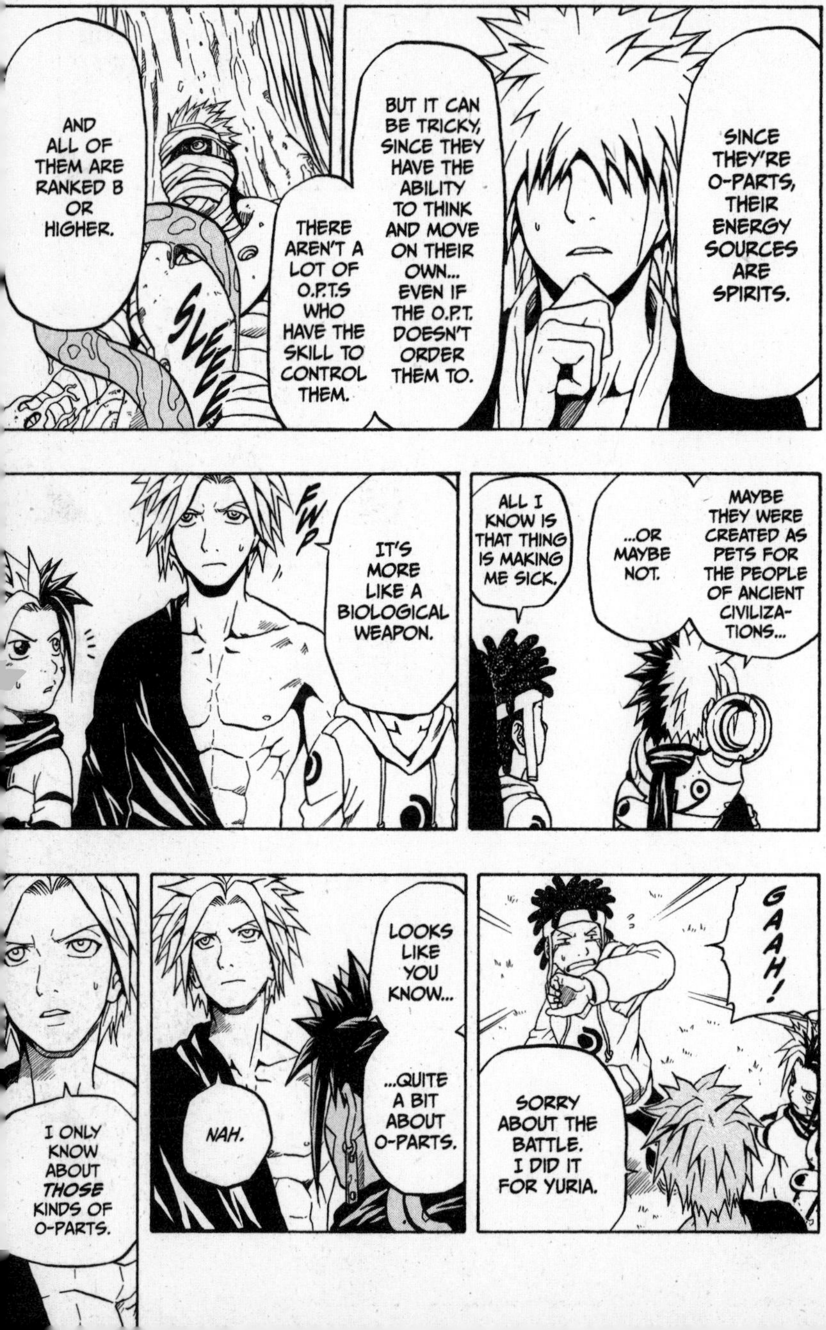
SINCE THEY'RE O-PARTS, THEIR ENERGY SOURCES ARE SPIRITS.
BUT IT CAN BE TRICKY, SINCE THEY HAVE THE ABILITY TO THINK AND MOVE ON THEIR OWN... EVEN IF THE O.P.T. DOESN'T ORDER THEM TO.
THERE AREN'T A LOT OF O.P.T.S WHO HAVE THE SKILL TO CONTROL THEM.
AND ALL OF THEM ARE RANKED B OR HIGHER.
MAYBE THEY WERE CREATED AS PETS FOR THE PEOPLE OF ANCIENT CIVILIZATIONS...
...OR MAYBE NOT.
ALL I KNOW IS THAT THING IS MAKING ME SICK.
FWP
IT'S MORE LIKE A BIOLOGICAL WEAPON.
GAAH!
SORRY ABOUT THE BATTLE. I DID IT FOR YURIA.
LOOKS LIKE YOU KNOW...
...QUITE A BIT ABOUT O-PARTS.
NAH.
I ONLY KNOW ABOUT *THOSE* KINDS OF O-PARTS.

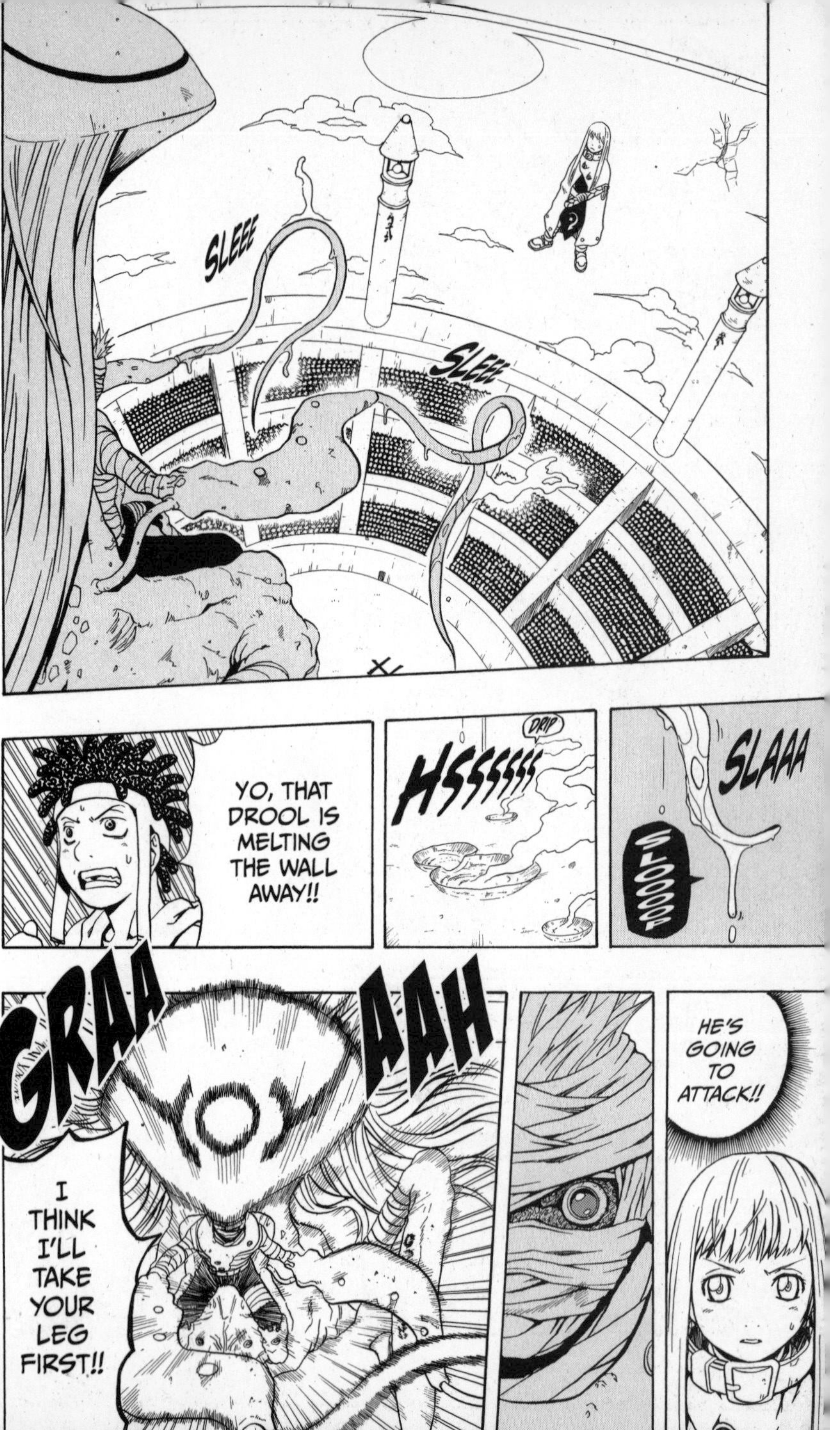
SLEEE
SLEEE
SLAAA
SLOOOOP
DRIP
HSSSSSS
YO, THAT DROOL IS MELTING THE WALL AWAY!!
HE'S GOING TO ATTACK!!
GRAAAAH
I THINK I'LL TAKE YOUR LEG FIRST!!

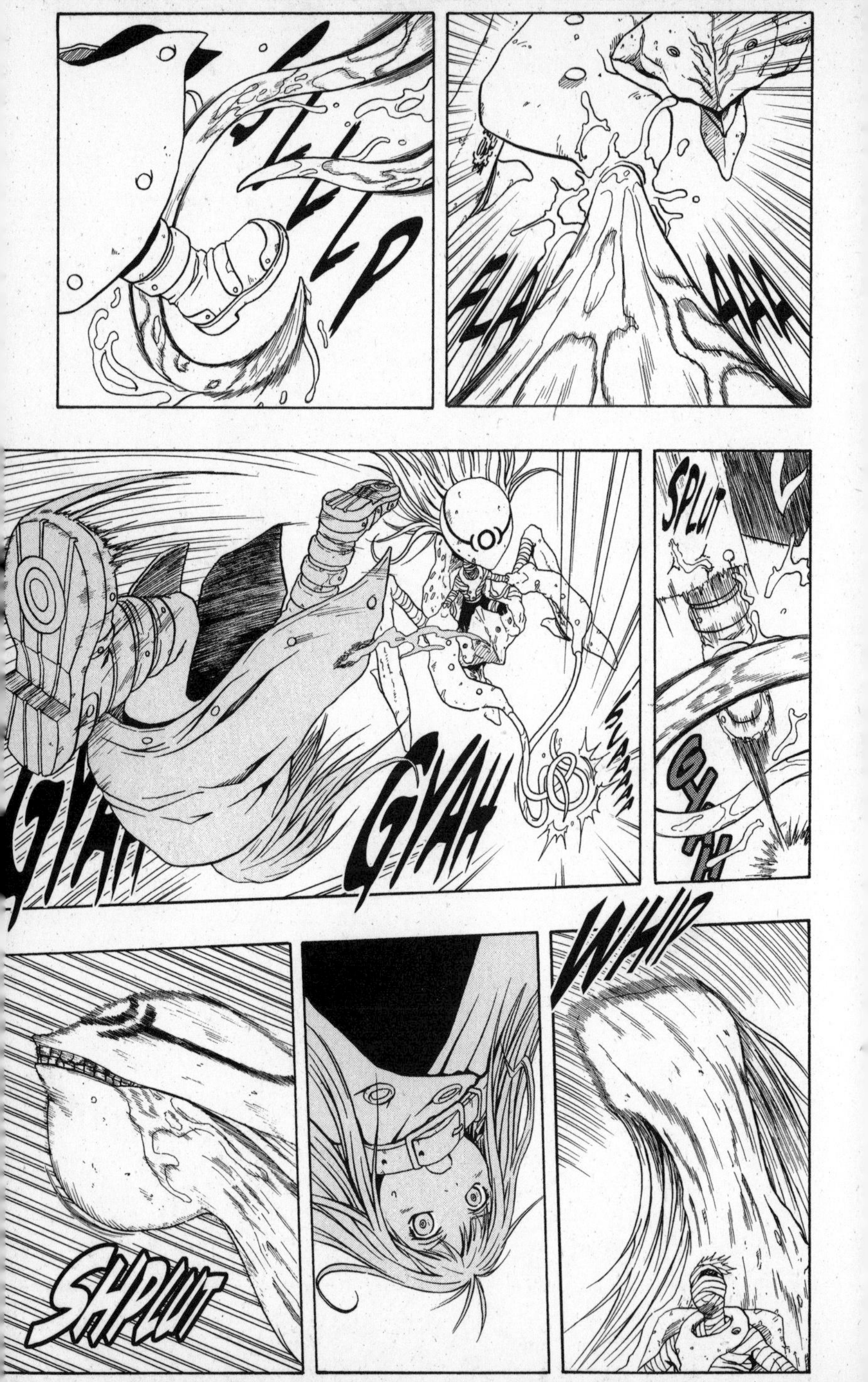
SPLUT
GYAH
GYAH
WHIP
SHPLUT

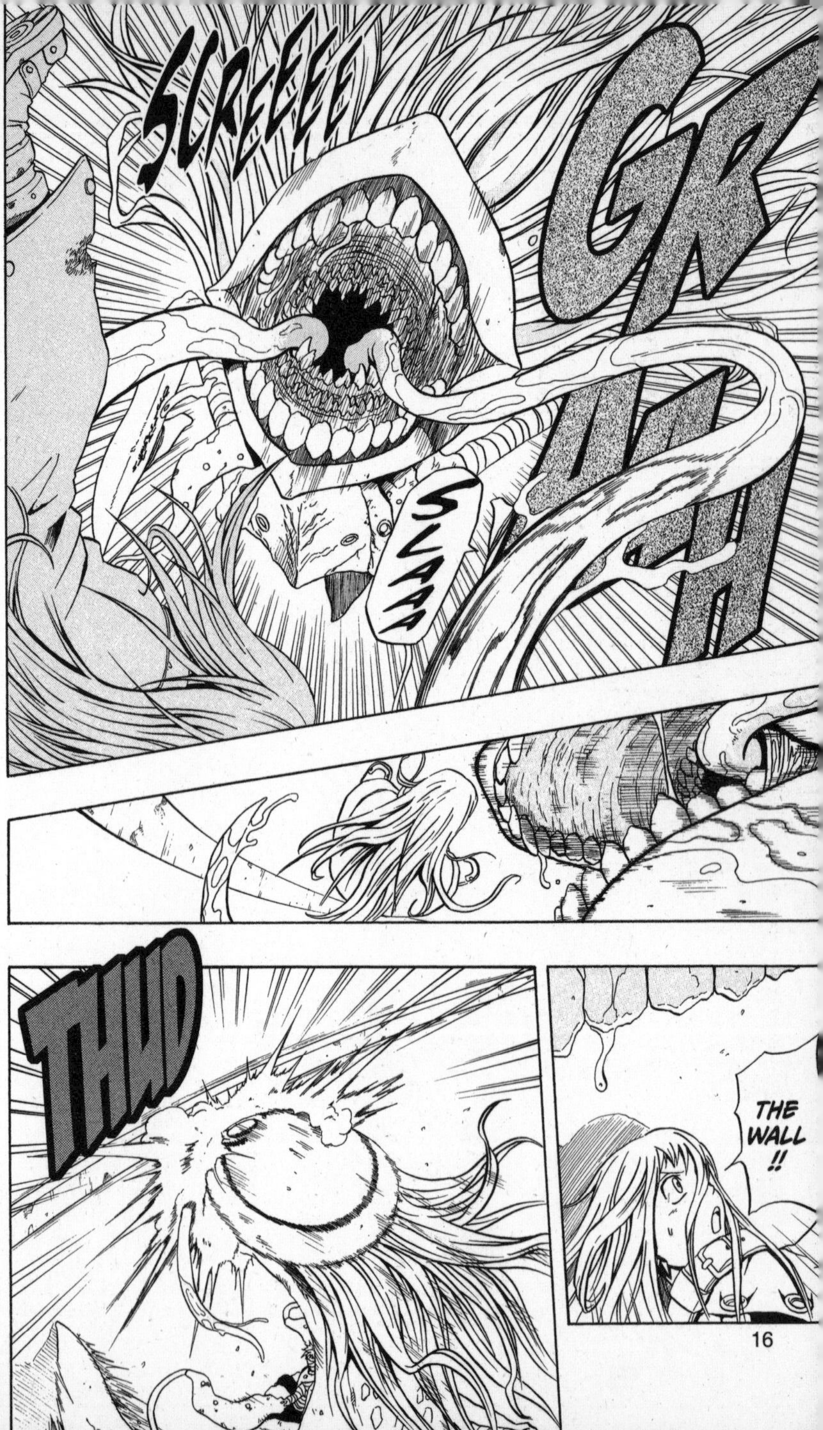
GRAH
SCREEEE
SLAAA
THE WALL!!
THUD

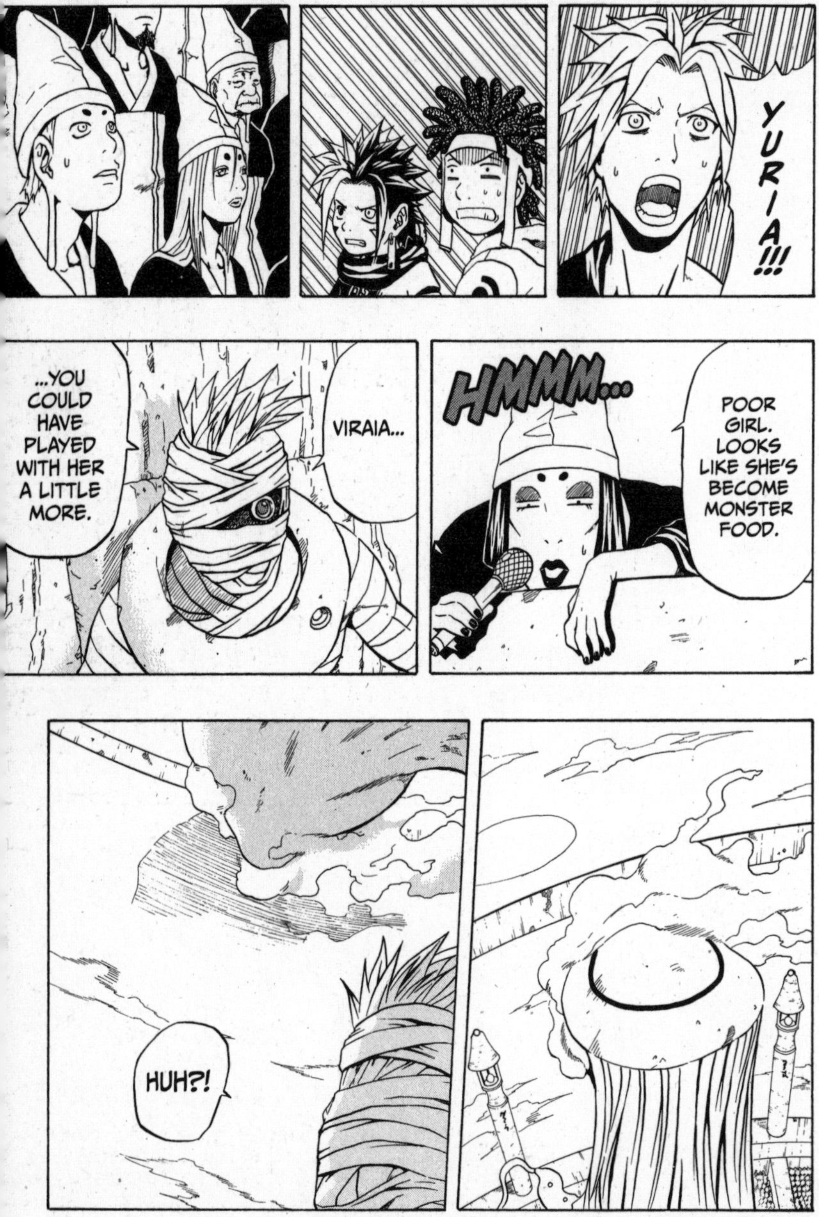
YURIA!!!
HMMMM...
POOR GIRL. LOOKS LIKE SHE'S BECOME MONSTER FOOD.
VIRAIA...
...YOU COULD HAVE PLAYED WITH HER A LITTLE MORE.
HUH?!

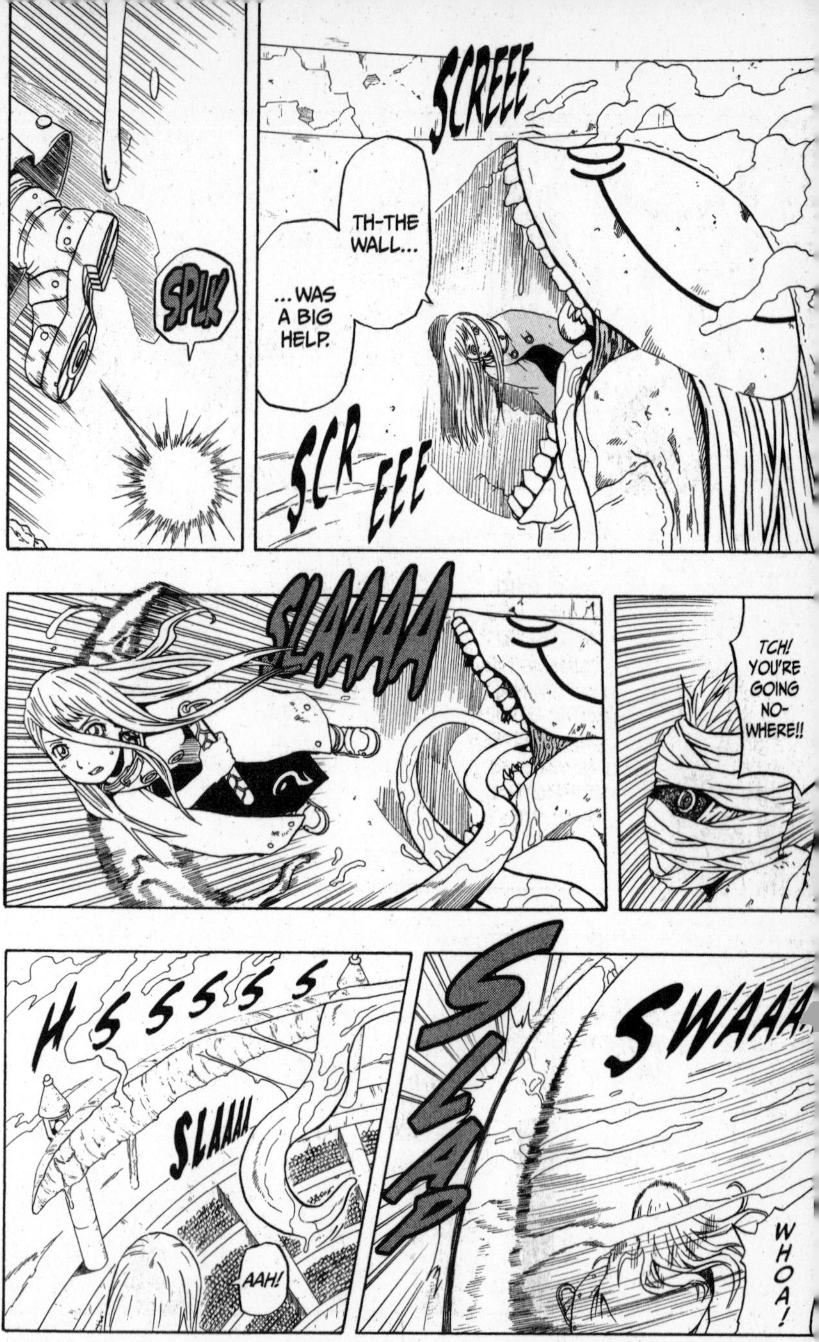
SCREEE
TH-THE WALL...
...WAS A BIG HELP.
SCR EEE
SPLIK
TCH! YOU'RE GOING NO-WHERE!!
SLAAAA
SWAAA
WHOA!
SLAP
HSSSSS
SLAAA
AAH!

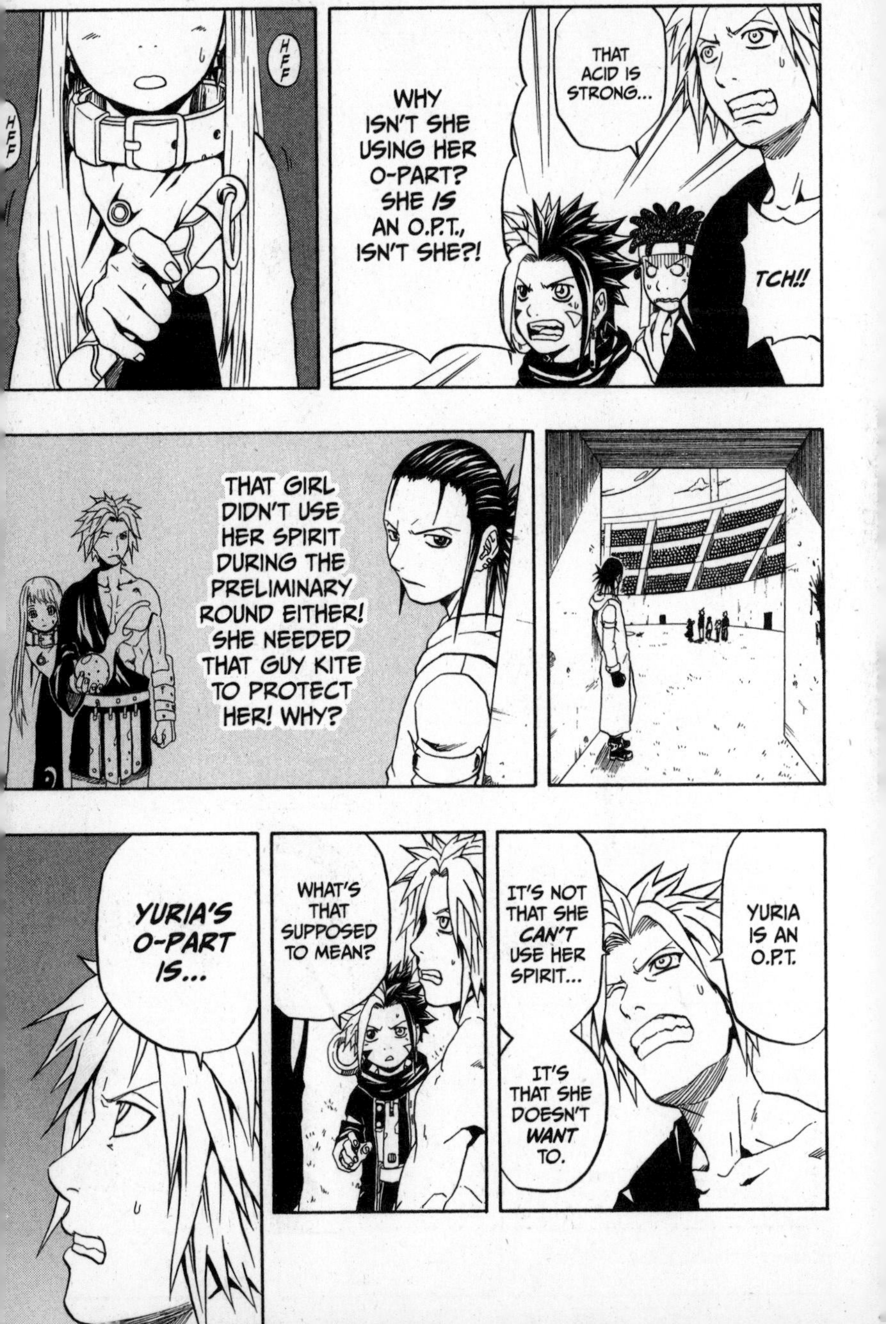
THAT ACID IS STRONG...
WHY ISN'T SHE USING HER O-PART? SHE *IS* AN O.P.T., ISN'T SHE?!
TCH!!
HFF
HFF
THAT GIRL DIDN'T USE HER SPIRIT DURING THE PRELIMINARY ROUND EITHER! SHE NEEDED THAT GUY KITE TO PROTECT HER! WHY?
YURIA IS AN O.P.T.
IT'S NOT THAT SHE *CAN'T* USE HER SPIRIT...
IT'S THAT SHE DOESN'T *WANT* TO.
WHAT'S THAT SUPPOSED TO MEAN?
YURIA'S O-PART IS...

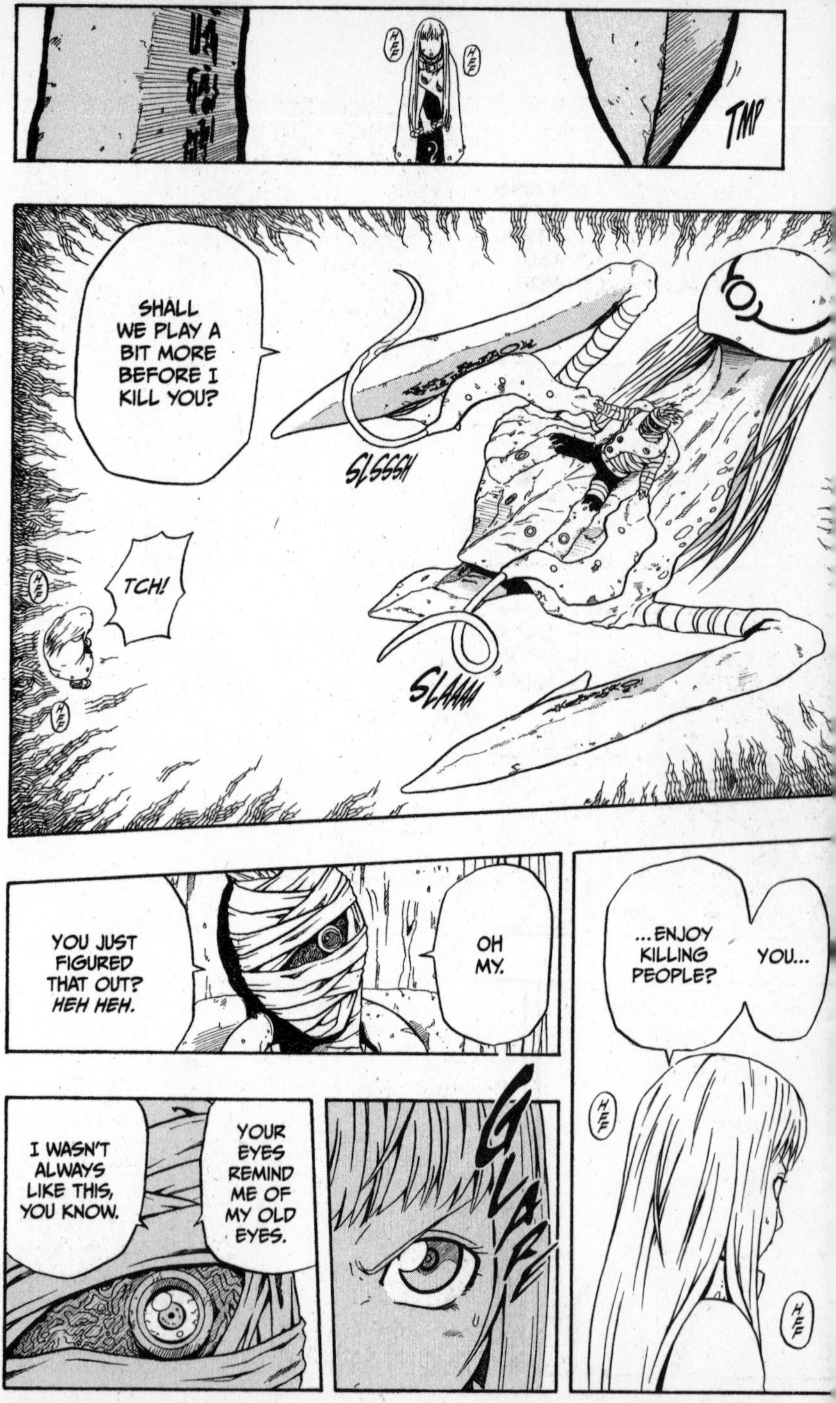
HEF
HEF
TMP
SHALL WE PLAY A BIT MORE BEFORE I KILL YOU?
SLSSSH
TCH!
HEF
HEF
SLAAAA
YOU...
...ENJOY KILLING PEOPLE?
HEF
HEF
OH MY.
YOU JUST FIGURED THAT OUT? HEH HEH.
GLARE
YOUR EYES REMIND ME OF MY OLD EYES.
I WASN'T ALWAYS LIKE THIS, YOU KNOW.

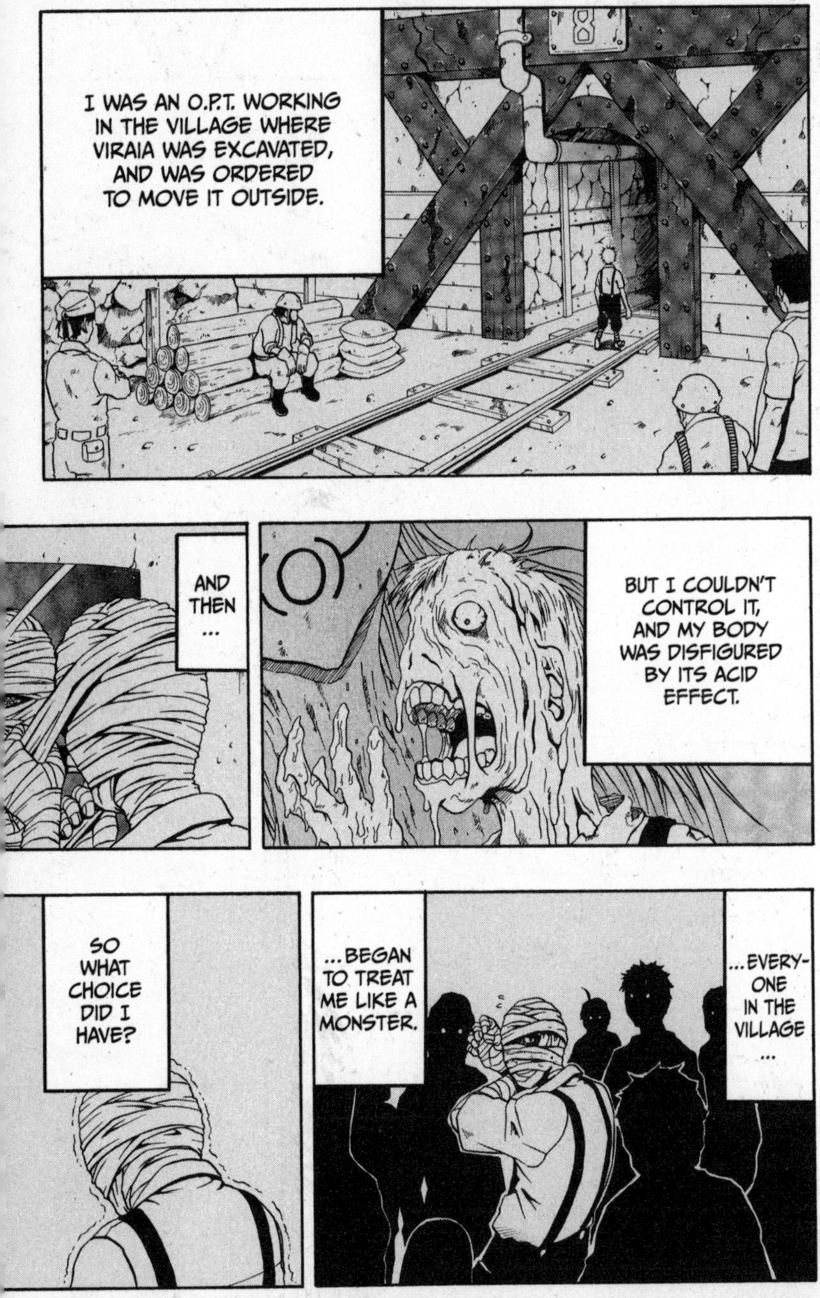
I WAS AN O.P.T. WORKING IN THE VILLAGE WHERE VIRAIA WAS EXCAVATED, AND WAS ORDERED TO MOVE IT OUTSIDE.
BUT I COULDN'T CONTROL IT, AND MY BODY WAS DISFIGURED BY ITS ACID EFFECT.
AND THEN ...
...EVERY-ONE IN THE VILLAGE ...
...BEGAN TO TREAT ME LIKE A MONSTER.
SO WHAT CHOICE DID I HAVE?

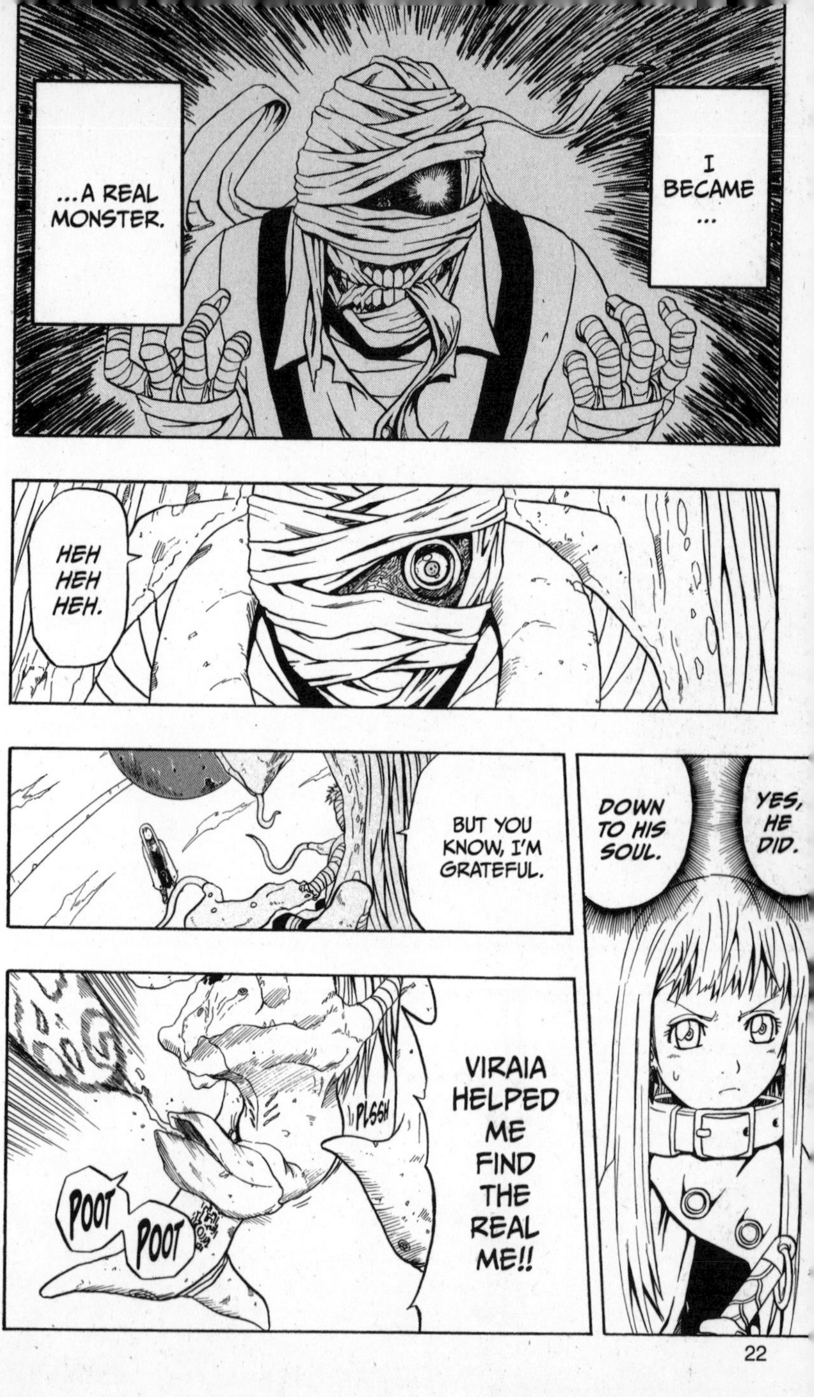
I BECAME ...
...A REAL MONSTER.
HEH HEH HEH.
YES, HE DID.
DOWN TO HIS SOUL.
BUT YOU KNOW, I'M GRATEFUL.
VIRAIA HELPED ME FIND THE REAL ME!!
PLSSH
POOT
POOT

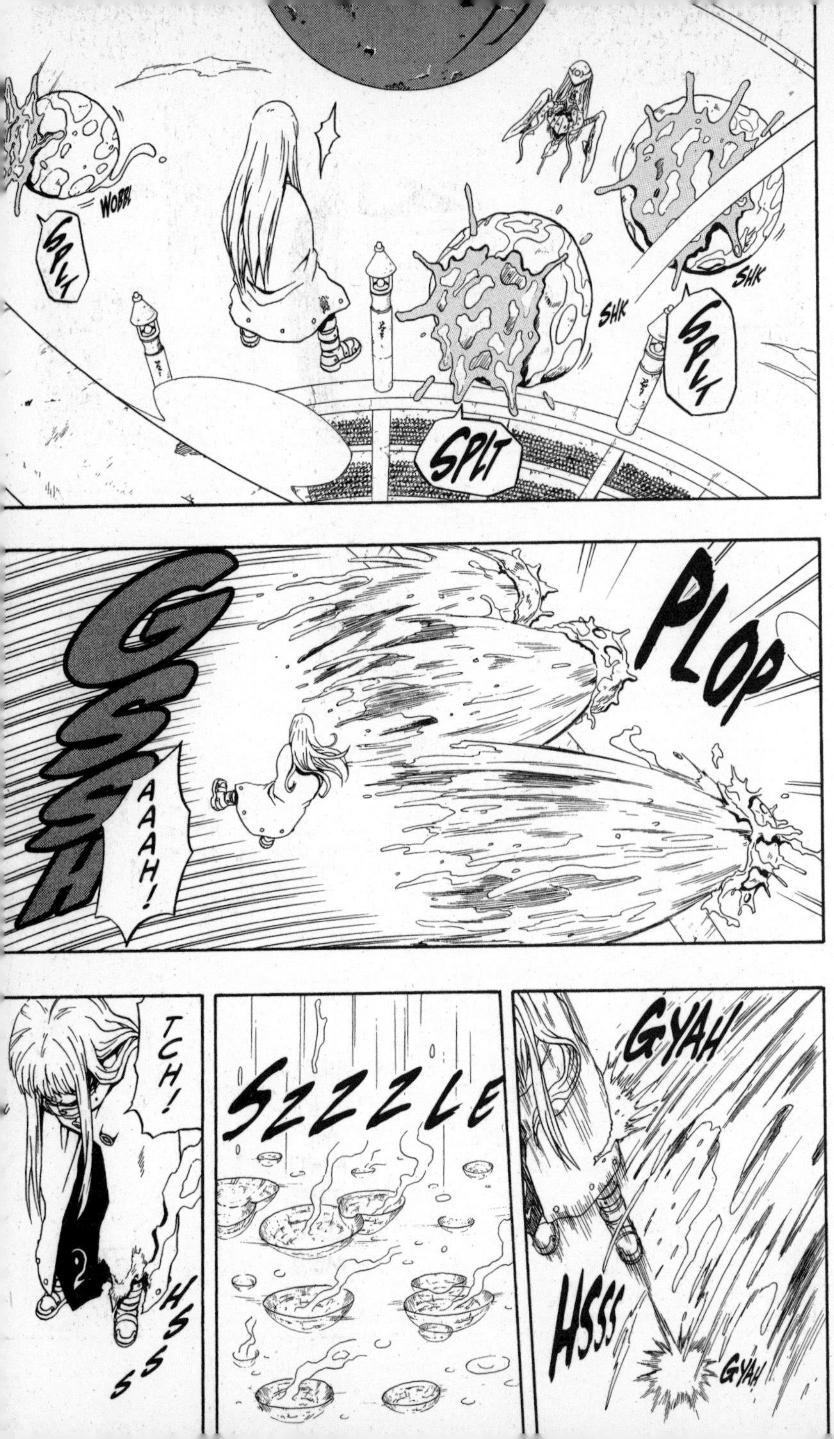
SHK
SPLK
SHK
SPLT
WOBBL
SPLK
PLOP
GSSSH
AAAAH!
GYAH
HSSS
GYAH
SZZZLE
TCH!
HSSSS

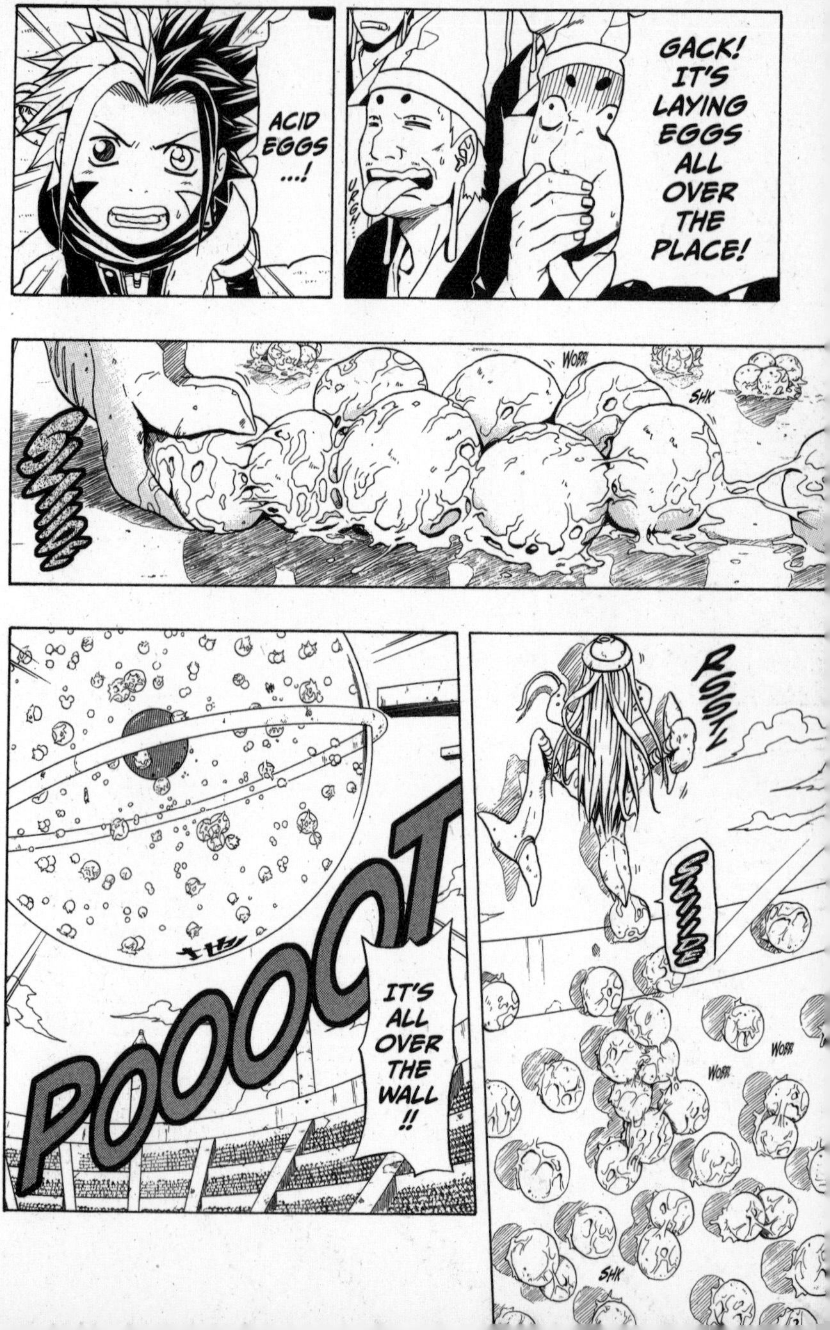
GACK! IT'S LAYING EGGS ALL OVER THE PLACE!
URGH...
ACID EGGS ...!
WOBB
SHK
WOBB
WOBB
SHK
POOOOT
IT'S ALL OVER THE WALL!!

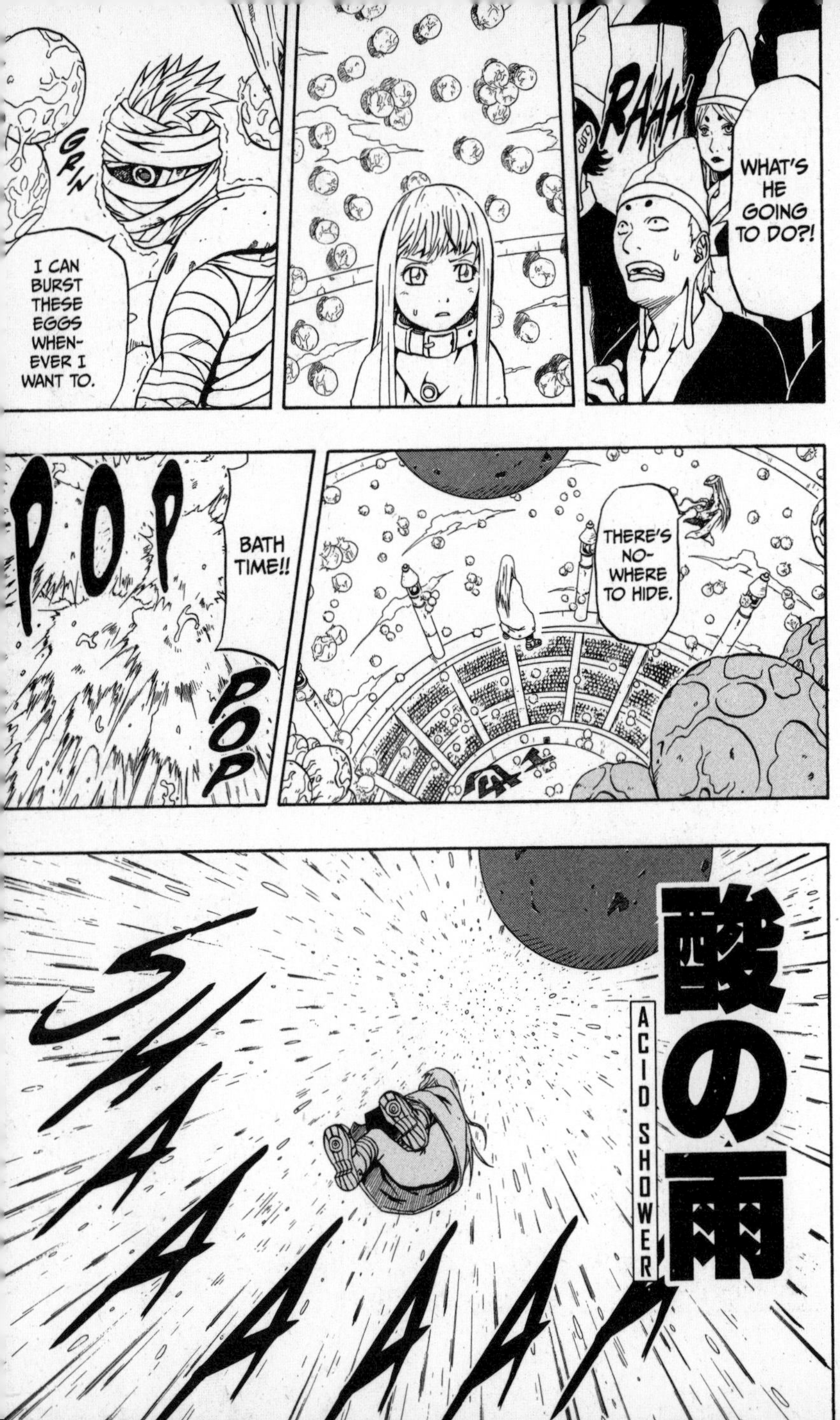
RAAH
WHAT'S HE GOING TO DO?!
GRIN
I CAN BURST THESE EGGS WHENEVER I WANT TO.
THERE'S NOWHERE TO HIDE.
POP
BATH TIME!!
POP
酸の雨
ACID SHOWER
SHAAAAA

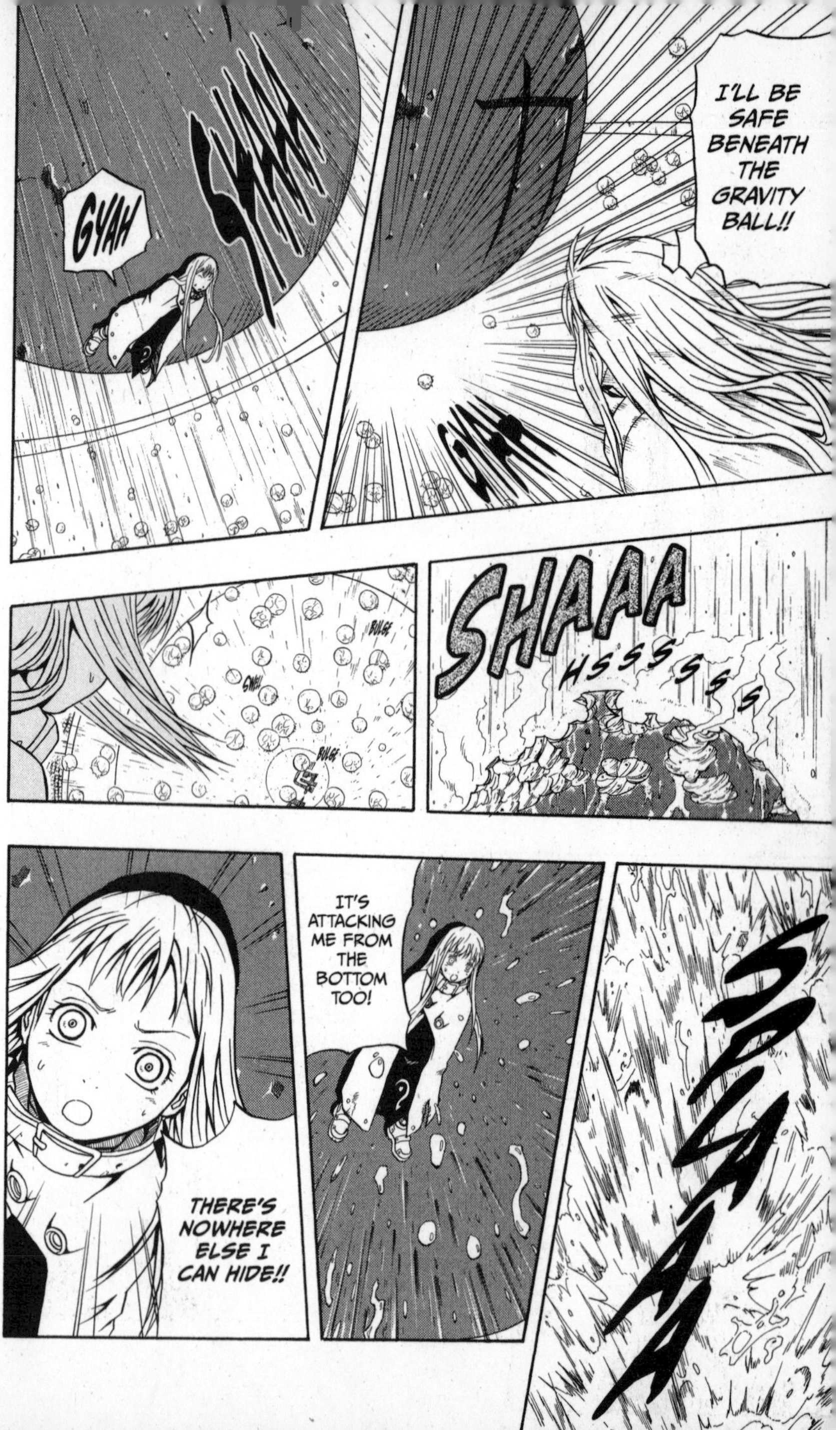
I'LL BE SAFE BENEATH THE GRAVITY BALL!!
GYAH
GYAH
SHAAA
HSSSSSS
BULGE
BULGE
IT'S ATTACKING ME FROM THE BOTTOM TOO!
THERE'S NOWHERE ELSE I CAN HIDE!!

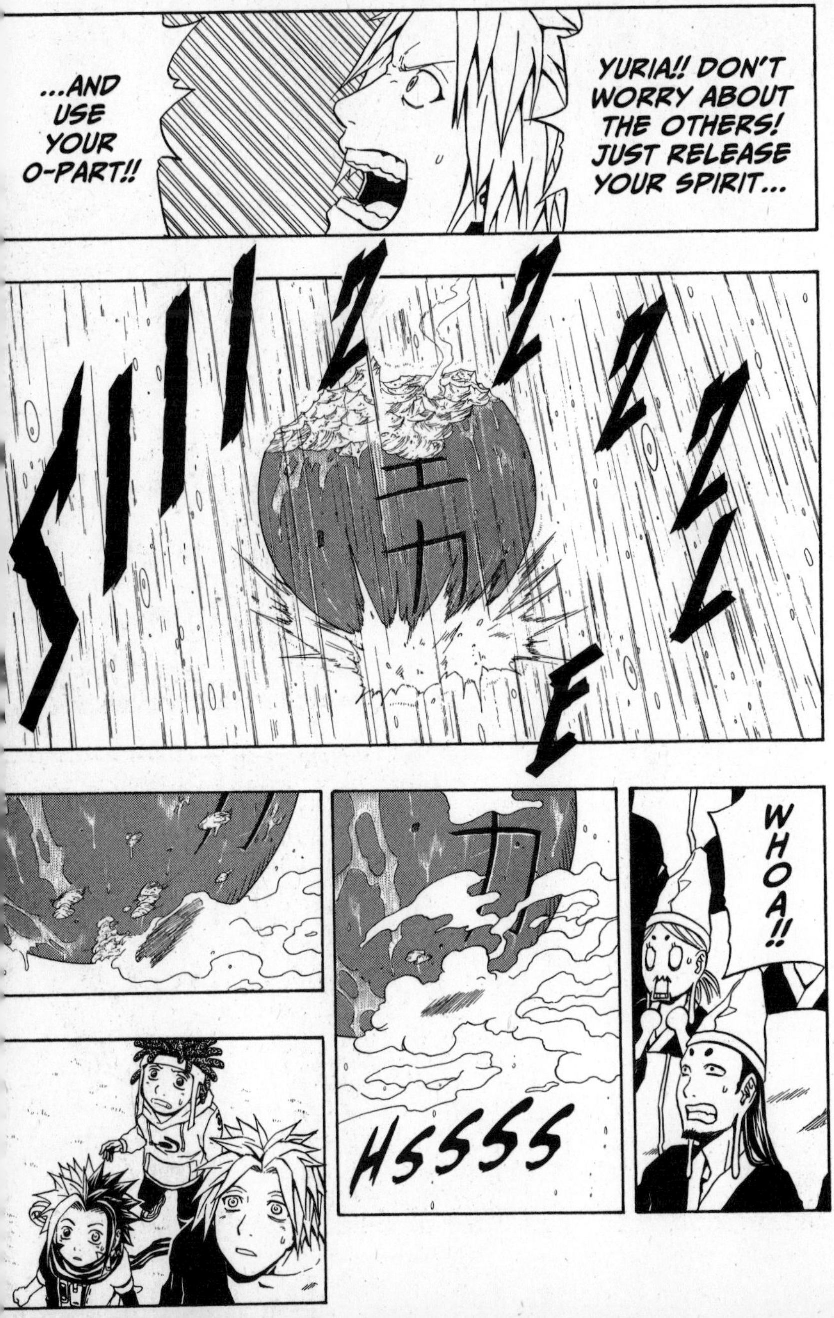
YURIA!! DON'T WORRY ABOUT THE OTHERS! JUST RELEASE YOUR SPIRIT...
...AND USE YOUR O-PART!!
WHOA!!
HSSSS

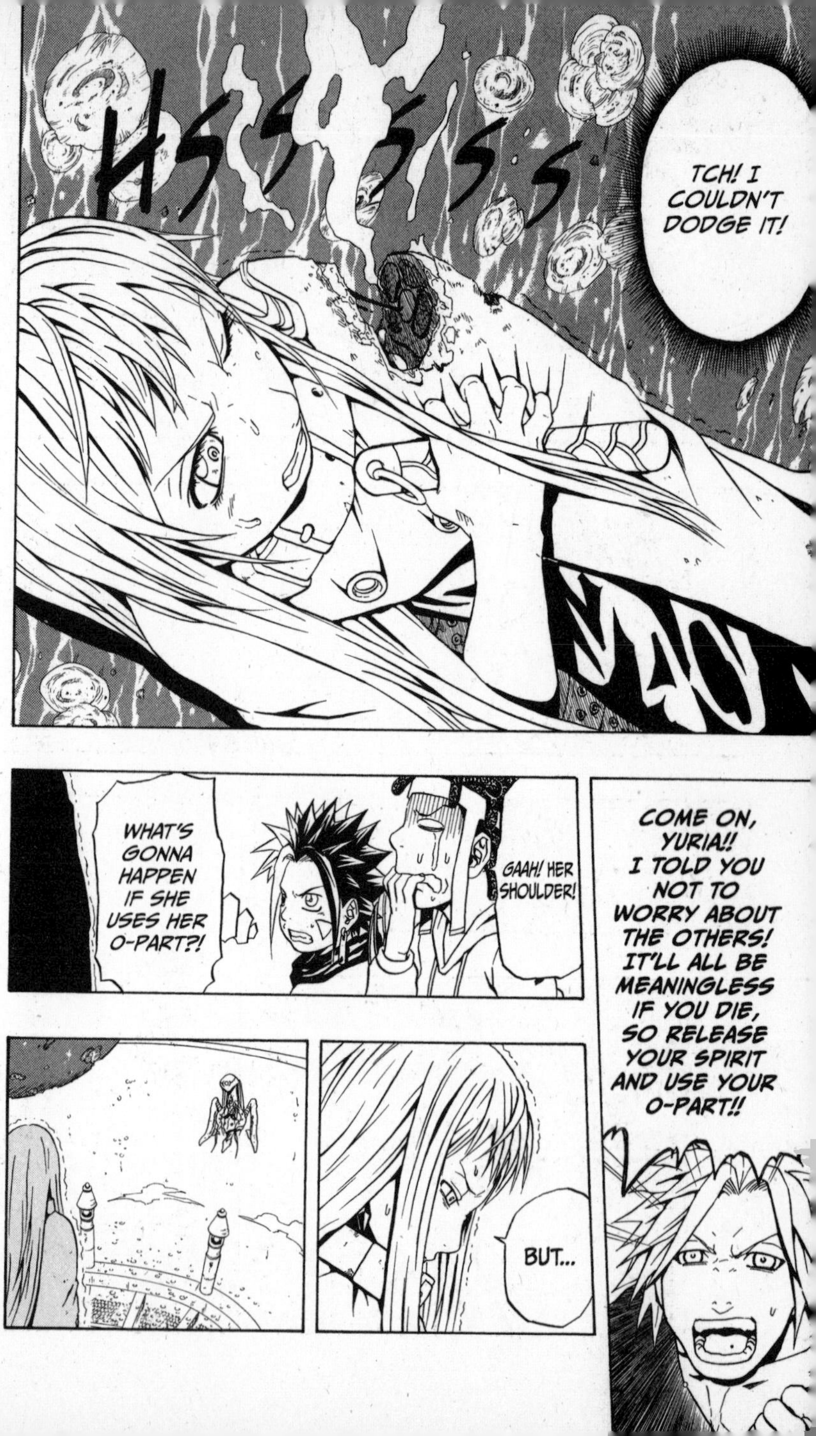
HSSSSS
TCH! I COULDN'T DODGE IT!
COME ON, YURIA!! I TOLD YOU NOT TO WORRY ABOUT THE OTHERS! IT'LL ALL BE MEANINGLESS IF YOU DIE, SO RELEASE YOUR SPIRIT AND USE YOUR O-PART!!
GAAH! HER SHOULDER!
WHAT'S GONNA HAPPEN IF SHE USES HER O-PART?!
BUT...

SHWAAA

POOT

GYAH

OH! FWAA

GYAH

GYAH

NO!!

HSSSS

HSSSS

SWAAA

AH!

NO!!

BWO MOOO

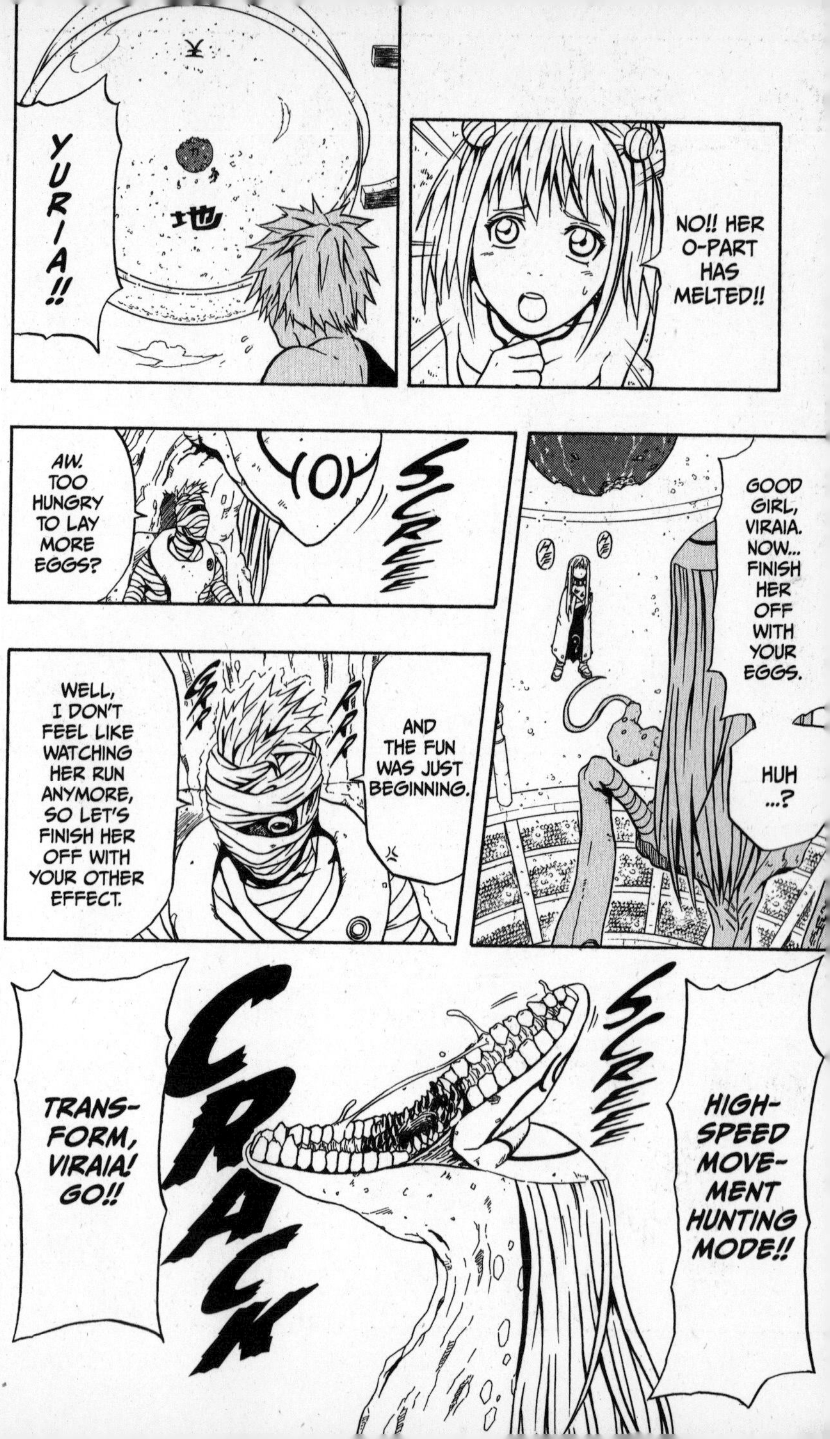
NO!! HER O-PART HAS MELTED!!
YURIA!!
GOOD GIRL, VIRAIA. NOW... FINISH HER OFF WITH YOUR EGGS.
HUH ...?
SCREEE
AW. TOO HUNGRY TO LAY MORE EGGS?
AND THE FUN WAS JUST BEGINNING.
WELL, I DON'T FEEL LIKE WATCHING HER RUN ANYMORE, SO LET'S FINISH HER OFF WITH YOUR OTHER EFFECT.
HIGH-SPEED MOVEMENT HUNTING MODE!!
SCREEE
CRACK
TRANS-FORM, VIRAIA! GO!!

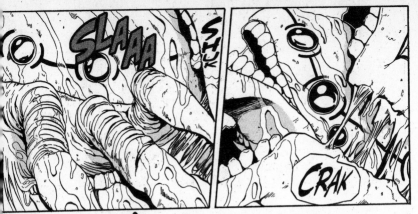

SLAAA
SHJK
CRAK

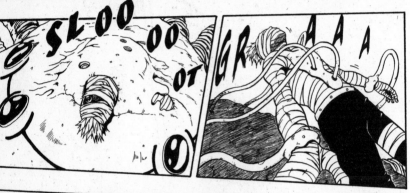

SL-OO
OO
OT
GRAAA

BLEH!

THAT'S NO TRANSFOR-MATION! IT'S JUST SHEDDING ITS SKIN!

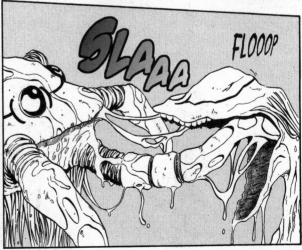

SLAAA
FLOOOP

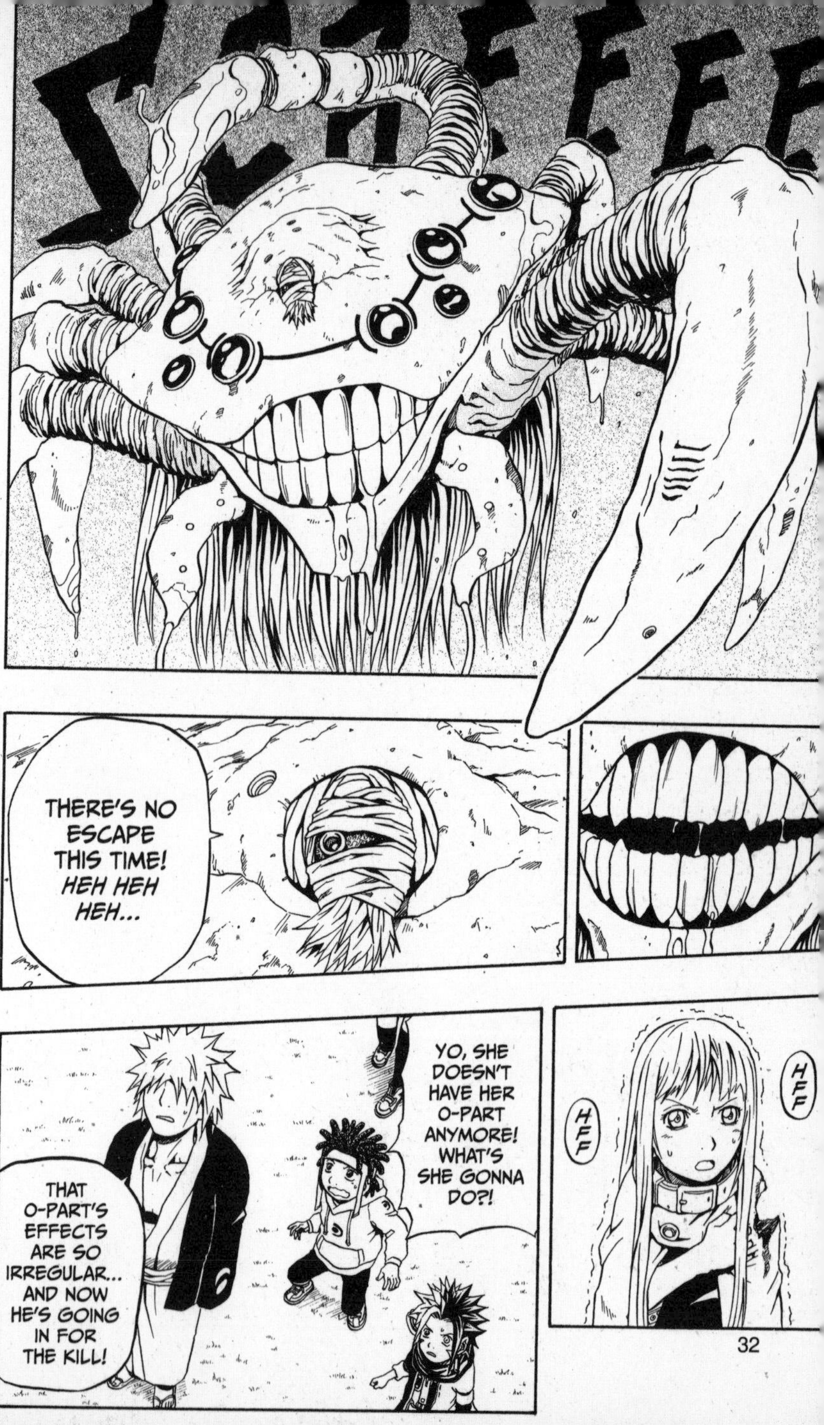
SCREEE
THERE'S NO ESCAPE THIS TIME! *HEH HEH HEH...*
HFF
HFF
YO, SHE DOESN'T HAVE HER O-PART ANYMORE! WHAT'S SHE GONNA DO?!
THAT O-PART'S EFFECTS ARE SO IRREGULAR... AND NOW HE'S GOING IN FOR THE KILL!

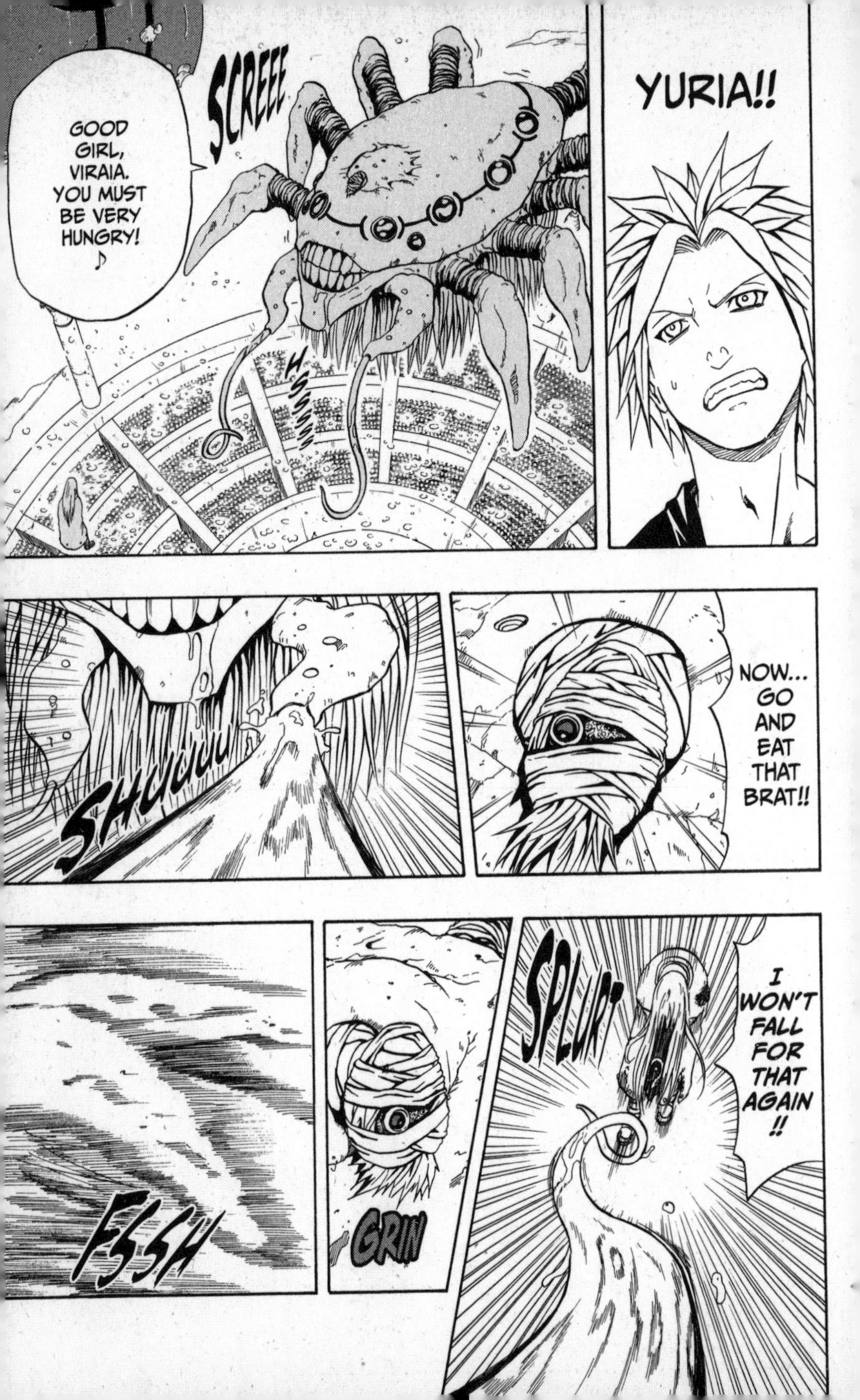
YURIA!!
SCREEE
GOOD GIRL, VIRAIA. YOU MUST BE VERY HUNGRY! ♪
NOW... GO AND EAT THAT BRAT!!
SPLURT
I WON'T FALL FOR THAT AGAIN!!
GRIN
FSSH

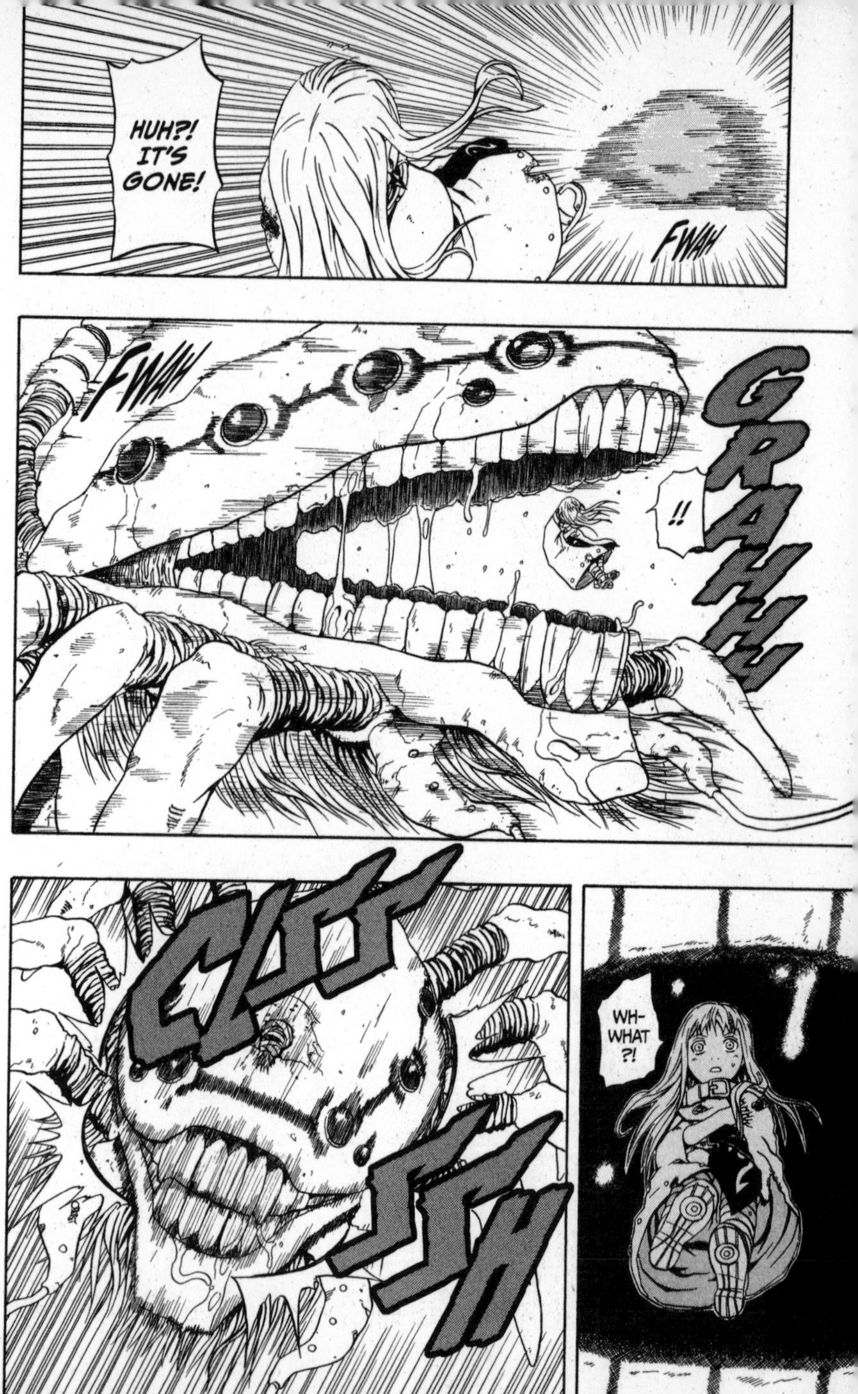
HUH?! IT'S GONE!
FWAH
GRAHHH
!!
FWAH
WH-WHAT?!
CLISSH

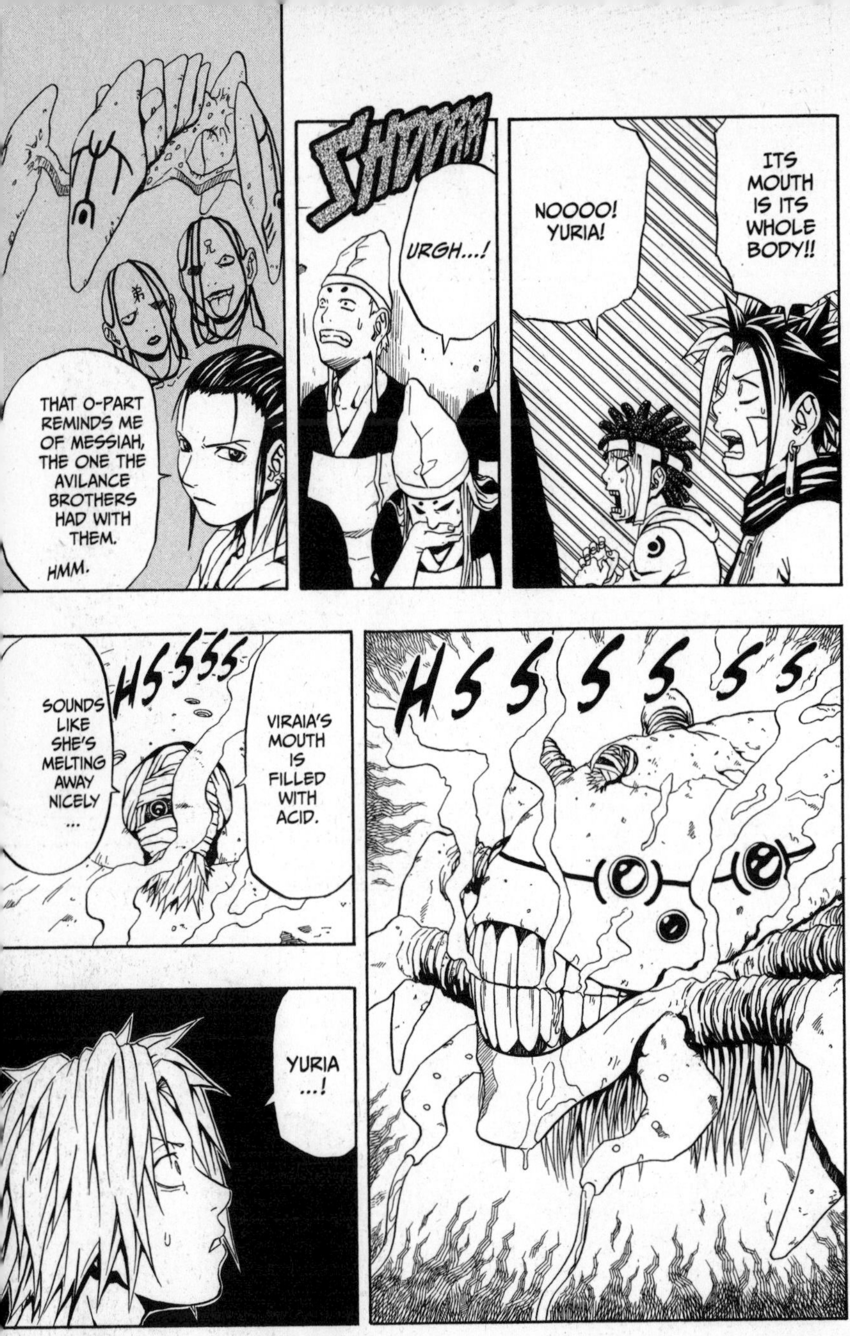
ITS MOUTH IS ITS WHOLE BODY!!
NOOOO! YURIA!
URGH...!
THAT O-PART REMINDS ME OF MESSIAH, THE ONE THE AVILANCE BROTHERS HAD WITH THEM.
HMM.
HSSSSSSS
VIRAIA'S MOUTH IS FILLED WITH ACID.
HSSSS
SOUNDS LIKE SHE'S MELTING AWAY NICELY...
YURIA...!

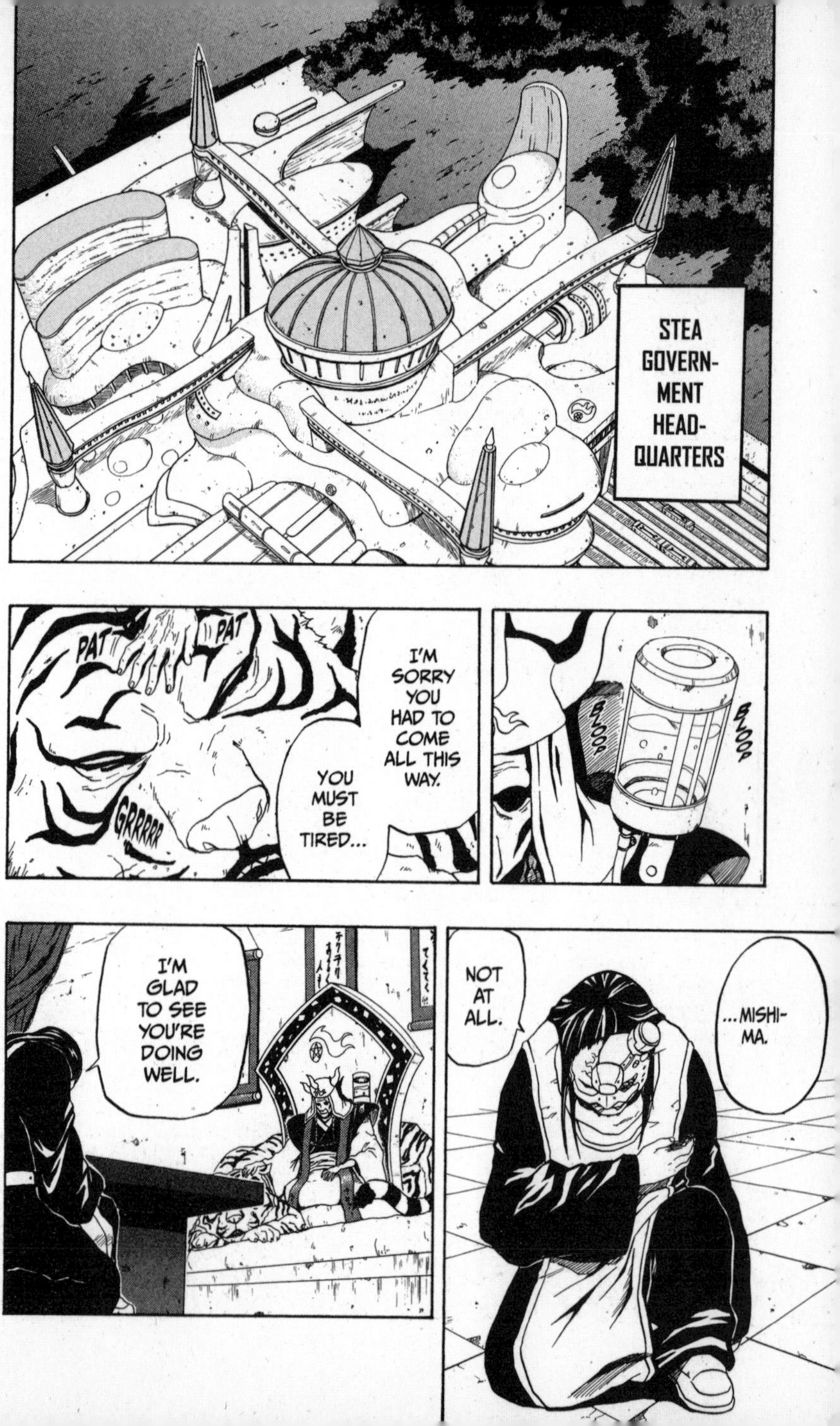
STEA GOVERNMENT HEADQUARTERS
BLOOP BLOOP
I'M SORRY YOU HAD TO COME ALL THIS WAY.
YOU MUST BE TIRED...
PAT PAT
GRRRRR
...MISHIMA.
NOT AT ALL.
I'M GLAD TO SEE YOU'RE DOING WELL.

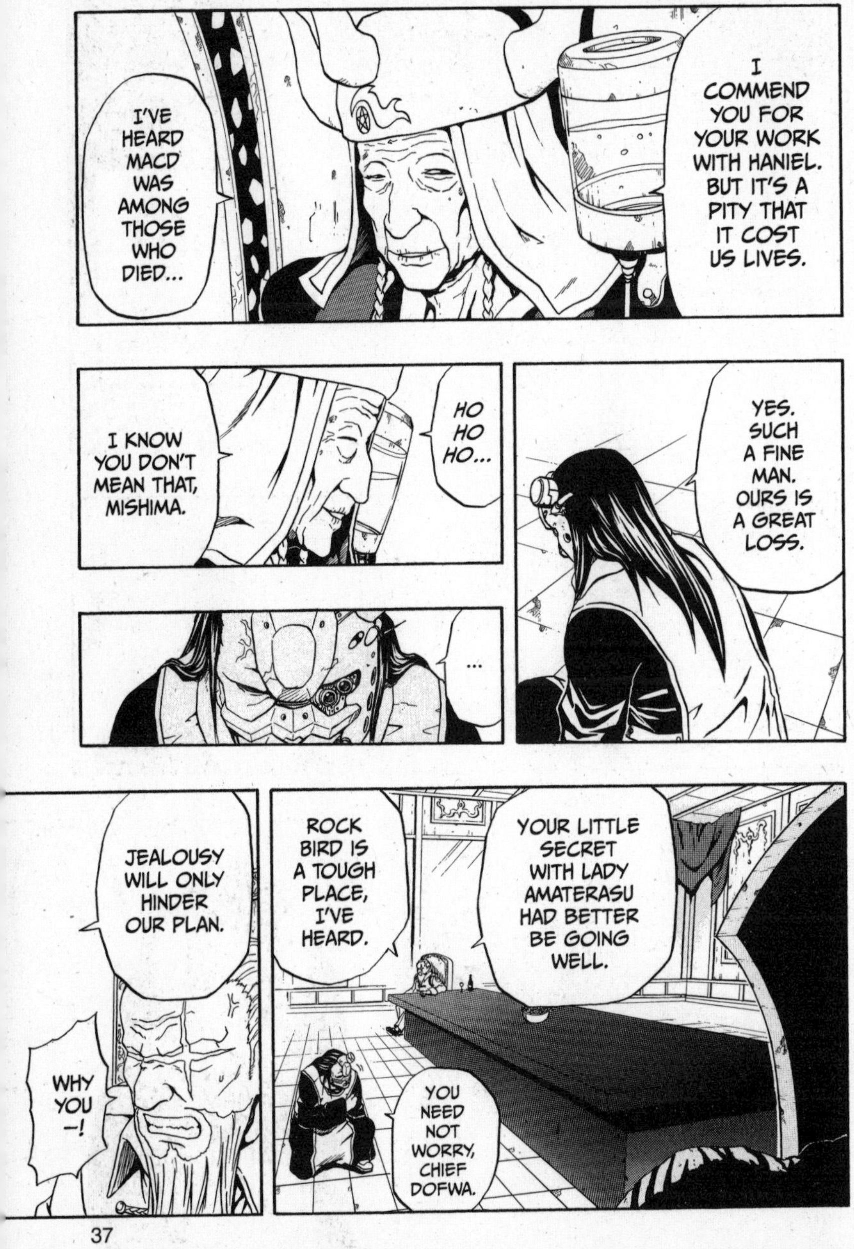
I COMMEND YOU FOR YOUR WORK WITH HANIEL. BUT IT'S A PITY THAT IT COST US LIVES.
I'VE HEARD MACD WAS AMONG THOSE WHO DIED...
YES. SUCH A FINE MAN. OURS IS A GREAT LOSS.
HO HO HO...
I KNOW YOU DON'T MEAN THAT, MISHIMA.
...
YOUR LITTLE SECRET WITH LADY AMATERASU HAD BETTER BE GOING WELL.
ROCK BIRD IS A TOUGH PLACE, I'VE HEARD.
YOU NEED NOT WORRY, CHIEF DOFWA.
JEALOUSY WILL ONLY HINDER OUR PLAN.
WHY YOU —!

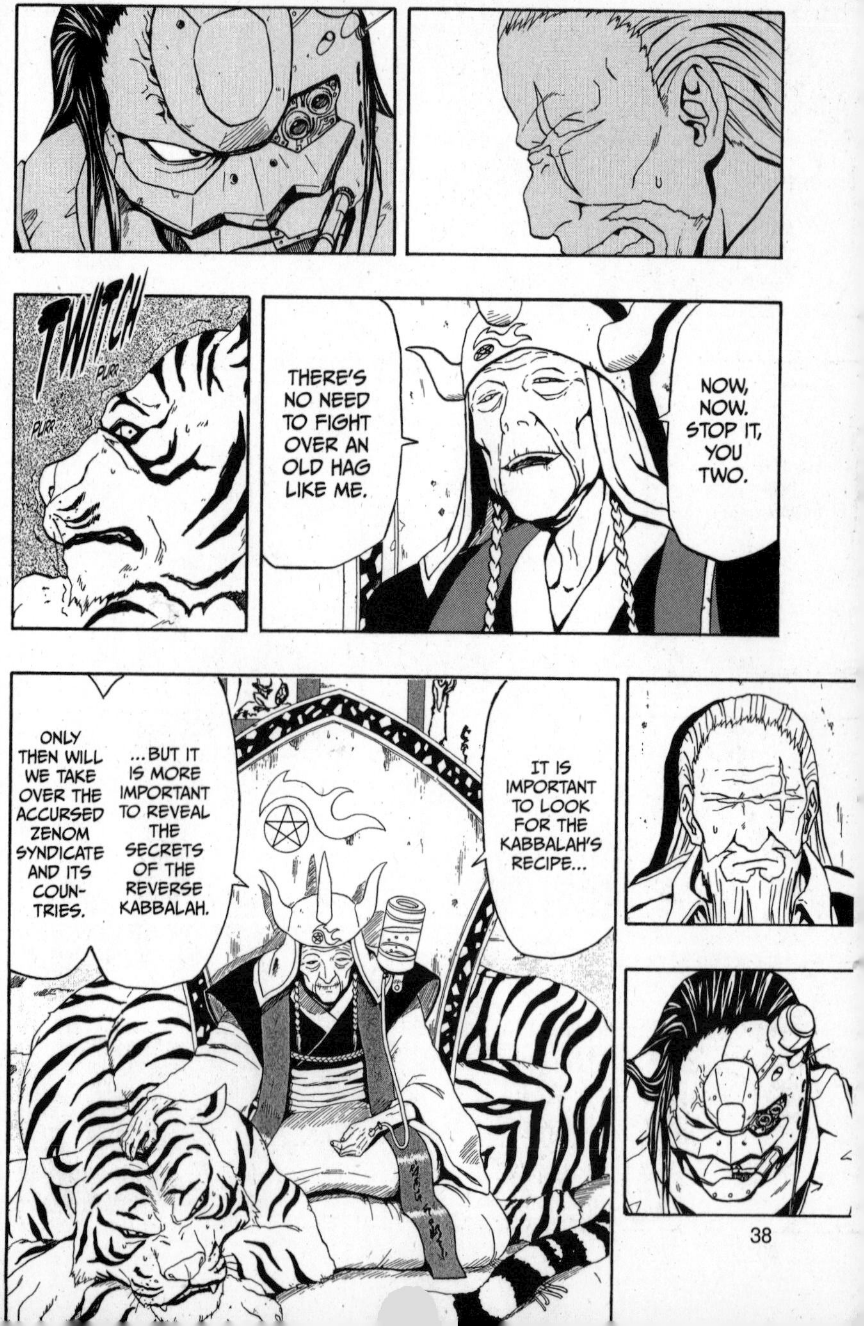
NOW, NOW. STOP IT, YOU TWO.
THERE'S NO NEED TO FIGHT OVER AN OLD HAG LIKE ME.
TWITCH
PURR
PURR
IT IS IMPORTANT TO LOOK FOR THE KABBALAH'S RECIPE...
...BUT IT IS MORE IMPORTANT TO REVEAL THE SECRETS OF THE REVERSE KABBALAH.
ONLY THEN WILL WE TAKE OVER THE ACCURSED ZENOM SYNDICATE AND ITS COUN-TRIES.

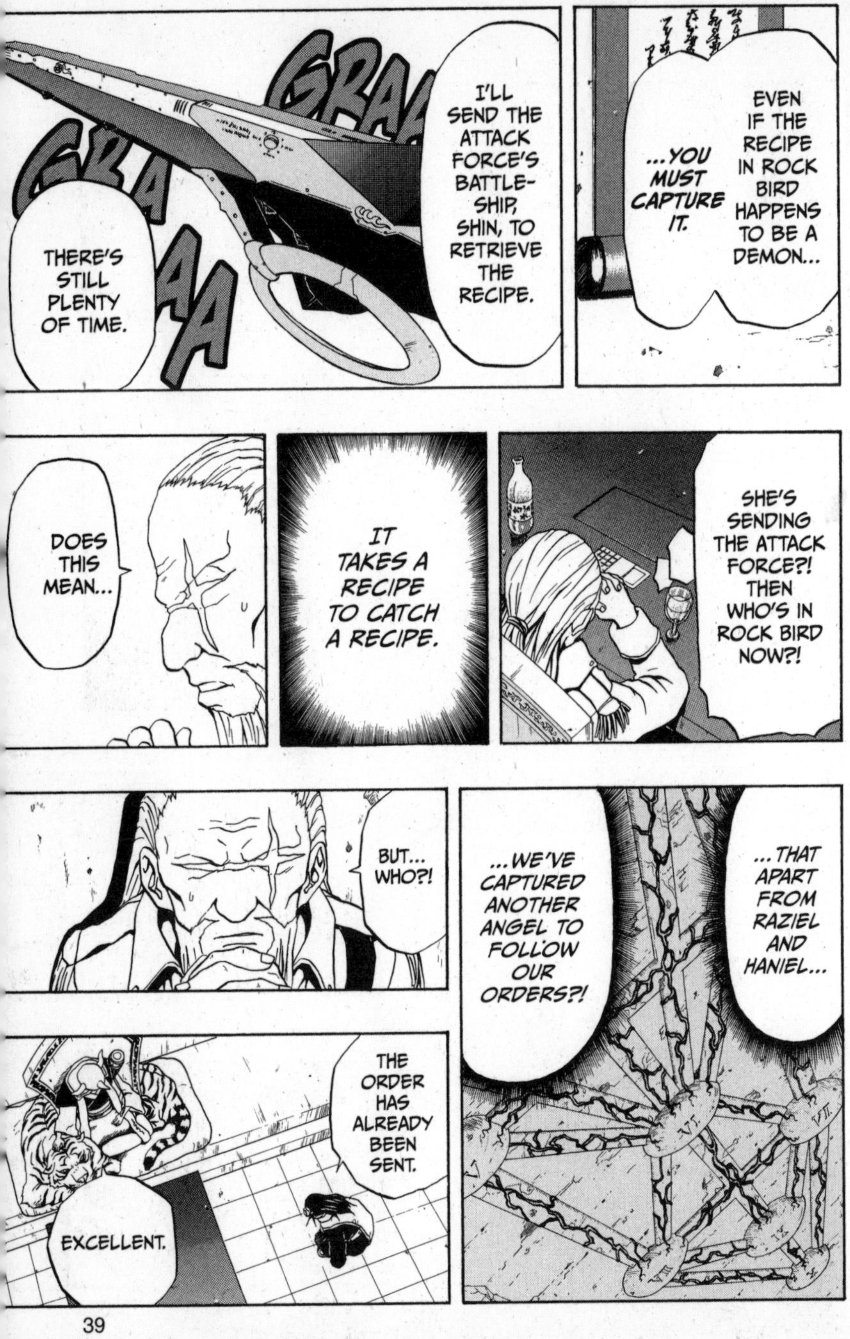
EVEN IF THE RECIPE IN ROCK BIRD HAPPENS TO BE A DEMON...
...YOU MUST CAPTURE IT.
I'LL SEND THE ATTACK FORCE'S BATTLESHIP, SHIN, TO RETRIEVE THE RECIPE.
GRAA
GRAAA
THERE'S STILL PLENTY OF TIME.
SHE'S SENDING THE ATTACK FORCE?! THEN WHO'S IN ROCK BIRD NOW?!
IT TAKES A RECIPE TO CATCH A RECIPE.
DOES THIS MEAN...
...THAT APART FROM RAZIEL AND HANIEL...
...WE'VE CAPTURED ANOTHER ANGEL TO FOLLOW OUR ORDERS?!
BUT... WHO?!
THE ORDER HAS ALREADY BEEN SENT.
EXCELLENT.

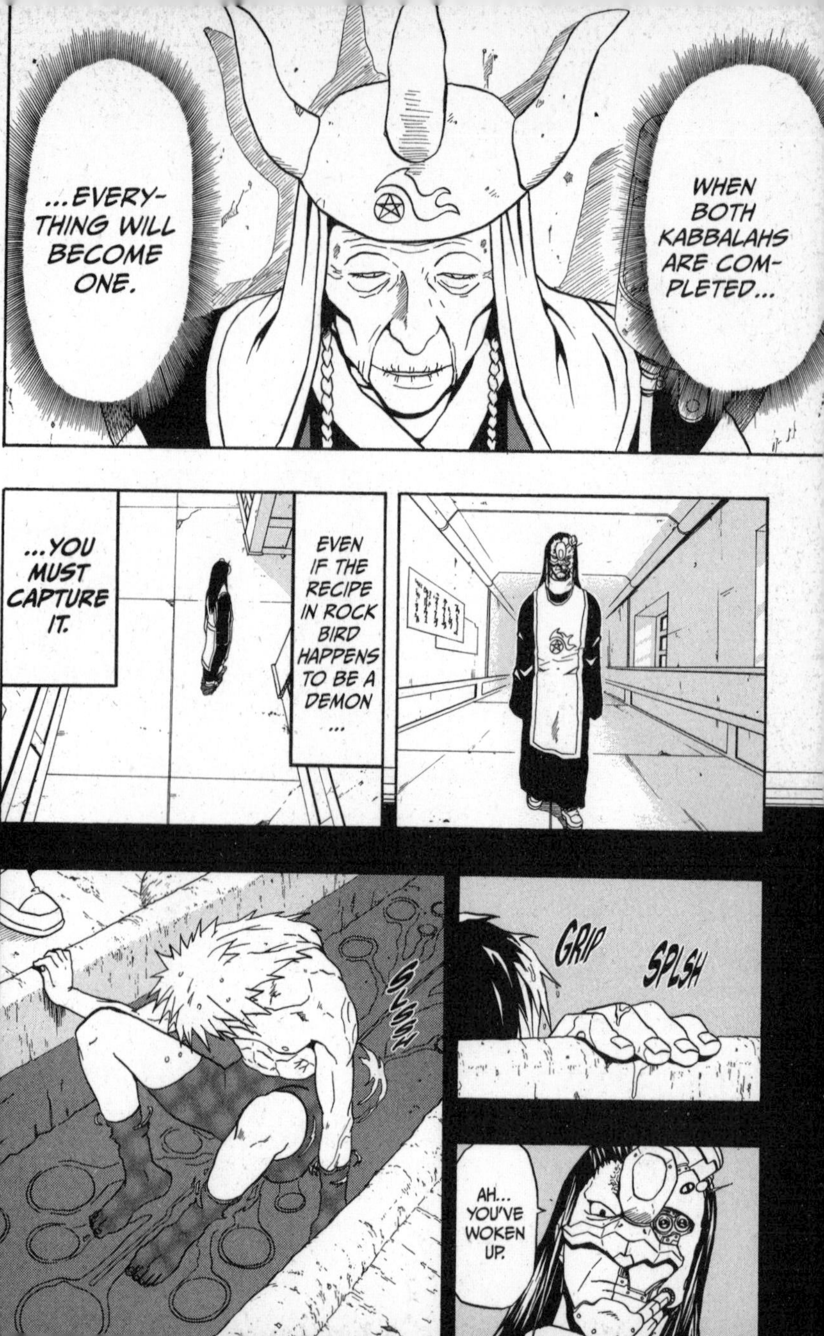
WHEN BOTH KABBALAHS ARE COMPLETED...
...EVERYTHING WILL BECOME ONE.
EVEN IF THE RECIPE IN ROCK BIRD HAPPENS TO BE A DEMON ...
...YOU MUST CAPTURE IT.
GRIP
SPLSH
AH... YOU'VE WOKEN UP.
SLSSH

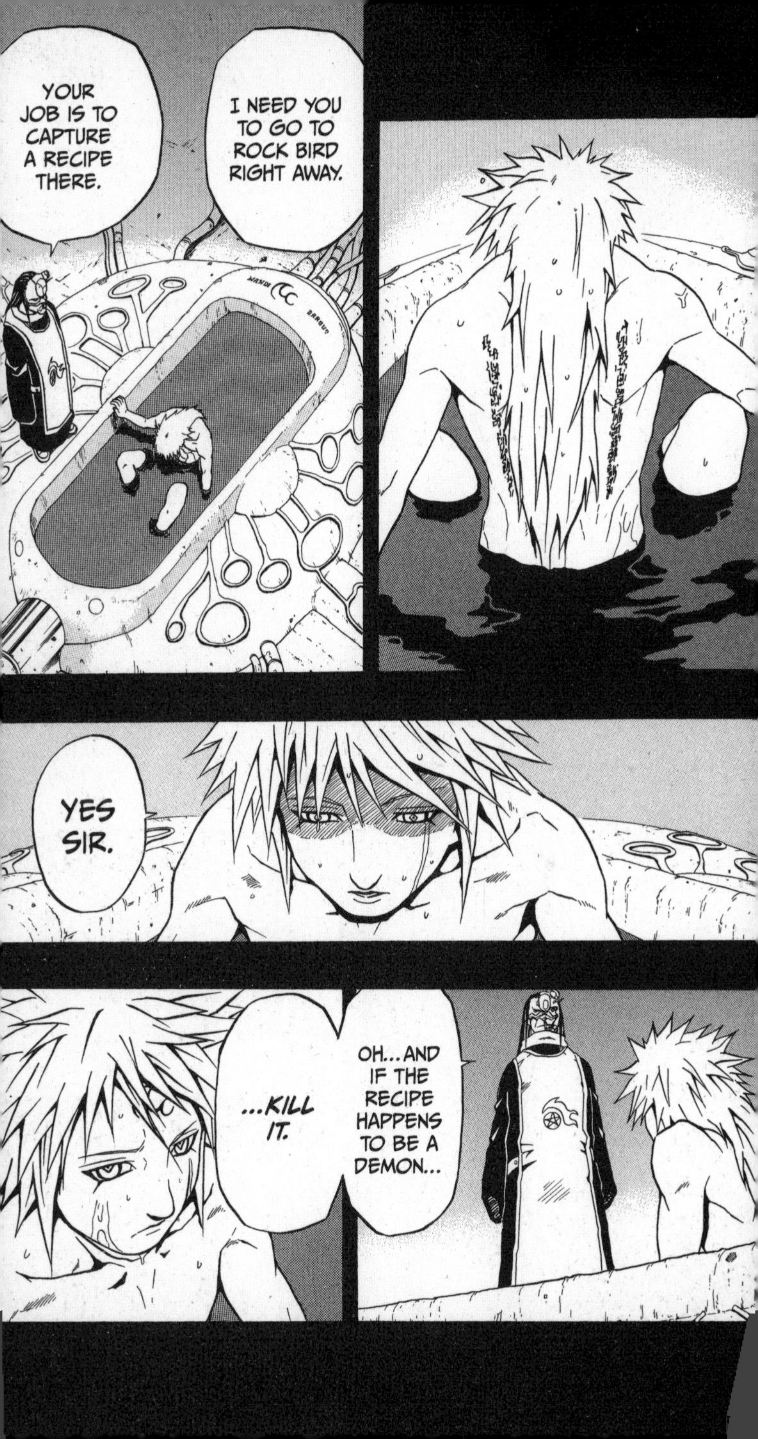

I NEED YOU TO GO TO ROCK BIRD RIGHT AWAY.
YOUR JOB IS TO CAPTURE A RECIPE THERE.
YES SIR.
OH...AND IF THE RECIPE HAPPENS TO BE A DEMON...
...KILL IT.

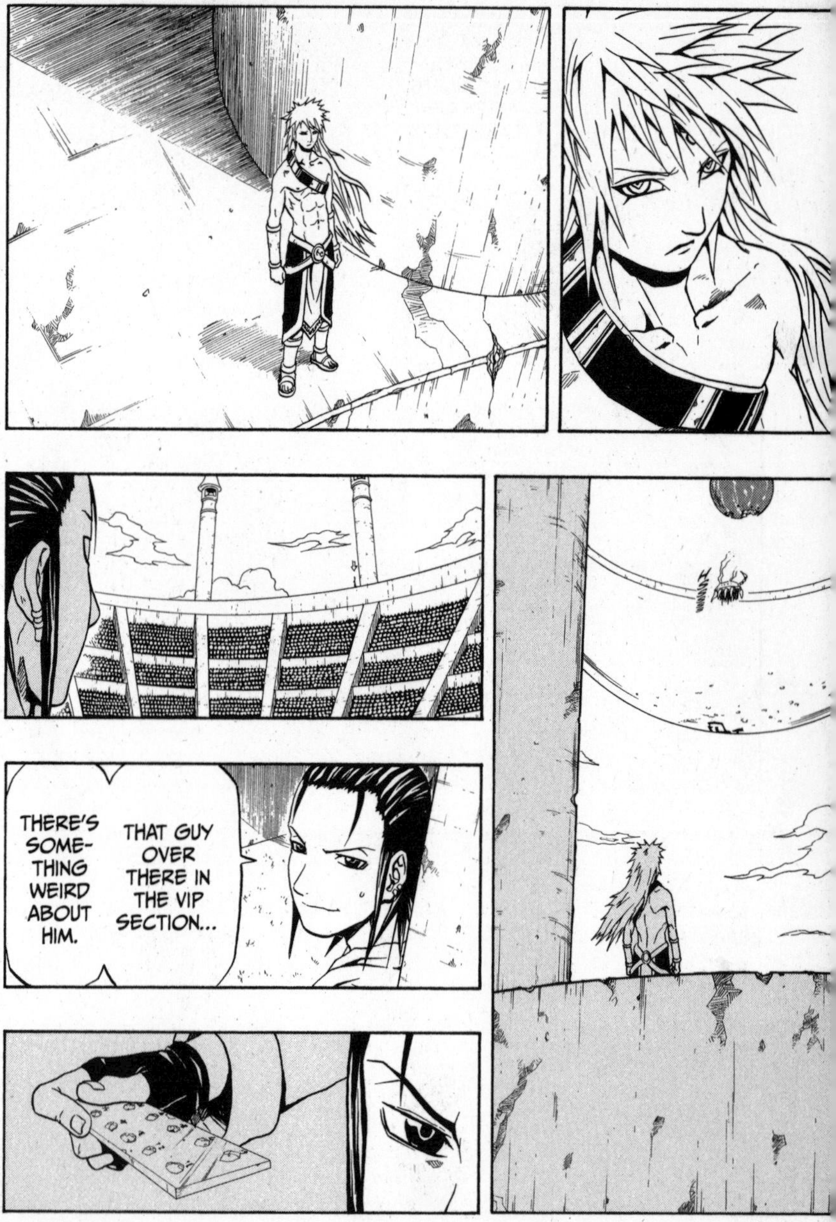
THAT GUY OVER THERE IN THE VIP SECTION...
THERE'S SOME-THING WEIRD ABOUT HIM.

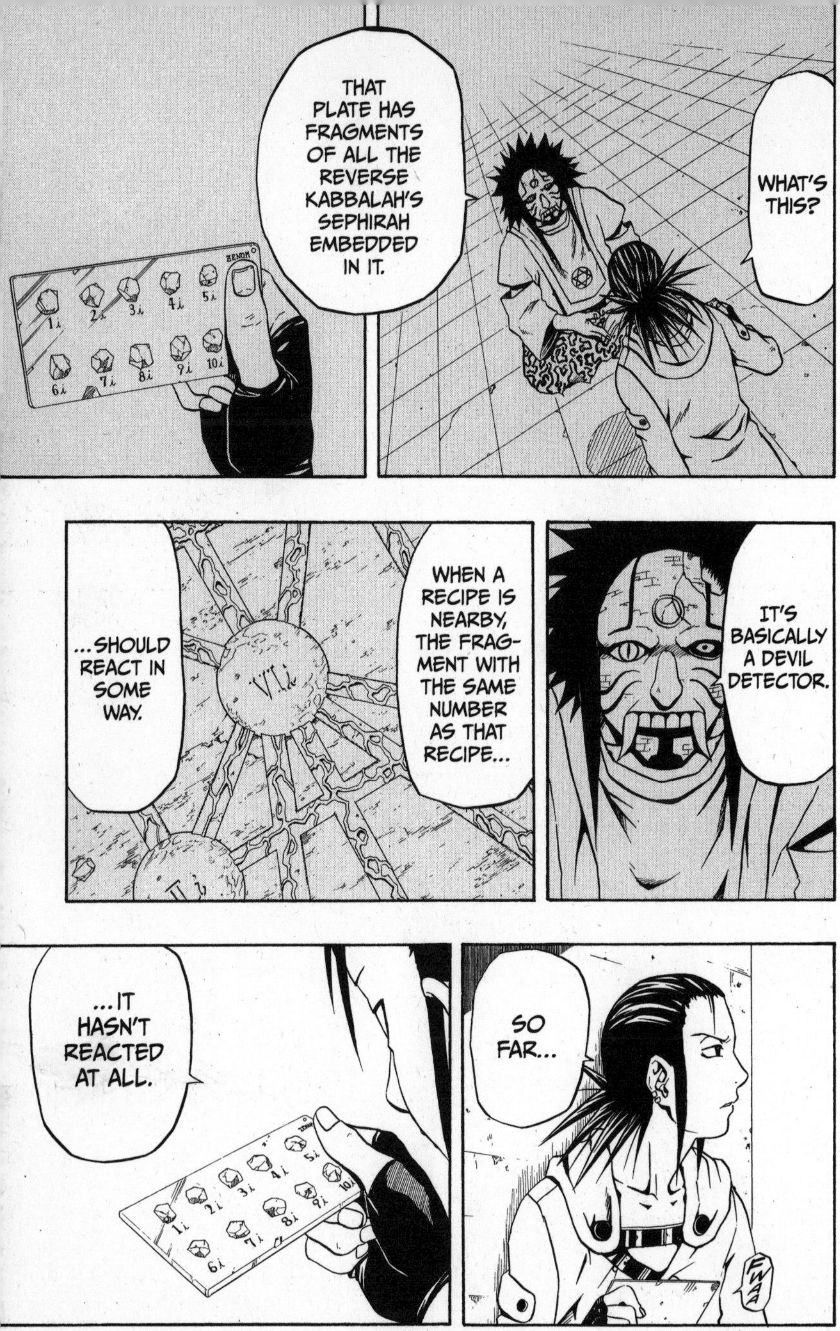
WHAT'S THIS?
THAT PLATE HAS FRAGMENTS OF ALL THE REVERSE KABBALAH'S SEPHIRAH EMBEDDED IN IT.
IT'S BASICALLY A DEVIL DETECTOR.
WHEN A RECIPE IS NEARBY, THE FRAG-MENT WITH THE SAME NUMBER AS THAT RECIPE...
...SHOULD REACT IN SOME WAY.
SO FAR...
FWAA
...IT HASN'T REACTED AT ALL.

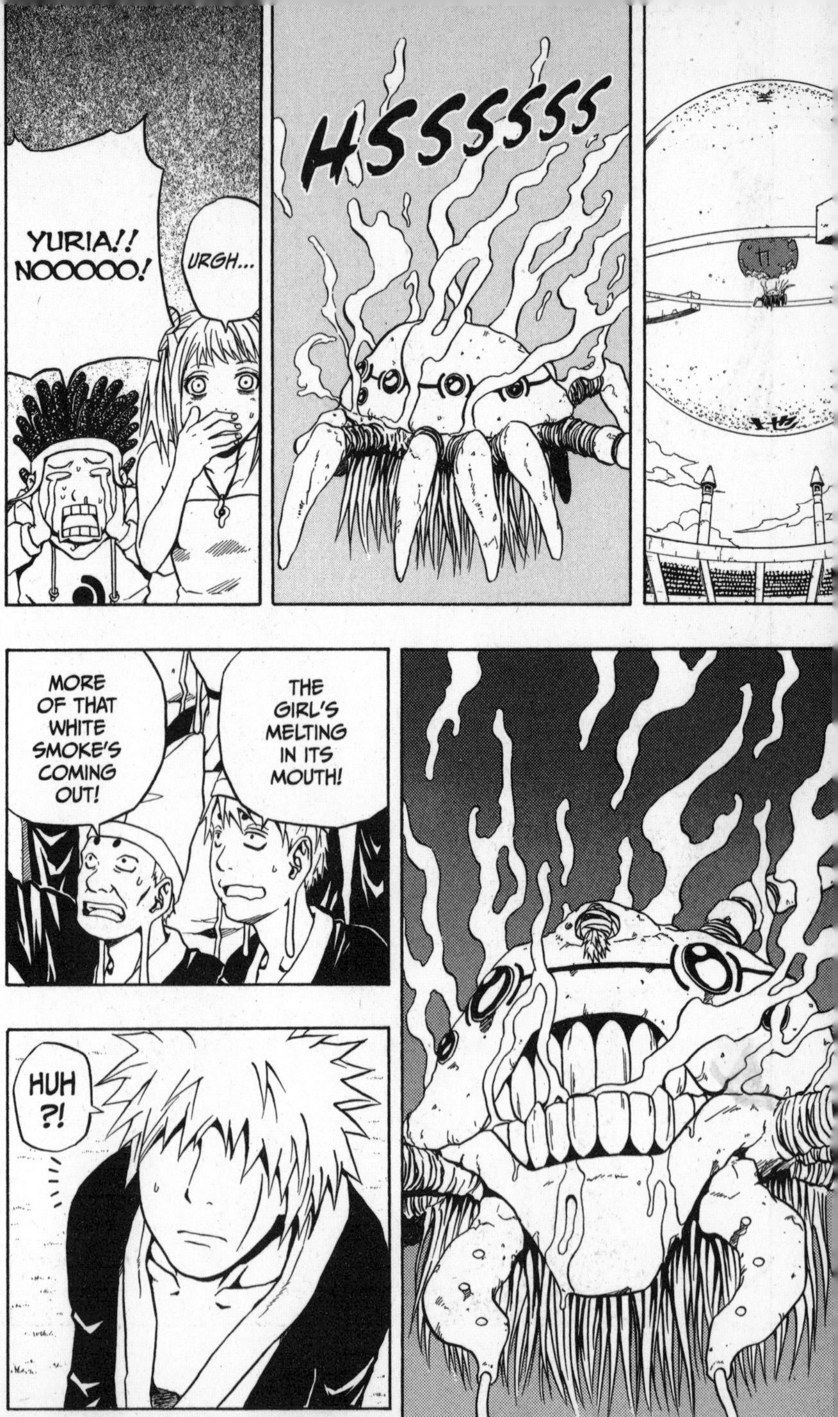
HSSSSSS
URGH...
YURIA!! NOOOOO!
THE GIRL'S MELTING IN ITS MOUTH!
MORE OF THAT WHITE SMOKE'S COMING OUT!
HUH ?!

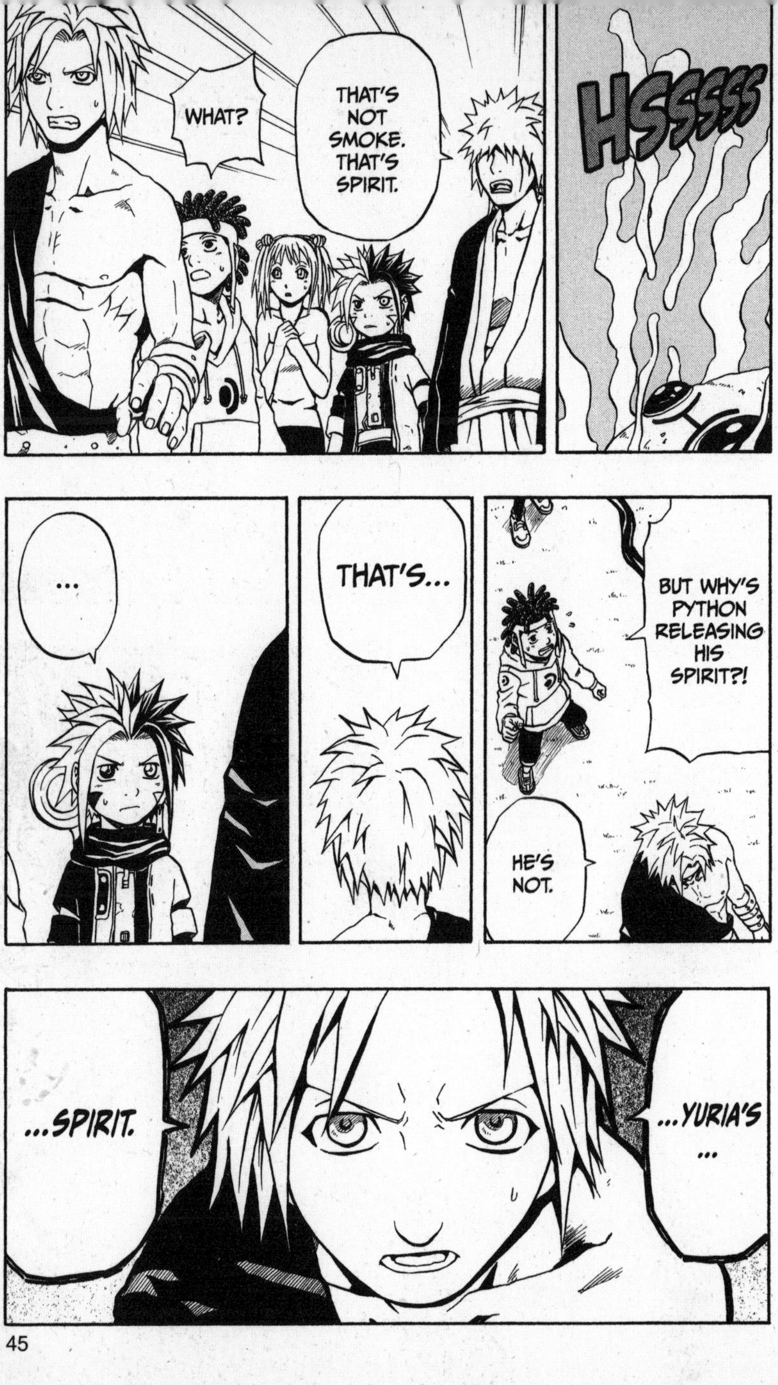
HSSSSS
THAT'S NOT SMOKE. THAT'S SPIRIT.
WHAT?
BUT WHY'S PYTHON RELEASING HIS SPIRIT?!
HE'S NOT.
THAT'S...
...
...YURIA'S ...
...SPIRIT.

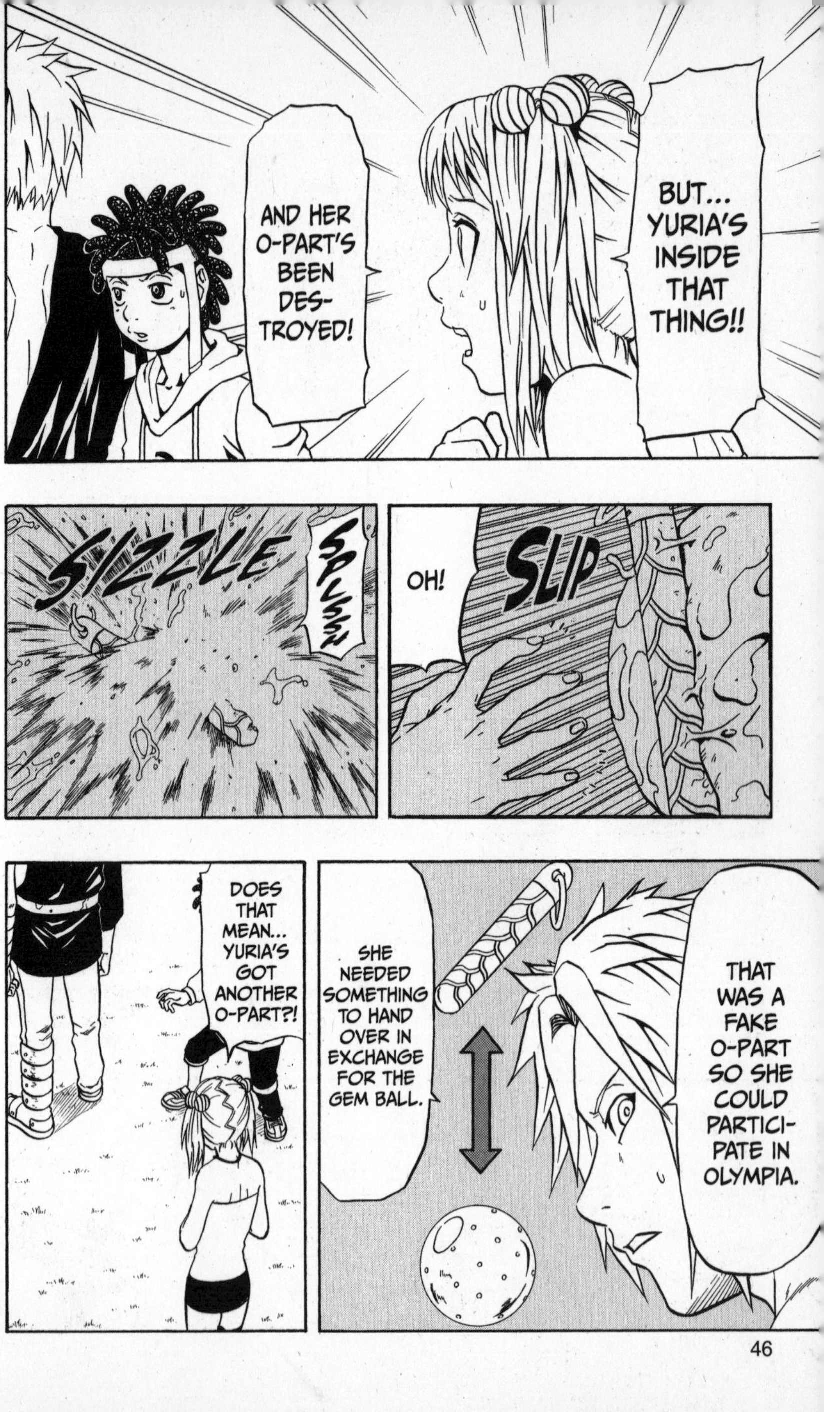
BUT... YURIA'S INSIDE THAT THING!!
AND HER O-PART'S BEEN DES-TROYED!
SLIP
OH!
SPLSSH
SIZZLE
THAT WAS A FAKE O-PART SO SHE COULD PARTICI-PATE IN OLYMPIA.
SHE NEEDED SOMETHING TO HAND OVER IN EXCHANGE FOR THE GEM BALL.
DOES THAT MEAN... YURIA'S GOT ANOTHER O-PART?!

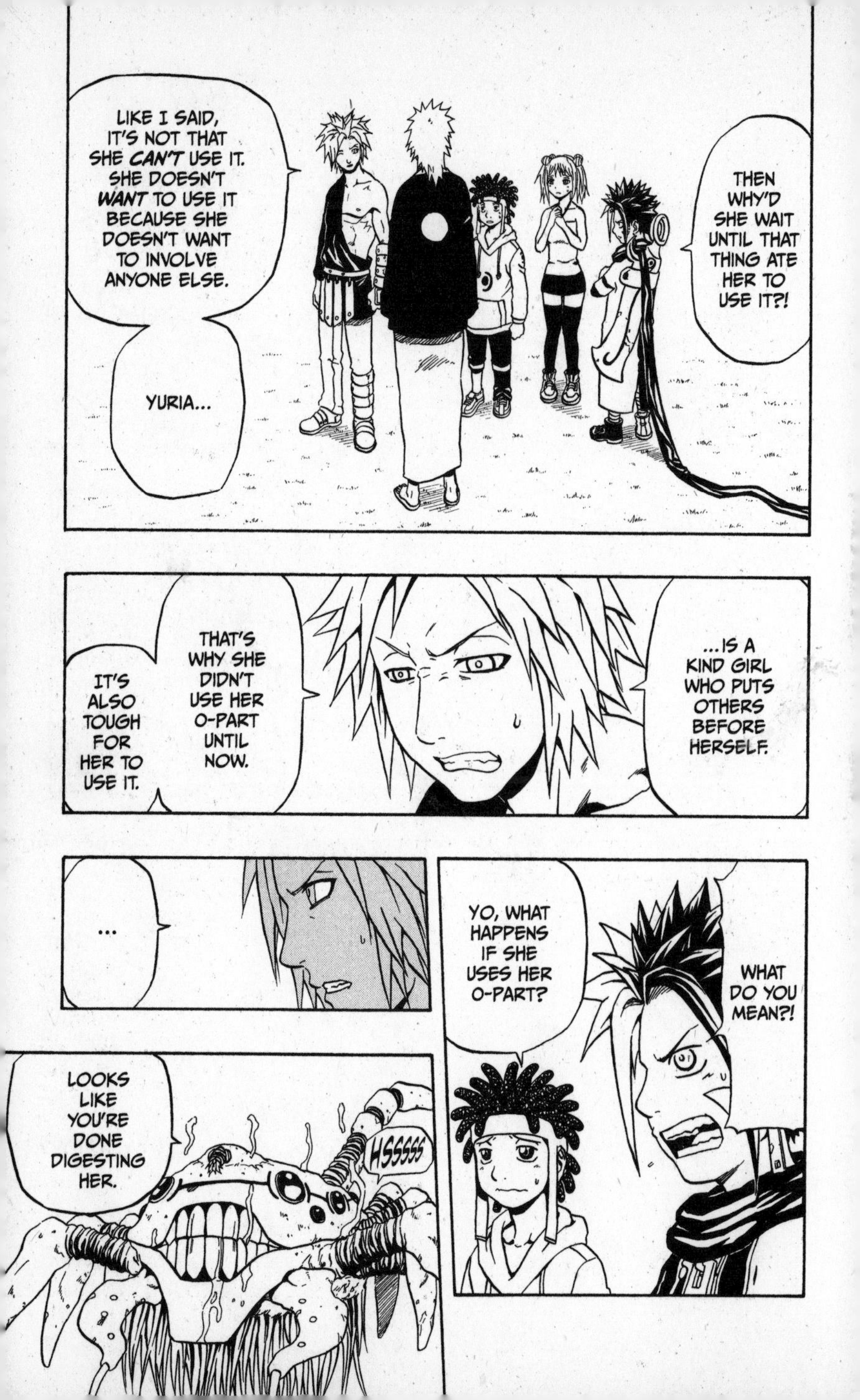
THEN WHY'D SHE WAIT UNTIL THAT THING ATE HER TO USE IT?!
LIKE I SAID, IT'S NOT THAT SHE *CAN'T* USE IT. SHE DOESN'T *WANT* TO USE IT BECAUSE SHE DOESN'T WANT TO INVOLVE ANYONE ELSE.
YURIA...
...IS A KIND GIRL WHO PUTS OTHERS BEFORE HERSELF.
THAT'S WHY SHE DIDN'T USE HER O-PART UNTIL NOW.
IT'S ALSO TOUGH FOR HER TO USE IT.
WHAT DO YOU MEAN?!
YO, WHAT HAPPENS IF SHE USES HER O-PART?
...
LOOKS LIKE YOU'RE DONE DIGESTING HER.
HSSSSS

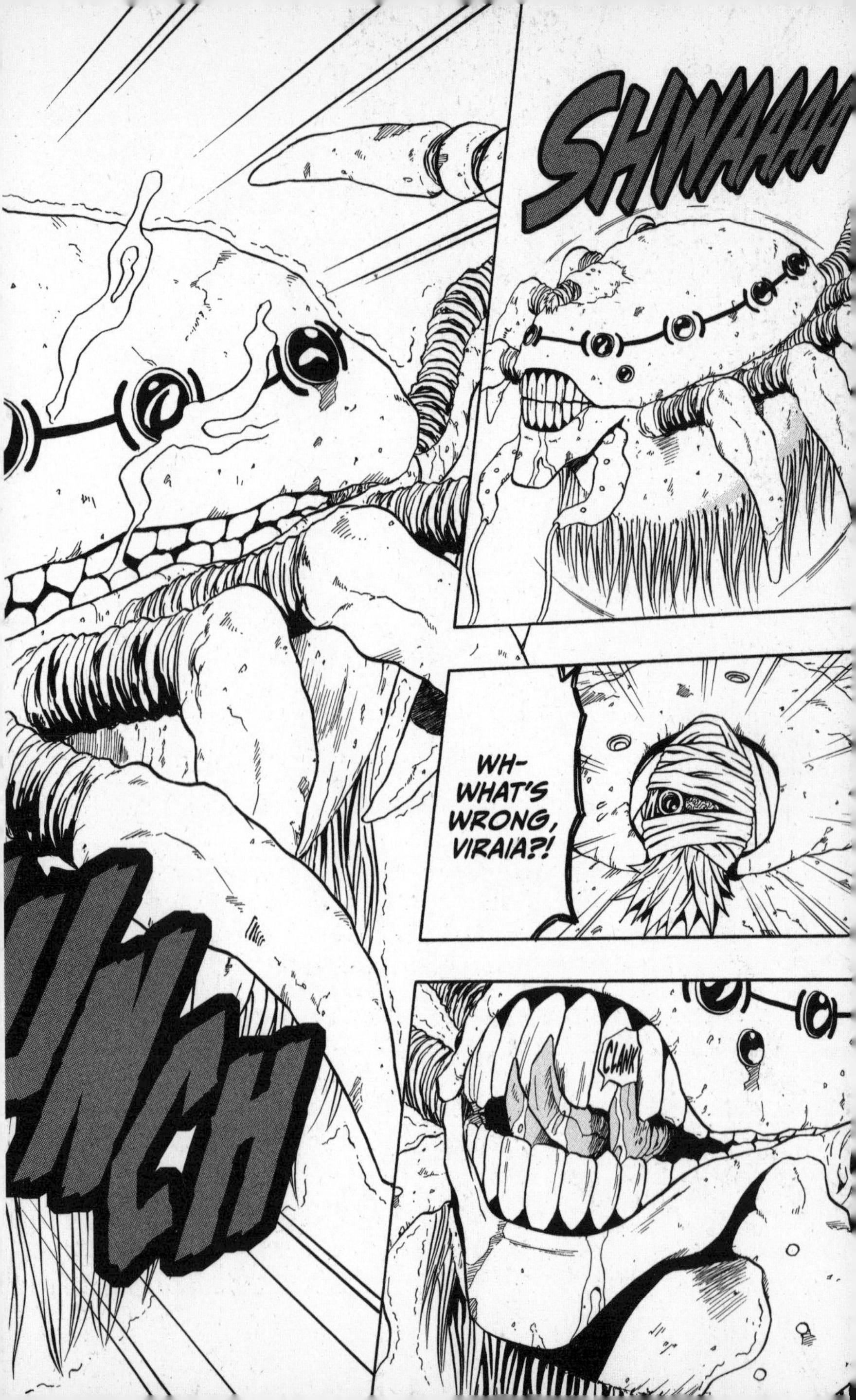
SHWAAA
WH-WHAT'S WRONG, VIRAIA?!
CLANK

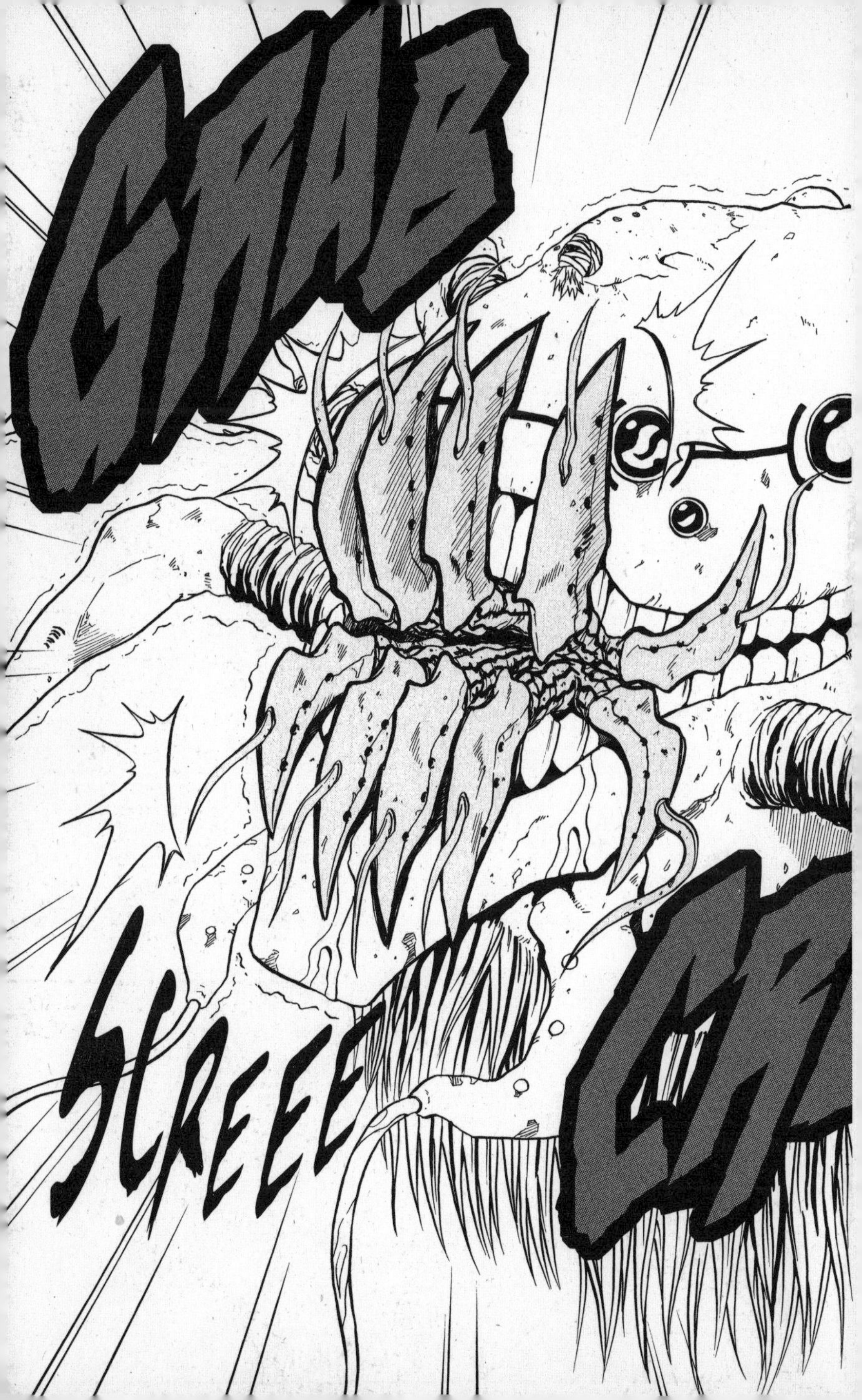
GRAB
SCREEE

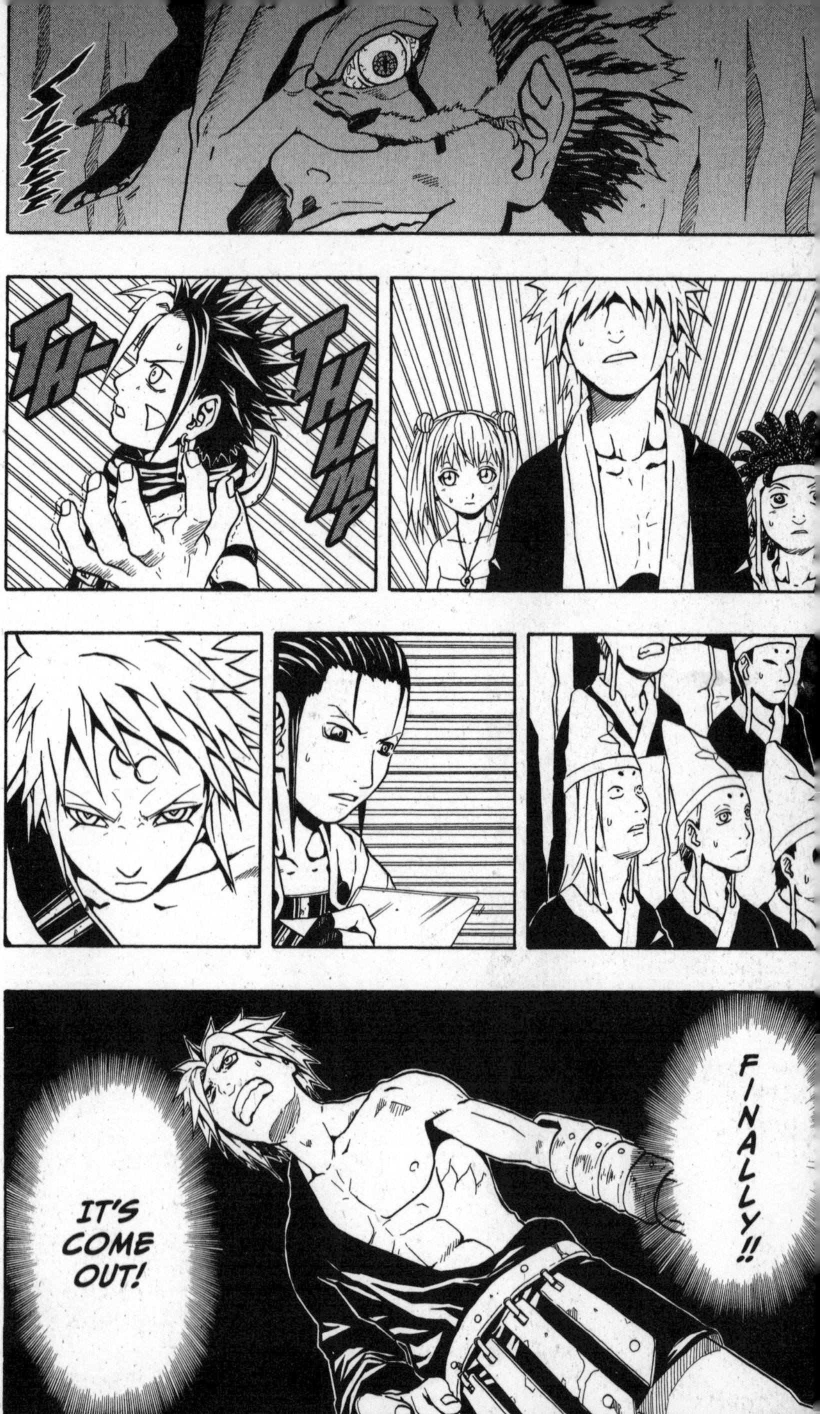
TH-
FINALLY!!
IT'S COME OUT!

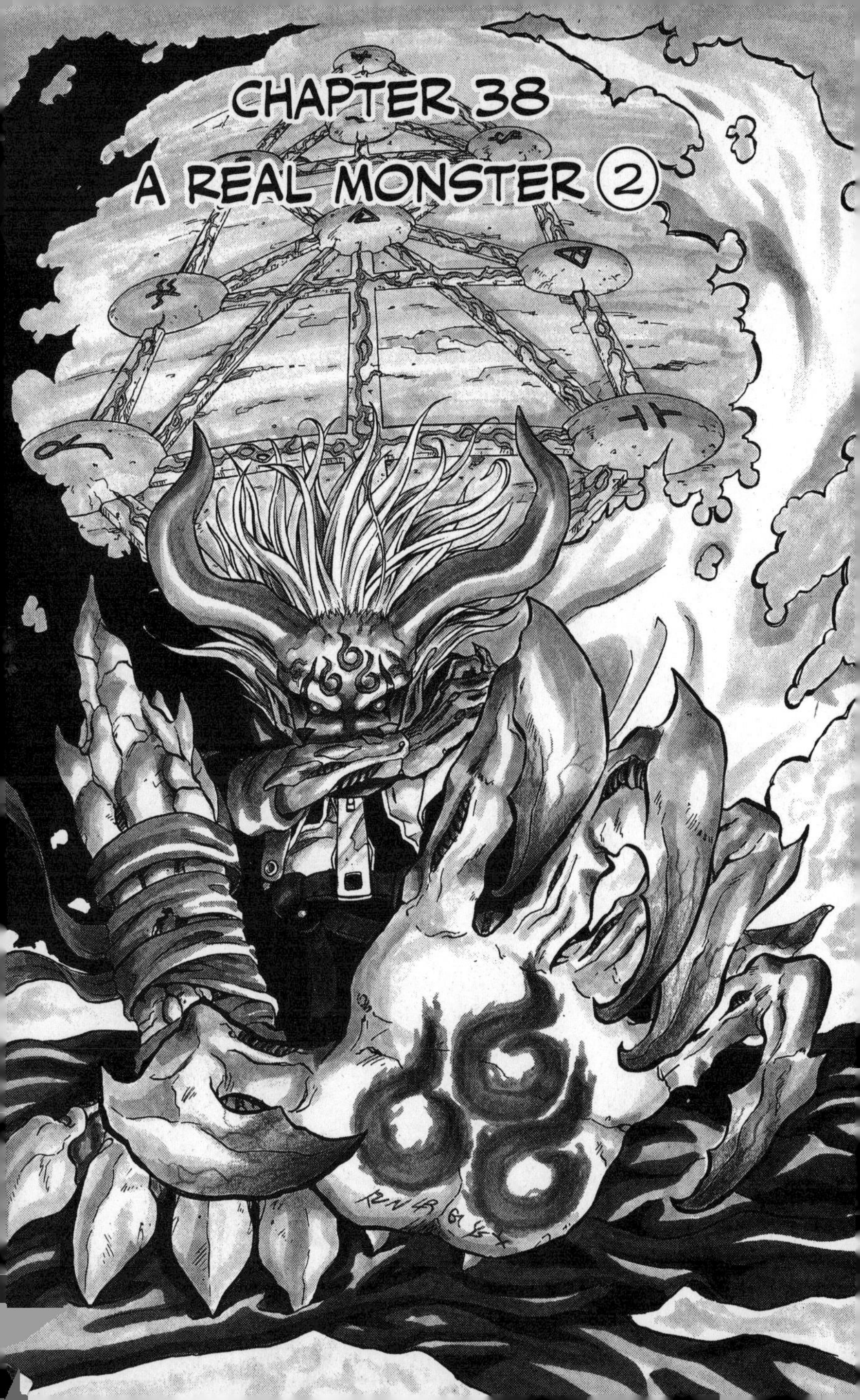
CHAPTER 38
A REAL MONSTER ②

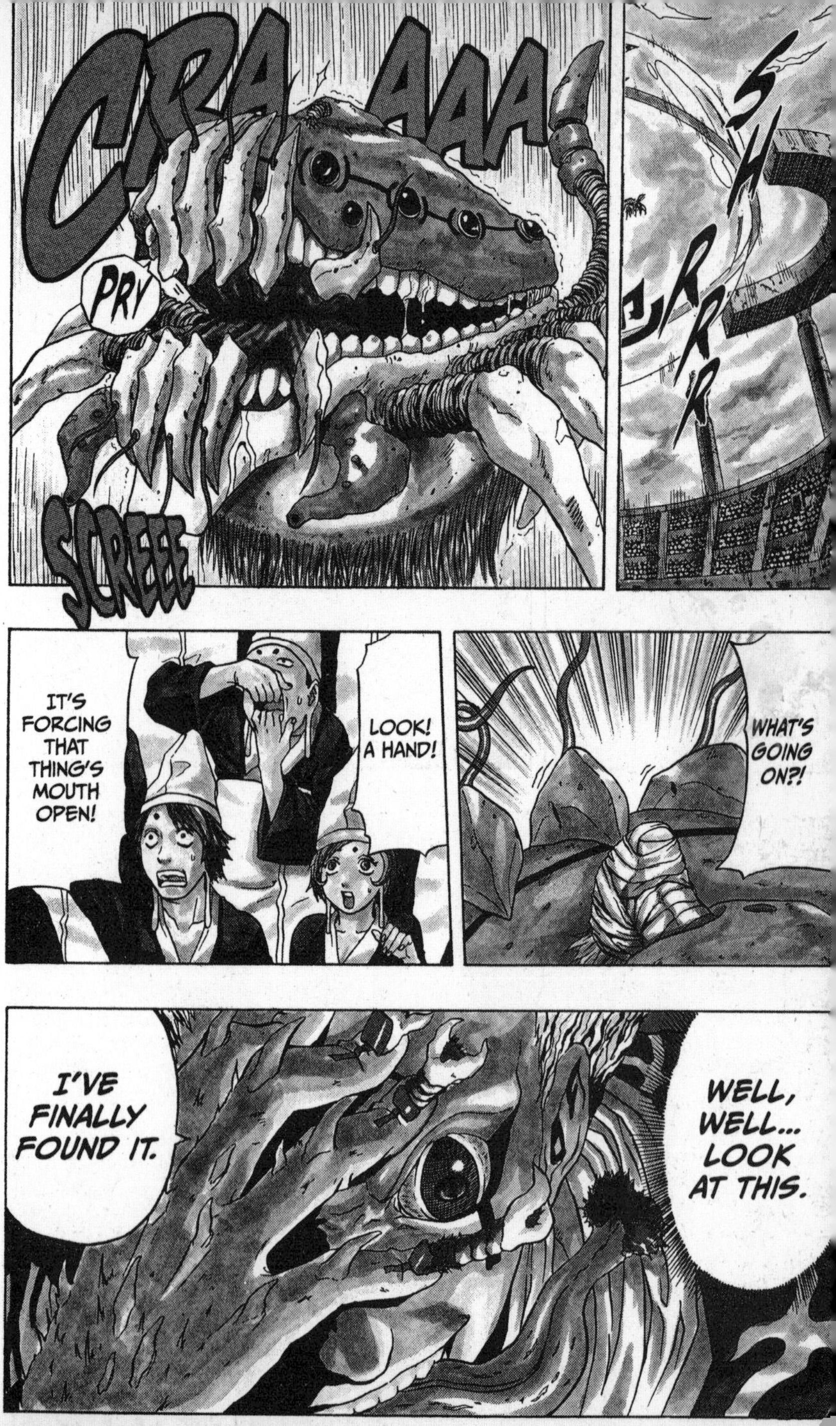
SHRRRR
CRAAAA
PRY
SCREEE
WHAT'S GOING ON?!
LOOK! A HAND!
IT'S FORCING THAT THING'S MOUTH OPEN!
WELL, WELL... LOOK AT THIS.
I'VE FINALLY FOUND IT.

URGH!

WH-WHAT'S GOING ON? WHY—?!

TH-THIS IS...

ZRRRRR

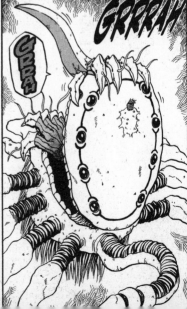

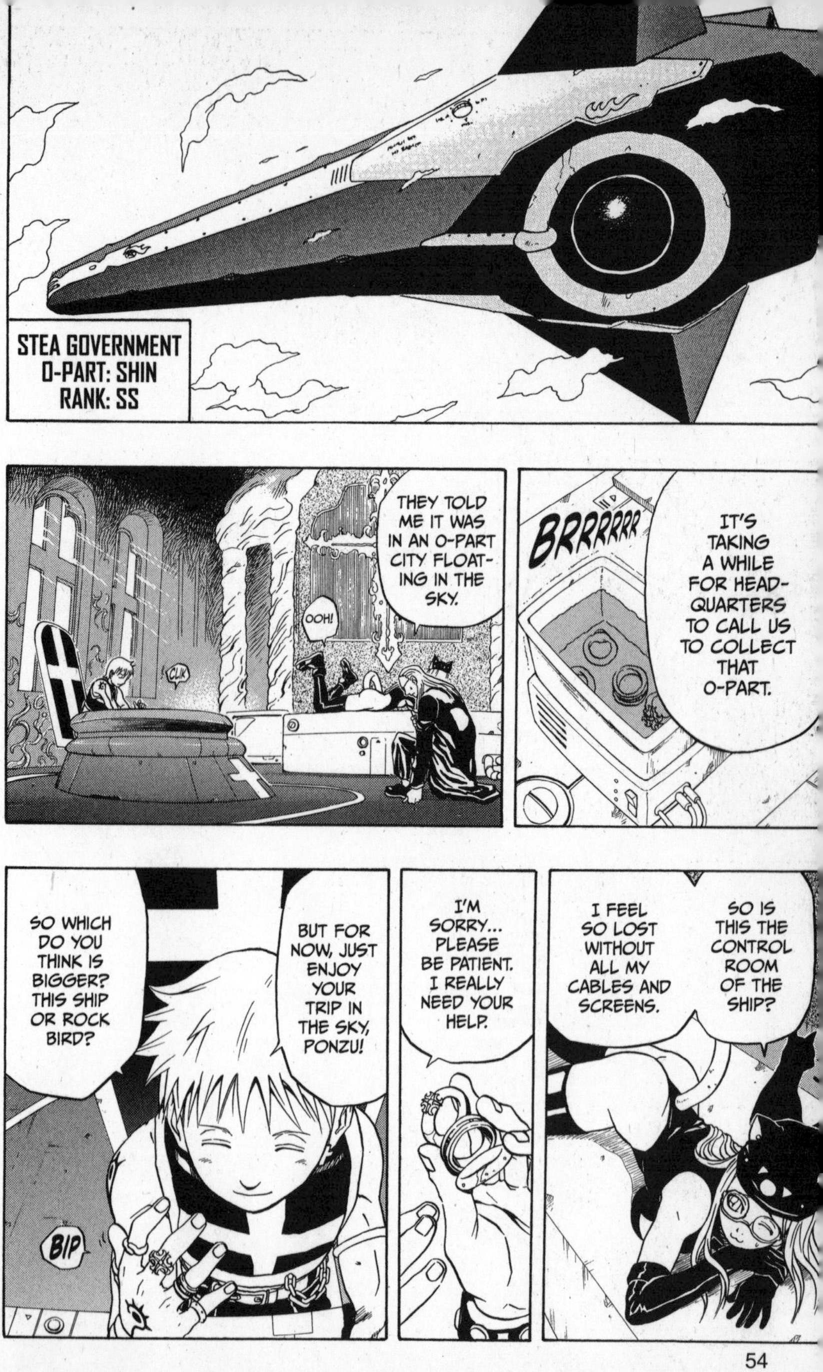
STEA GOVERNMENT
O-PART: SHIN
RANK: SS
IT'S TAKING A WHILE FOR HEAD-QUARTERS TO CALL US TO COLLECT THAT O-PART.
BRRRRRR
THEY TOLD ME IT WAS IN AN O-PART CITY FLOAT-ING IN THE SKY.
OOH!
CLIK
SO IS THIS THE CONTROL ROOM OF THE SHIP?
I FEEL SO LOST WITHOUT ALL MY CABLES AND SCREENS.
I'M SORRY... PLEASE BE PATIENT. I REALLY NEED YOUR HELP.
BUT FOR NOW, JUST ENJOY YOUR TRIP IN THE SKY, PONZU!
SO WHICH DO YOU THINK IS BIGGER? THIS SHIP OR ROCK BIRD?
BIP

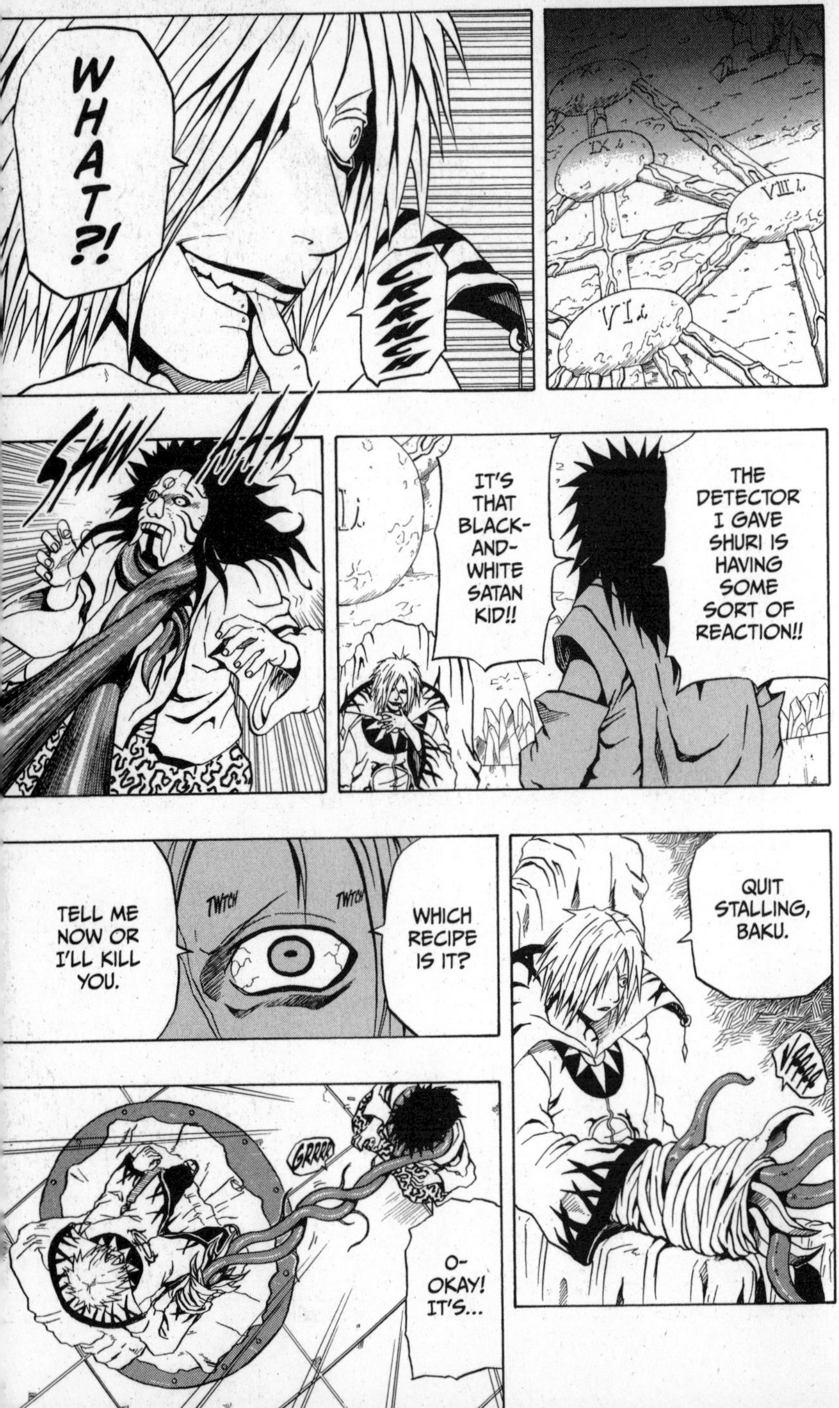
WHAT?!
THE DETECTOR I GAVE SHURI IS HAVING SOME SORT OF REACTION!!
IT'S THAT BLACK-AND-WHITE SATAN KID!!
SHWAAAA
QUIT STALLING, BAKU.
TWTCH
TWTCH
WHICH RECIPE IS IT?
TELL ME NOW OR I'LL KILL YOU.
GRRRR
O-OKAY! IT'S...

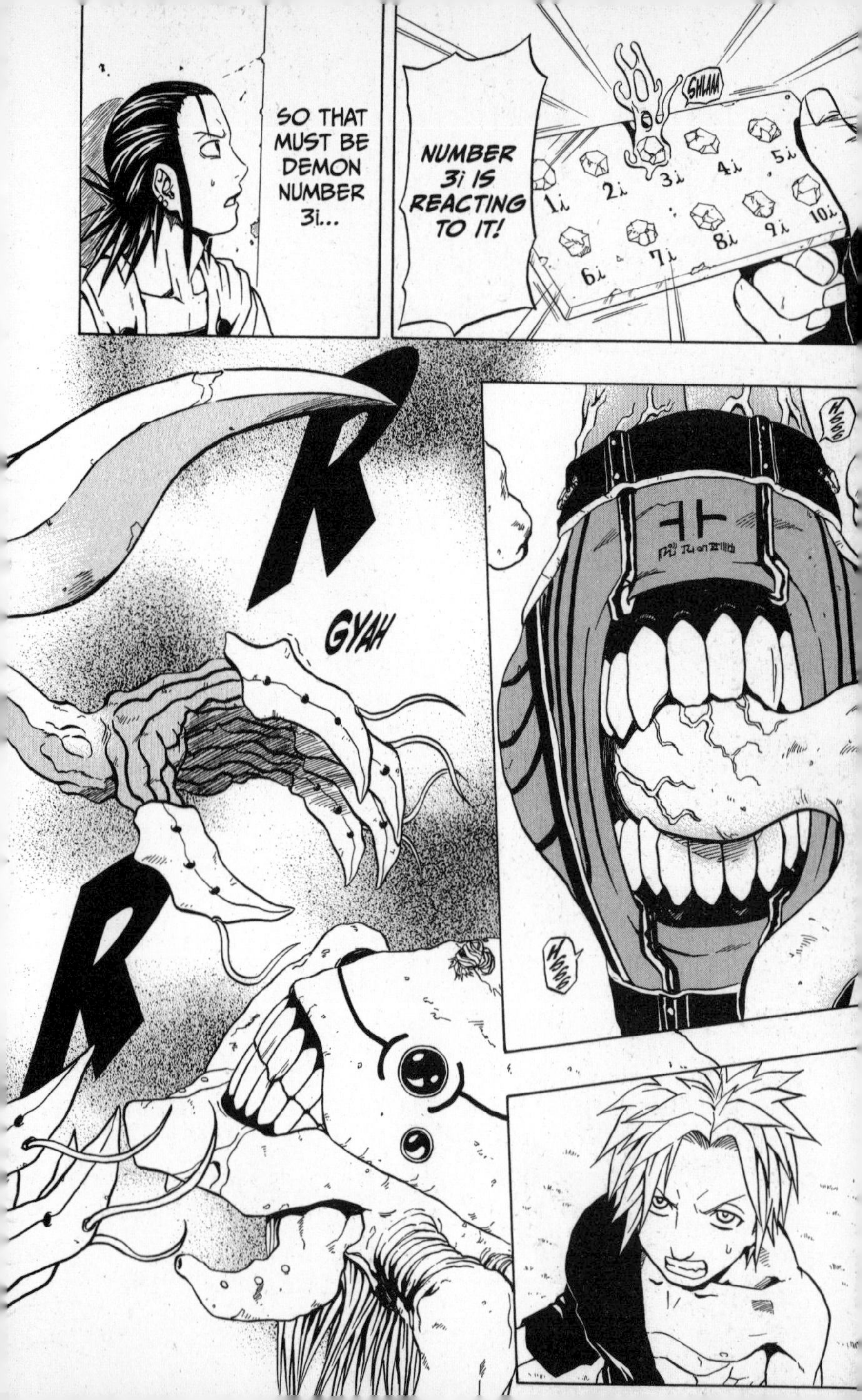
NUMBER 3i IS REACTING TO IT!
SHLAAA
1i 2i 3i 4i 5i 6i 7i 8i 9i 10i
SO THAT MUST BE DEMON NUMBER 3i...
NGGG
NGGG
R
GYAH
R

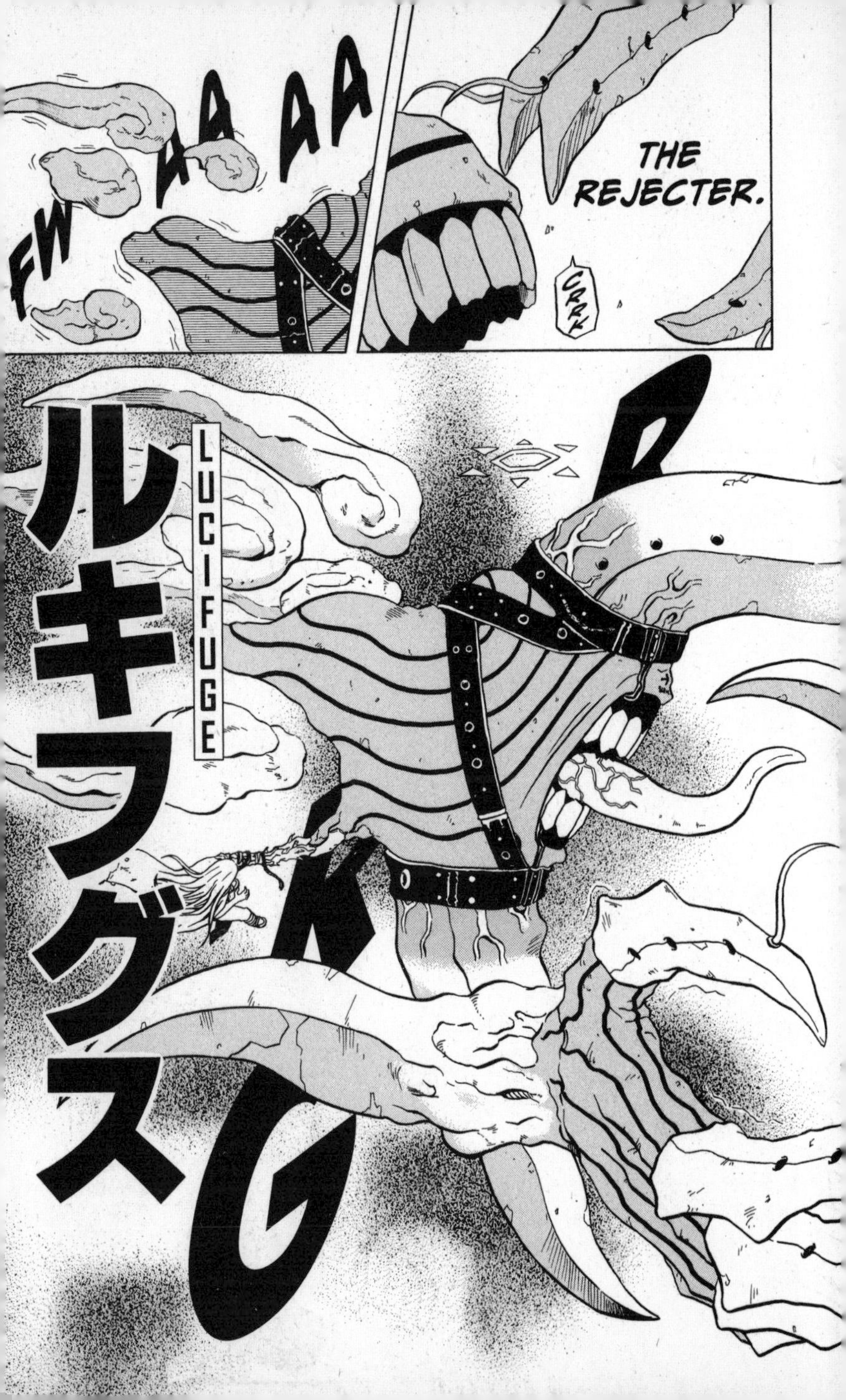
THE REJECTER.
CRRK
FWAAAAA
ルキフグス
LUCIFUGE

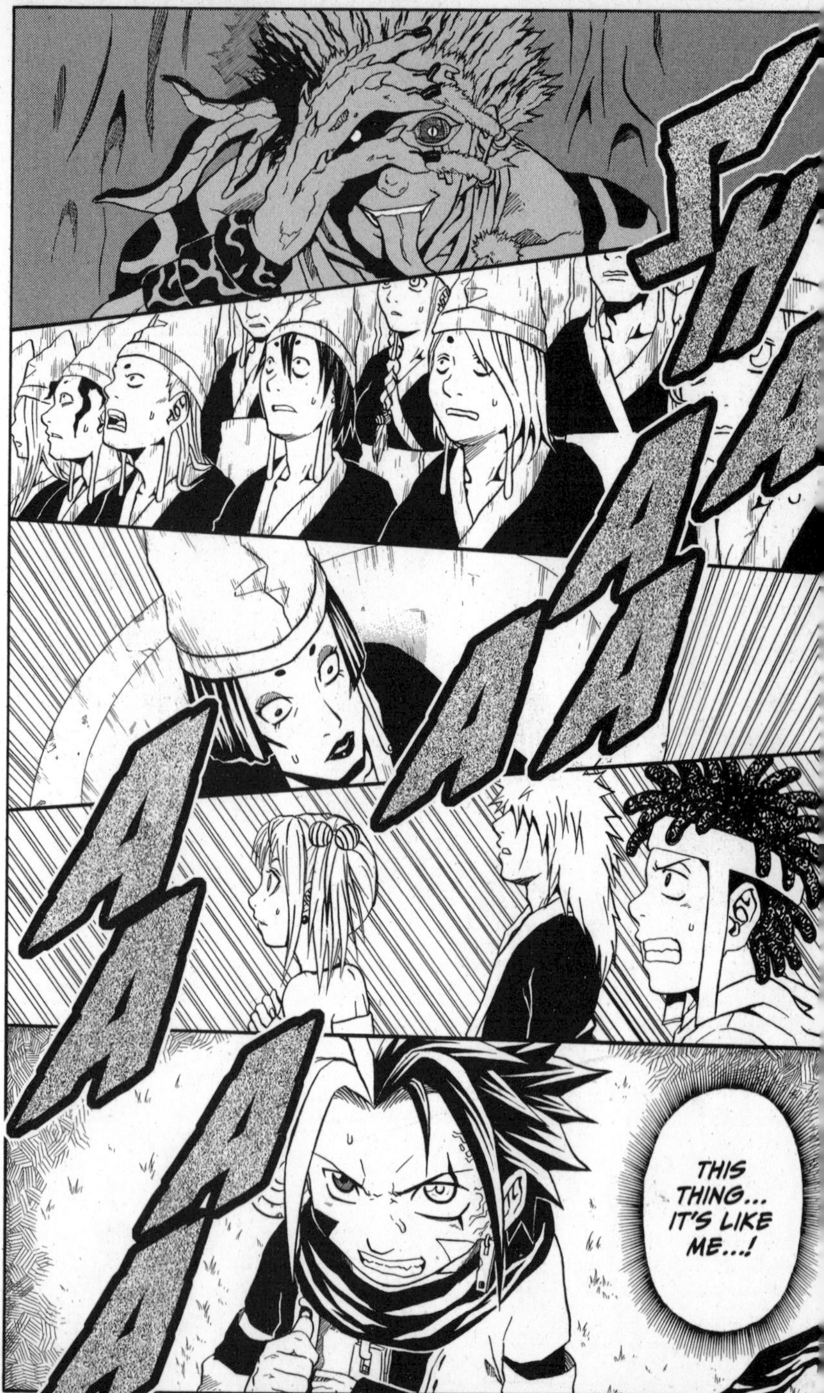
THIS THING... IT'S LIKE ME...!

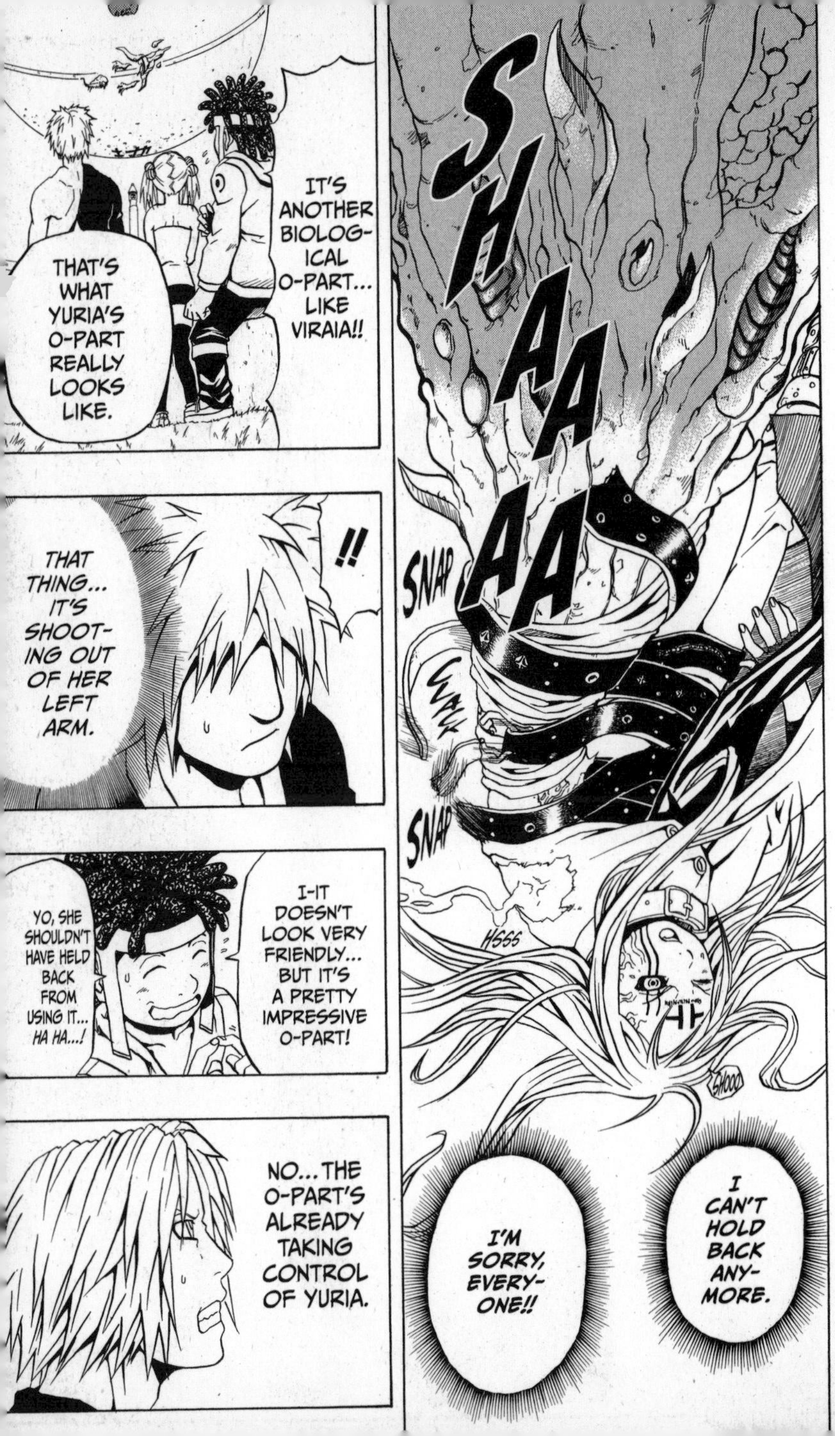
SHAAAA
SNAP
SNAP
HSSS
I CAN'T HOLD BACK ANYMORE.
I'M SORRY, EVERYONE!!
IT'S ANOTHER BIOLOGICAL O-PART... LIKE VIRAIA!!
THAT'S WHAT YURIA'S O-PART REALLY LOOKS LIKE.
!!
THAT THING... IT'S SHOOTING OUT OF HER LEFT ARM.
I-IT DOESN'T LOOK VERY FRIENDLY... BUT IT'S A PRETTY IMPRESSIVE O-PART!
YO, SHE SHOULDN'T HAVE HELD BACK FROM USING IT... HA HA...!
NO... THE O-PART'S ALREADY TAKING CONTROL OF YURIA.

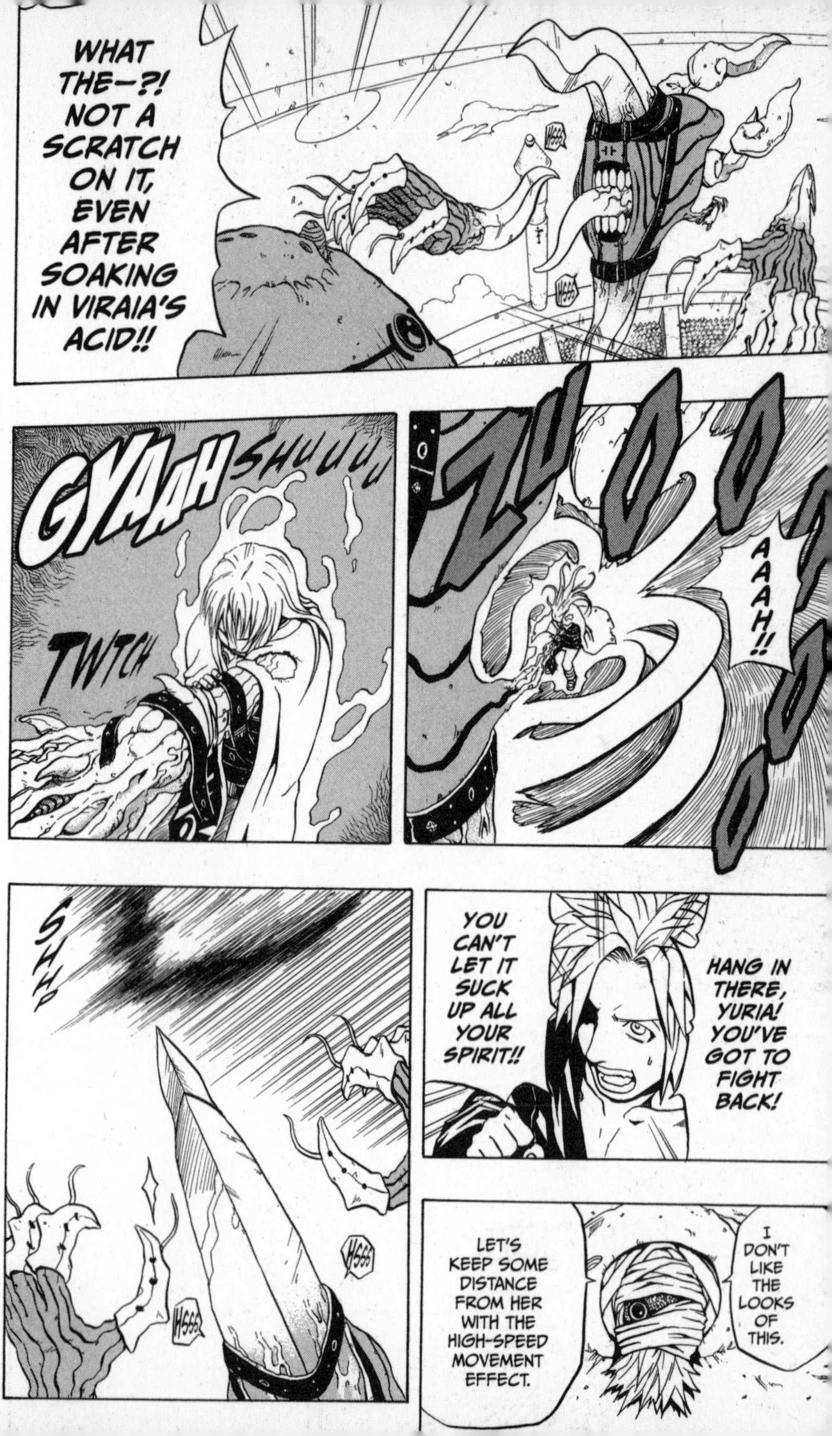
WHAT THE—?! NOT A SCRATCH ON IT, EVEN AFTER SOAKING IN VIRAIA'S ACID!!
HSSS
HSSS
ZUOOOOO
AAAAH!!
GYAAH
SHUUUU
TWTCH
HANG IN THERE, YURIA! YOU'VE GOT TO FIGHT BACK!
YOU CAN'T LET IT SUCK UP ALL YOUR SPIRIT!!
I DON'T LIKE THE LOOKS OF THIS.
LET'S KEEP SOME DISTANCE FROM HER WITH THE HIGH-SPEED MOVEMENT EFFECT.
SHHH
HSSS
HSSS

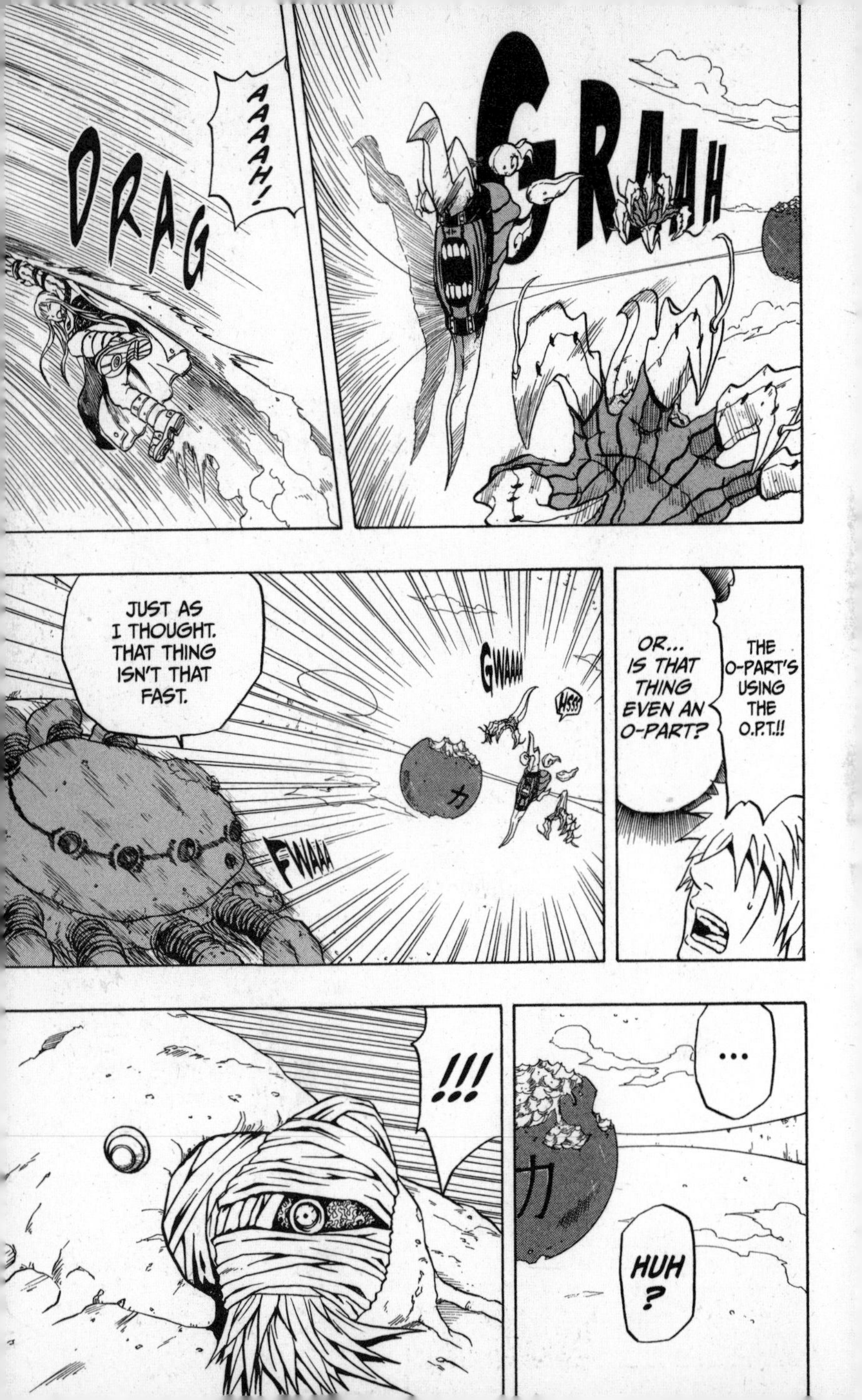
GRAAAH
AAAAAH!
DRAG
THE O-PART'S USING THE O.P.T.!!
OR... IS THAT THING EVEN AN O-PART?
JUST AS I THOUGHT. THAT THING ISN'T THAT FAST.
GWAAAA
HSSS
FWAAA
...
HUH?
!!!

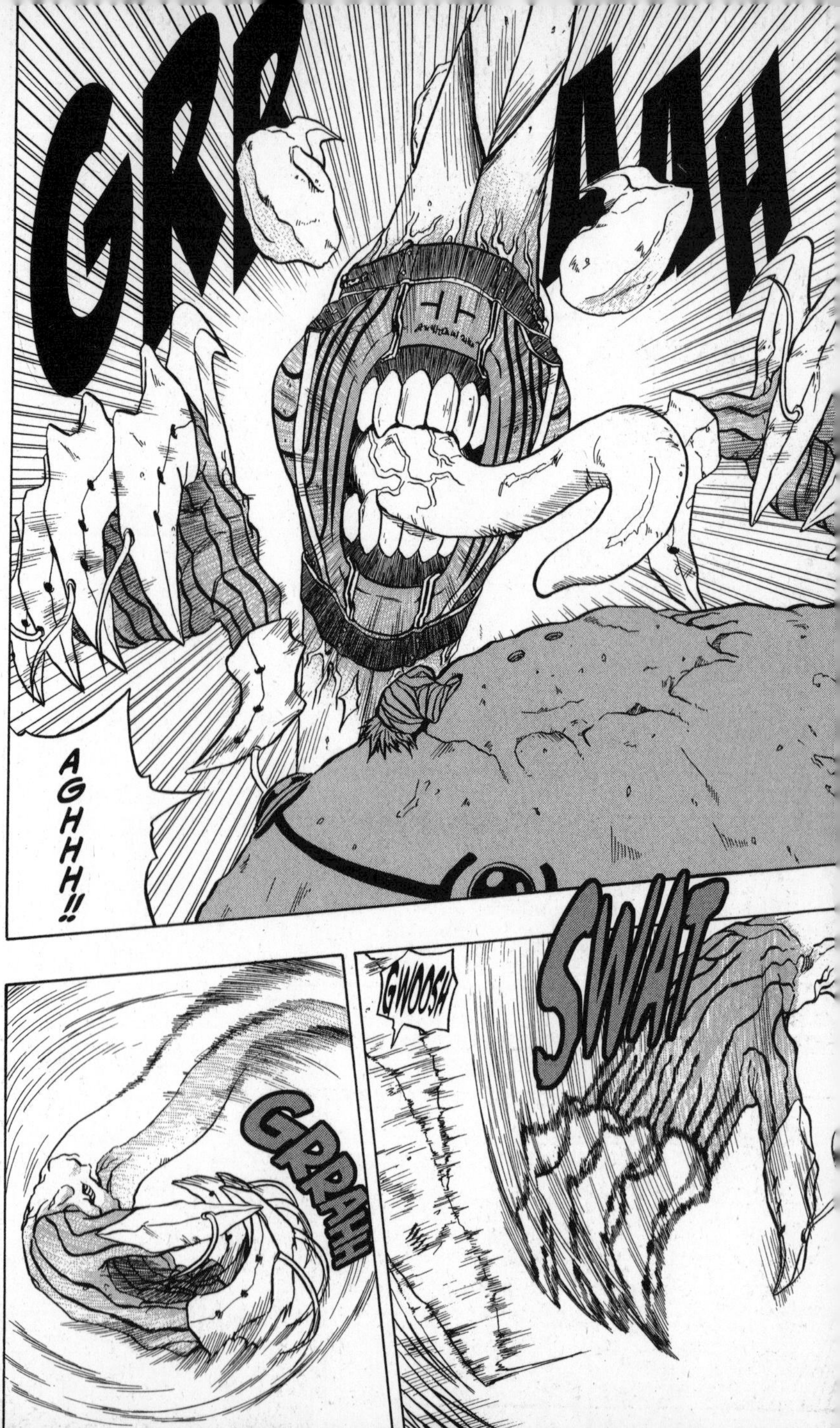
GRR
AAA
AGHHHH!!
SWHT
GWOOSH
GRRAHH

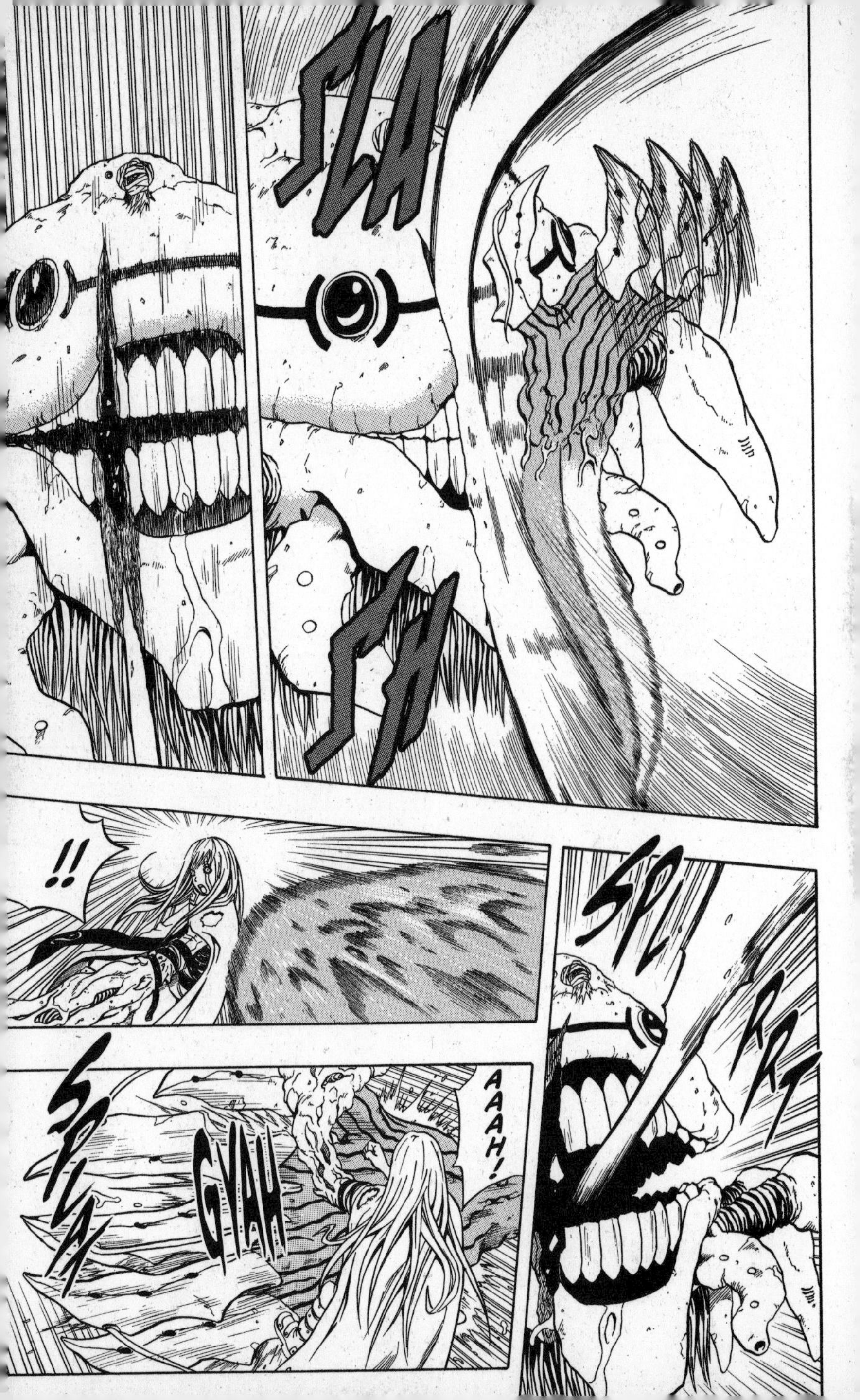
SLA
SH
SPL
RRT
!!
AAAH!
GYAH

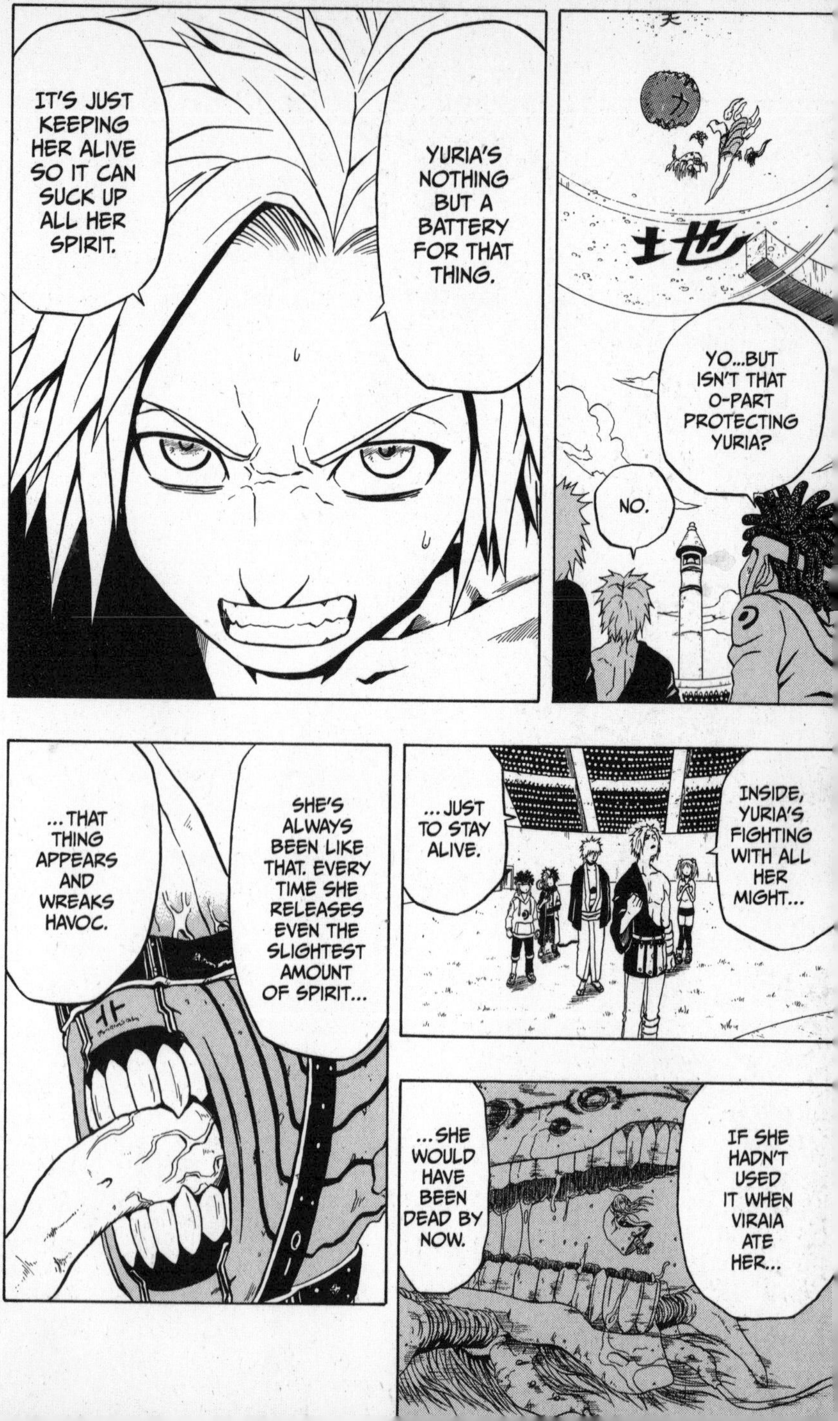
YO...BUT ISN'T THAT O-PART PROTECTING YURIA?
NO.
YURIA'S NOTHING BUT A BATTERY FOR THAT THING.
IT'S JUST KEEPING HER ALIVE SO IT CAN SUCK UP ALL HER SPIRIT.
INSIDE, YURIA'S FIGHTING WITH ALL HER MIGHT...
...JUST TO STAY ALIVE.
IF SHE HADN'T USED IT WHEN VIRAIA ATE HER...
...SHE WOULD HAVE BEEN DEAD BY NOW.
SHE'S ALWAYS BEEN LIKE THAT. EVERY TIME SHE RELEASES EVEN THE SLIGHTEST AMOUNT OF SPIRIT...
...THAT THING APPEARS AND WREAKS HAVOC.

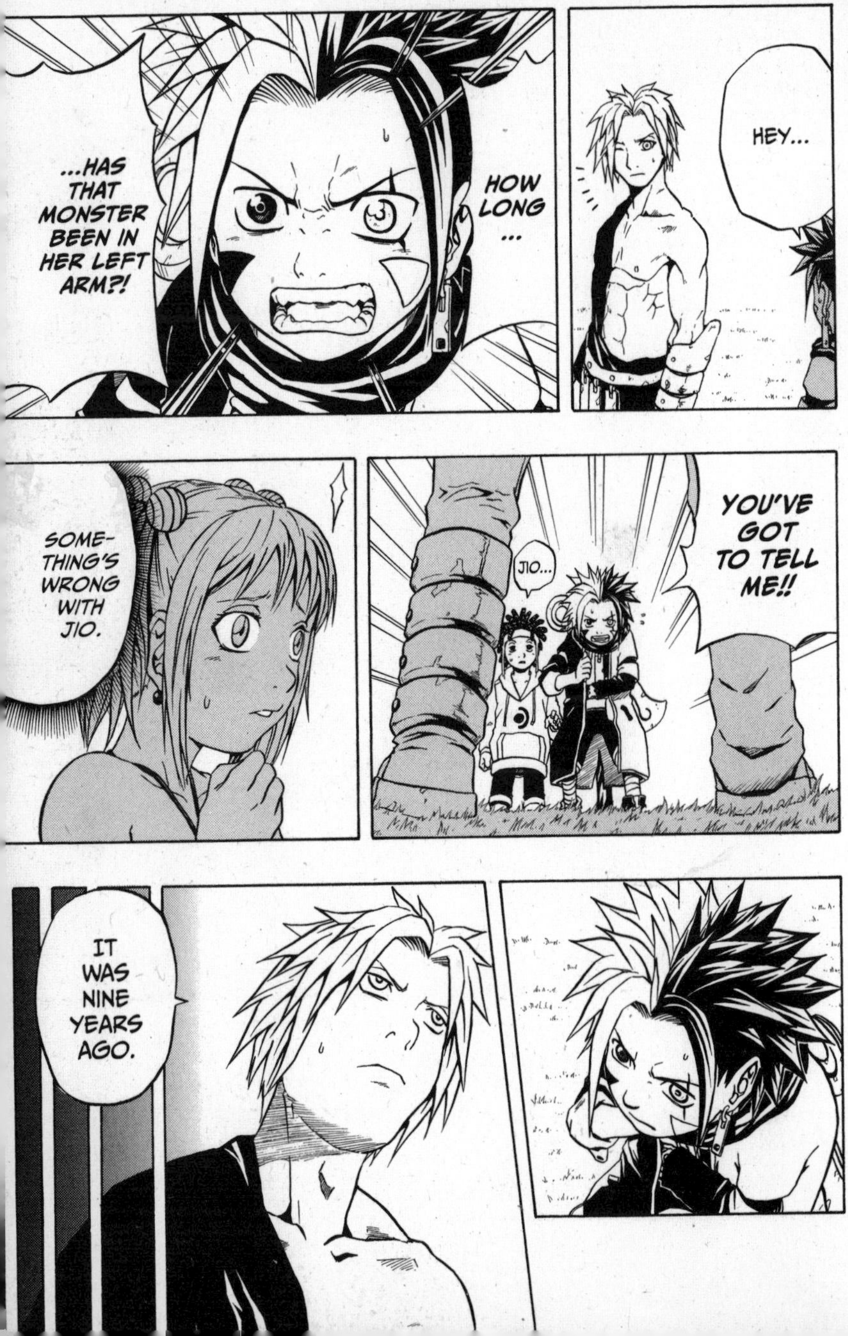
HEY...
HOW LONG ...
...HAS THAT MONSTER BEEN IN HER LEFT ARM?!
YOU'VE GOT TO TELL ME!!
JIO...
SOME-THING'S WRONG WITH JIO.
IT WAS NINE YEARS AGO.

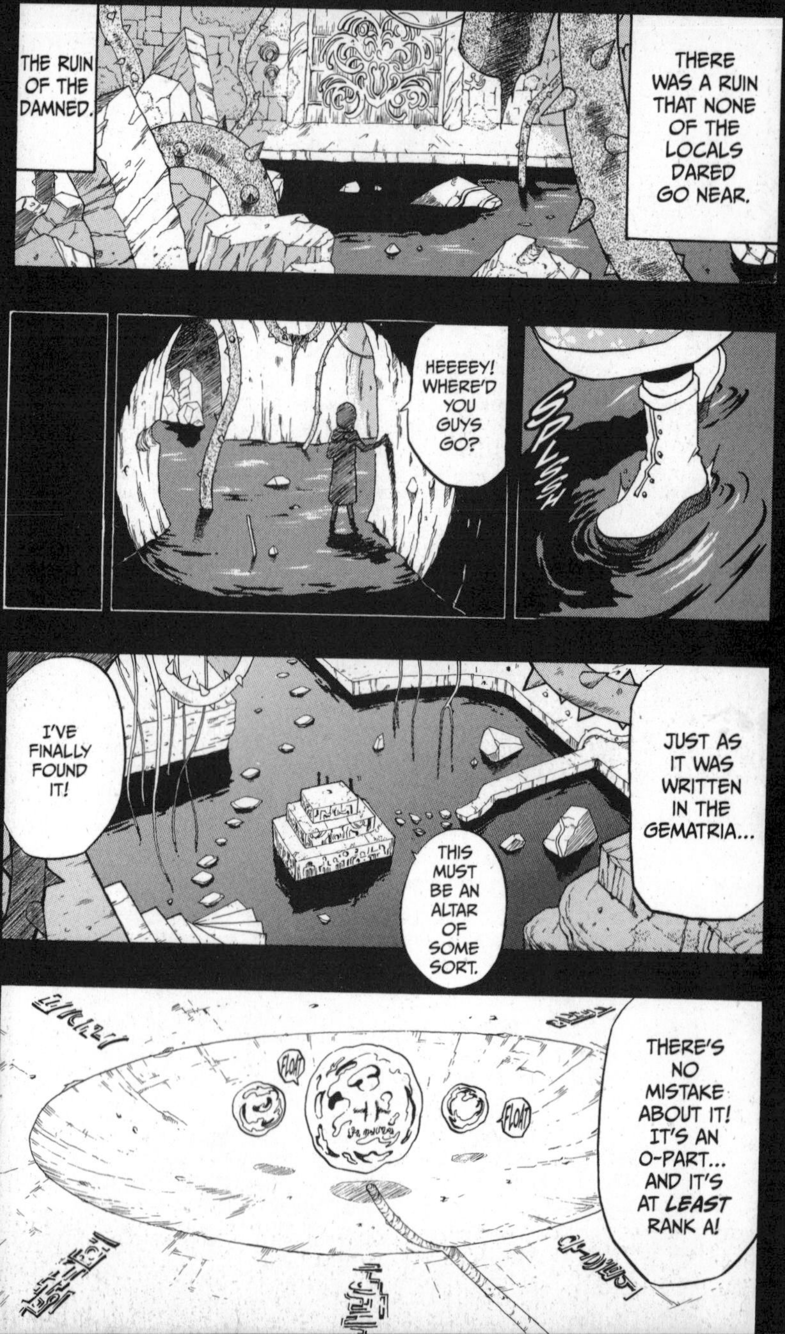
THERE WAS A RUIN THAT NONE OF THE LOCALS DARED GO NEAR.
THE RUIN OF THE DAMNED.
SPLOSH
HEEEEY! WHERE'D YOU GUYS GO?
JUST AS IT WAS WRITTEN IN THE GEMATRIA...
I'VE FINALLY FOUND IT!
THIS MUST BE AN ALTAR OF SOME SORT.
THERE'S NO MISTAKE ABOUT IT! IT'S AN O-PART... AND IT'S AT *LEAST* RANK A!
FLOAT
FLOAT

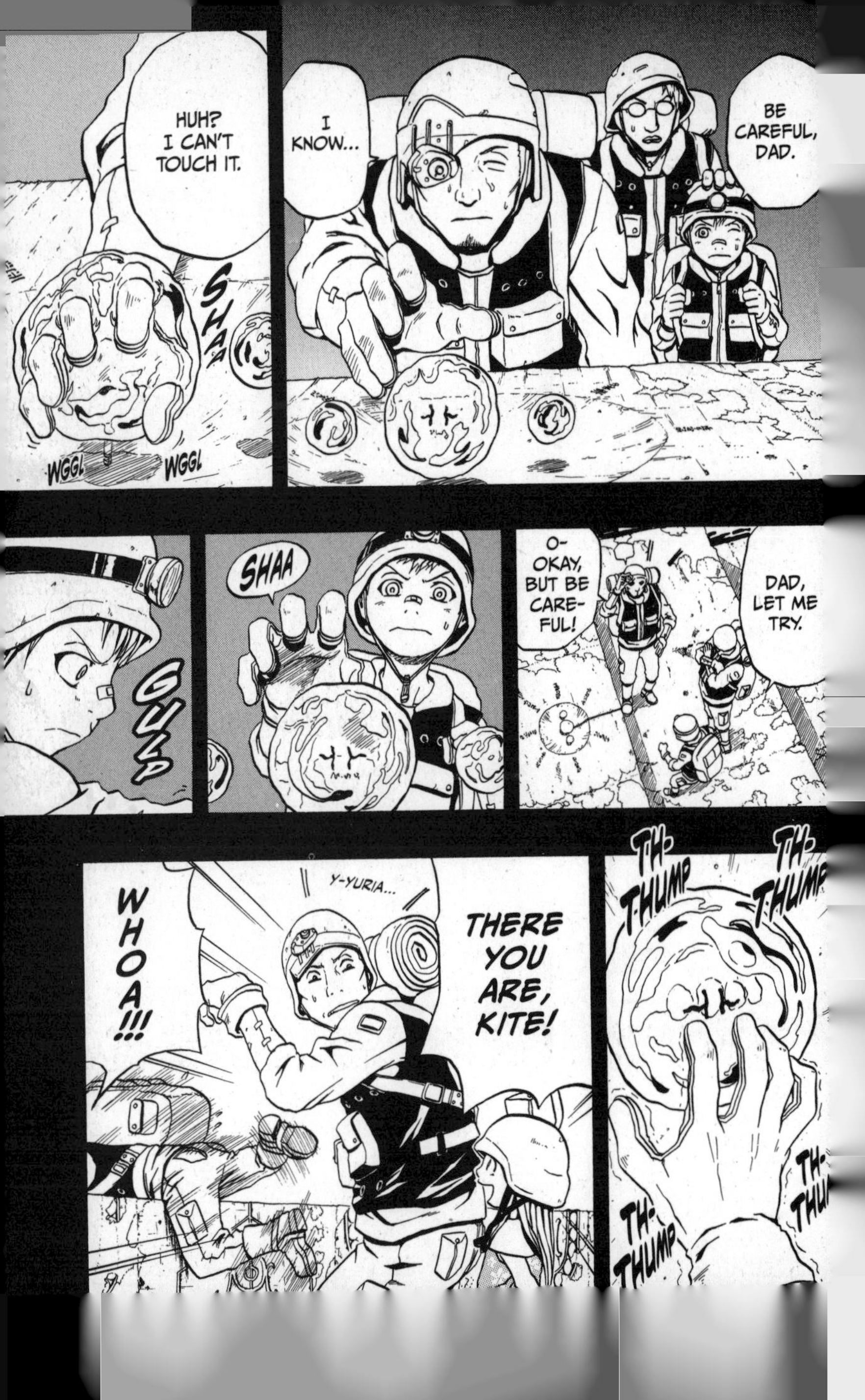
BE CAREFUL, DAD.
I KNOW...
HUH? I CAN'T TOUCH IT.
SHAA
WGGL
WGGL
DAD, LET ME TRY.
O-OKAY, BUT BE CARE-FUL!
SHAA
GULP
TH-THUMP
TH-THUMP
TH-THUMP
THERE YOU ARE, KITE!
Y-YURIA...
WHOA!!!

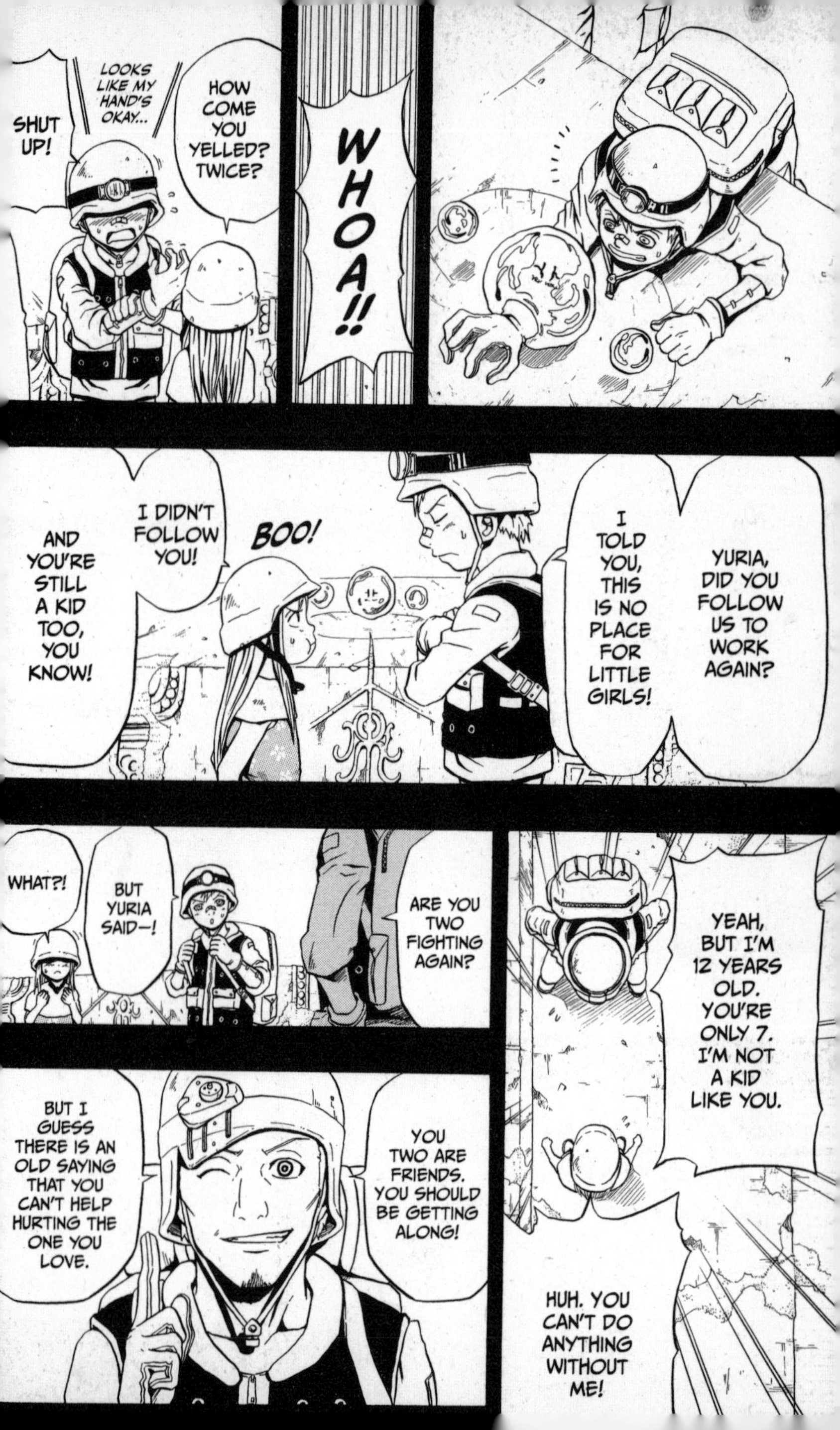
WHOA!!
HOW COME YOU YELLED? TWICE?
LOOKS LIKE MY HAND'S OKAY...
SHUT UP!
YURIA, DID YOU FOLLOW US TO WORK AGAIN?
I TOLD YOU, THIS IS NO PLACE FOR LITTLE GIRLS!
BOO!
I DIDN'T FOLLOW YOU!
AND YOU'RE STILL A KID TOO, YOU KNOW!
YEAH, BUT I'M 12 YEARS OLD. YOU'RE ONLY 7. I'M NOT A KID LIKE YOU.
HUH. YOU CAN'T DO ANYTHING WITHOUT ME!
ARE YOU TWO FIGHTING AGAIN?
BUT YURIA SAID—!
WHAT?!
YOU TWO ARE FRIENDS. YOU SHOULD BE GETTING ALONG!
BUT I GUESS THERE IS AN OLD SAYING THAT YOU CAN'T HELP HURTING THE ONE YOU LOVE.

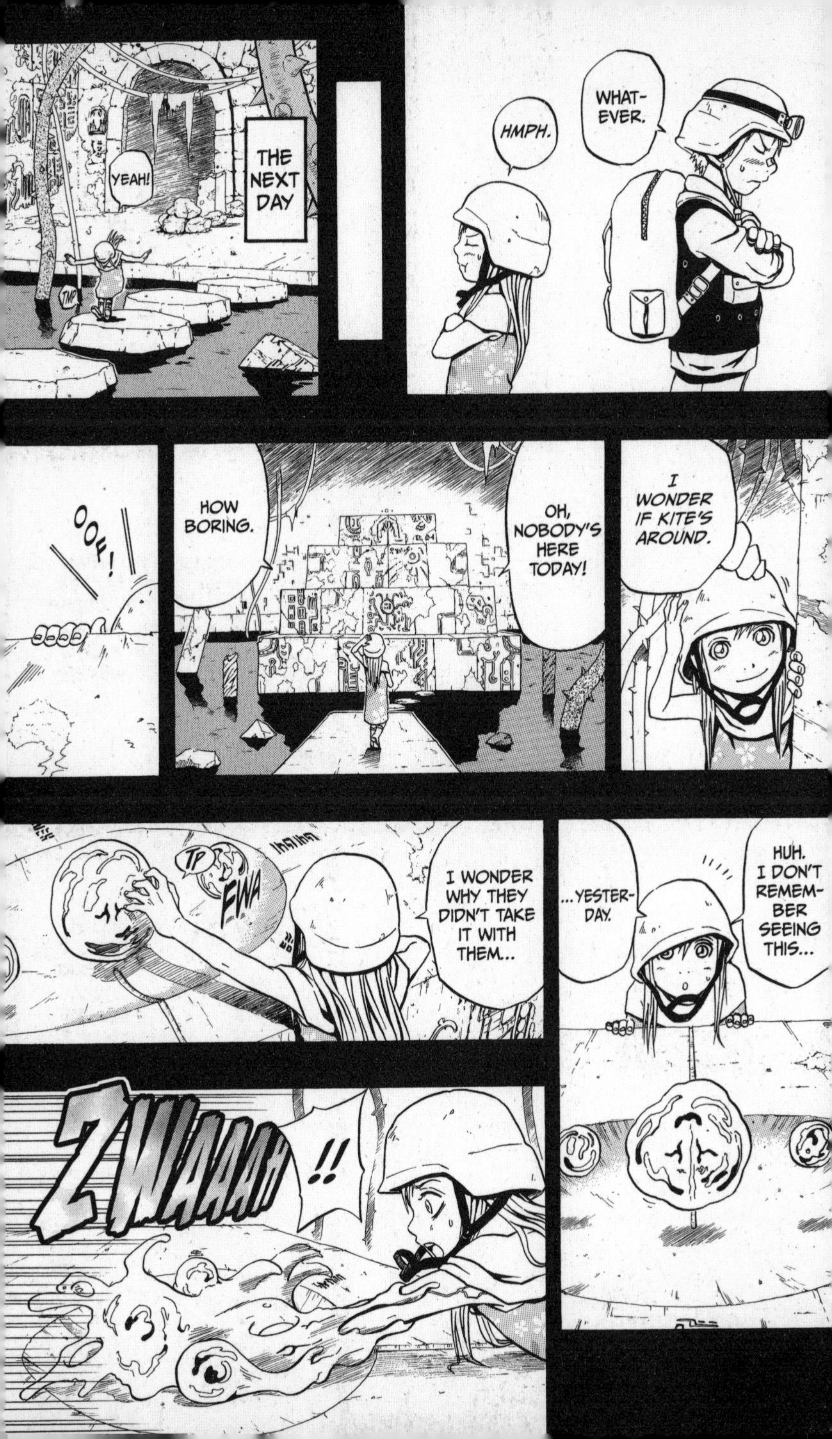
WHAT-EVER.
HMPH.
THE NEXT DAY
YEAH!
TMP
I WONDER IF KITE'S AROUND.
OH, NOBODY'S HERE TODAY!
HOW BORING.
OOF!
HUH. I DON'T REMEM-BER SEEING THIS...
...YESTER-DAY.
I WONDER WHY THEY DIDN'T TAKE IT WITH THEM...
TP
FWA
ZWAAAH
!!

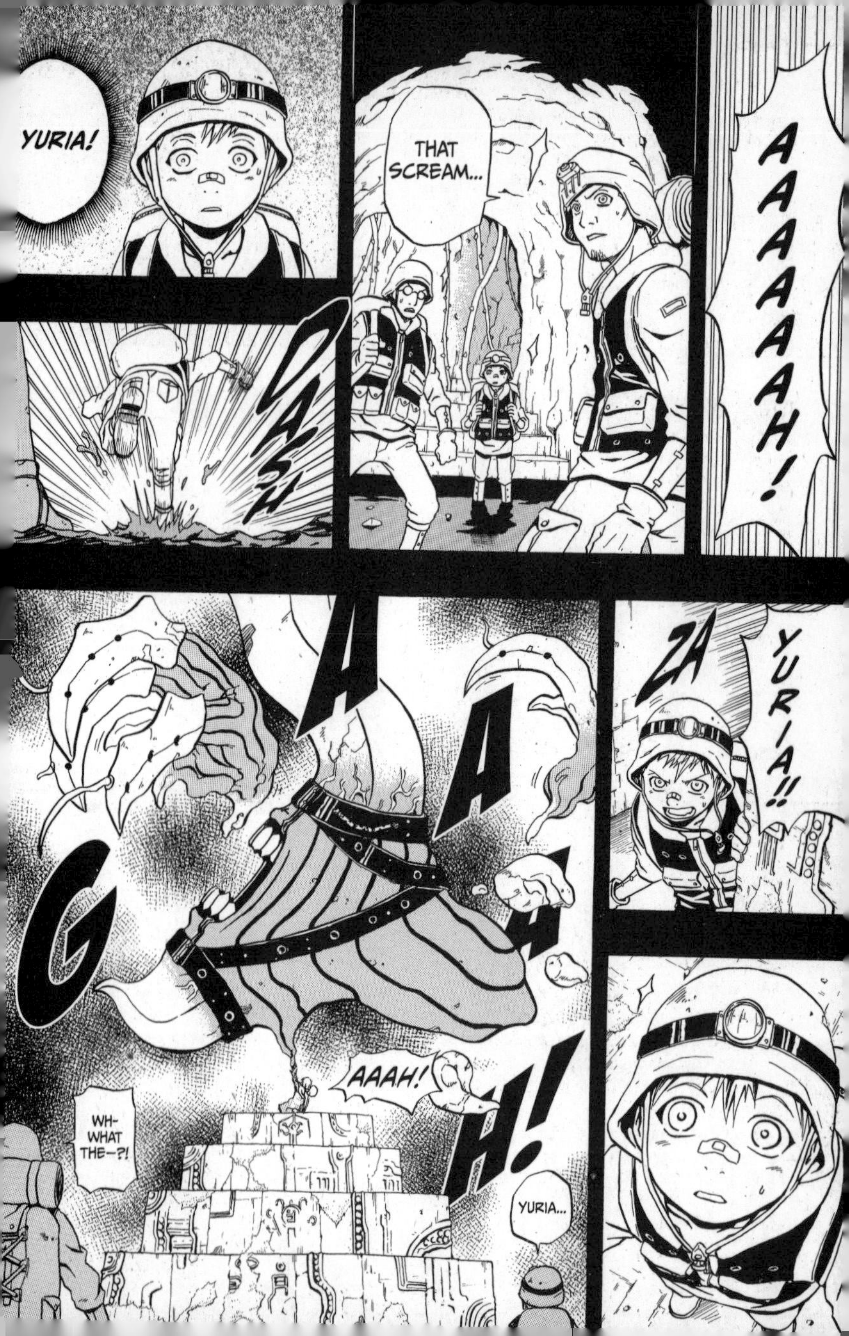
AAAAAAAH!
THAT SCREAM...
YURIA!
DASH
ZA
YURIA!!
GAAHH!
AAAH!
YURIA...
WH- WHAT THE--?!

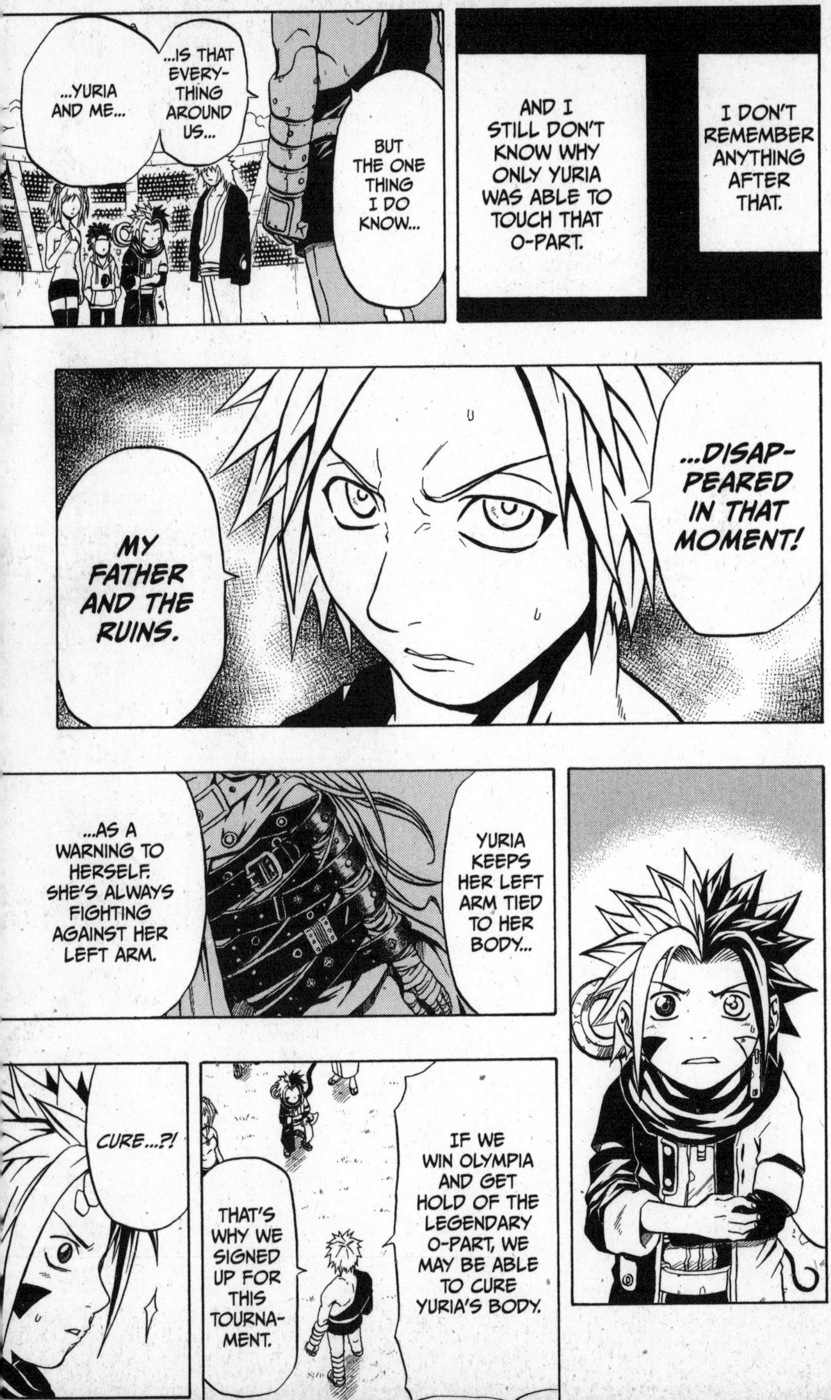
I DON'T REMEMBER ANYTHING AFTER THAT.
AND I STILL DON'T KNOW WHY ONLY YURIA WAS ABLE TO TOUCH THAT O-PART.
BUT THE ONE THING I DO KNOW...
...IS THAT EVERY-THING AROUND US...
...YURIA AND ME...
...DISAP-PEARED IN THAT MOMENT!
MY FATHER AND THE RUINS.
YURIA KEEPS HER LEFT ARM TIED TO HER BODY...
...AS A WARNING TO HERSELF. SHE'S ALWAYS FIGHTING AGAINST HER LEFT ARM.
IF WE WIN OLYMPIA AND GET HOLD OF THE LEGENDARY O-PART, WE MAY BE ABLE TO CURE YURIA'S BODY.
THAT'S WHY WE SIGNED UP FOR THIS TOURNA-MENT.
CURE...?!

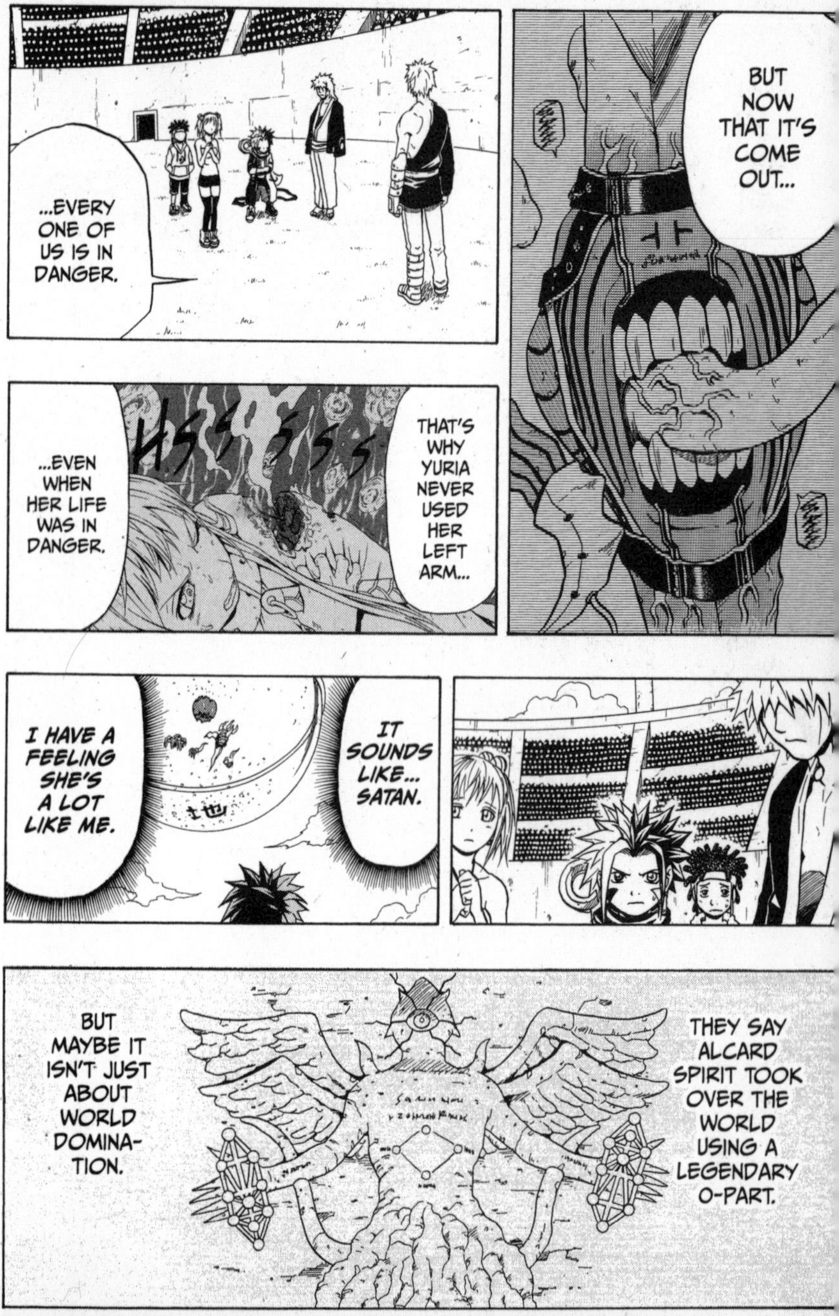
BUT NOW THAT IT'S COME OUT...
...EVERY ONE OF US IS IN DANGER.
THAT'S WHY YURIA NEVER USED HER LEFT ARM...
HSSSSS
...EVEN WHEN HER LIFE WAS IN DANGER.
IT SOUNDS LIKE... SATAN.
I HAVE A FEELING SHE'S A LOT LIKE ME.
THEY SAY ALCARD SPIRIT TOOK OVER THE WORLD USING A LEGENDARY O-PART.
BUT MAYBE IT ISN'T JUST ABOUT WORLD DOMINATION.

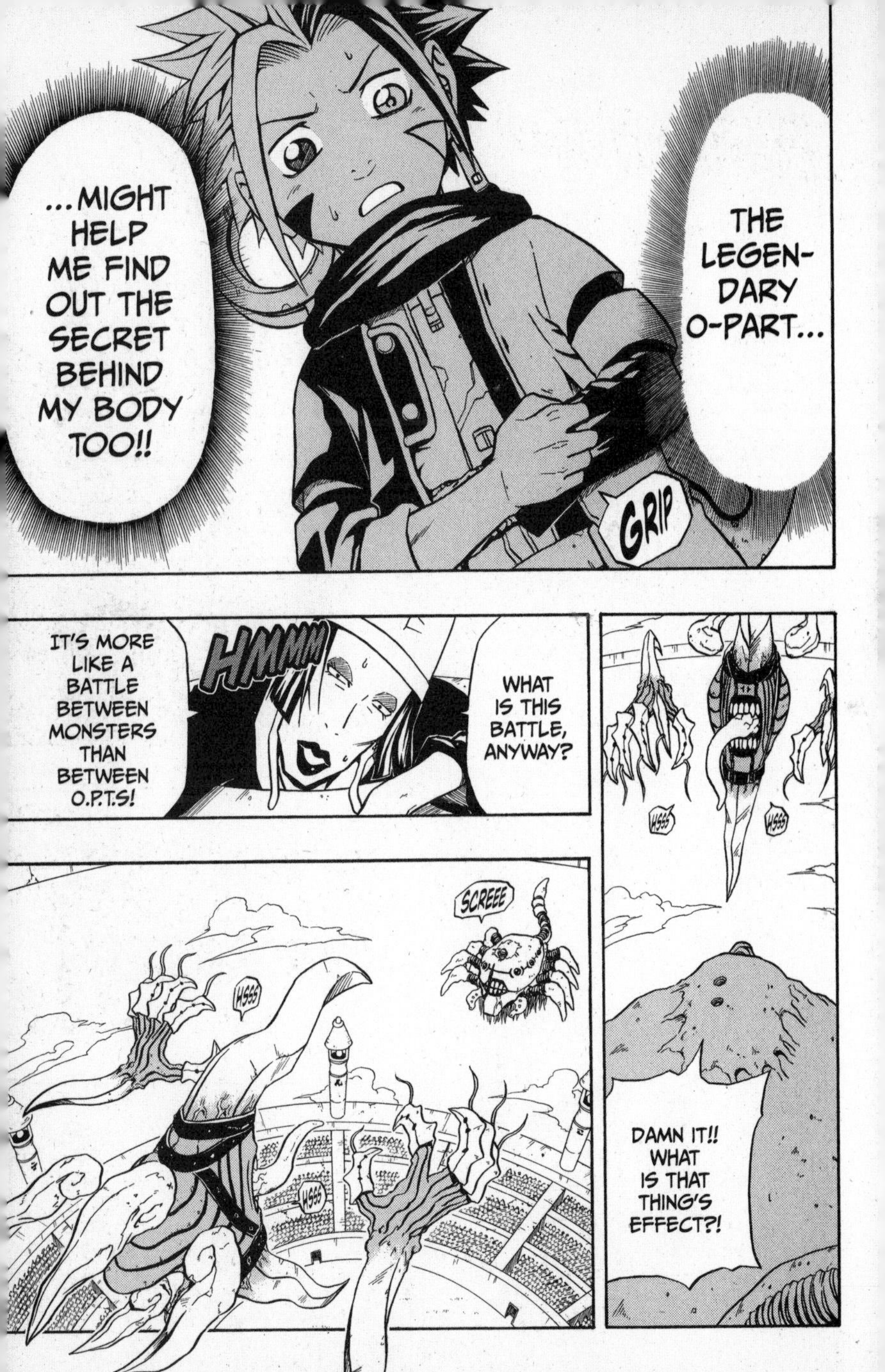
THE LEGEN-DARY O-PART...
...MIGHT HELP ME FIND OUT THE SECRET BEHIND MY BODY TOO!!
GRIP
HSSS
HSSS
DAMN IT!! WHAT IS THAT THING'S EFFECT?!
WHAT IS THIS BATTLE, ANYWAY?
HMMM
IT'S MORE LIKE A BATTLE BETWEEN MONSTERS THAN BETWEEN O.P.T.S!
SCREEE
HSSS
HSSS

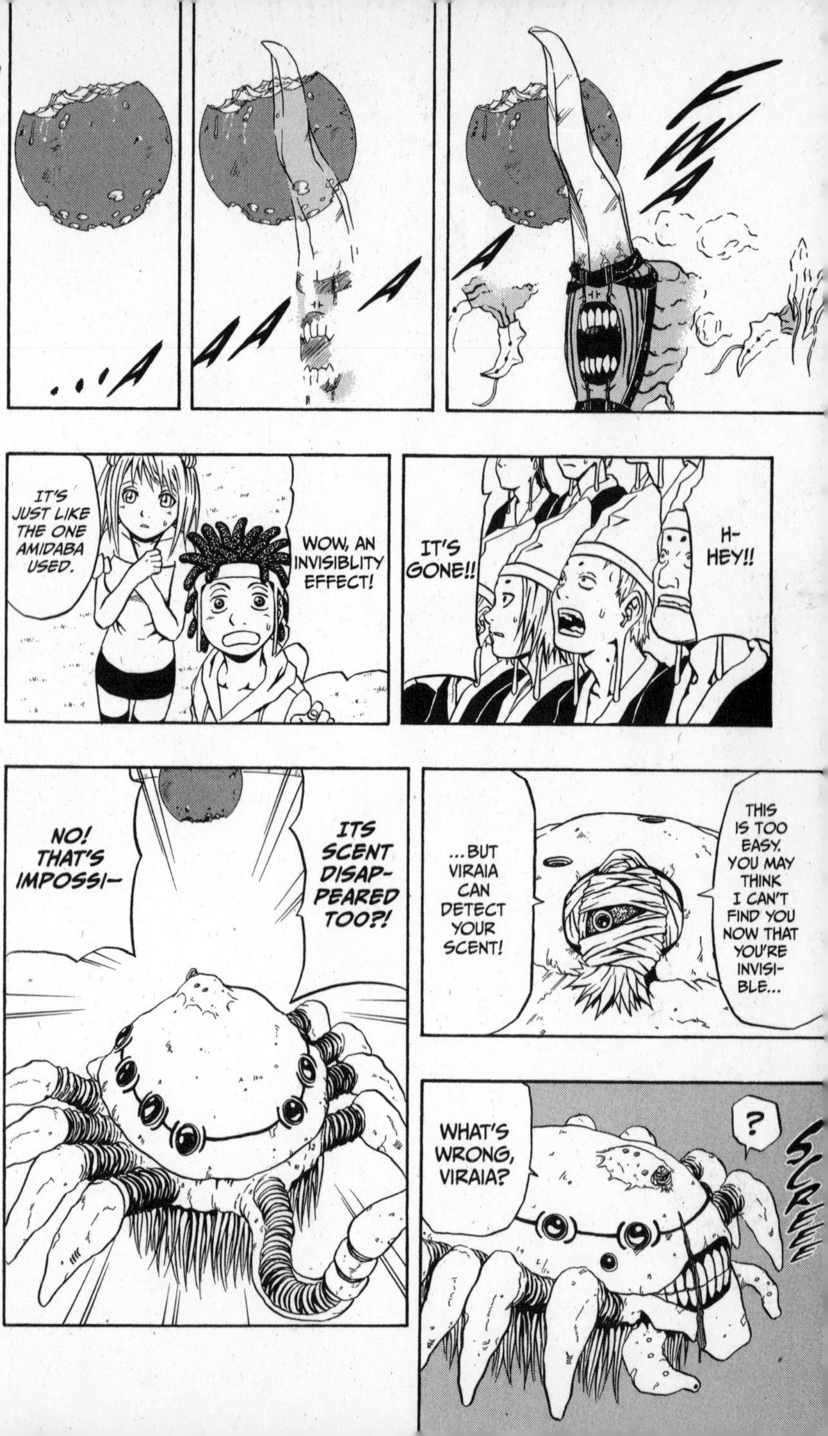
FWAA
AAA
...'A
H-HEY!!
IT'S GONE!!
WOW, AN INVISIBLITY EFFECT!
IT'S JUST LIKE THE ONE AMIDABA USED.
THIS IS TOO EASY. YOU MAY THINK I CAN'T FIND YOU NOW THAT YOU'RE INVISI-BLE...
...BUT VIRAIA CAN DETECT YOUR SCENT!
?
SCREEE
WHAT'S WRONG, VIRAIA?
ITS SCENT DISAP-PEARED TOO?!
NO! THAT'S IMPOSSI-

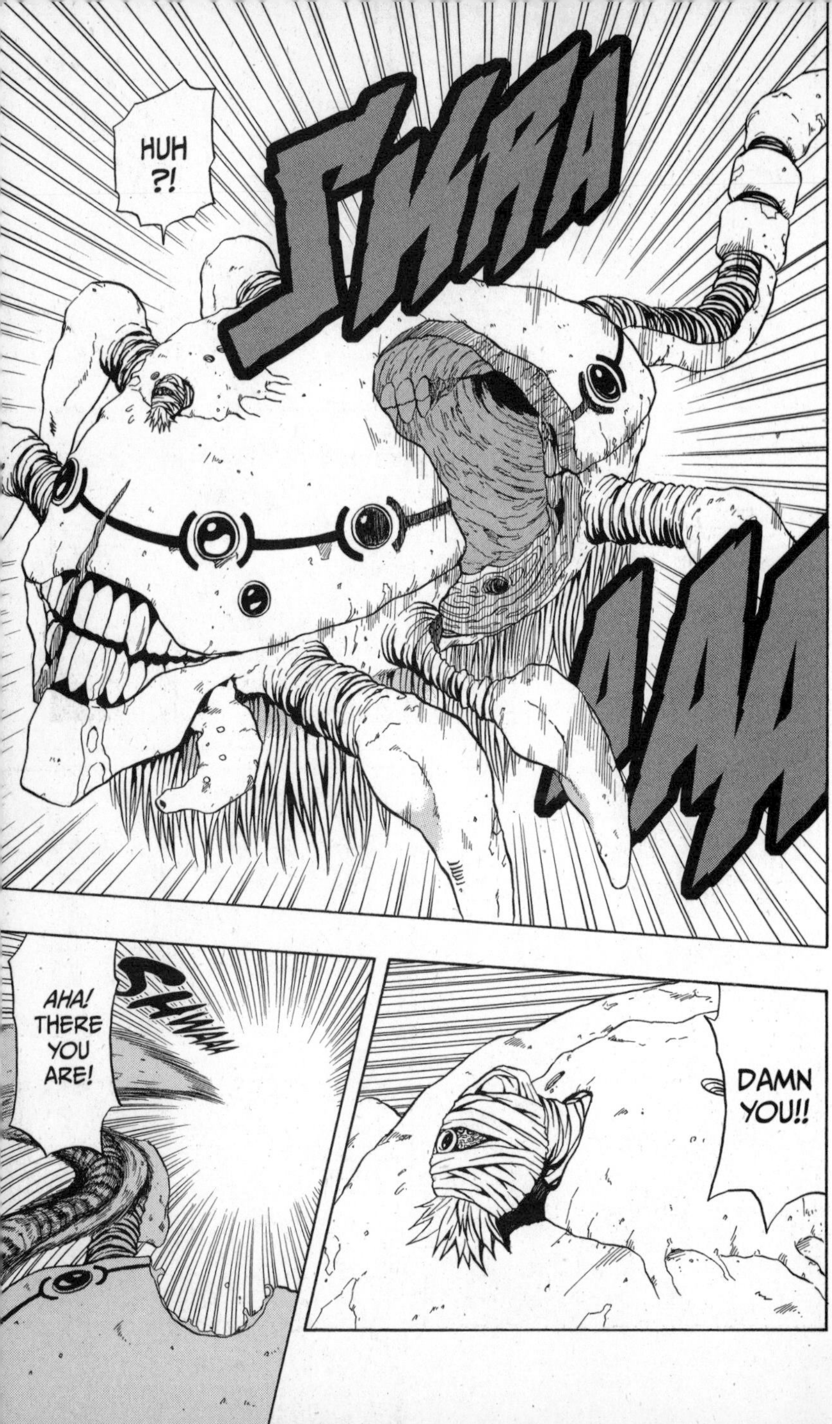
SHAA
AAAA
HUH ?!
DAMN YOU!!
SHWAAA
AHA! THERE YOU ARE!

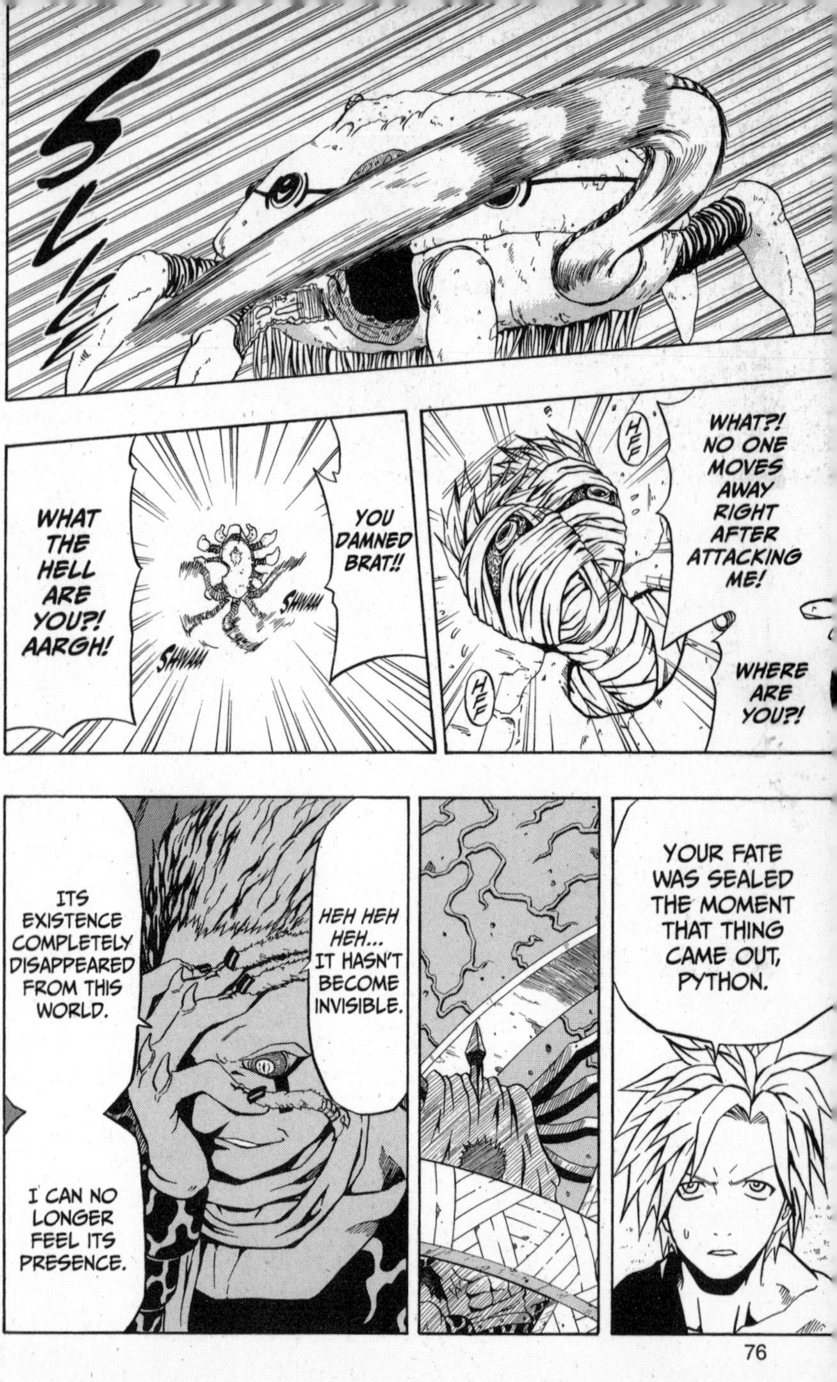
HEF
WHAT?! NO ONE MOVES AWAY RIGHT AFTER ATTACKING ME!
HEF
WHERE ARE YOU?!
YOU DAMNED BRAT!!
WHAT THE HELL ARE YOU?! AARGH!
YOUR FATE WAS SEALED THE MOMENT THAT THING CAME OUT, PYTHON.
HEH HEH HEH... IT HASN'T BECOME INVISIBLE.
ITS EXISTENCE COMPLETELY DISAPPEARED FROM THIS WORLD.
I CAN NO LONGER FEEL ITS PRESENCE.

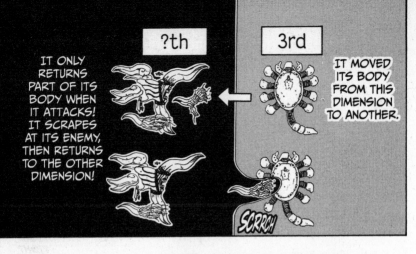

3rd
IT MOVED ITS BODY FROM THIS DIMENSION TO ANOTHER.
SCRRCH
?th
IT ONLY RETURNS PART OF ITS BODY WHEN IT ATTACKS! IT SCRAPES AT ITS ENEMY, THEN RETURNS TO THE OTHER DIMENSION!
A DEMON THAT CAN MOVE BETWEEN DIMEN-SIONS...
...THAT CAN REJECT EVERYTHING AROUND IT AND RETREAT TO A PARALLEL VOID...
WHAT AMAZING POWERS! IT MUST BE...
SEPHIRAH 3i...
...LUCIFUGE THE REJECTER.

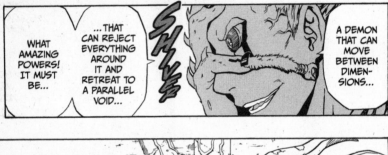

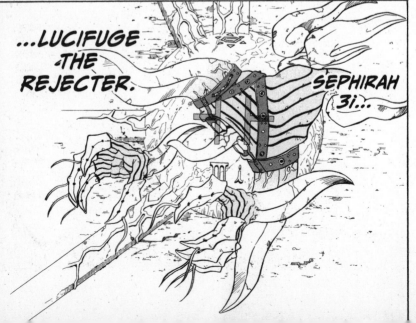

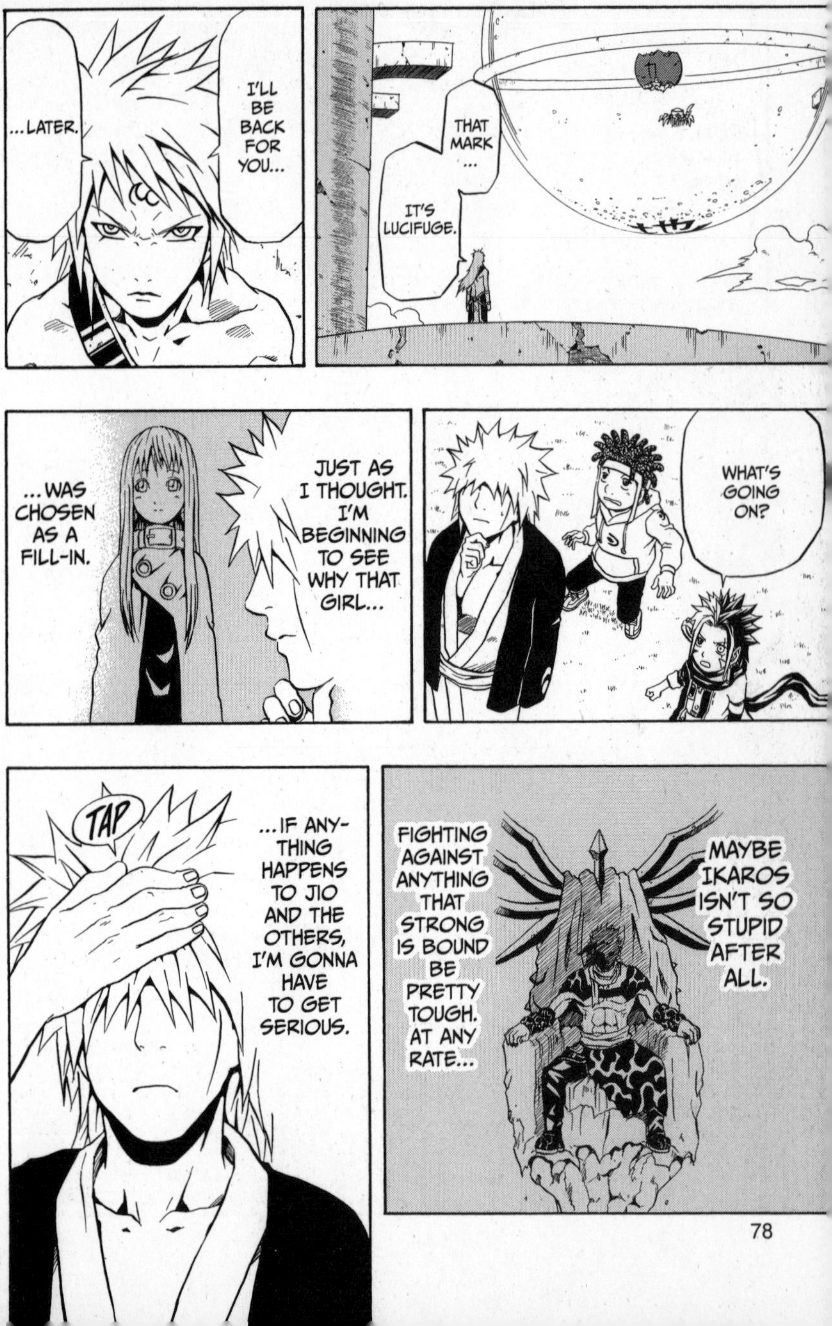
THAT MARK...
IT'S LUCIFUGE.
I'LL BE BACK FOR YOU...
...LATER.
WHAT'S GOING ON?
JUST AS I THOUGHT. I'M BEGINNING TO SEE WHY THAT GIRL...
...WAS CHOSEN AS A FILL-IN.
MAYBE IKAROS ISN'T SO STUPID AFTER ALL.
FIGHTING AGAINST ANYTHING THAT STRONG IS BOUND BE PRETTY TOUGH. AT ANY RATE...
TAP
...IF ANY-THING HAPPENS TO JIO AND THE OTHERS, I'M GONNA HAVE TO GET SERIOUS.

WHERE ARE YOU ATTACK-ING ME FROM?! WHERE ARE YOU?!

AAAAARGH!

I'M SORRY...

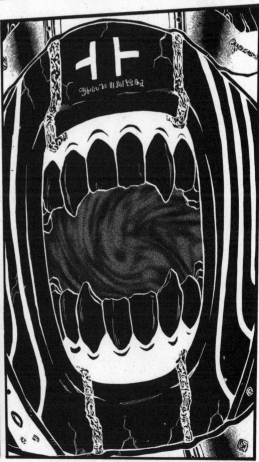

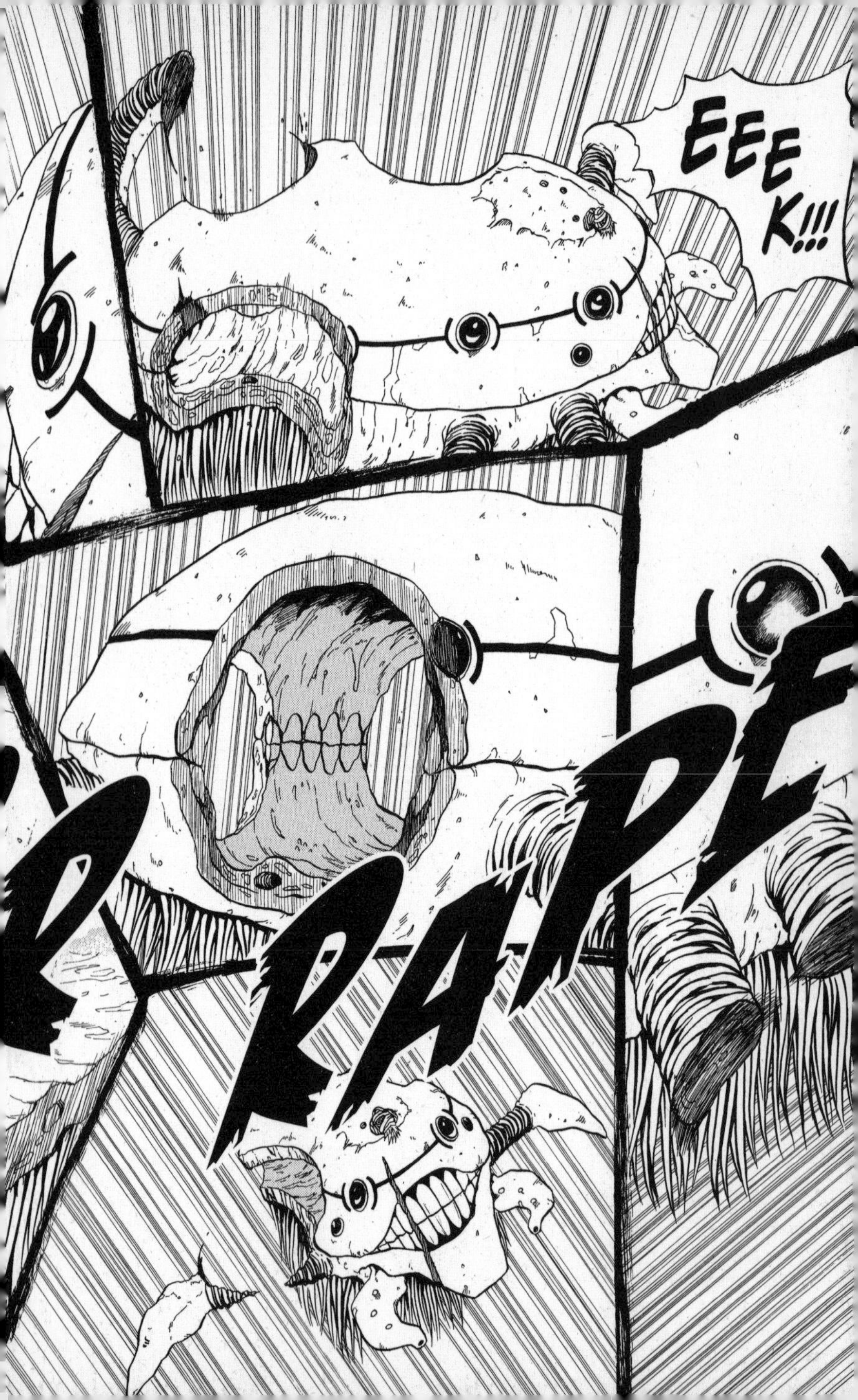
EEEK!!!

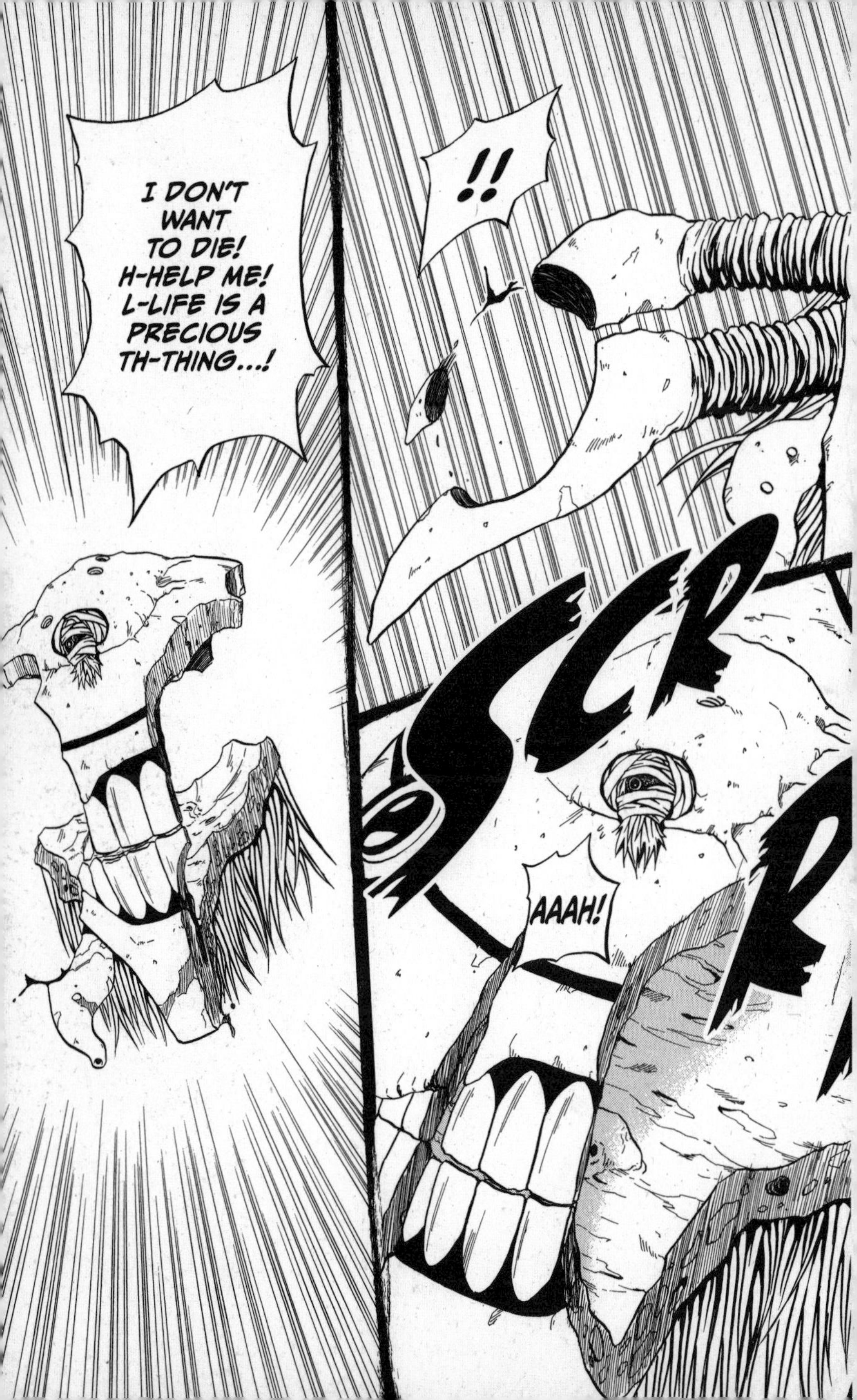
!!
SCRR
AAAH!
I DON'T WANT TO DIE! H-HELP ME! L-LIFE IS A PRECIOUS TH-THING...!

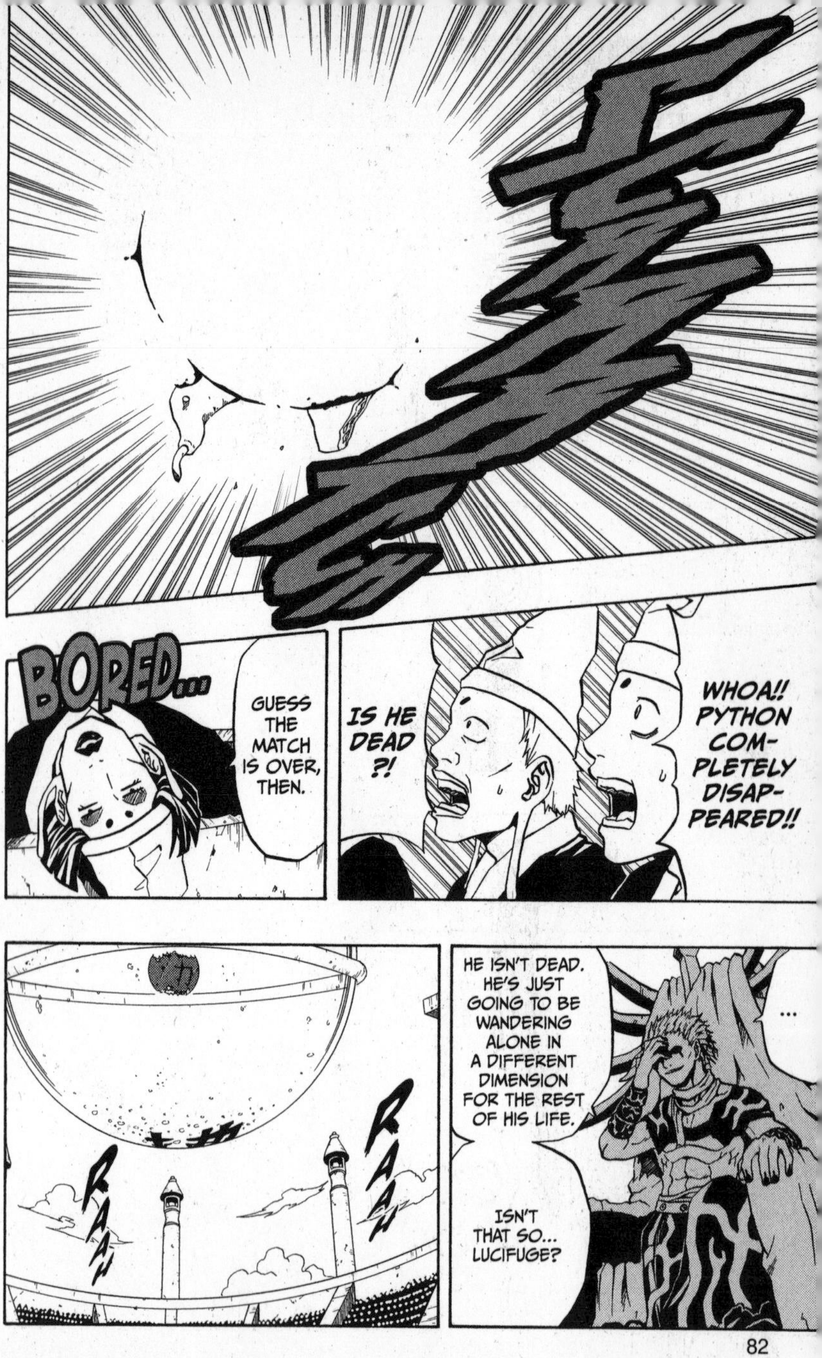
WHOA!! PYTHON COMPLETELY DISAPPEARED!!
IS HE DEAD?!
GUESS THE MATCH IS OVER, THEN.
BORED...
...
HE ISN'T DEAD. HE'S JUST GOING TO BE WANDERING ALONE IN A DIFFERENT DIMENSION FOR THE REST OF HIS LIFE.
ISN'T THAT SO... LUCIFUGE?
RAAAH
RAAAH

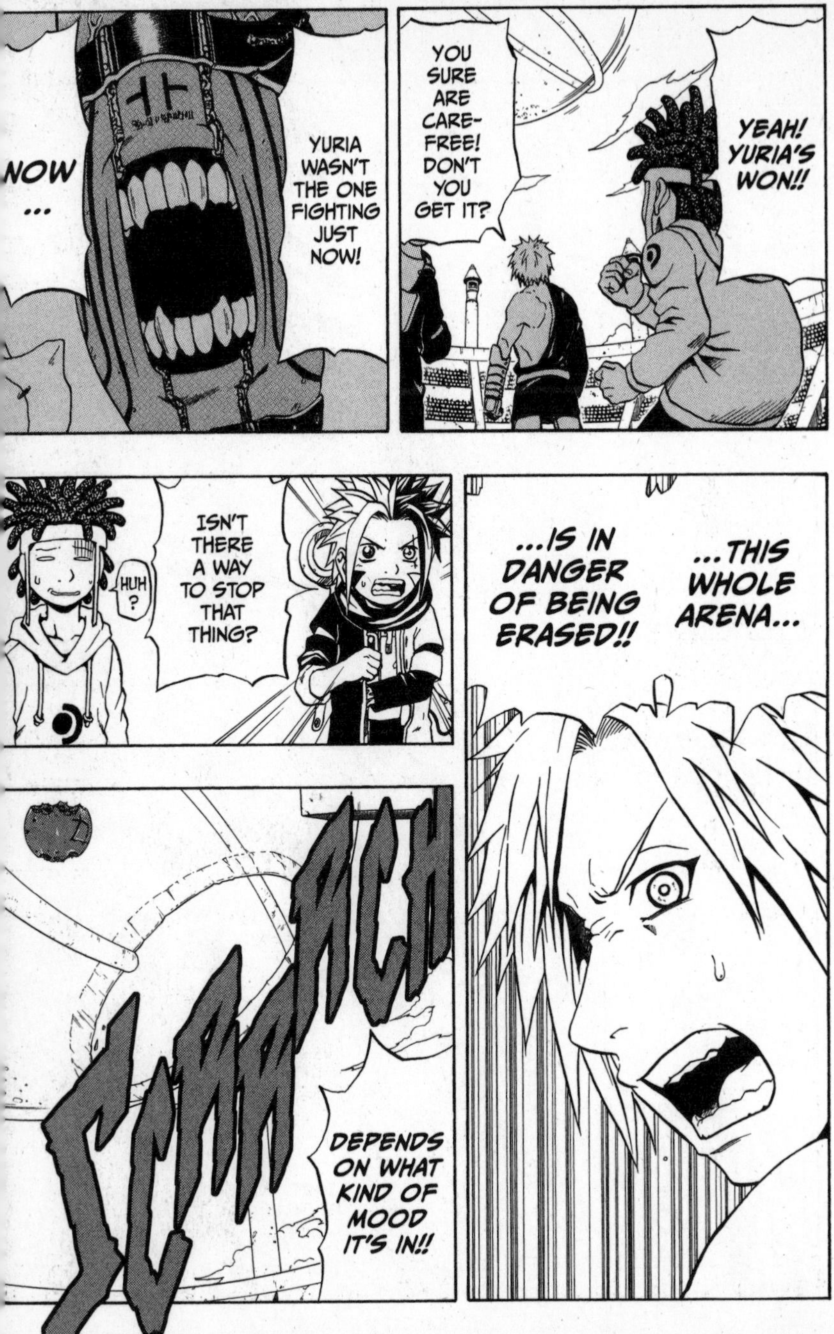
YEAH! YURIA'S WON!!
YOU SURE ARE CARE-FREE! DON'T YOU GET IT?
YURIA WASN'T THE ONE FIGHTING JUST NOW!
NOW ...
...THIS WHOLE ARENA...
...IS IN DANGER OF BEING ERASED!!
ISN'T THERE A WAY TO STOP THAT THING?
HUH?
SCRAAACH
DEPENDS ON WHAT KIND OF MOOD IT'S IN!!

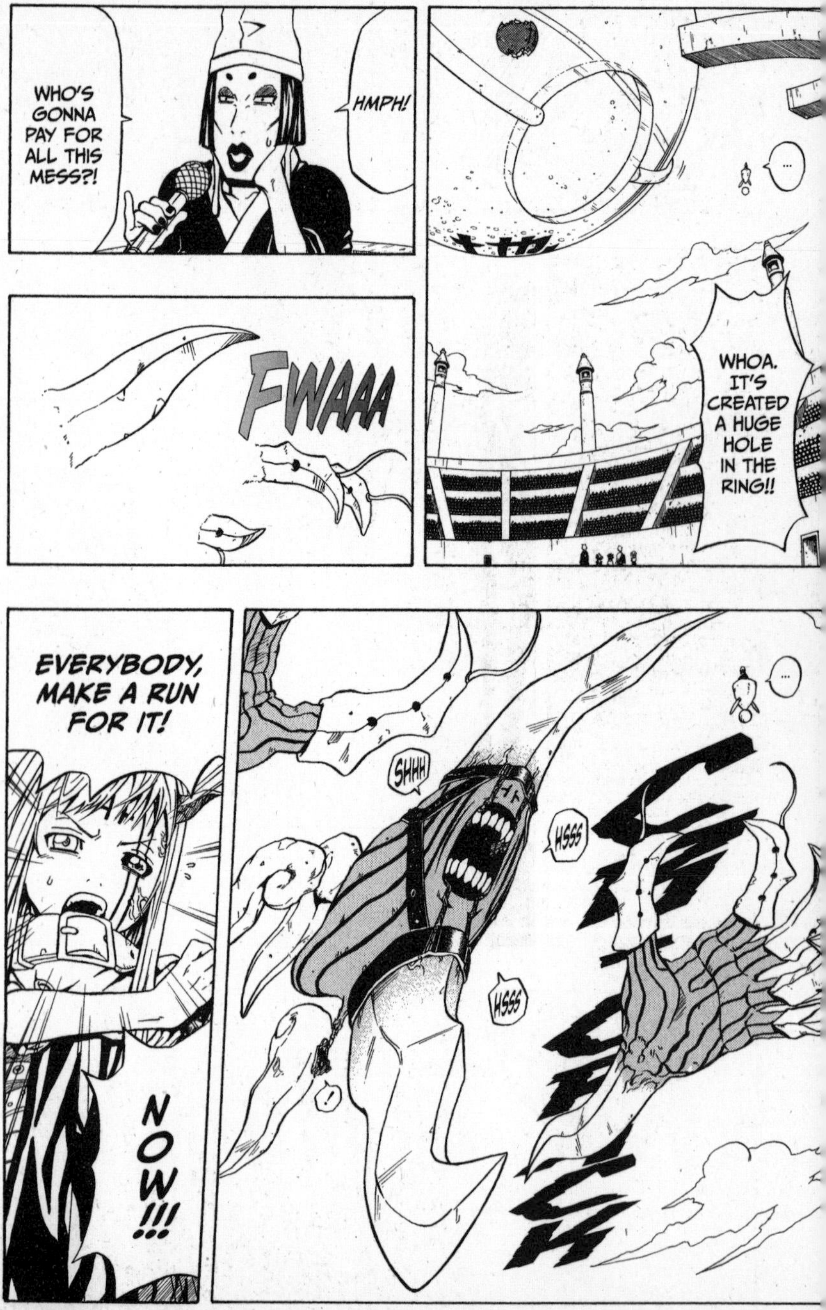
...
WHOA. IT'S CREATED A HUGE HOLE IN THE RING!!
HMPH!
WHO'S GONNA PAY FOR ALL THIS MESS?!
FWAAA
...
SHHH
HSSS
HSSS
!
EVERYBODY, MAKE A RUN FOR IT!
NOW!!!

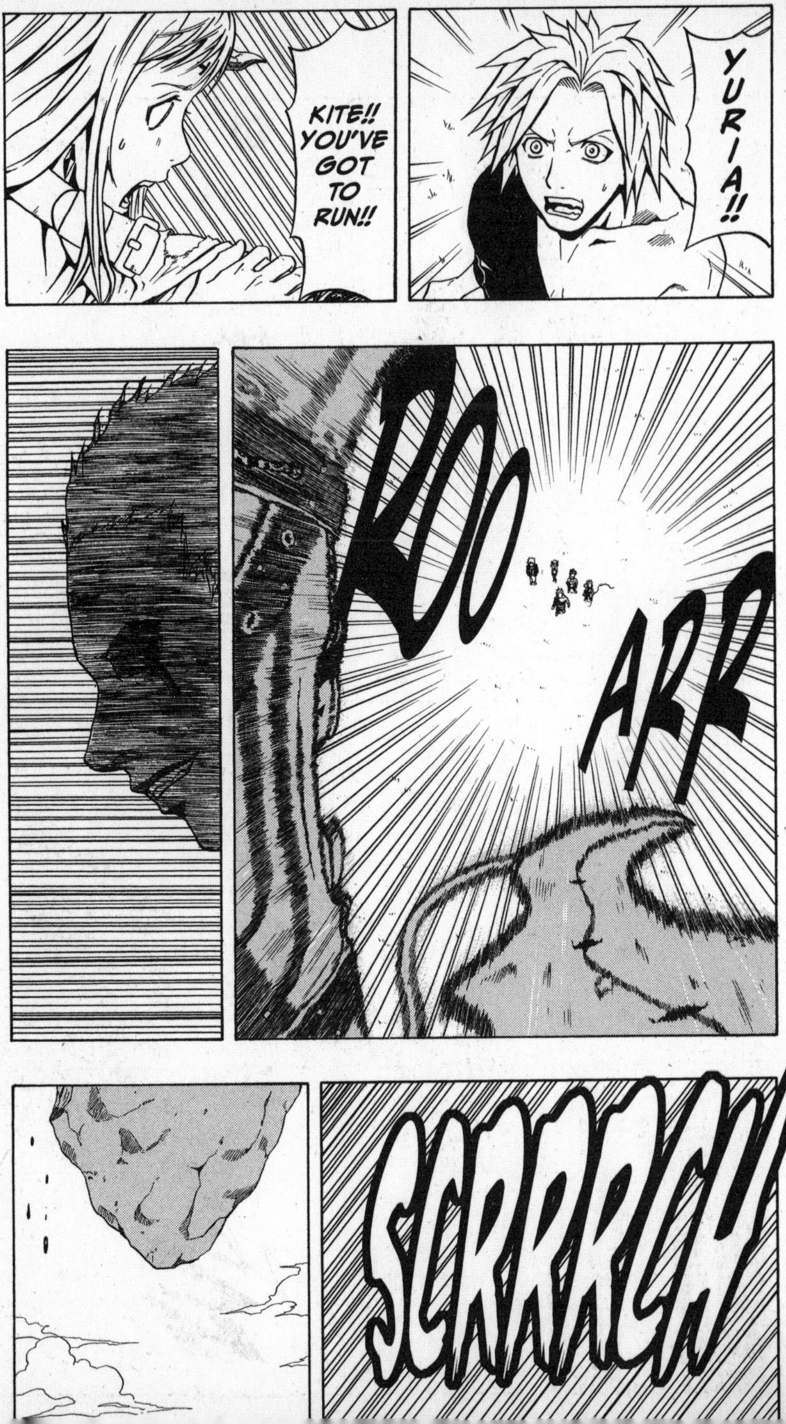
YURIA!!
KITE!! YOU'VE GOT TO RUN!!
KOO
ARR
SCRRRCH!

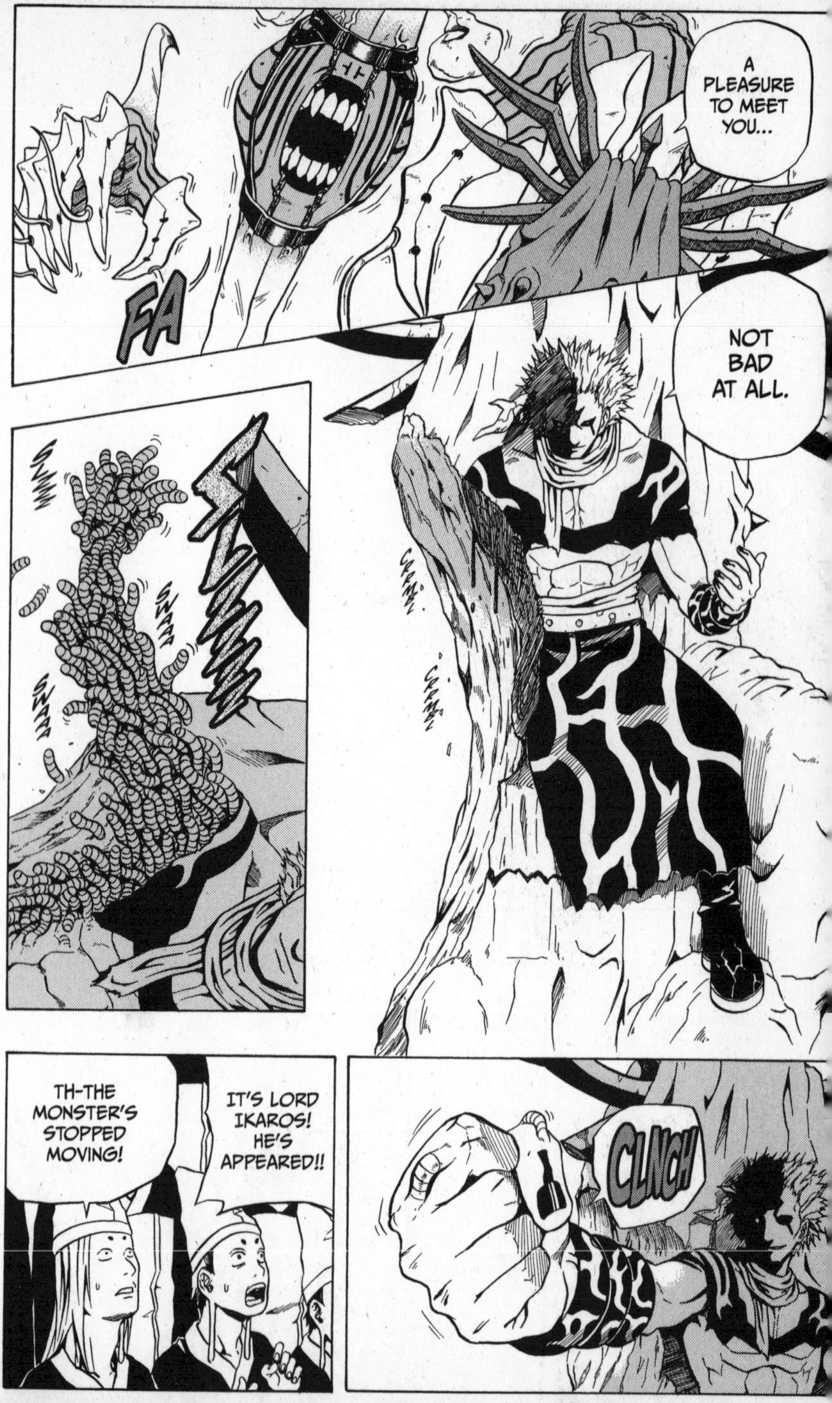
A PLEASURE TO MEET YOU...
FA
NOT BAD AT ALL.
CLINCH
IT'S LORD IKAROS! HE'S APPEARED!!
TH-THE MONSTER'S STOPPED MOVING!

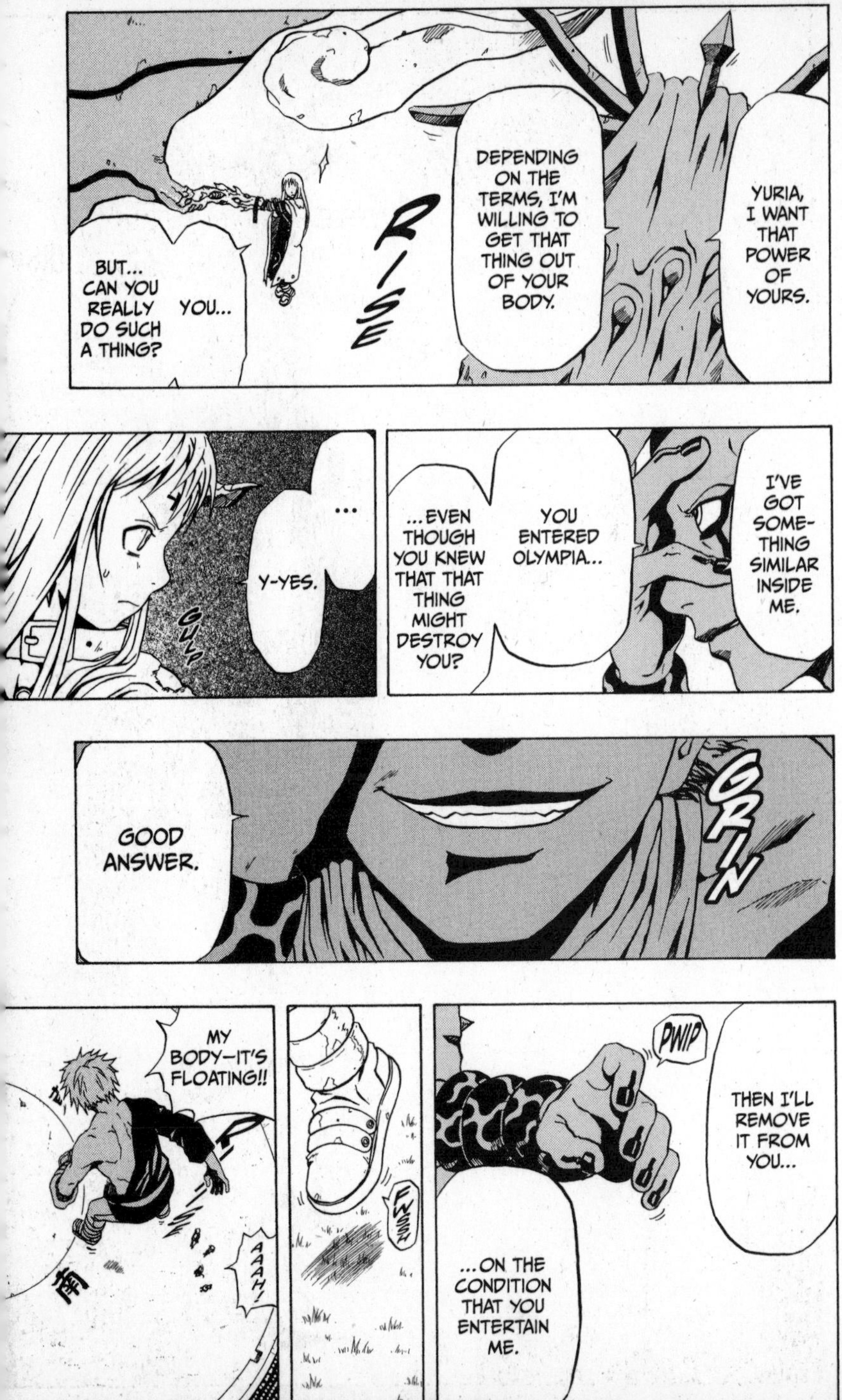
YURIA, I WANT THAT POWER OF YOURS.
DEPENDING ON THE TERMS, I'M WILLING TO GET THAT THING OUT OF YOUR BODY.
RISE
YOU...
BUT... CAN YOU REALLY DO SUCH A THING?
I'VE GOT SOME-THING SIMILAR INSIDE ME.
YOU ENTERED OLYMPIA...
...EVEN THOUGH YOU KNEW THAT THAT THING MIGHT DESTROY YOU?
...
Y-YES.
GULP
GRIN
GOOD ANSWER.
THEN I'LL REMOVE IT FROM YOU...
PWIP
...ON THE CONDITION THAT YOU ENTERTAIN ME.
FWSSH
MY BODY—IT'S FLOATING!!
AAAH!

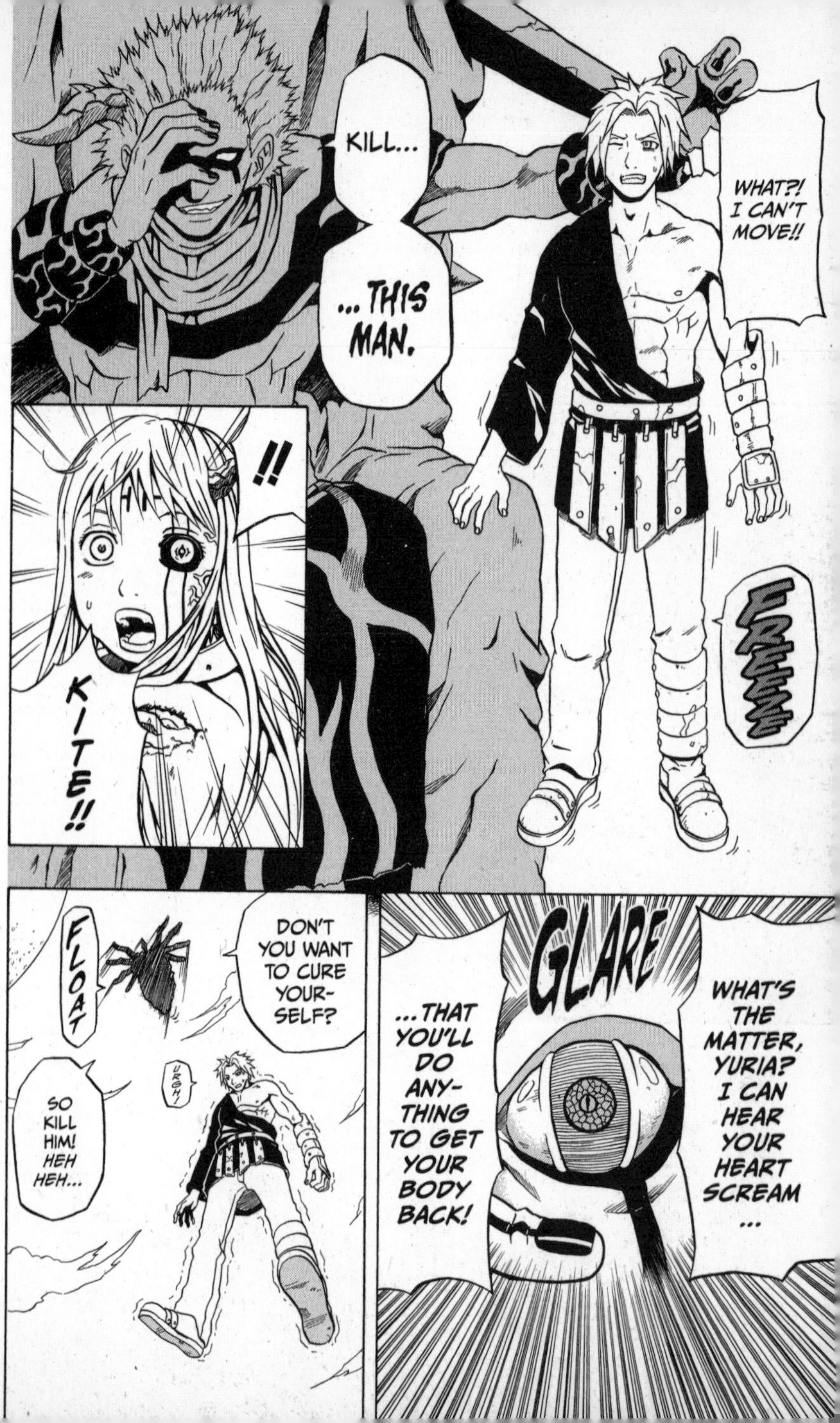
WHAT?! I CAN'T MOVE!!
KILL...
...THIS MAN.
FREEZE
!!
KITE!!
GLARE
WHAT'S THE MATTER, YURIA? I CAN HEAR YOUR HEART SCREAM...
...THAT YOU'LL DO ANYTHING TO GET YOUR BODY BACK!
DON'T YOU WANT TO CURE YOUR-SELF?
FLOAT
SO KILL HIM! HEH HEH...
URGH!

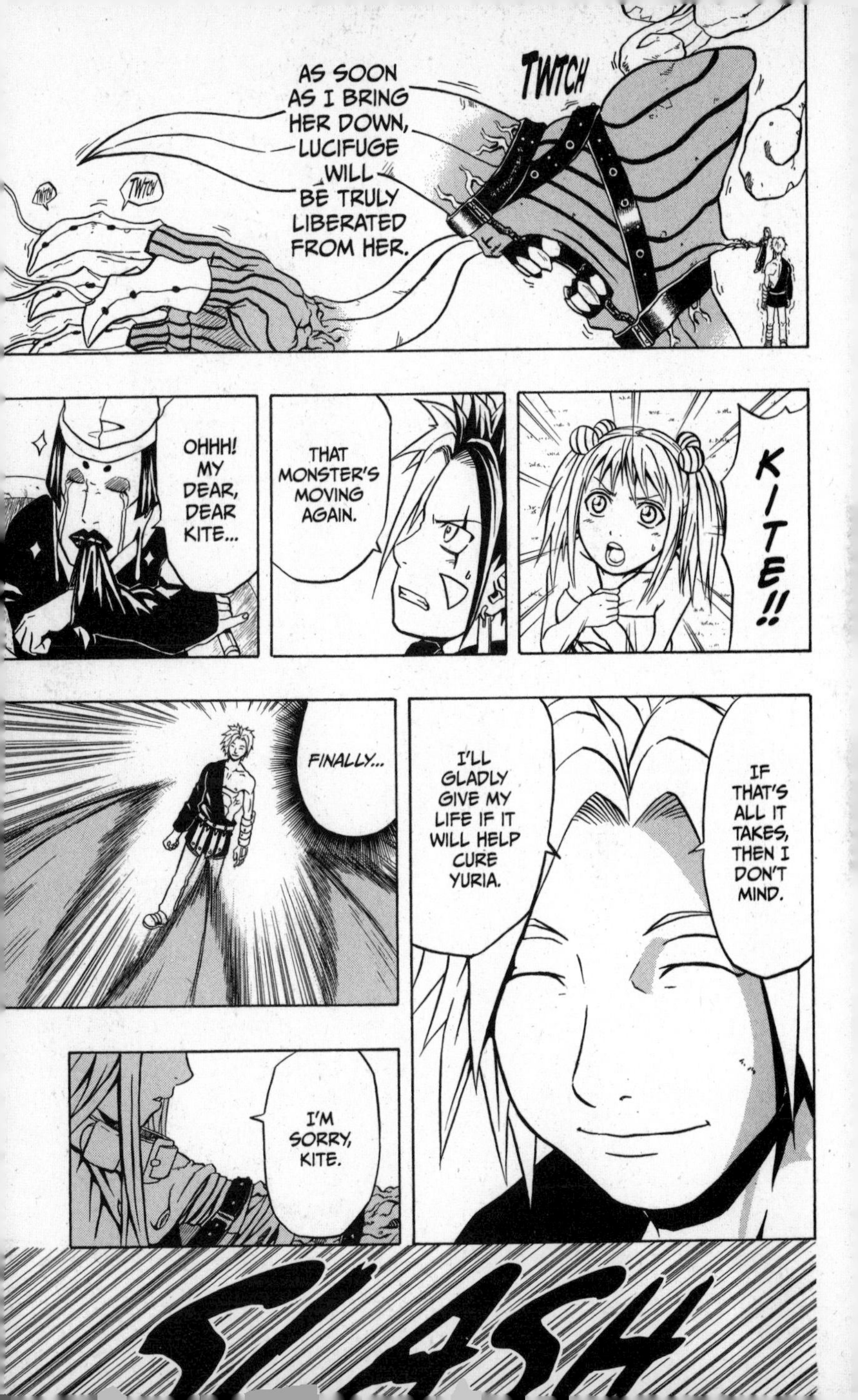
TWITCH
AS SOON AS I BRING HER DOWN, LUCIFUGE WILL BE TRULY LIBERATED FROM HER.
TWITCH
TWITCH
KITE!!
THAT MONSTER'S MOVING AGAIN.
OHHH! MY DEAR, DEAR KITE...
IF THAT'S ALL IT TAKES, THEN I DON'T MIND.
I'LL GLADLY GIVE MY LIFE IF IT WILL HELP CURE YURIA.
FINALLY...
I'M SORRY, KITE.
SLASH

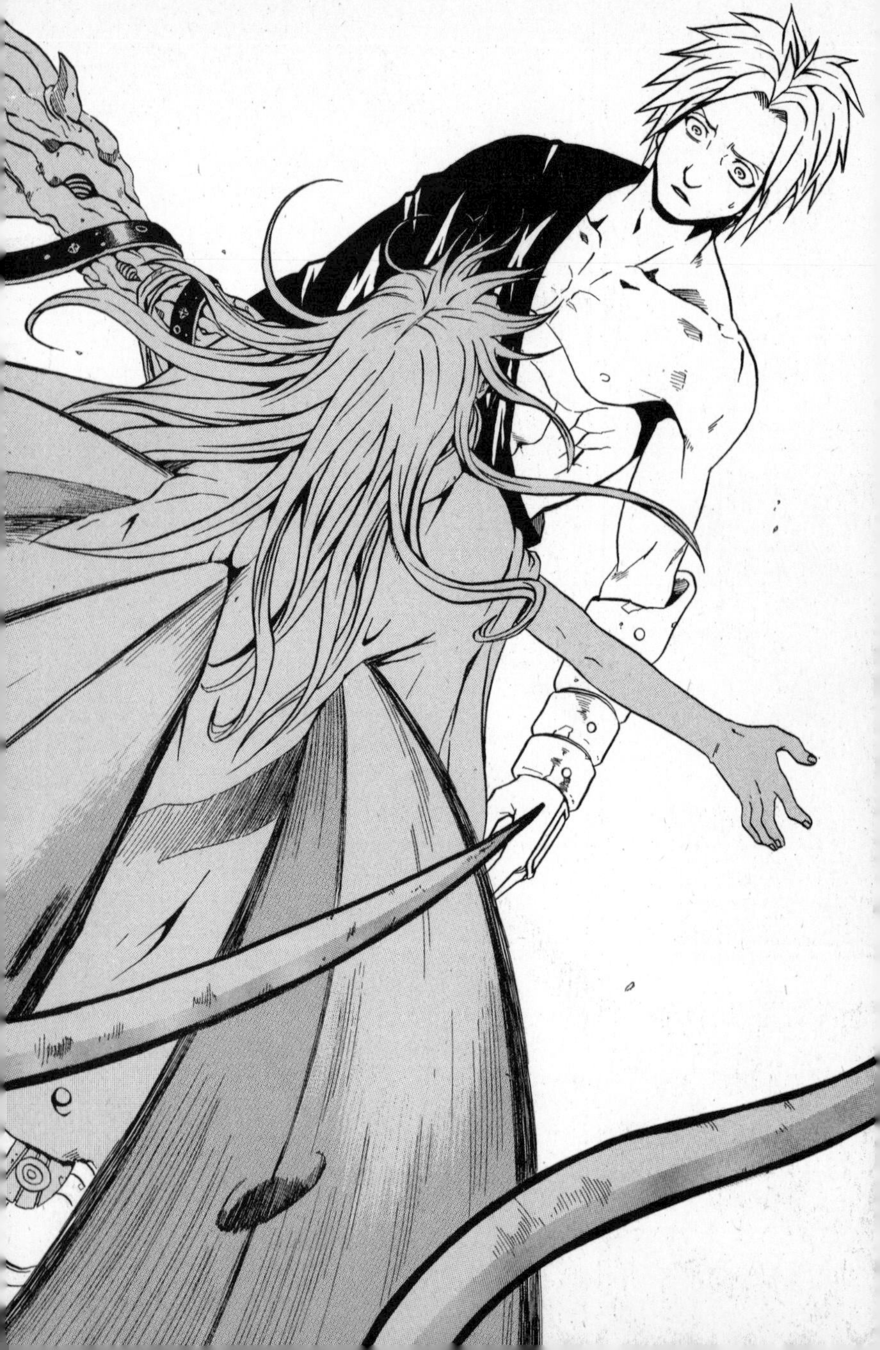

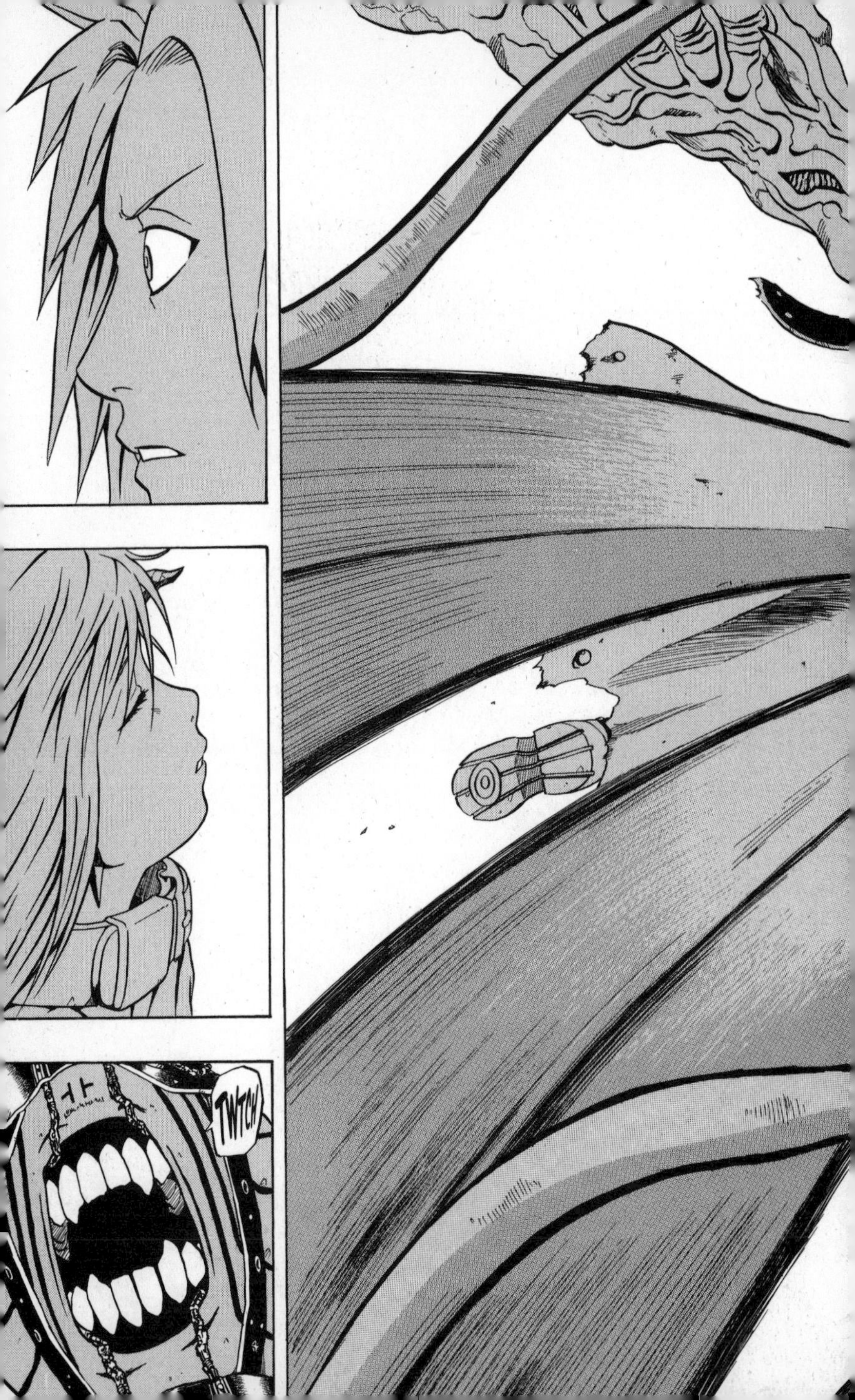
TWITCH

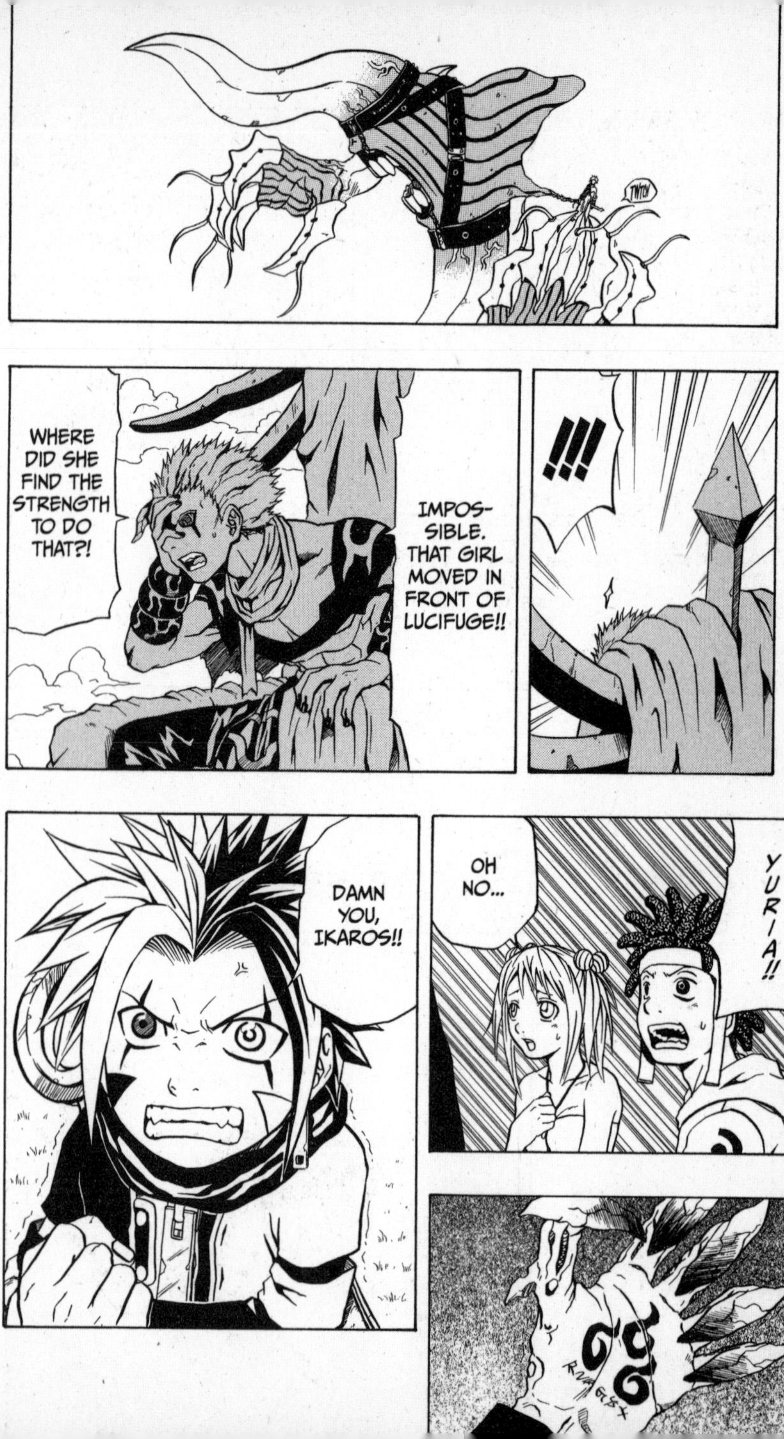
TWITCH
!!!!
IMPOS-SIBLE. THAT GIRL MOVED IN FRONT OF LUCIFUGE!!
WHERE DID SHE FIND THE STRENGTH TO DO THAT?!
YURIA!!
OH NO...
DAMN YOU, IKAROS!!

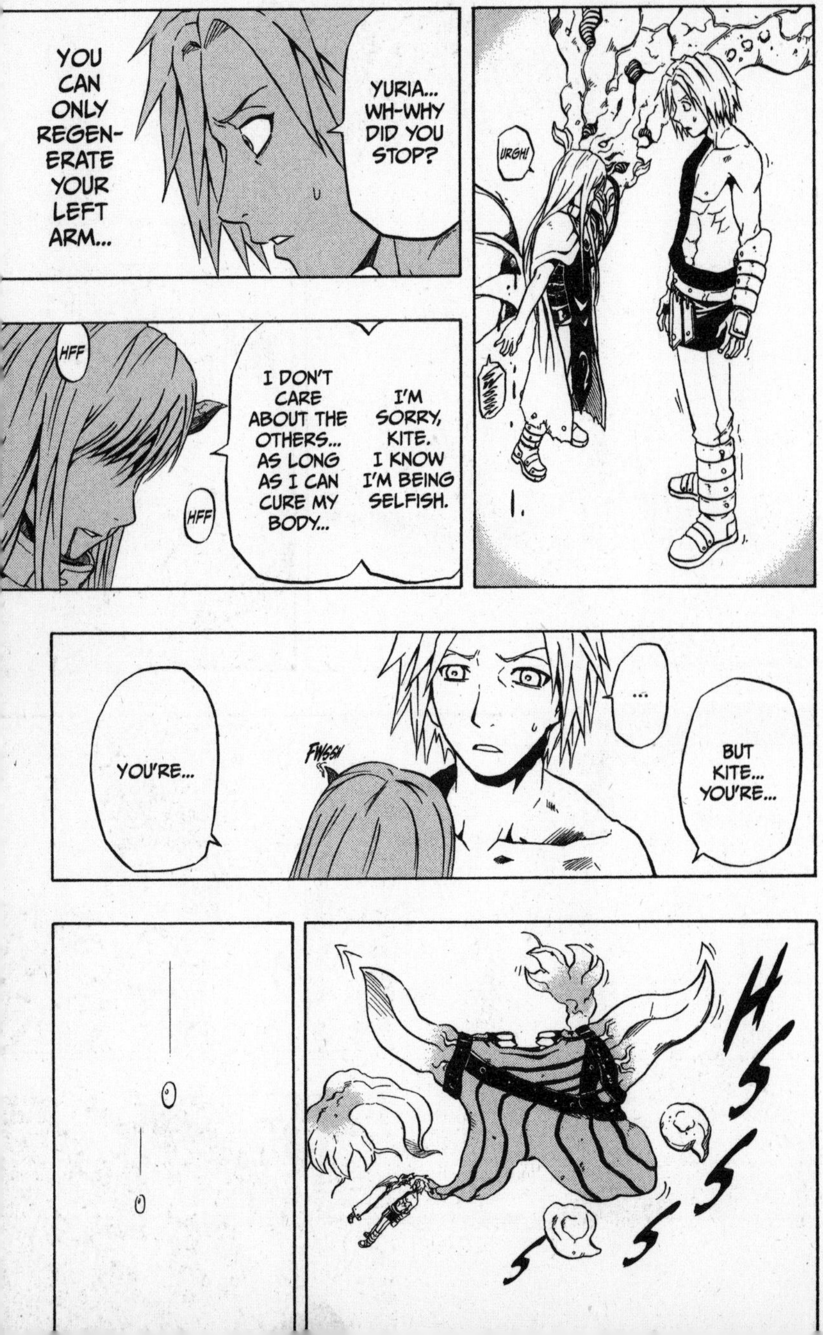
URGH!
YURIA... WH-WHY DID YOU STOP?
YOU CAN ONLY REGENERATE YOUR LEFT ARM...
HFF
I'M SORRY, KITE. I KNOW I'M BEING SELFISH.
I DON'T CARE ABOUT THE OTHERS... AS LONG AS I CAN CURE MY BODY...
HFF
BUT KITE... YOU'RE...
...
FWSSH
YOU'RE...
HSSSSS

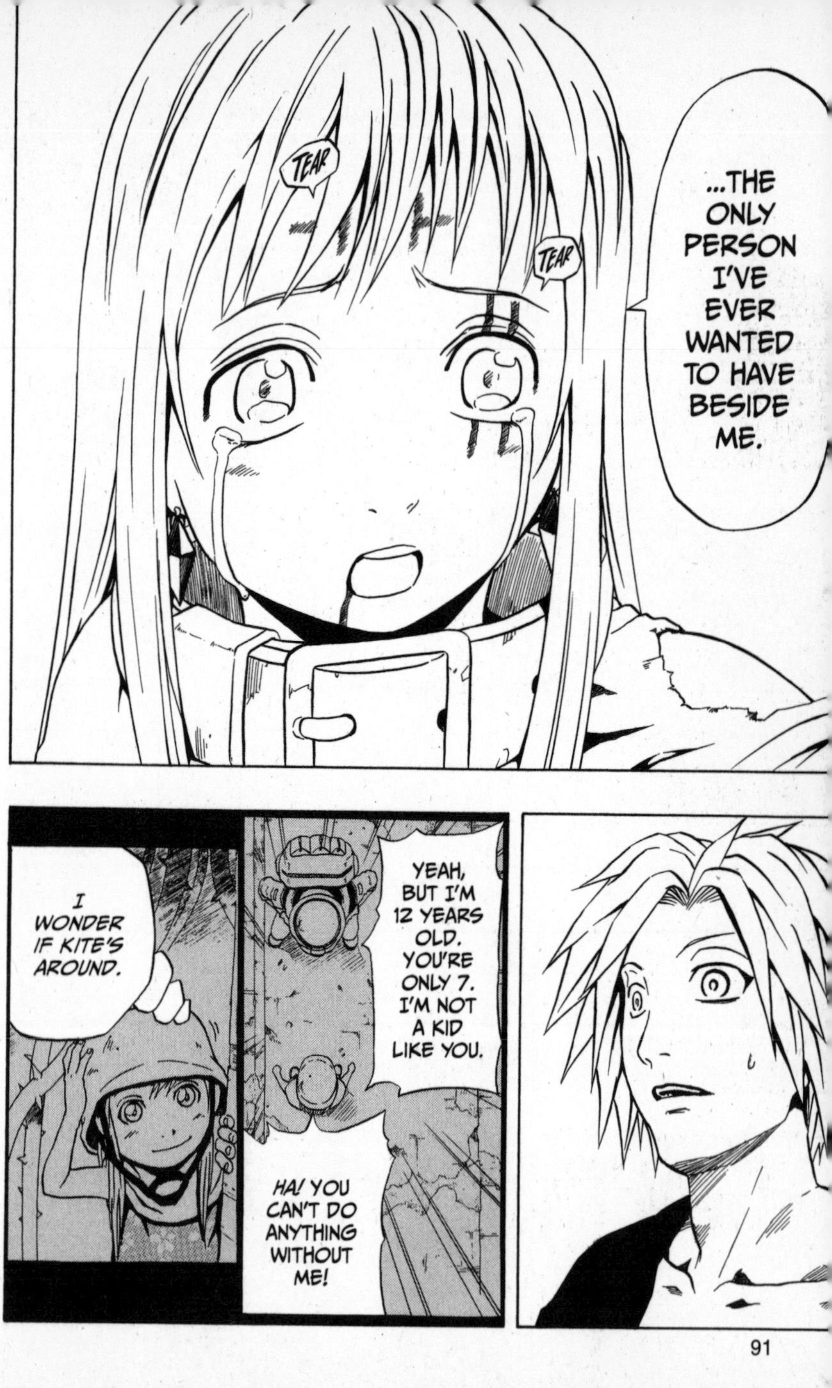
TEAR
TEAR
...THE ONLY PERSON I'VE EVER WANTED TO HAVE BESIDE ME.
YEAH, BUT I'M 12 YEARS OLD. YOU'RE ONLY 7. I'M NOT A KID LIKE YOU.
HA! YOU CAN'T DO ANYTHING WITHOUT ME!
I WONDER IF KITE'S AROUND.

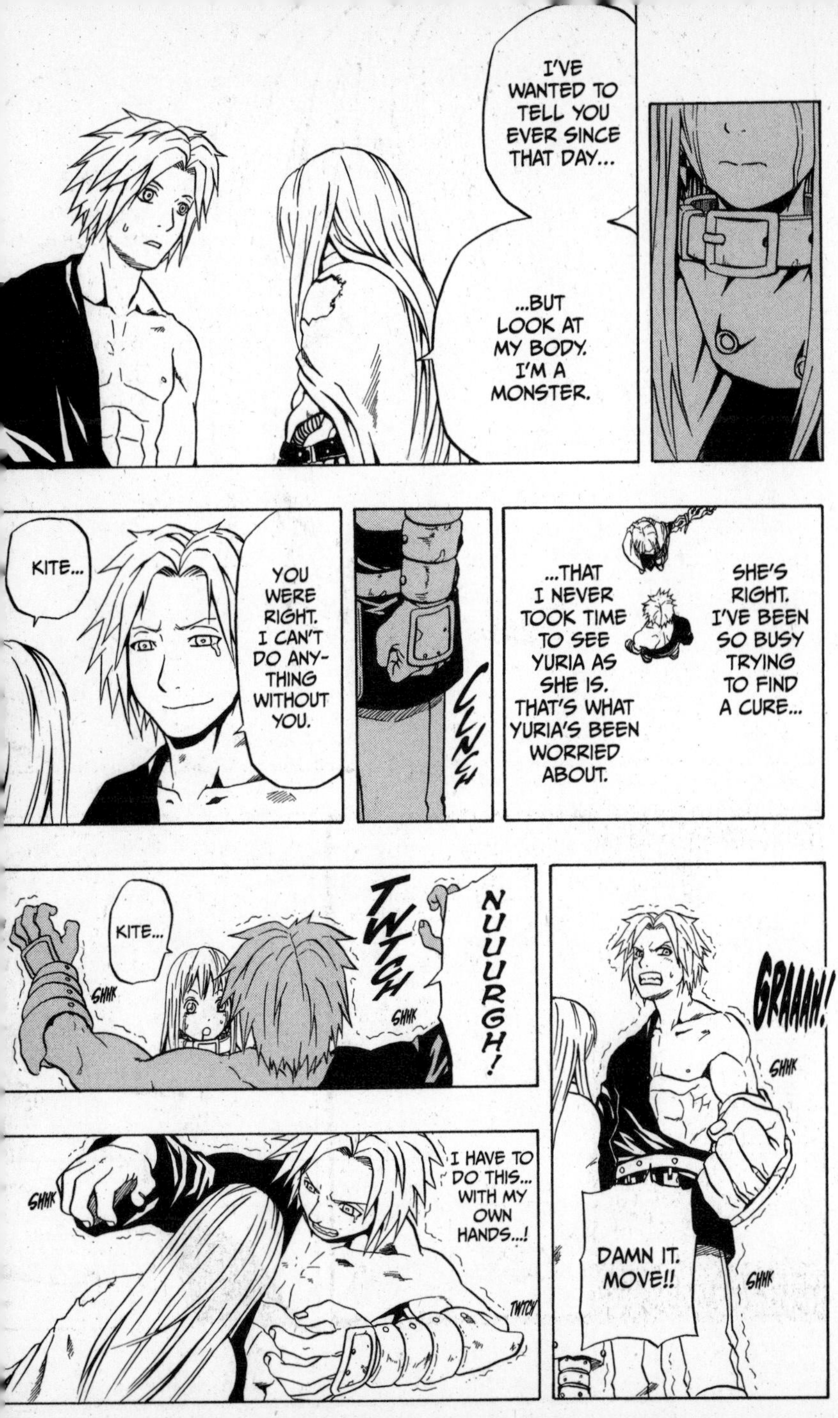

I'VE WANTED TO TELL YOU EVER SINCE THAT DAY...
...BUT LOOK AT MY BODY. I'M A MONSTER.
SHE'S RIGHT. I'VE BEEN SO BUSY TRYING TO FIND A CURE...
...THAT I NEVER TOOK TIME TO SEE YURIA AS SHE IS. THAT'S WHAT YURIA'S BEEN WORRIED ABOUT.
CLNCH
YOU WERE RIGHT. I CAN'T DO ANY-THING WITHOUT YOU.
KITE...
GRAAAH!
SHHK
DAMN IT. MOVE!!
SHHK
NUUURGH!
TWITCH
SHHK
KITE...
SHHK
I HAVE TO DO THIS... WITH MY OWN HANDS...!
SHHK
TWITCH

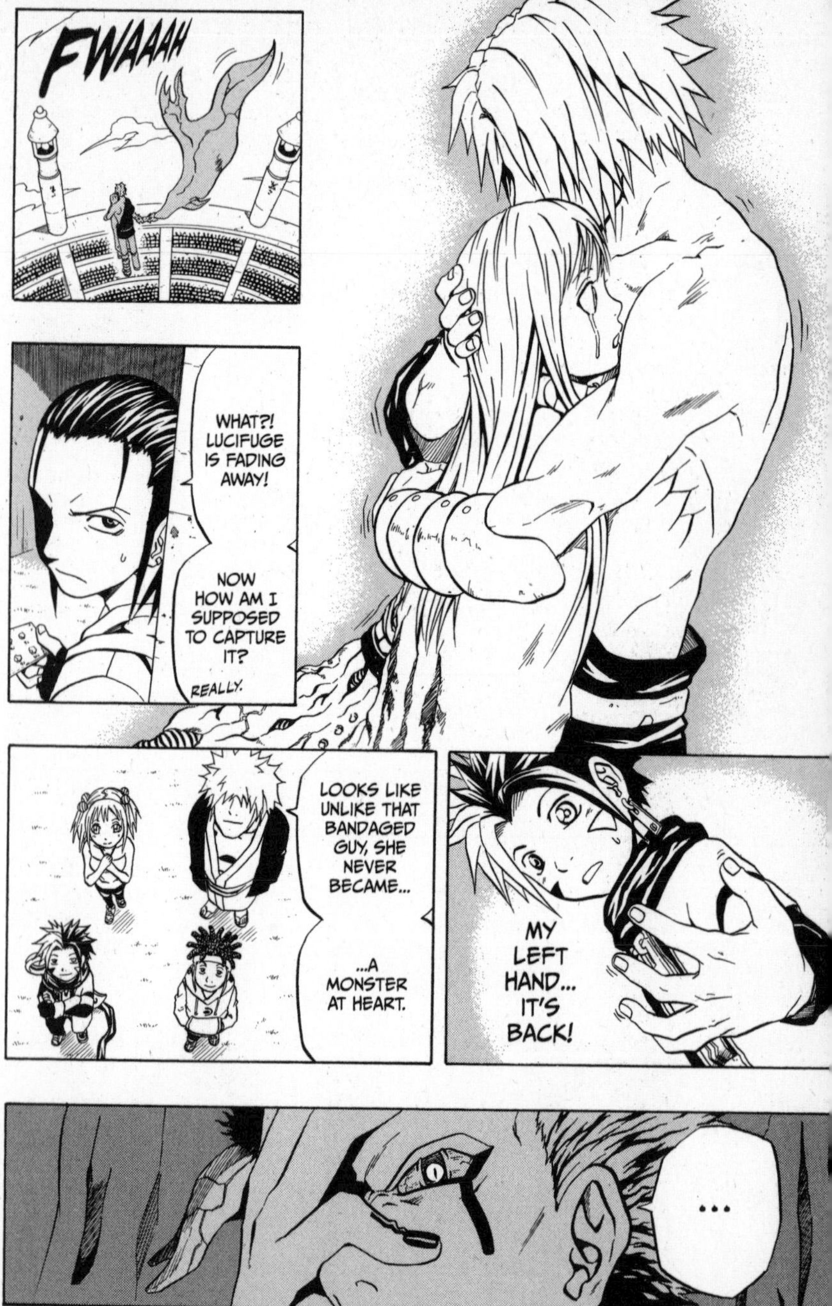
FWAAAH
WHAT?! LUCIFUGE IS FADING AWAY!
NOW HOW AM I SUPPOSED TO CAPTURE IT?
REALLY.
MY LEFT HAND... IT'S BACK!
LOOKS LIKE UNLIKE THAT BANDAGED GUY, SHE NEVER BECAME...
...A MONSTER AT HEART.
...

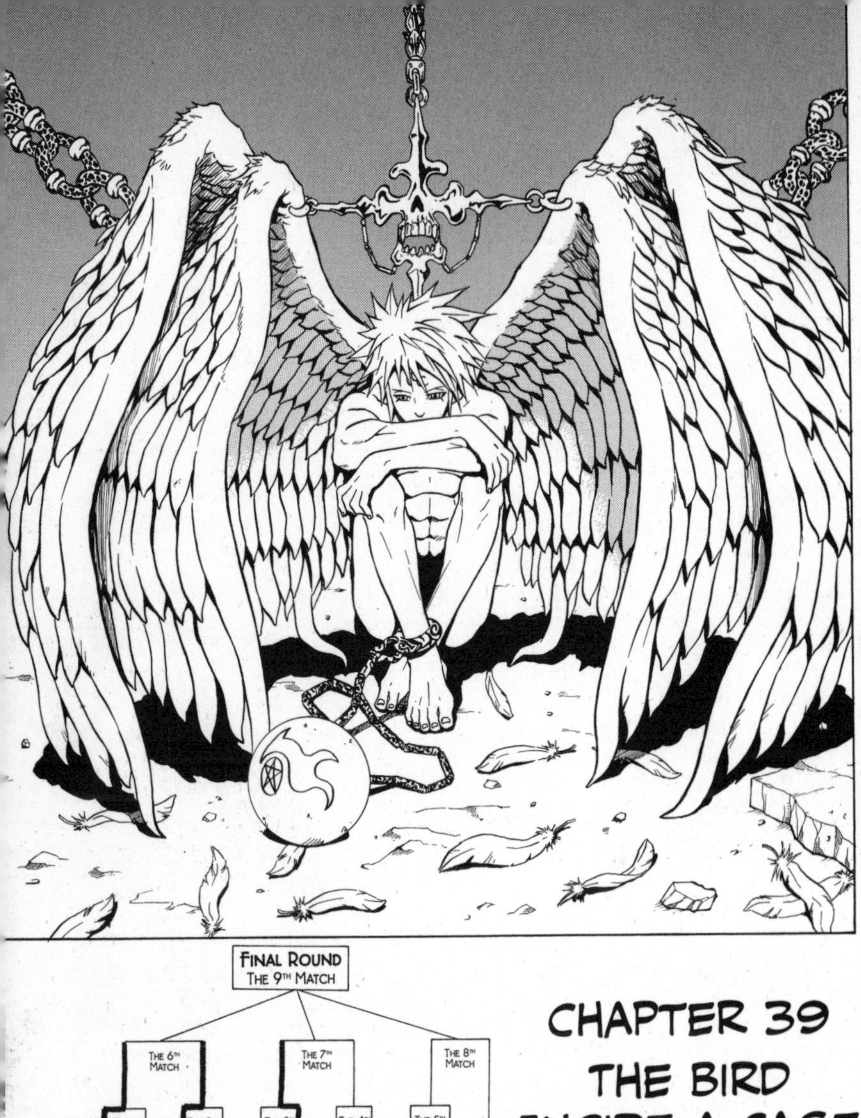

CHAPTER 39
THE BIRD INSIDE A CAGE

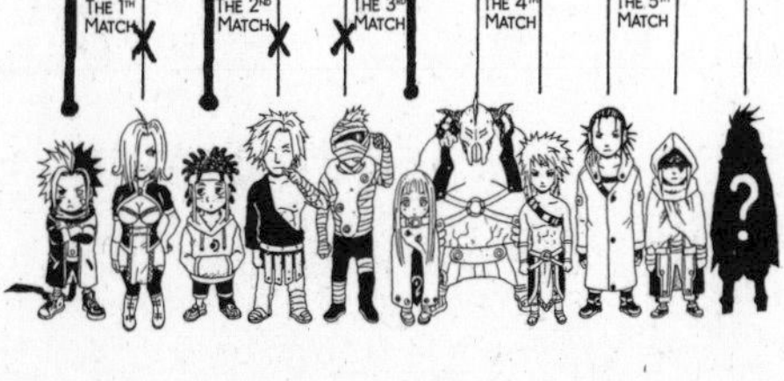

FINAL ROUND
THE 9TH MATCH
THE 6TH MATCH
THE 7TH MATCH
THE 8TH MATCH
THE 1ST MATCH
THE 2ND MATCH
THE 3RD MATCH
THE 4TH MATCH
THE 5TH MATCH
?

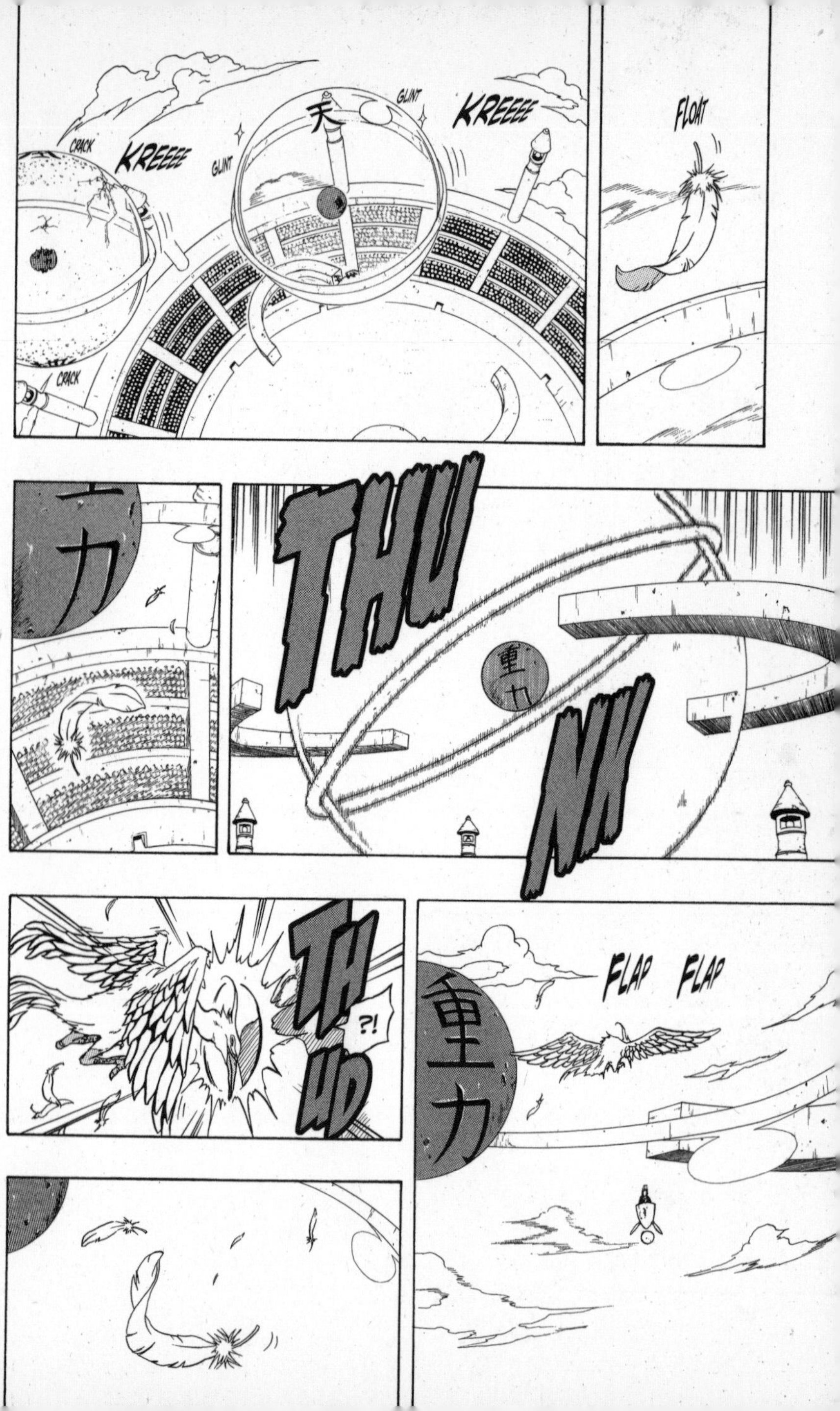
FLOAT
GLINT
KREEEE
天
CRACK
KREEEE
GLINT
CRACK
THUNK
重力
力
FLAP FLAP
重力
THUD
?!

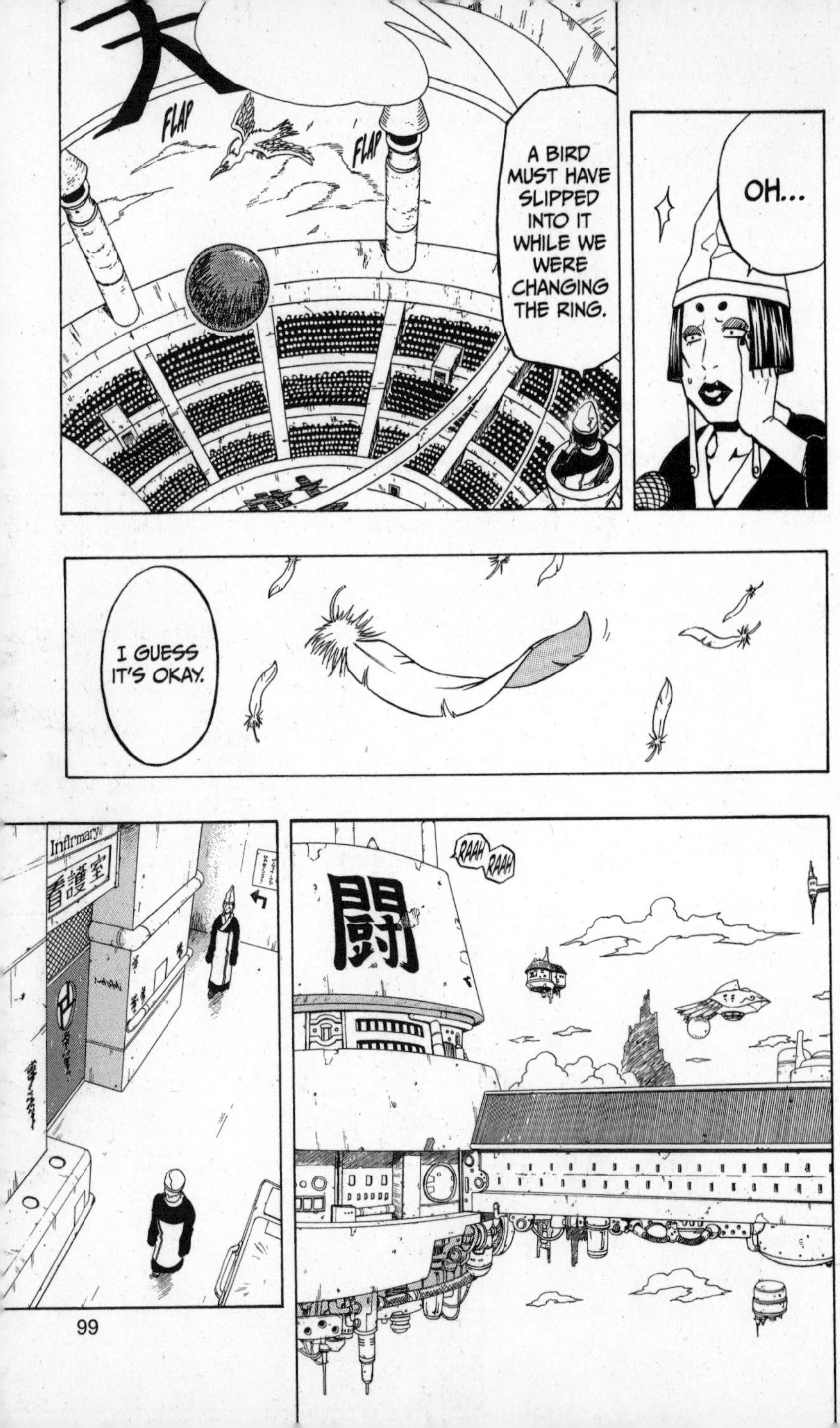
OH...
A BIRD MUST HAVE SLIPPED INTO IT WHILE WE WERE CHANGING THE RING.
FLAP
FLAP
I GUESS IT'S OKAY.
RAAH
RAAH
Infirmary
看護室

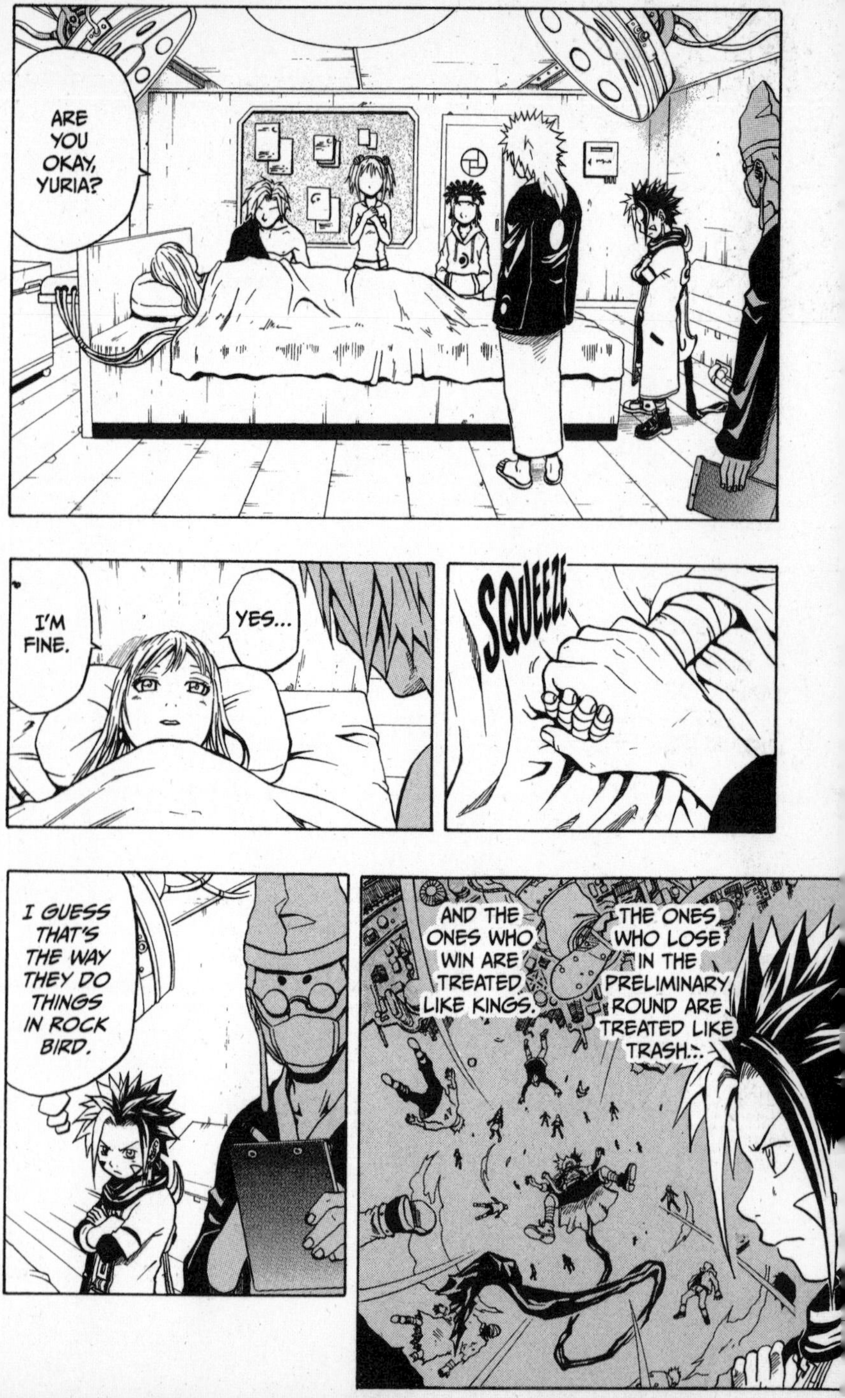
ARE YOU OKAY, YURIA?
SQUEEZE
YES...
I'M FINE.
THE ONES WHO LOSE IN THE PRELIMINARY ROUND ARE TREATED LIKE TRASH...
AND THE ONES WHO WIN ARE TREATED LIKE KINGS.
I GUESS THAT'S THE WAY THEY DO THINGS IN ROCK BIRD.

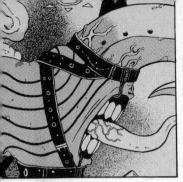

WE'RE LUCKY THAT THING WENT AWAY.

NO.

YURIA'S HEART MADE THAT THING DISAPPEAR.

I KNOW IT.

IT WASN'T LUCK.

I THINK THAT'S WHAT IT WAS.

WELL...

WHAAA?

...

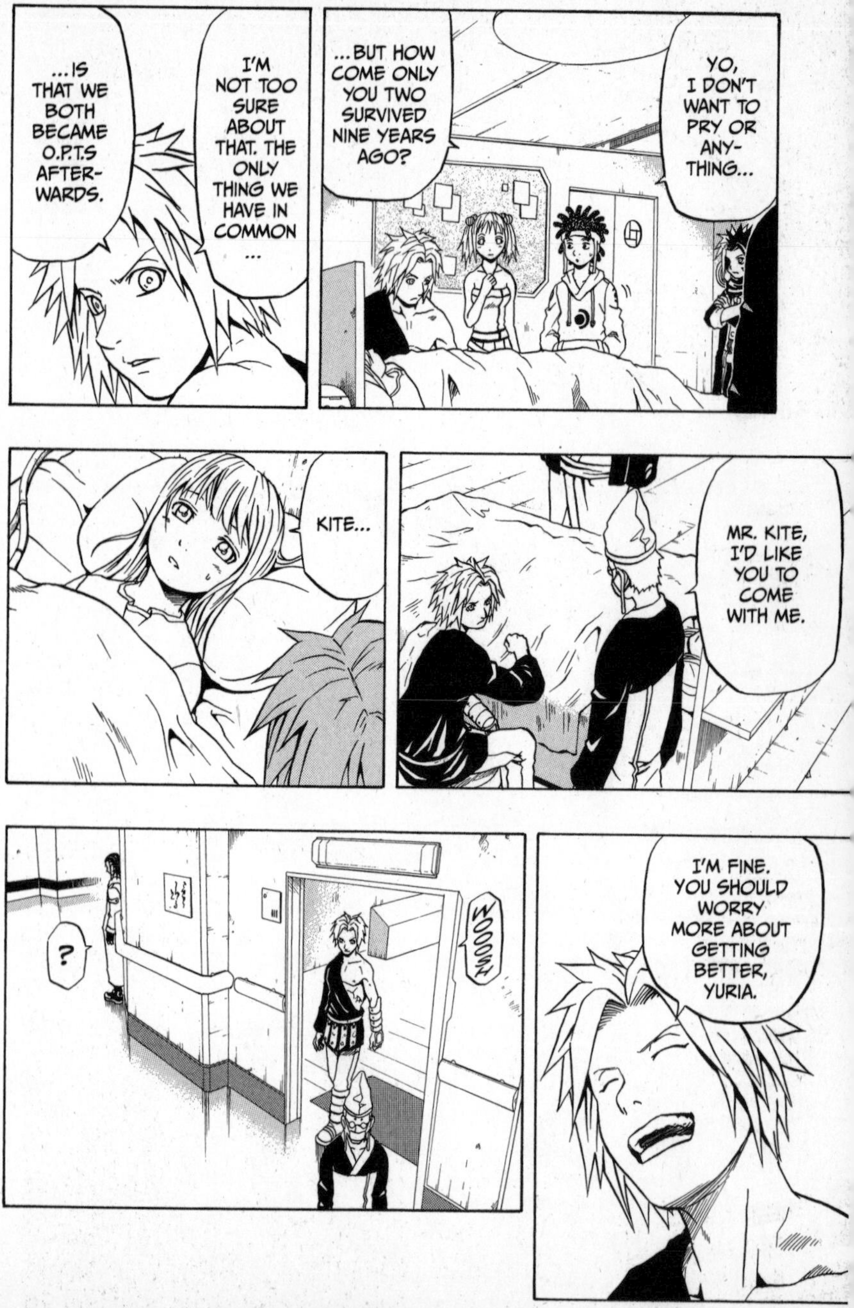
YO, I DON'T WANT TO PRY OR ANY-THING...
...BUT HOW COME ONLY YOU TWO SURVIVED NINE YEARS AGO?
I'M NOT TOO SURE ABOUT THAT. THE ONLY THING WE HAVE IN COMMON ...
...IS THAT WE BOTH BECAME O.P.T.S AFTER-WARDS.
MR. KITE, I'D LIKE YOU TO COME WITH ME.
KITE...
I'M FINE. YOU SHOULD WORRY MORE ABOUT GETTING BETTER, YURIA.
WOOOSH
?

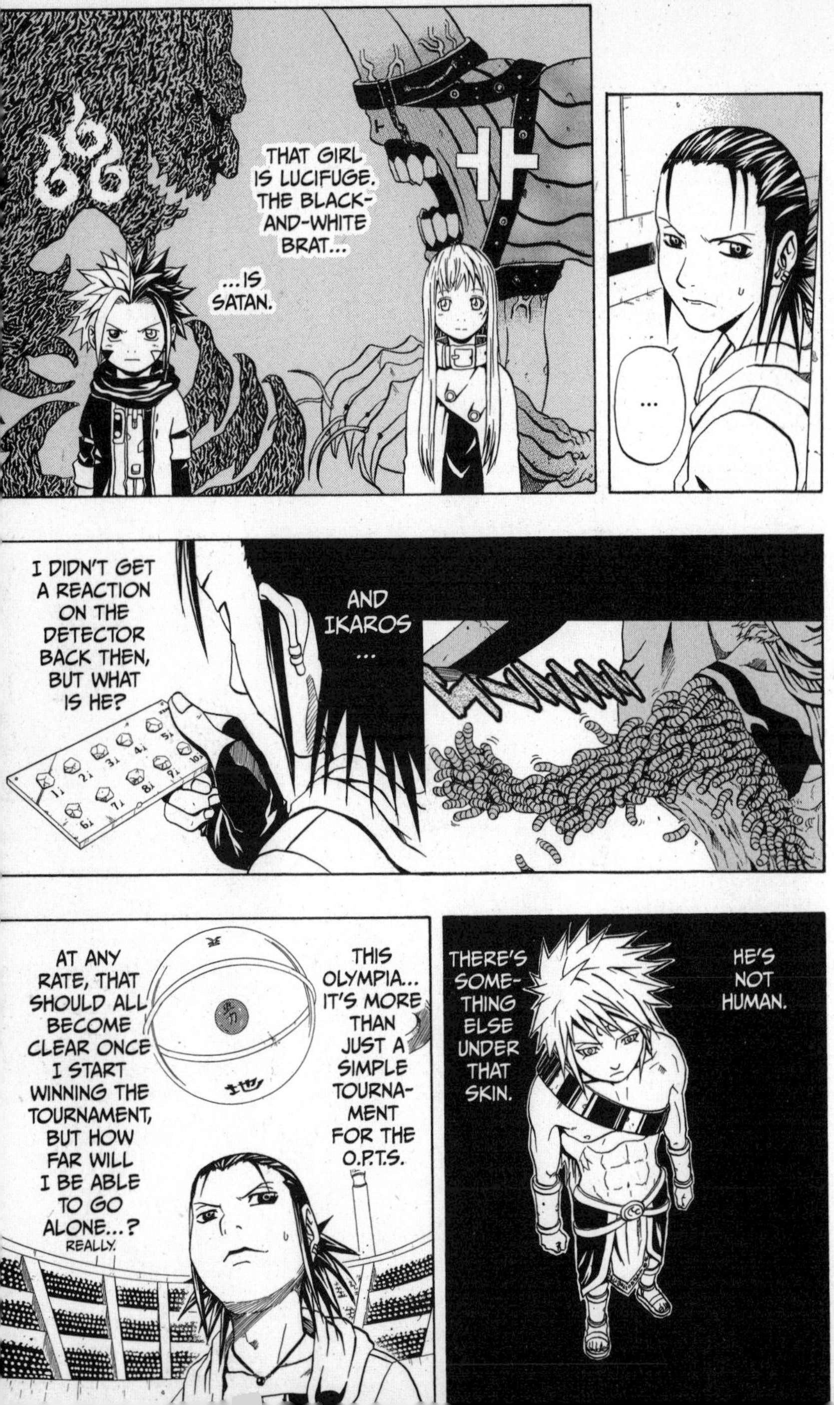
...
THAT GIRL IS LUCIFUGE. THE BLACK-AND-WHITE BRAT...
...IS SATAN.
AND IKAROS ...
I DIDN'T GET A REACTION ON THE DETECTOR BACK THEN, BUT WHAT IS HE?
HE'S NOT HUMAN.
THERE'S SOMETHING ELSE UNDER THAT SKIN.
THIS OLYMPIA... IT'S MORE THAN JUST A SIMPLE TOURNAMENT FOR THE O.P.T.S.
AT ANY RATE, THAT SHOULD ALL BECOME CLEAR ONCE I START WINNING THE TOURNAMENT, BUT HOW FAR WILL I BE ABLE TO GO ALONE...?
REALLY.

C-CRACK!

!!!

WHERE ARE YOU TAKING ME?

B6

TH UD

C-CRACK

C-CRACK

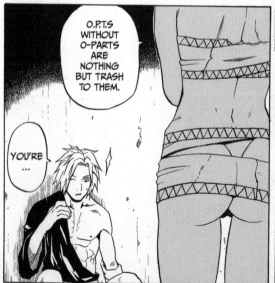

O.P.T.S WITHOUT O-PARTS ARE NOTHING BUT TRASH TO THEM.

YOU'RE ...

URGH ...

TH-THUMP   TH-THUMP

WHERE AM I?

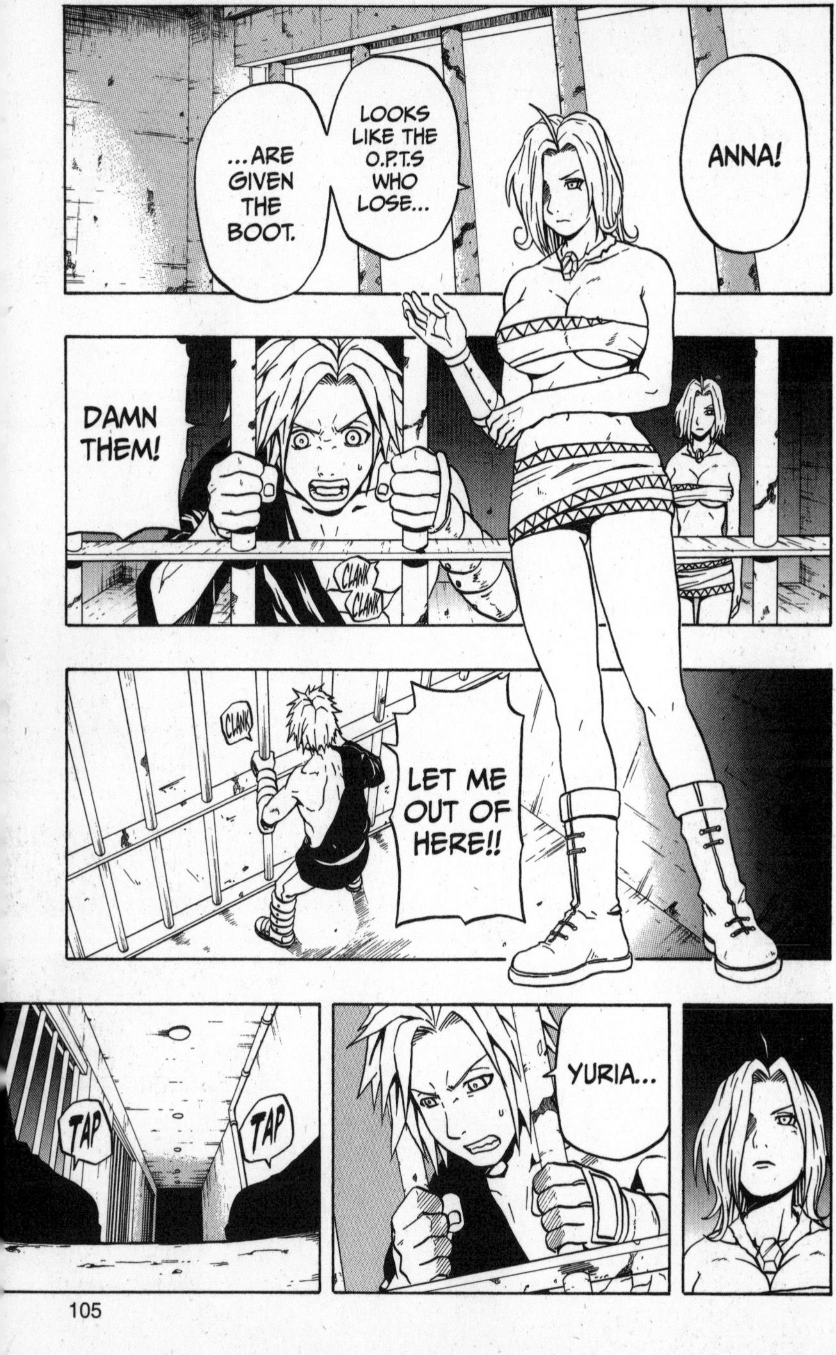
ANNA!
LOOKS LIKE THE O.P.T.S WHO LOSE...
...ARE GIVEN THE BOOT.
DAMN THEM!
CLANK
CLANK
LET ME OUT OF HERE!!
CLANK
YURIA...
TAP
TAP

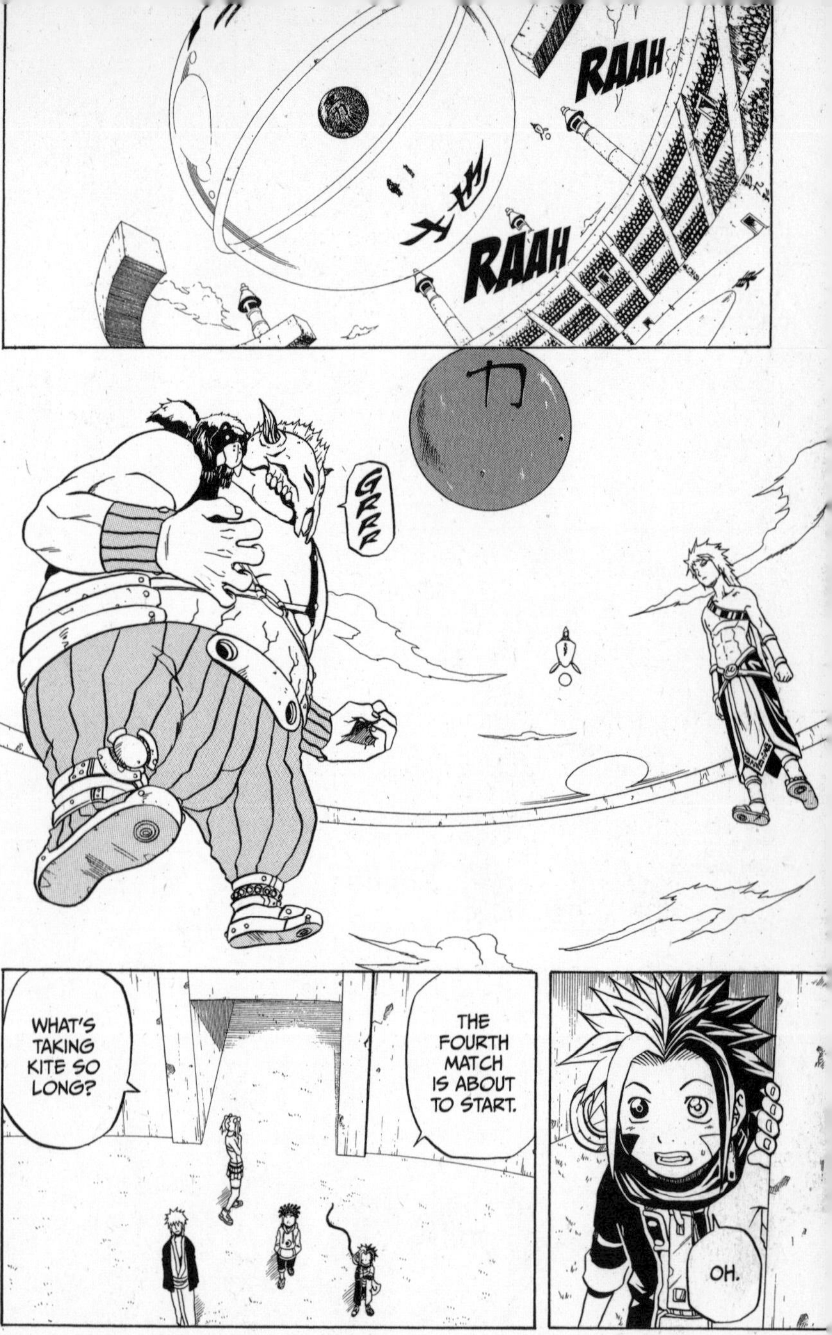
RAAH
RAAH
GRRR
OH.
THE FOURTH MATCH IS ABOUT TO START.
WHAT'S TAKING KITE SO LONG?

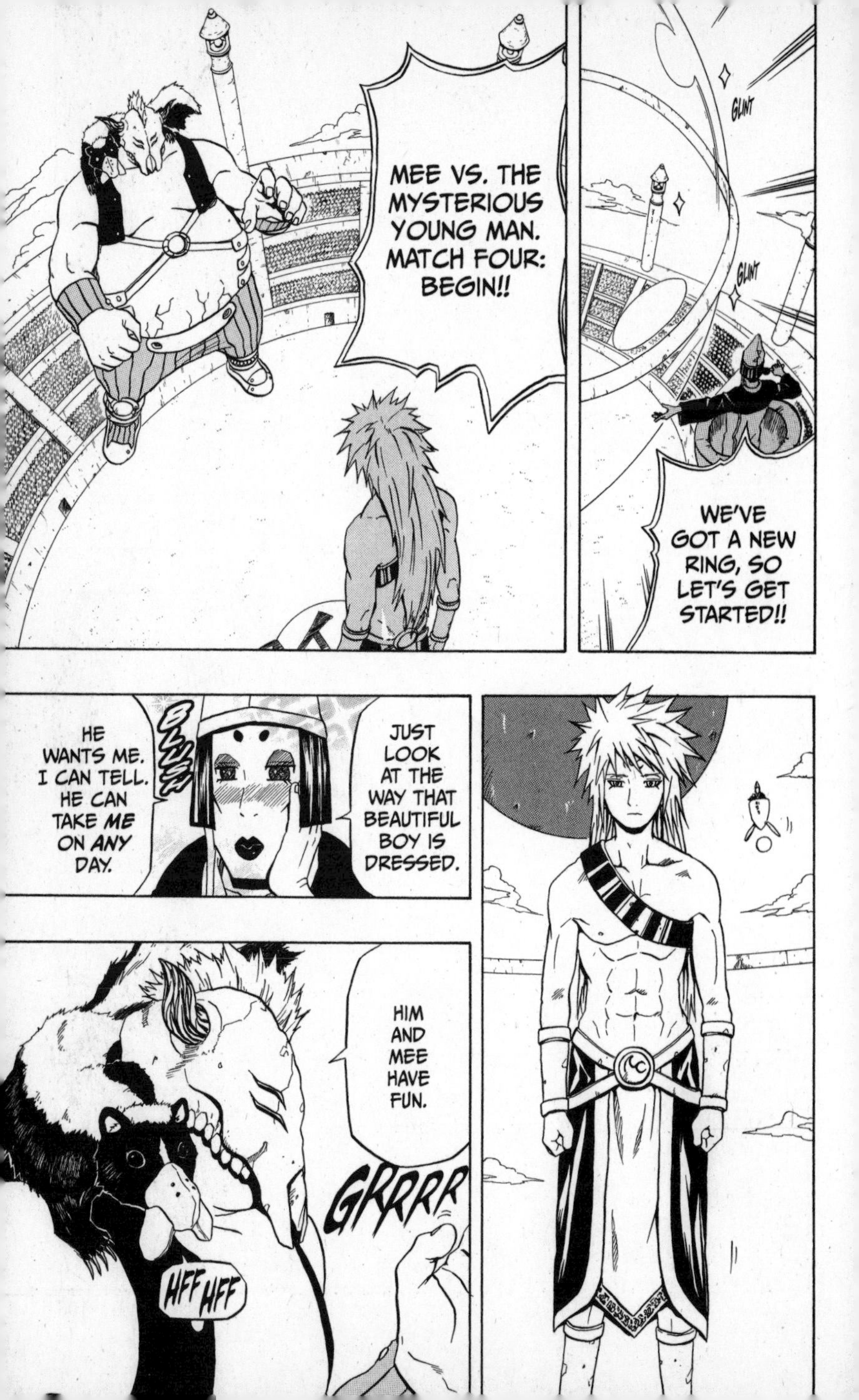
GLINT
GLINT
WE'VE GOT A NEW RING, SO LET'S GET STARTED!!
MEE VS. THE MYSTERIOUS YOUNG MAN. MATCH FOUR: BEGIN!!
JUST LOOK AT THE WAY THAT BEAUTIFUL BOY IS DRESSED.
HE WANTS ME. I CAN TELL. HE CAN TAKE *ME* ON *ANY* DAY.
HIM AND MEE HAVE FUN.
GRRRR
HFF HFF

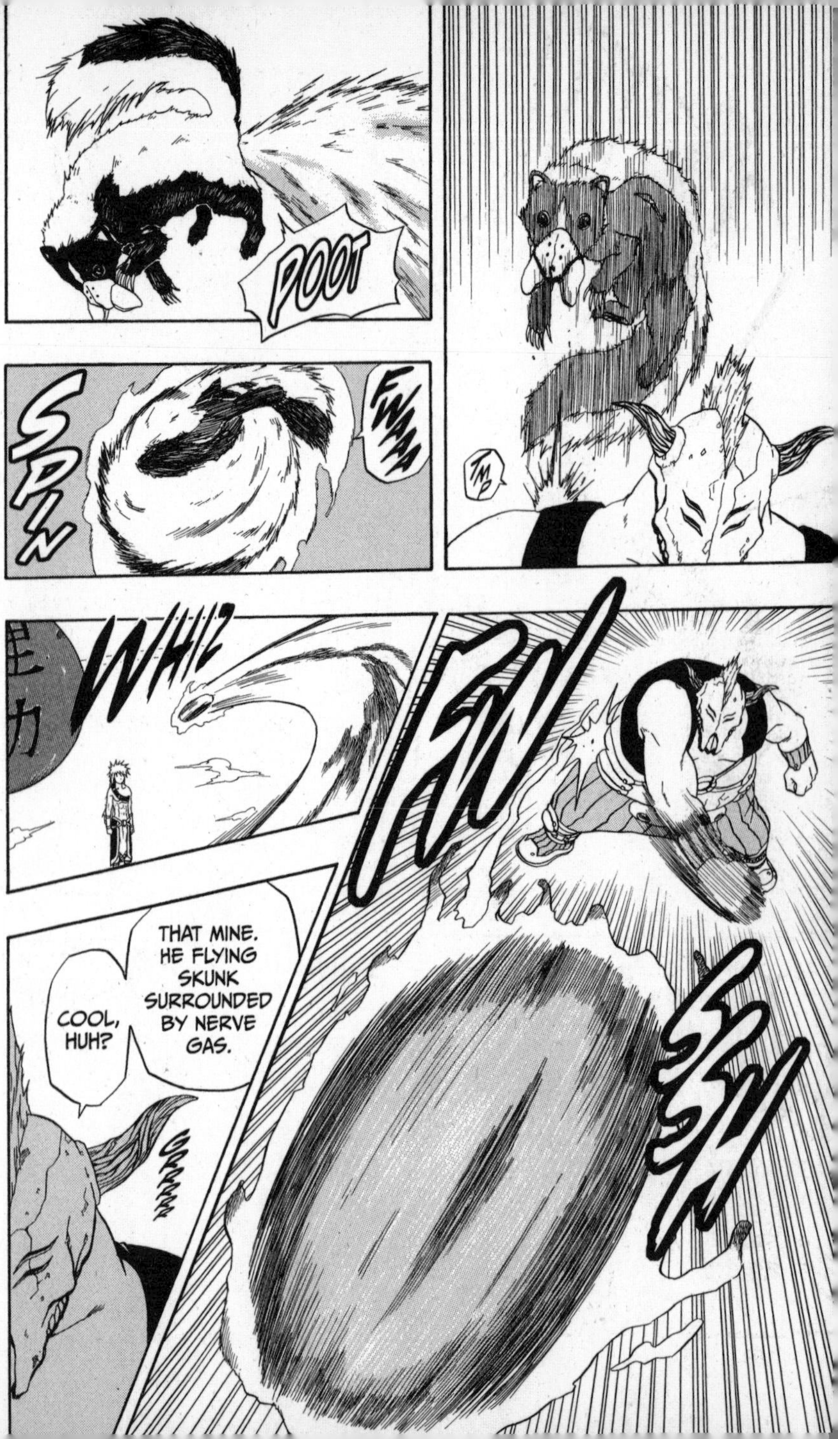
TMP
POOT
FWAAA
SPIN
FW
WHIZ
THAT MINE. HE FLYING SKUNK SURROUNDED BY NERVE GAS.
COOL, HUH?
GRRRRR

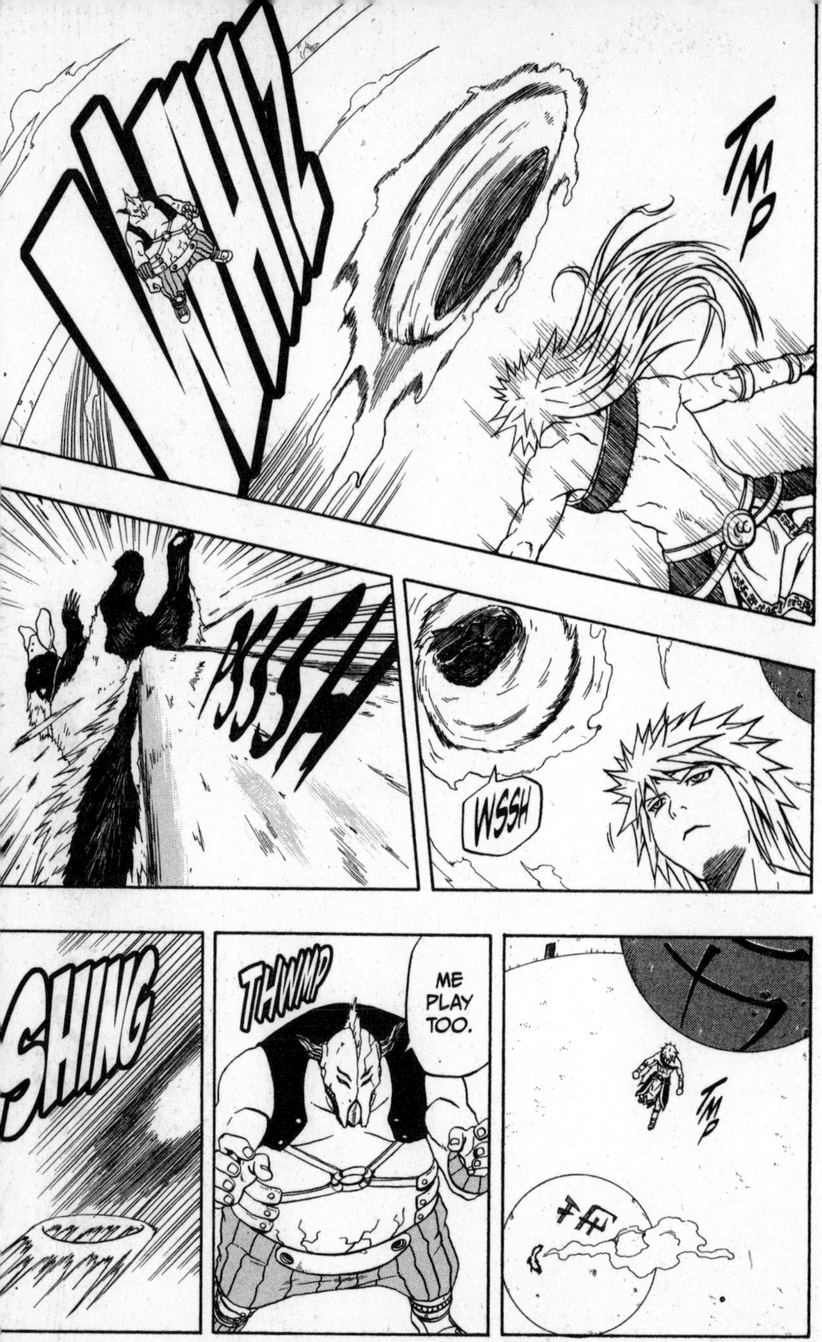
TMP
WSSH
PSSH
TMP
ME PLAY TOO.
THWMP
SHING

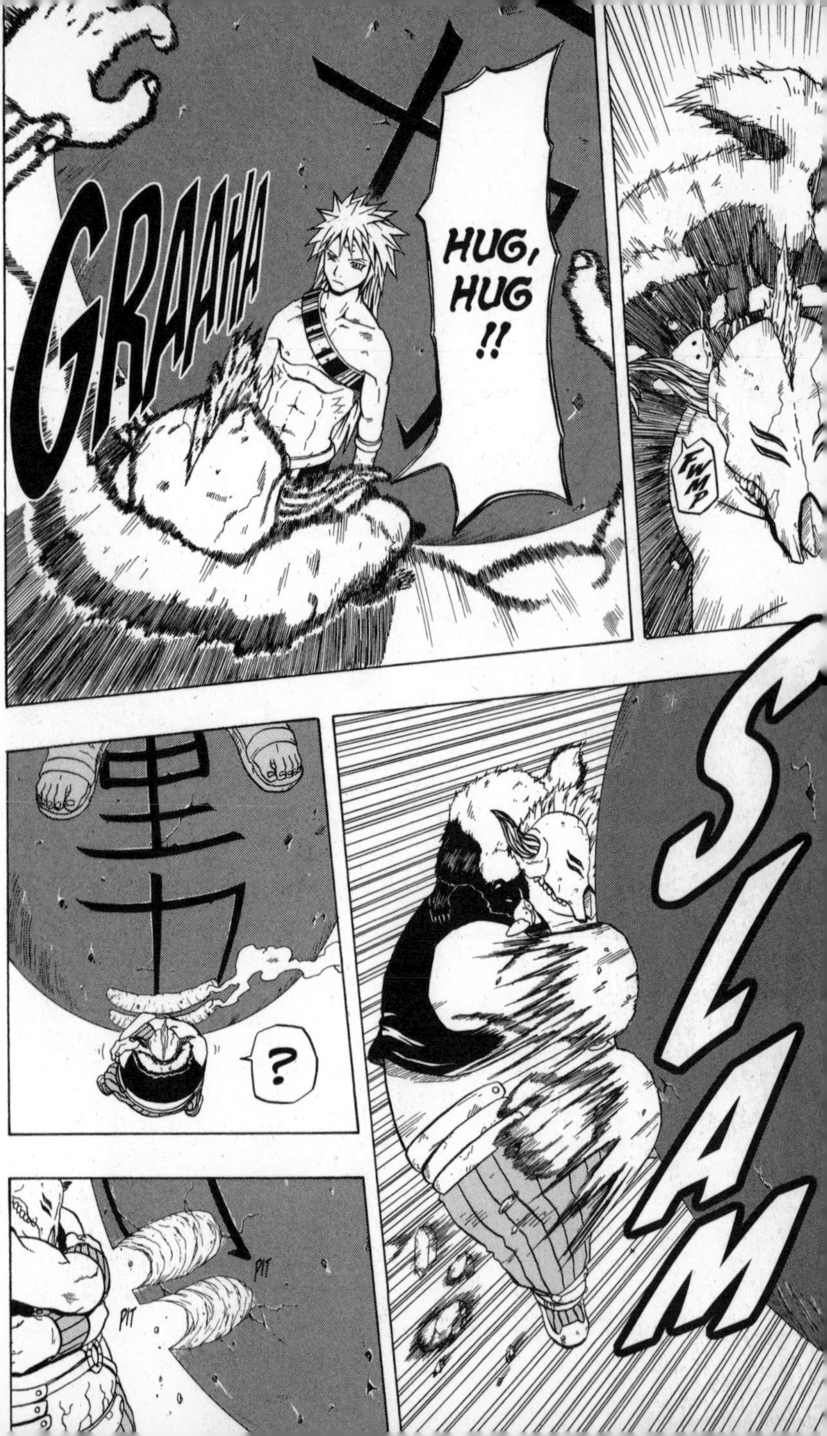
FWMP
HUG, HUG !!
GRAAHH
SLAM
?
PIT
PIT

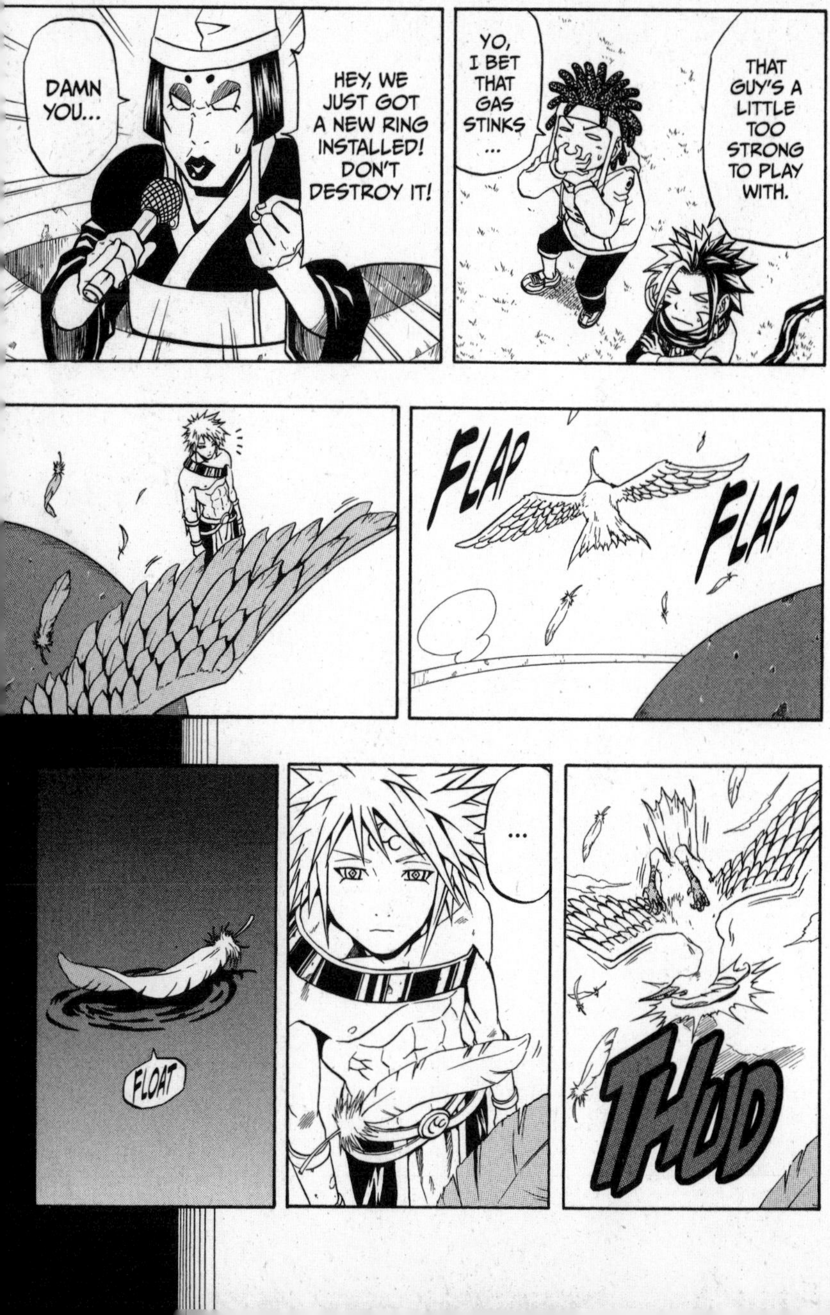
THAT GUY'S A LITTLE TOO STRONG TO PLAY WITH.
YO, I BET THAT GAS STINKS ...
HEY, WE JUST GOT A NEW RING INSTALLED! DON'T DESTROY IT!
DAMN YOU...
FLAP
FLAP
THUD
...
FLOAT

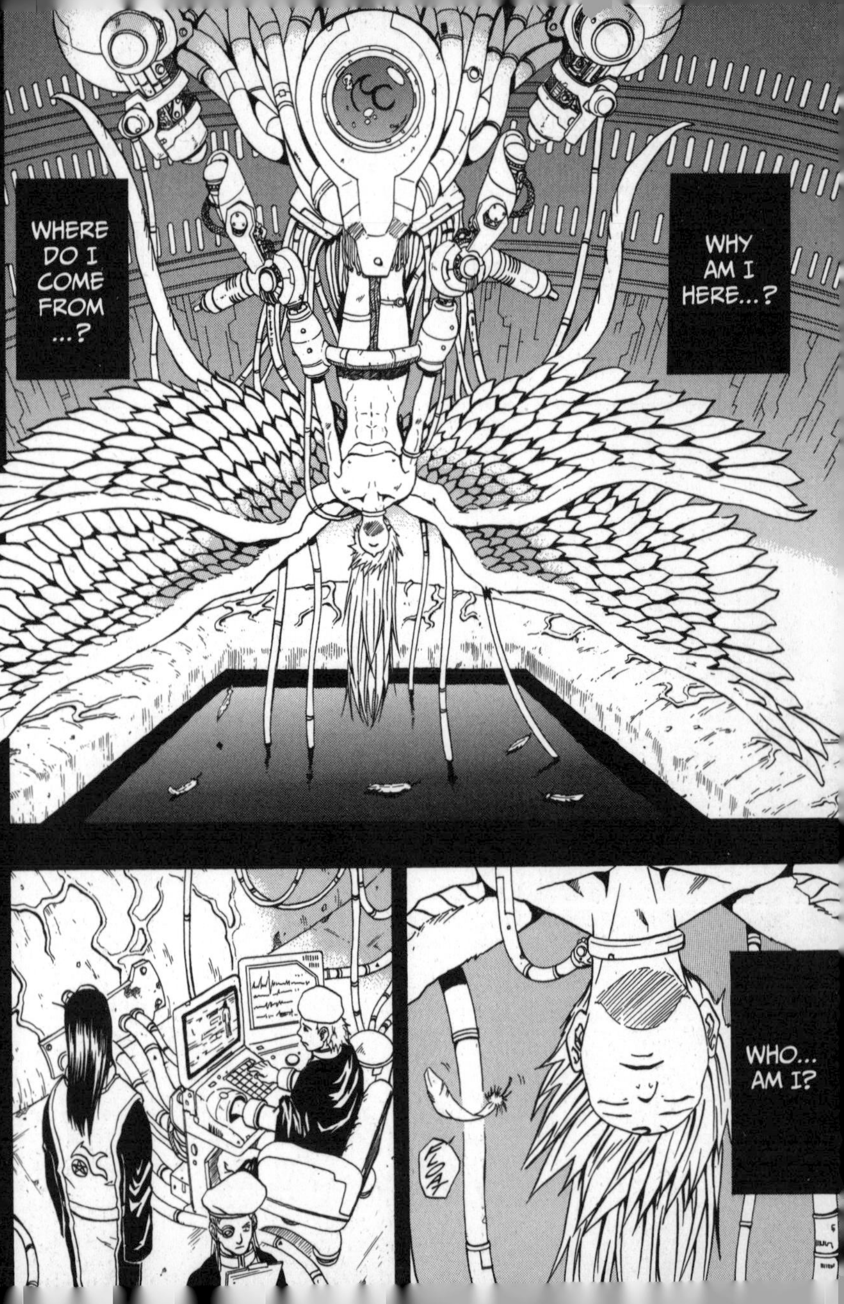
WHY AM I HERE...?
WHERE DO I COME FROM ...?
WHO... AM I?

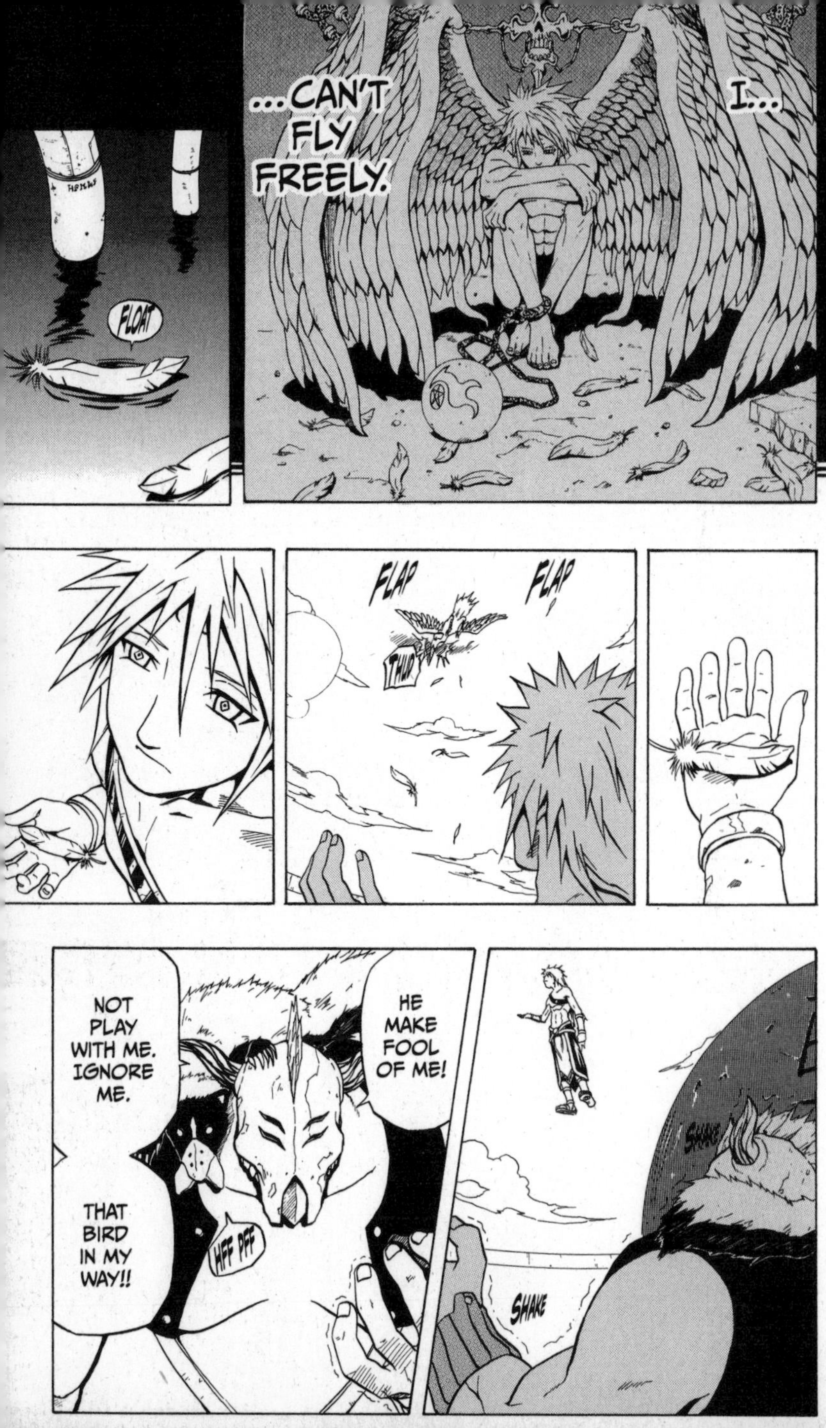
I...
...CAN'T FLY FREELY.
FLOAT
FLAP
FLAP
THUD
SHAKE
SHAKE
HE MAKE FOOL OF ME!
NOT PLAY WITH ME. IGNORE ME.
HFF PFF
THAT BIRD IN MY WAY!!

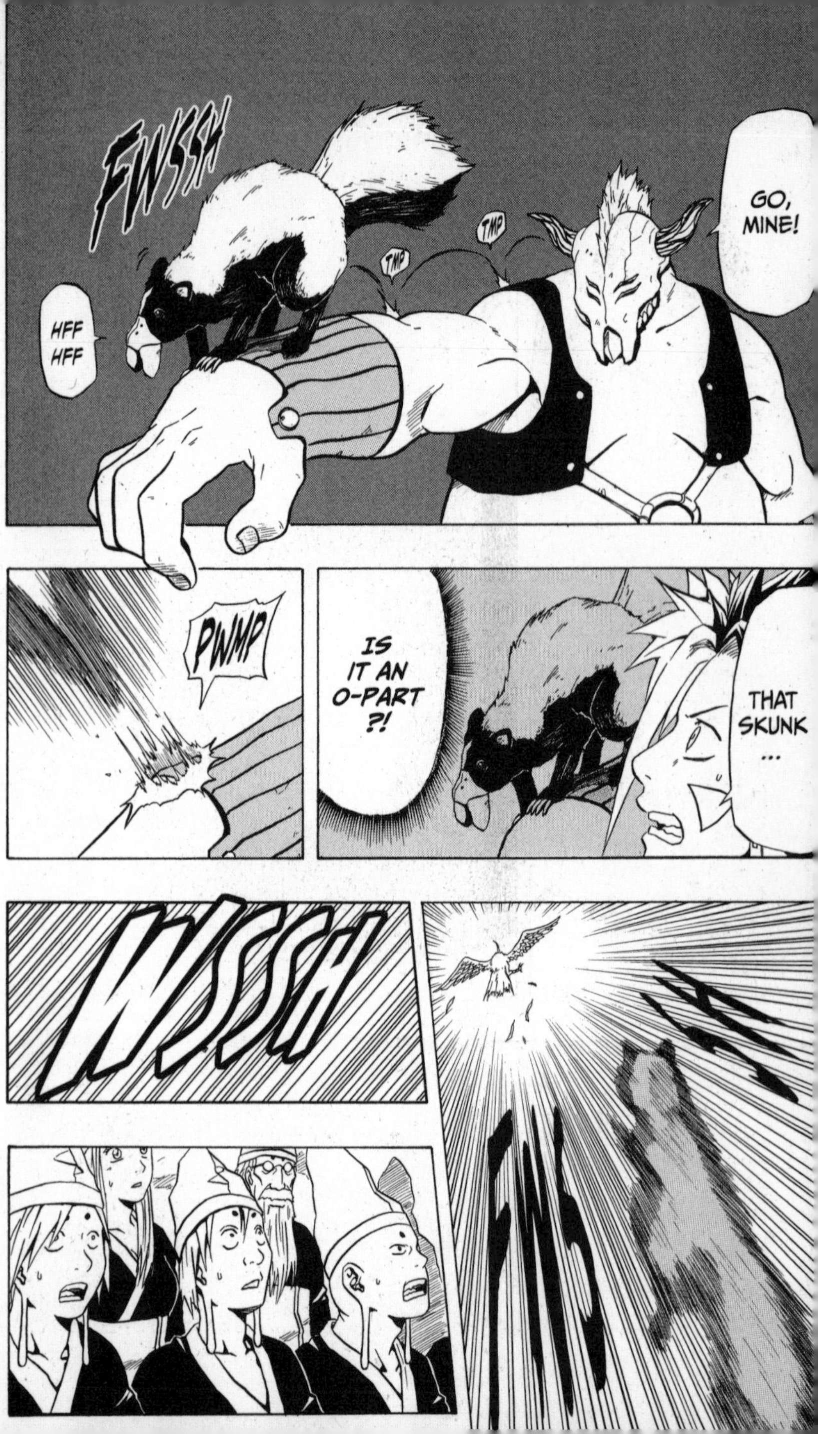
GO, MINE!
TMP
TMP
FWSSH
HFF HFF
THAT SKUNK ...
IS IT AN O-PART ?!
PWMP
WSSCH

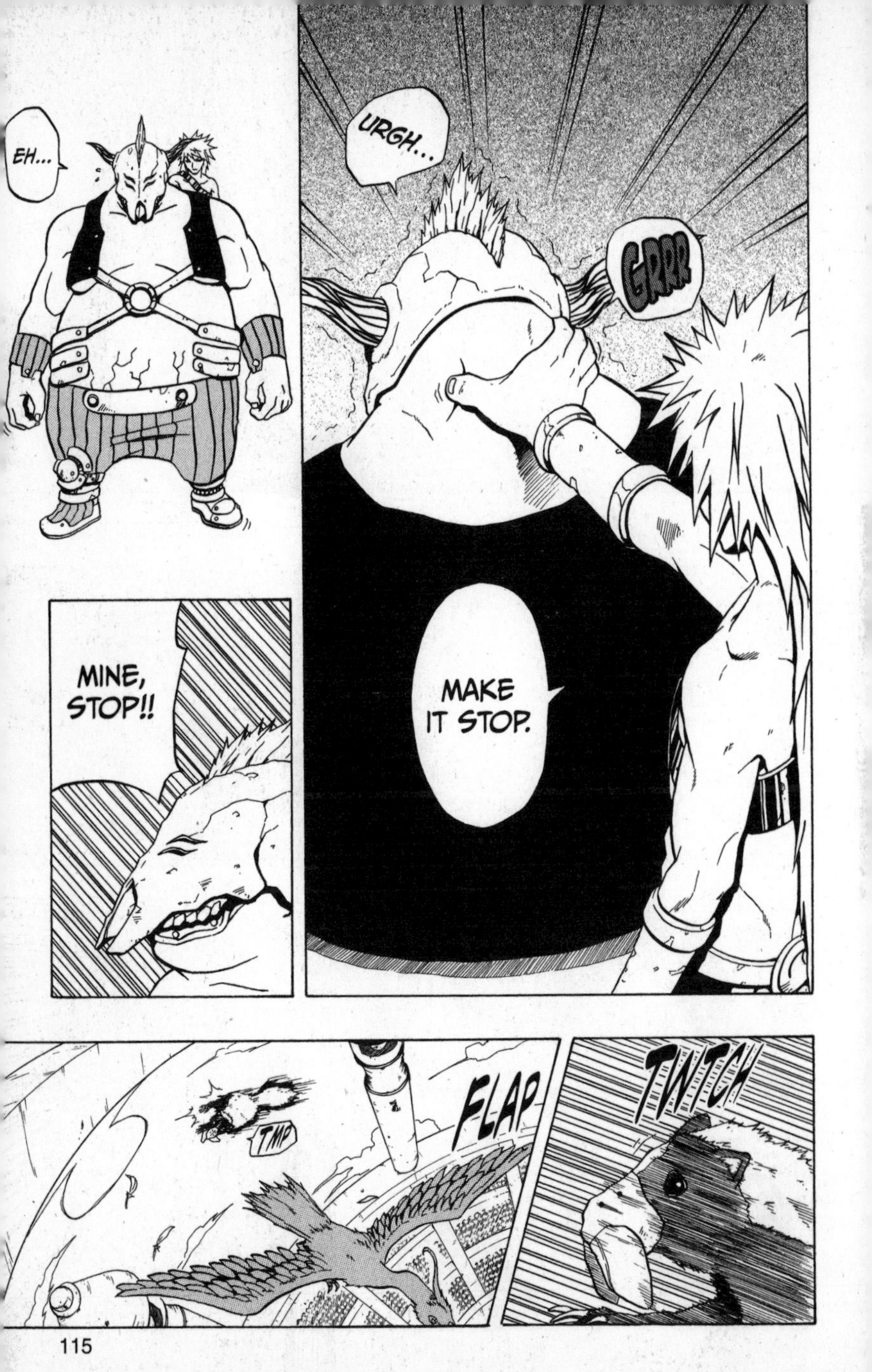
URGH...
GRRR
MAKE IT STOP.
EH...
MINE, STOP!!
TWITCH
FLAP
TMP

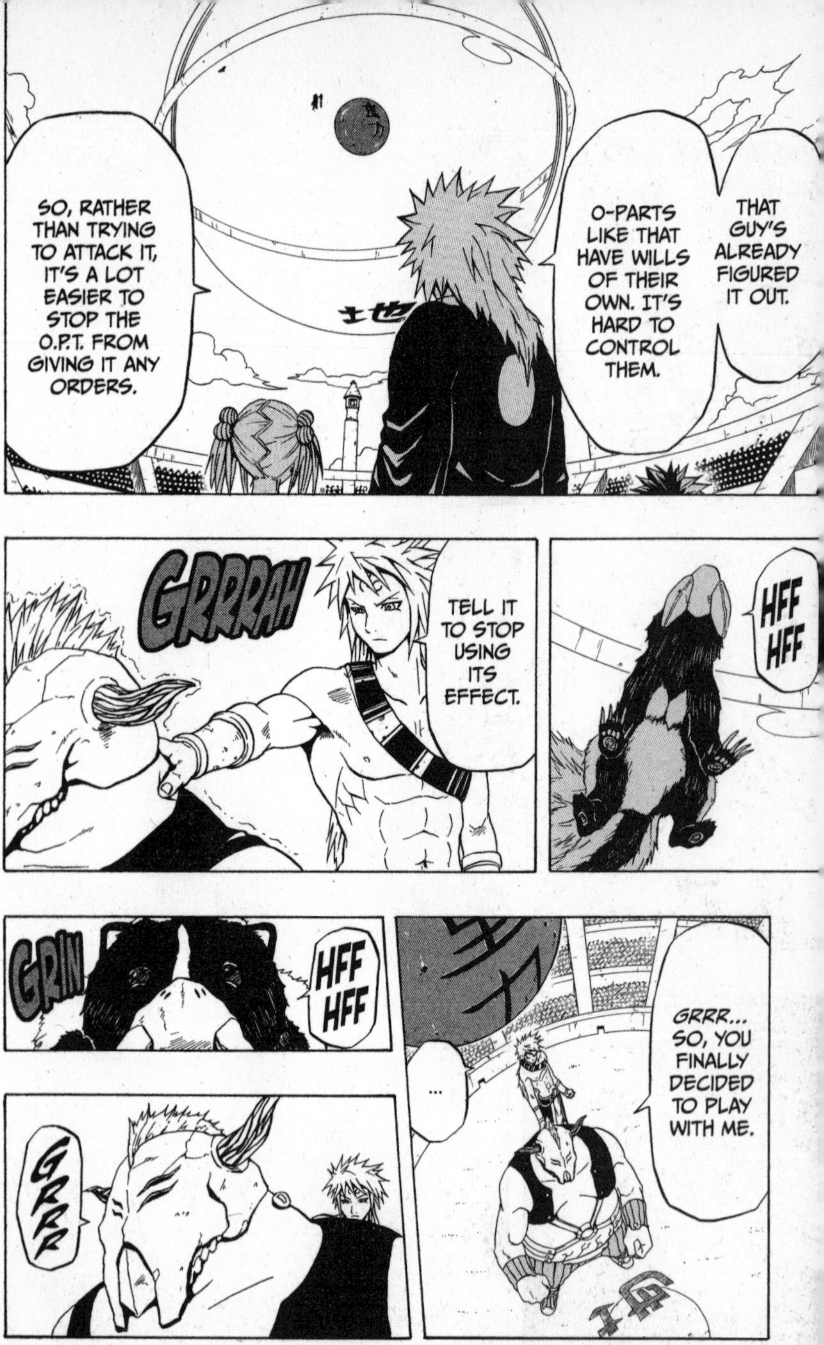
THAT GUY'S ALREADY FIGURED IT OUT.
O-PARTS LIKE THAT HAVE WILLS OF THEIR OWN. IT'S HARD TO CONTROL THEM.
SO, RATHER THAN TRYING TO ATTACK IT, IT'S A LOT EASIER TO STOP THE O.P.T. FROM GIVING IT ANY ORDERS.
HFF HFF
TELL IT TO STOP USING ITS EFFECT.
GRRRAH
GRRR... SO, YOU FINALLY DECIDED TO PLAY WITH ME.
...
HFF HFF
GRIN
GRRR

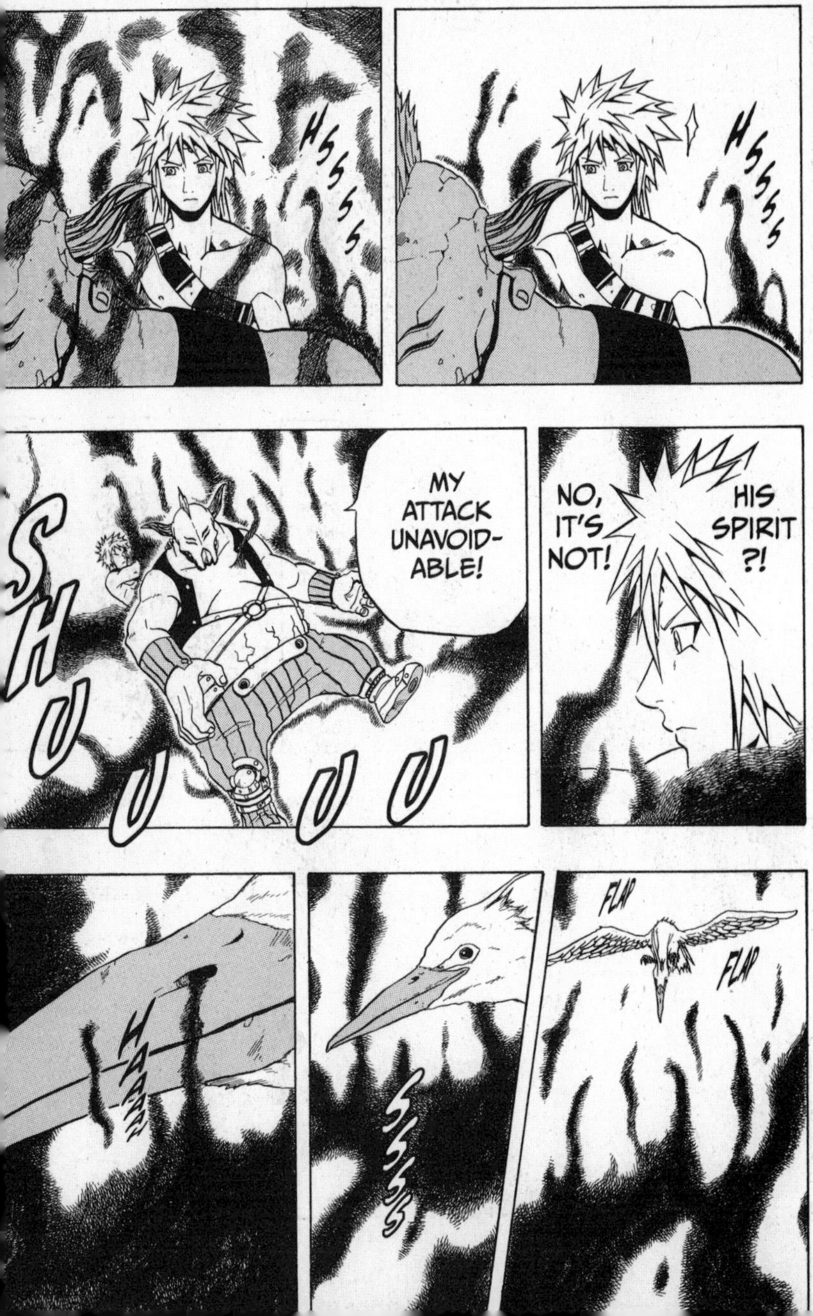
HSSSSS
HSSSSS
HIS SPIRIT?!
NO, IT'S NOT!
MY ATTACK UNAVOID-ABLE!
SHUUUUU
FLAP
FLAP
SSSSS

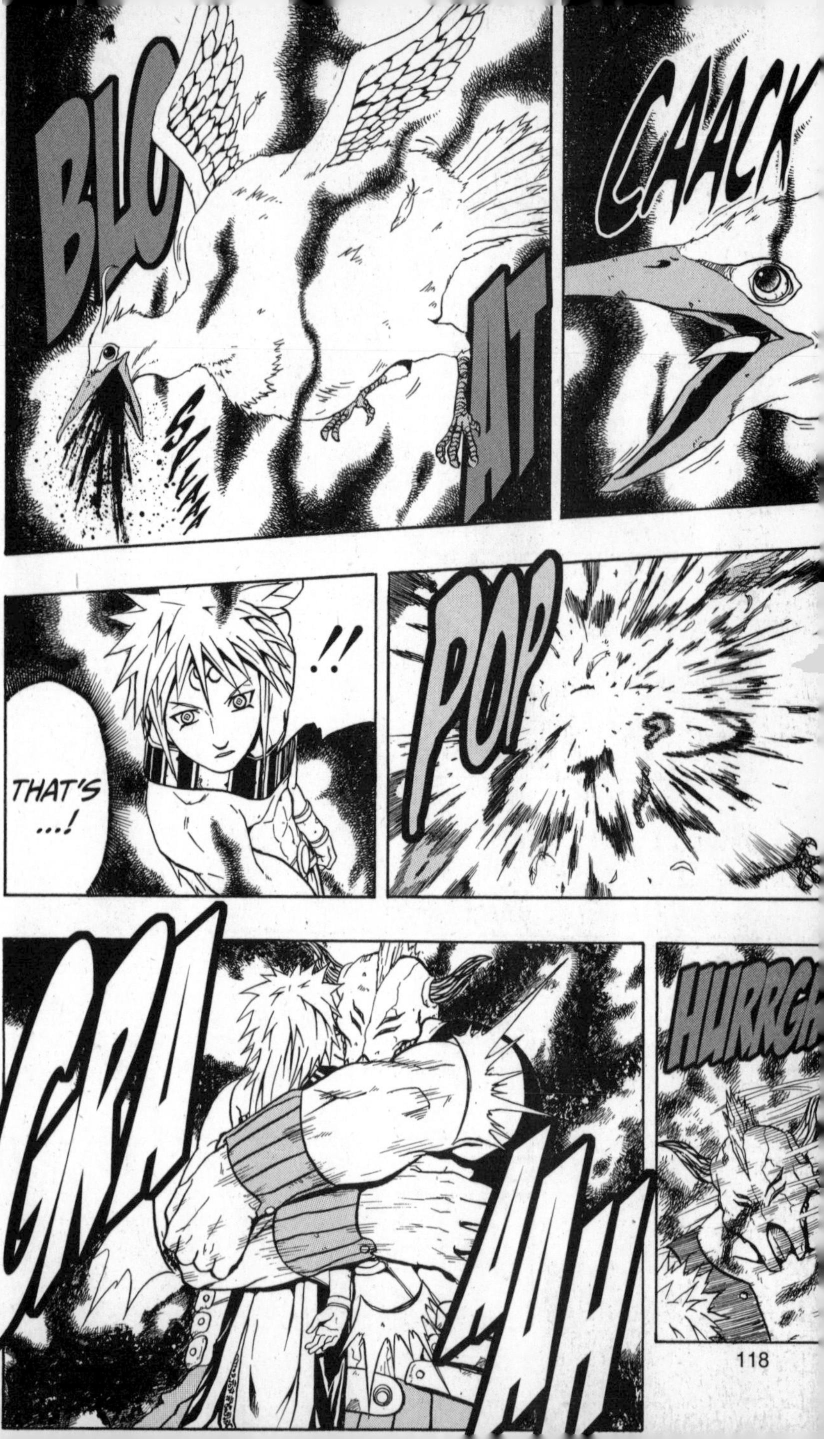
CAACK
BLU
AT
SQUAAA
POP
!!
THAT'S ...!
HURRGH
GRA
AAH

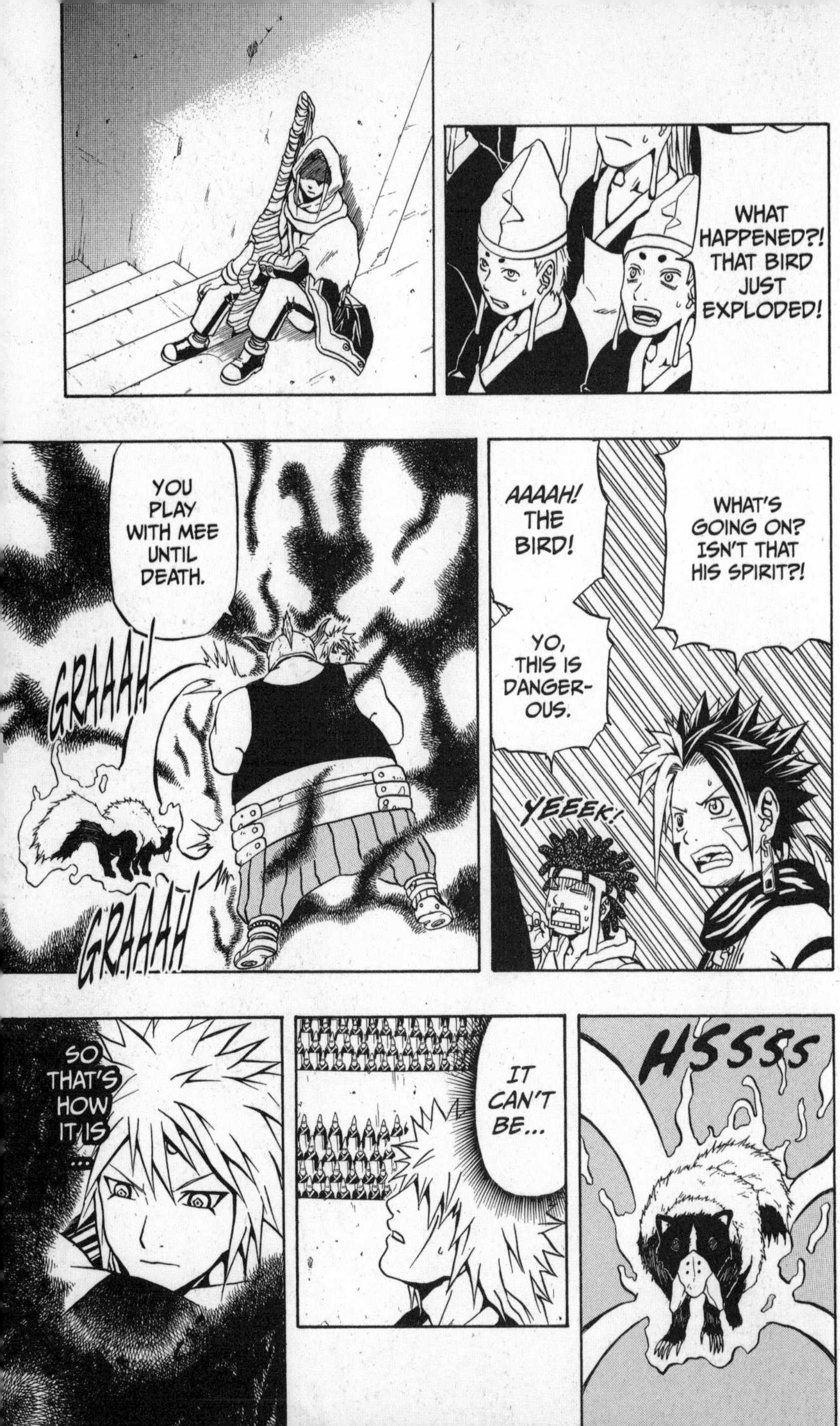
WHAT HAPPENED?! THAT BIRD JUST EXPLODED!
WHAT'S GOING ON? ISN'T THAT HIS SPIRIT?!
AAAAH! THE BIRD!
YO, THIS IS DANGER-OUS.
YEEEK!
YOU PLAY WITH MEE UNTIL DEATH.
GRAAAH
GRAAAH
HSSSS
IT CAN'T BE...
SO THAT'S HOW IT IS...

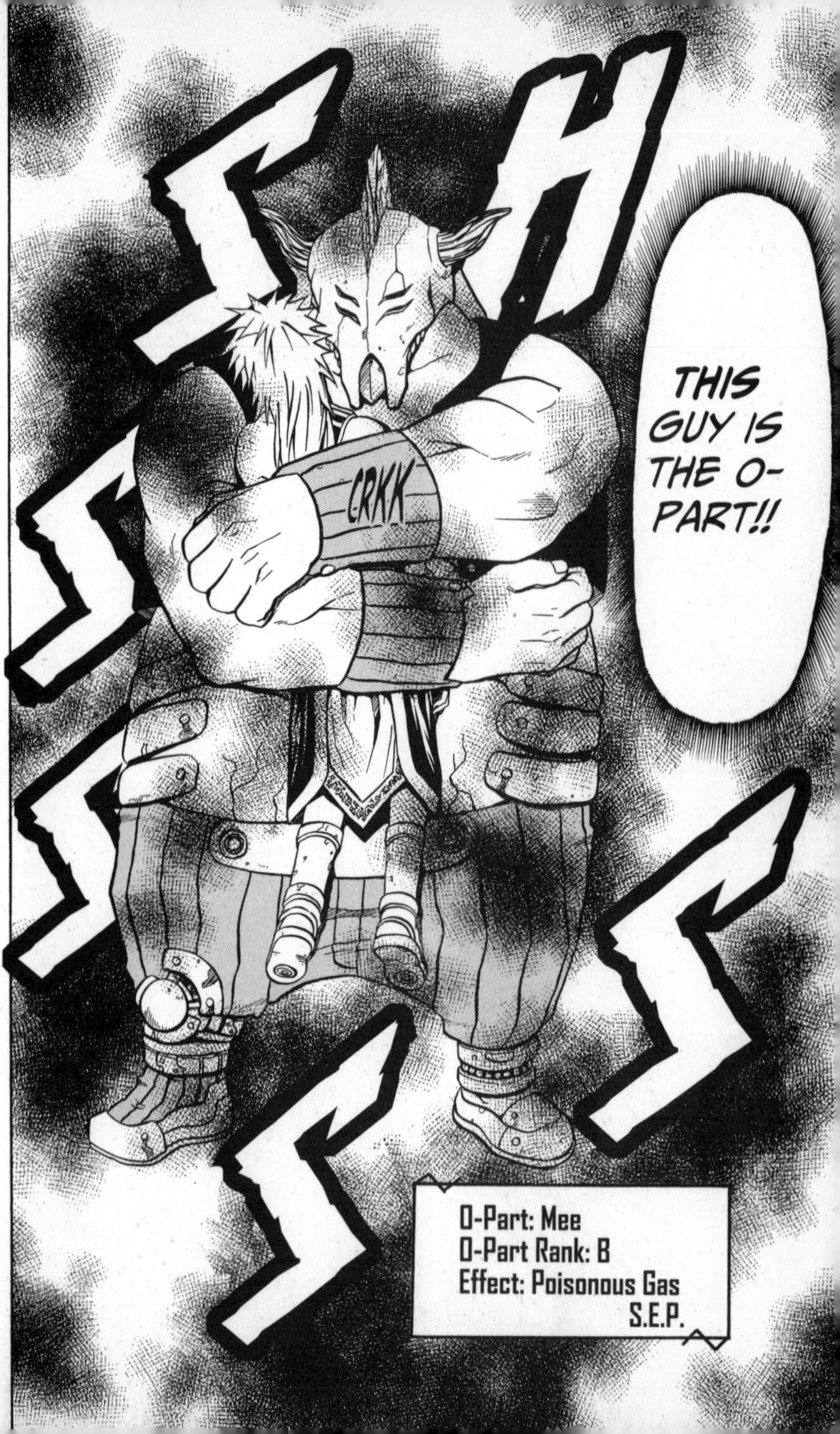
THIS GUY IS THE O-PART!!
CRKK
O-Part: Mee
O-Part Rank: B
Effect: Poisonous Gas
S.E.P.

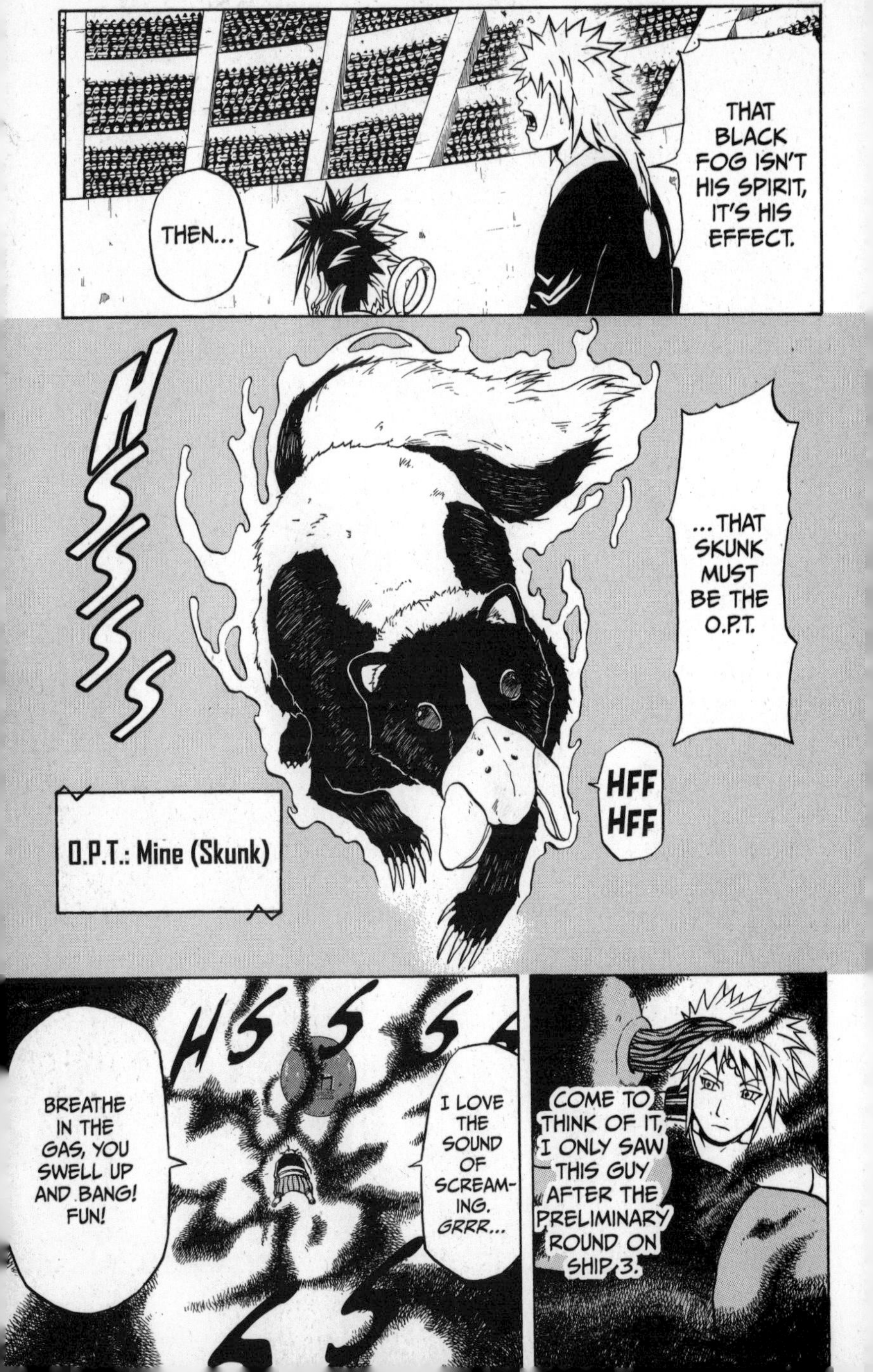
THAT BLACK FOG ISN'T HIS SPIRIT, IT'S HIS EFFECT.
THEN...
...THAT SKUNK MUST BE THE O.P.T.
HFF HFF
HISSSSS
O.P.T.: Mine (Skunk)
COME TO THINK OF IT, I ONLY SAW THIS GUY AFTER THE PRELIMINARY ROUND ON SHIP 3.
HSSS
I LOVE THE SOUND OF SCREAMING. GRRR...
BREATHE IN THE GAS, YOU SWELL UP AND BANG! FUN!

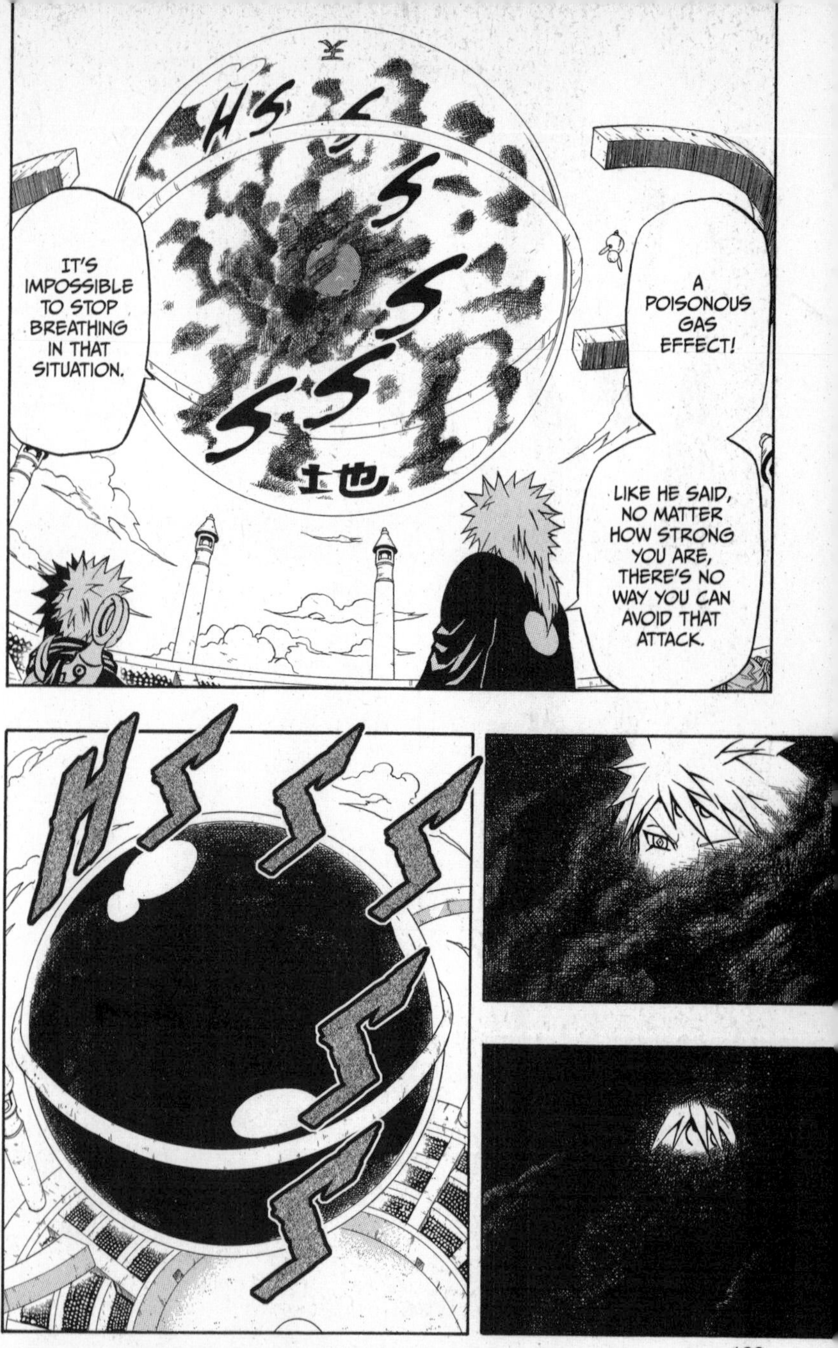
HSSSSSS
A POISONOUS GAS EFFECT!
LIKE HE SAID, NO MATTER HOW STRONG YOU ARE, THERE'S NO WAY YOU CAN AVOID THAT ATTACK.
IT'S IMPOSSIBLE TO STOP BREATHING IN THAT SITUATION.
HSSSS

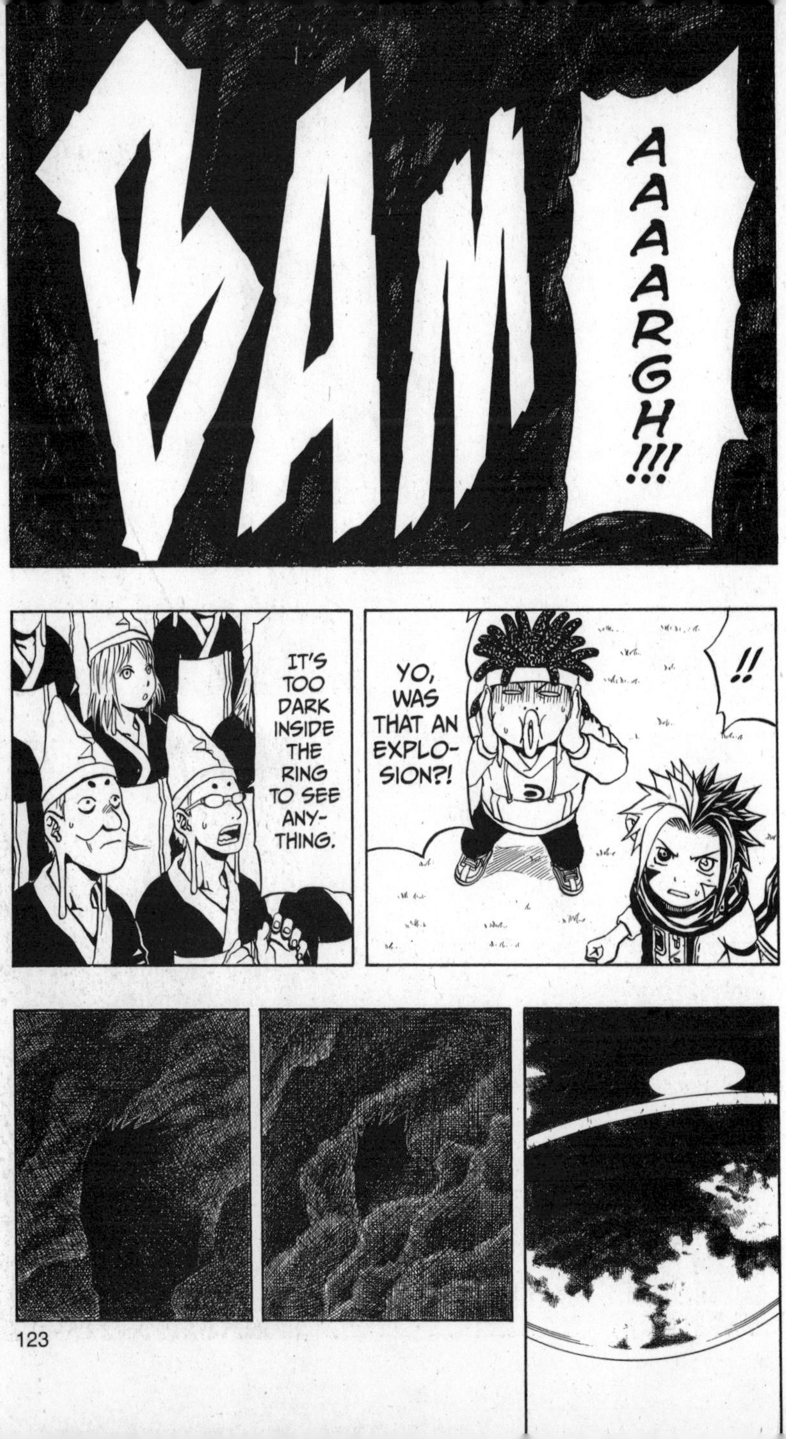
AAAARGH!!!
BAM
!!
YO, WAS THAT AN EXPLOSION?!
IT'S TOO DARK INSIDE THE RING TO SEE ANYTHING.

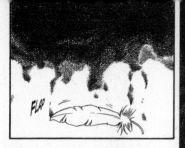

FLAP

HE
WON.

WHOA,
THAT
BLOND
GUY
BLEW
UP IN
THE
GAS!

YUP...
PRETTY
STRONG
EFFECT.

DUN
DUN

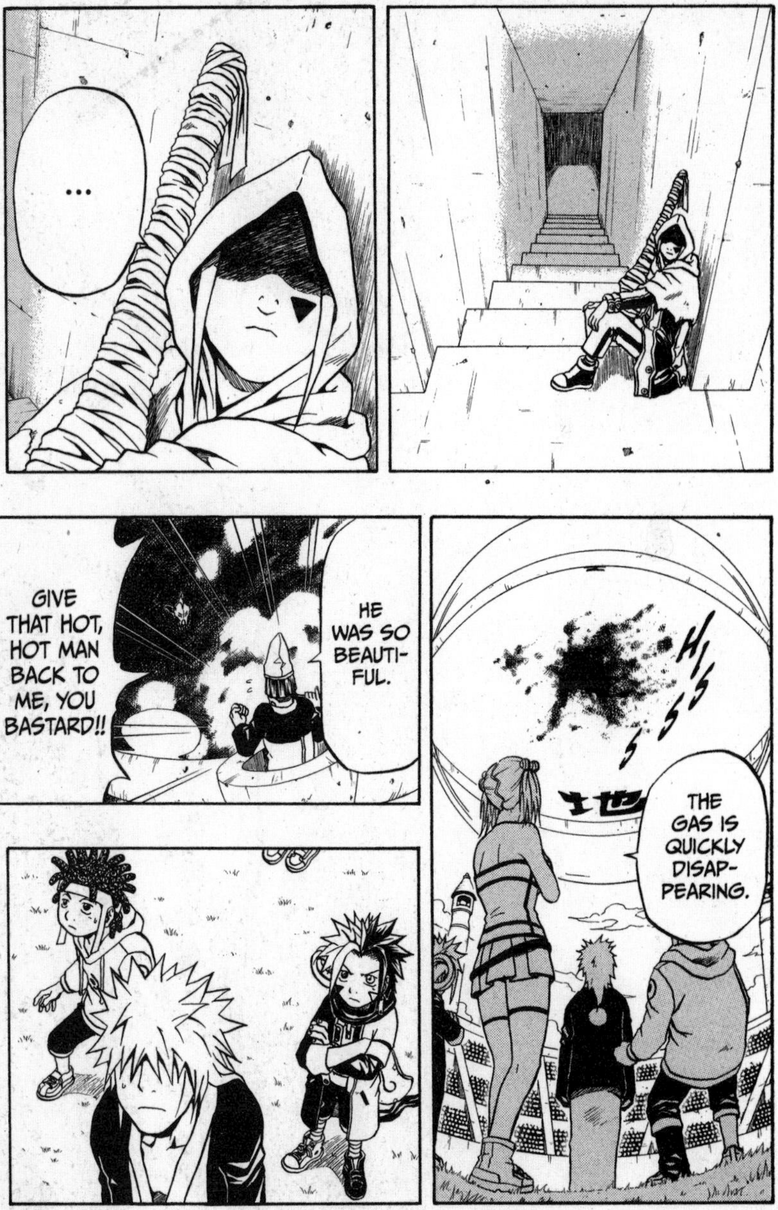
...
HISSSS
THE GAS IS QUICKLY DISAPPEARING.
HE WAS SO BEAUTIFUL.
GIVE THAT HOT, HOT MAN BACK TO ME, YOU BASTARD!!

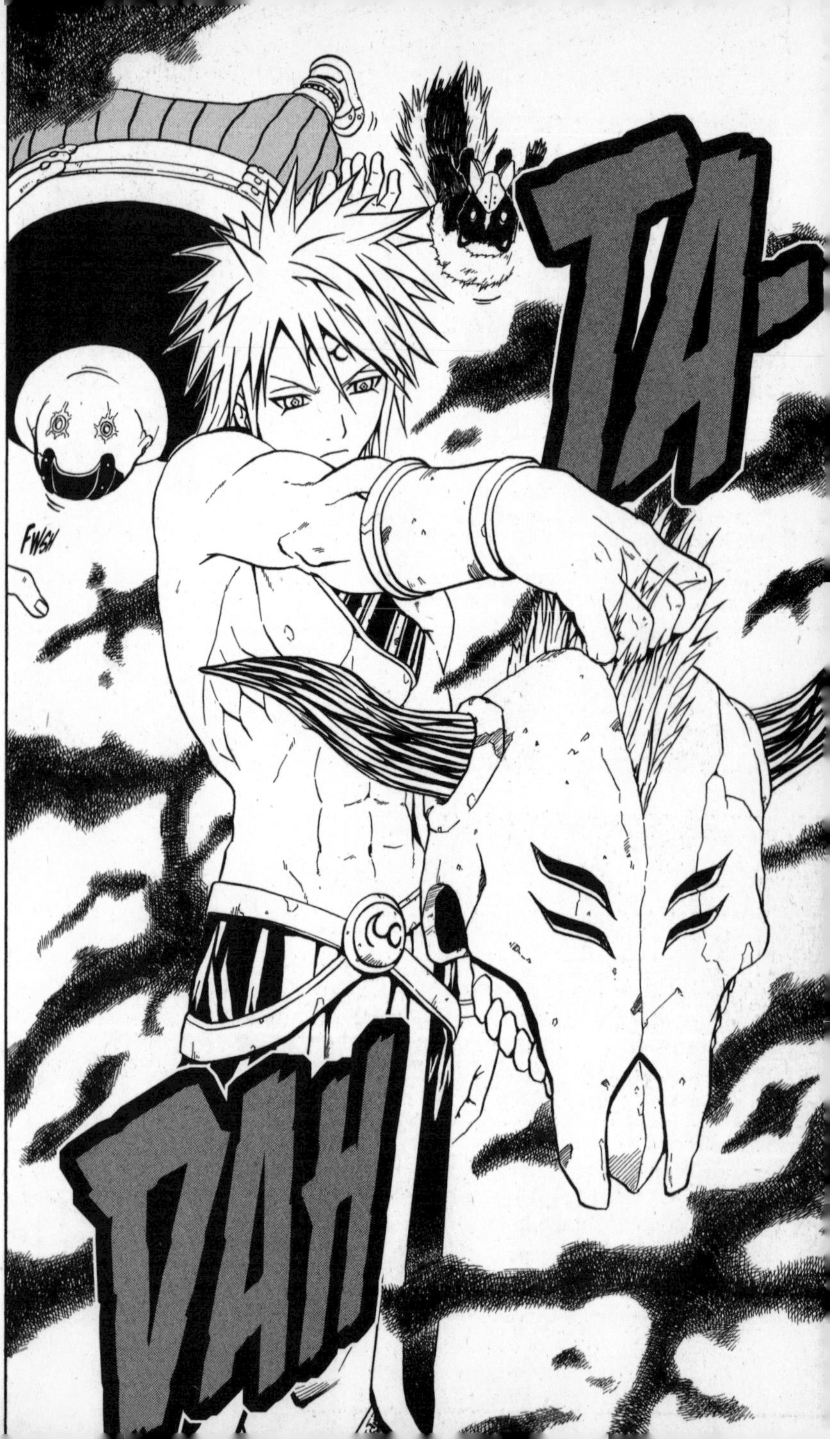
TA
FWSH
DAH

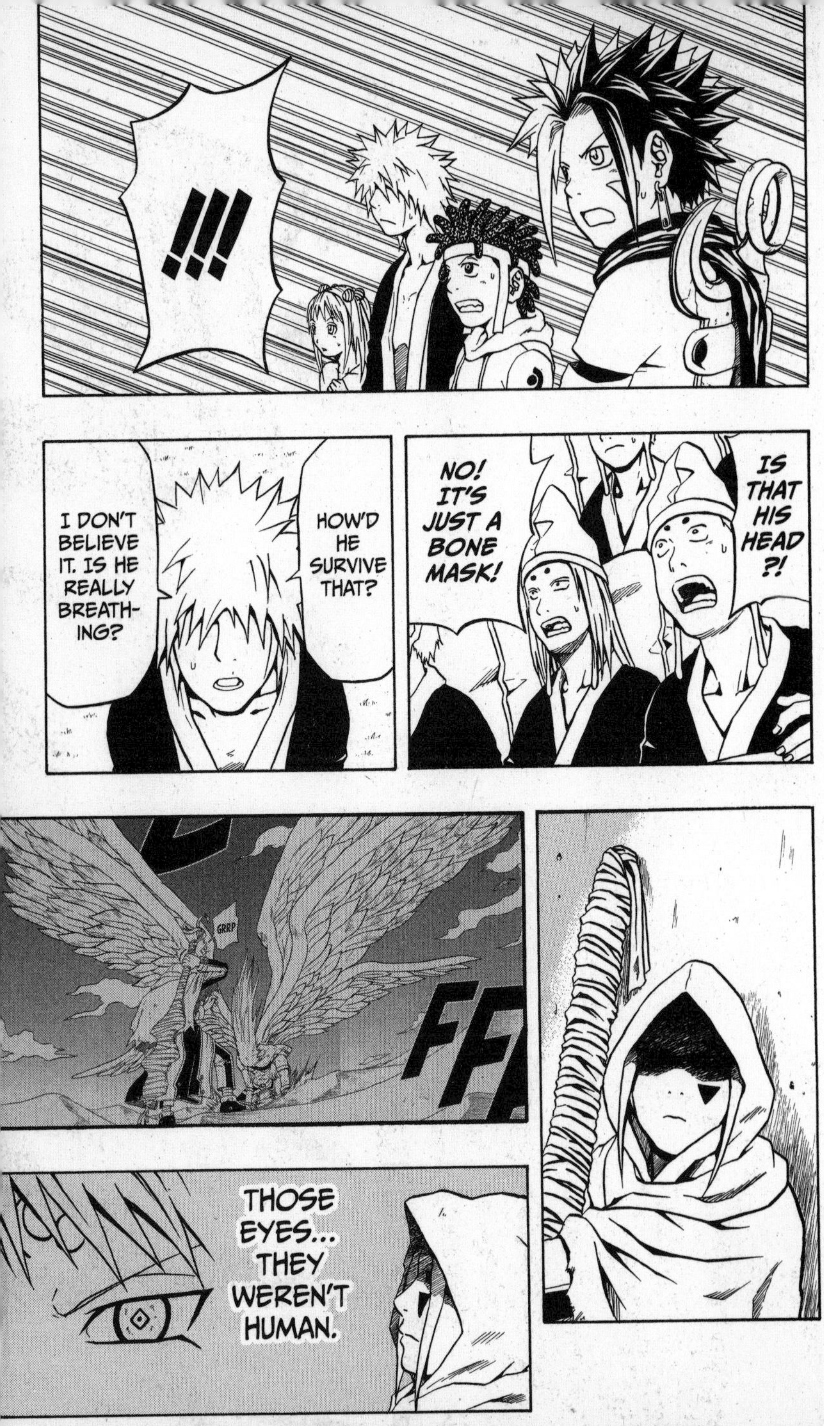
!!!
IS THAT HIS HEAD?!
NO! IT'S JUST A BONE MASK!
HOW'D HE SURVIVE THAT?
I DON'T BELIEVE IT. IS HE REALLY BREATH-ING?
GRRP
FF
THOSE EYES... THEY WEREN'T HUMAN.

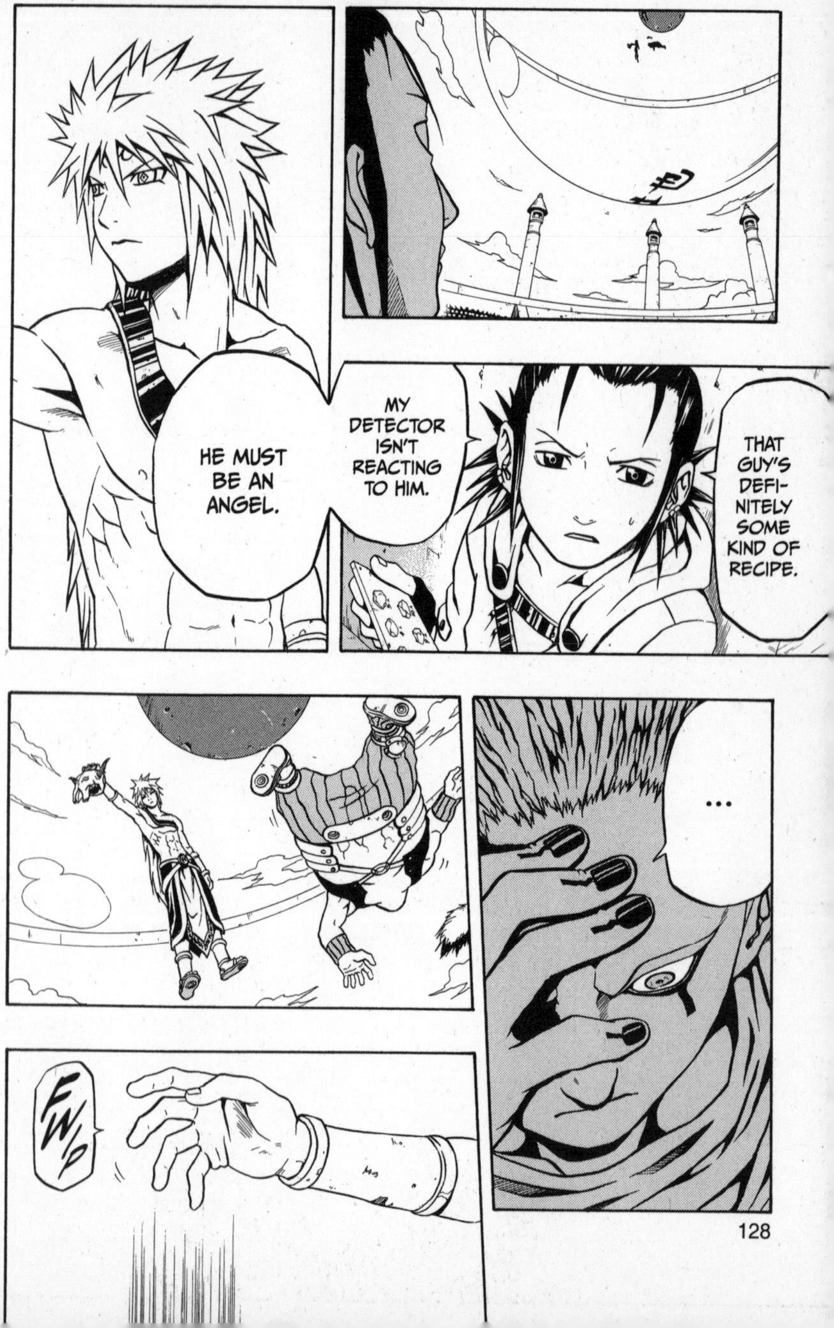
THAT GUY'S DEFI-NITELY SOME KIND OF RECIPE.
MY DETECTOR ISN'T REACTING TO HIM.
HE MUST BE AN ANGEL.
...
FWIP

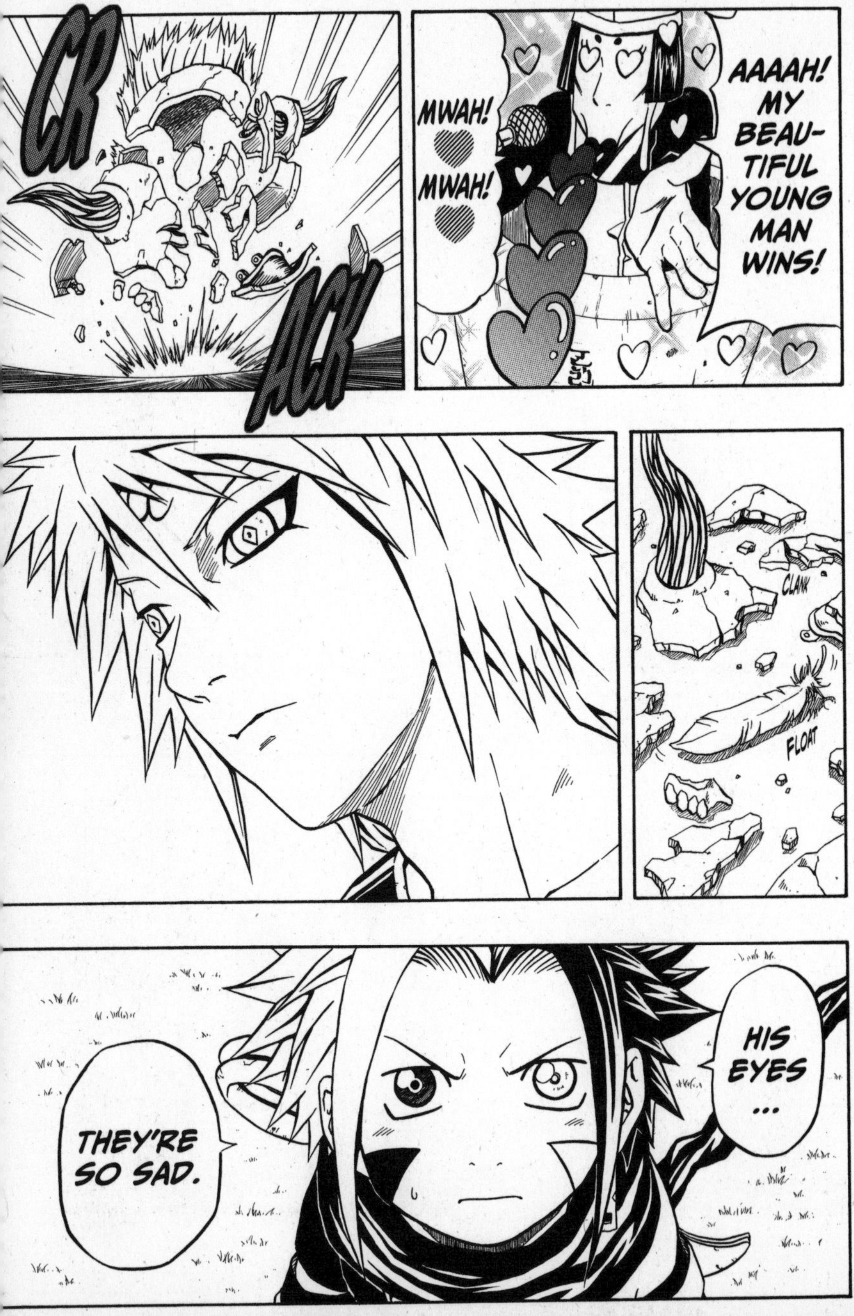
AAAAH! MY BEAU-TIFUL YOUNG MAN WINS!
MWAH! MWAH!
CRACK
CLANK
FLOAT
HIS EYES...
THEY'RE SO SAD.

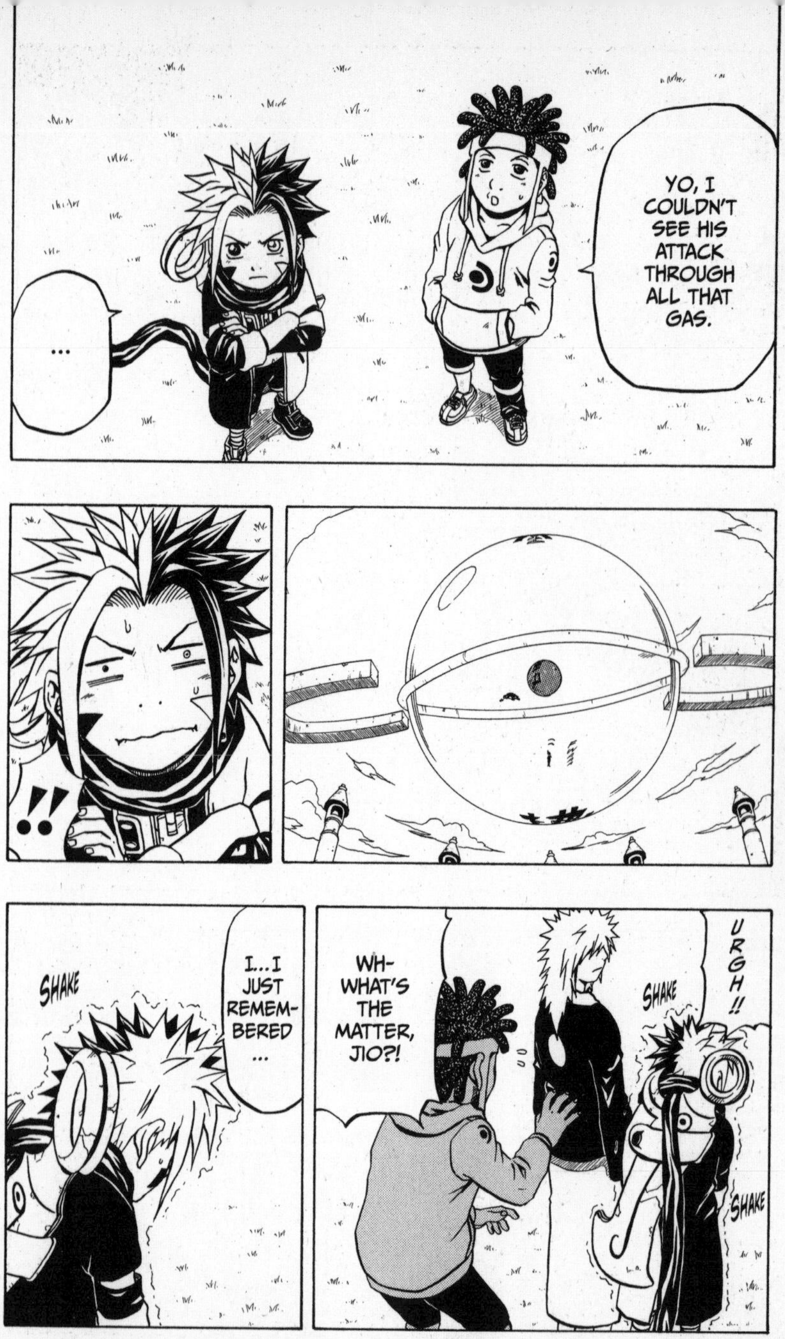
YO, I COULDN'T SEE HIS ATTACK THROUGH ALL THAT GAS.
...
!!
URGH!!
SHAKE
SHAKE
WH- WHAT'S THE MATTER, JIO?!
I...I JUST REMEM-BERED...
SHAKE

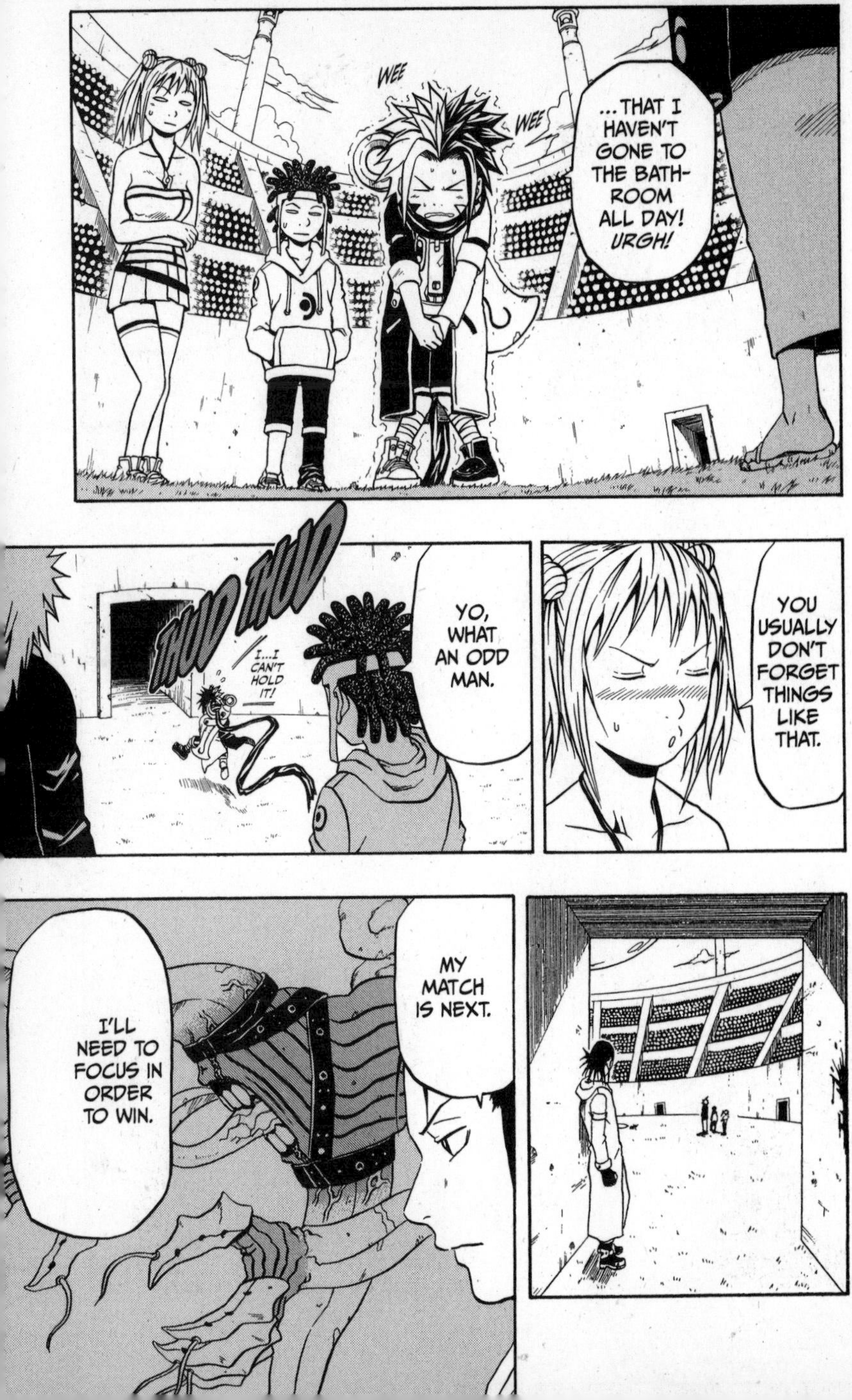
...THAT I HAVEN'T GONE TO THE BATH-ROOM ALL DAY! URGH!
WEE
WEE
YOU USUALLY DON'T FORGET THINGS LIKE THAT.
YO, WHAT AN ODD MAN.
THUD THUD
I...I CAN'T HOLD IT!
MY MATCH IS NEXT.
I'LL NEED TO FOCUS IN ORDER TO WIN.

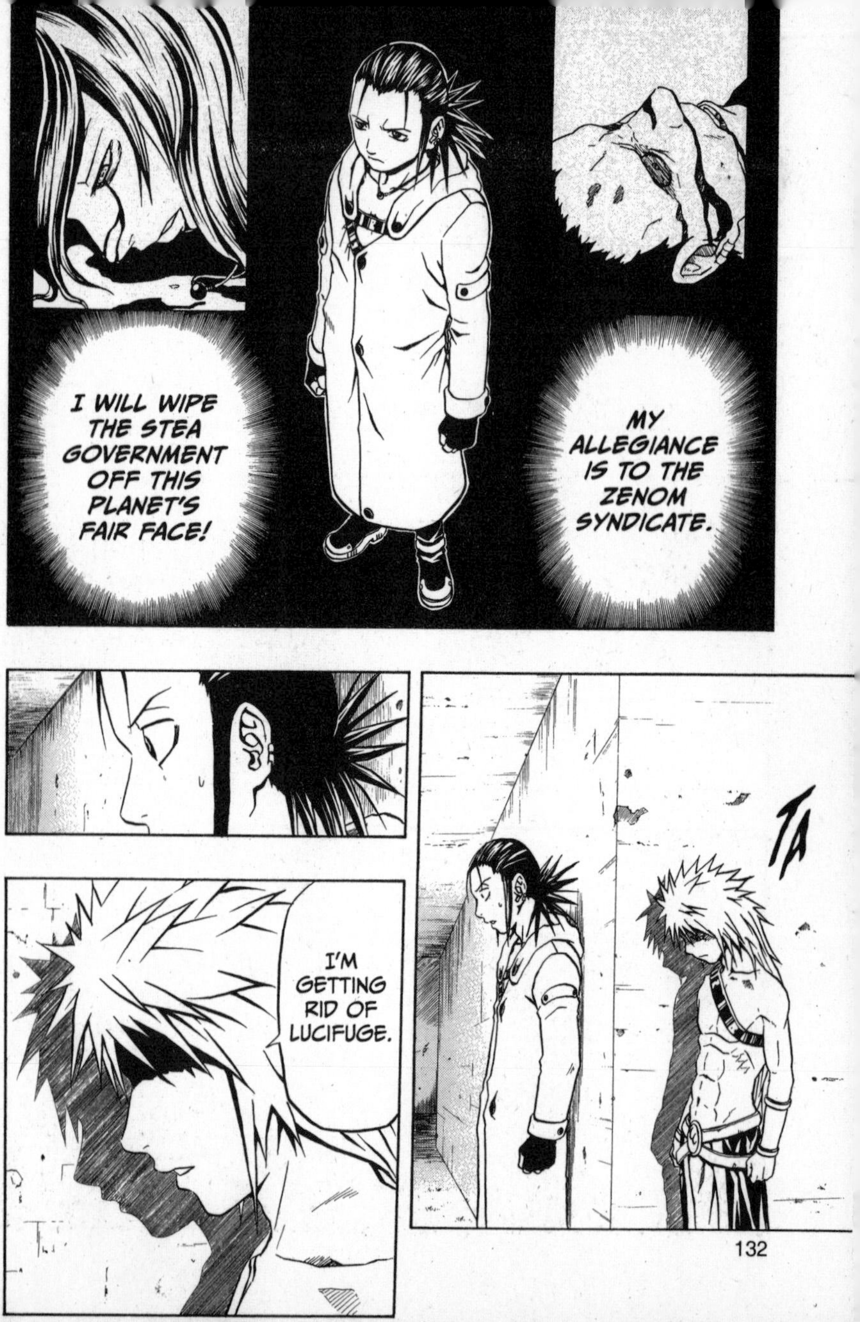
MY ALLEGIANCE IS TO THE ZENOM SYNDICATE.
I WILL WIPE THE STEA GOVERNMENT OFF THIS PLANET'S FAIR FACE!
TA
I'M GETTING RID OF LUCIFUGE.

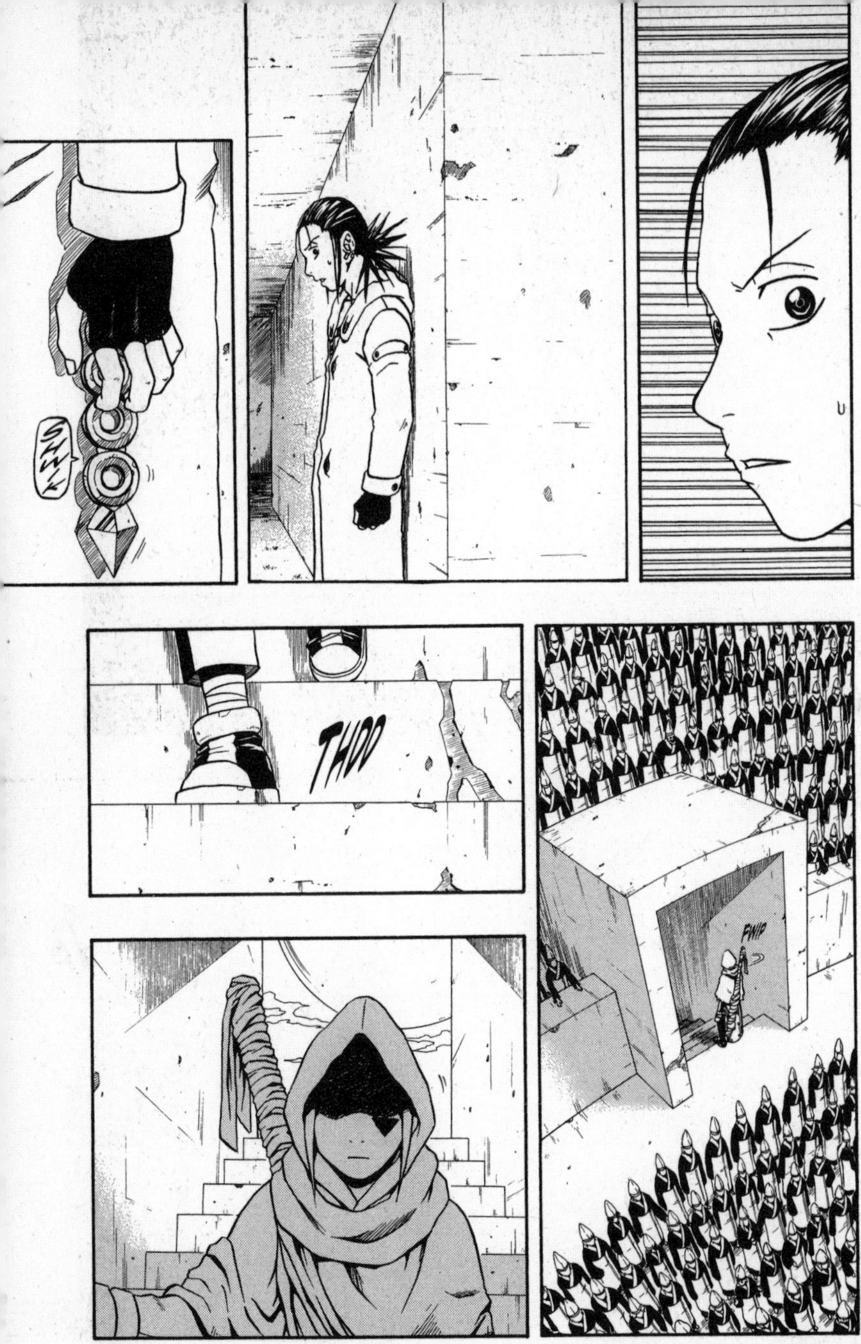
SHWIK
FWIP
THDD

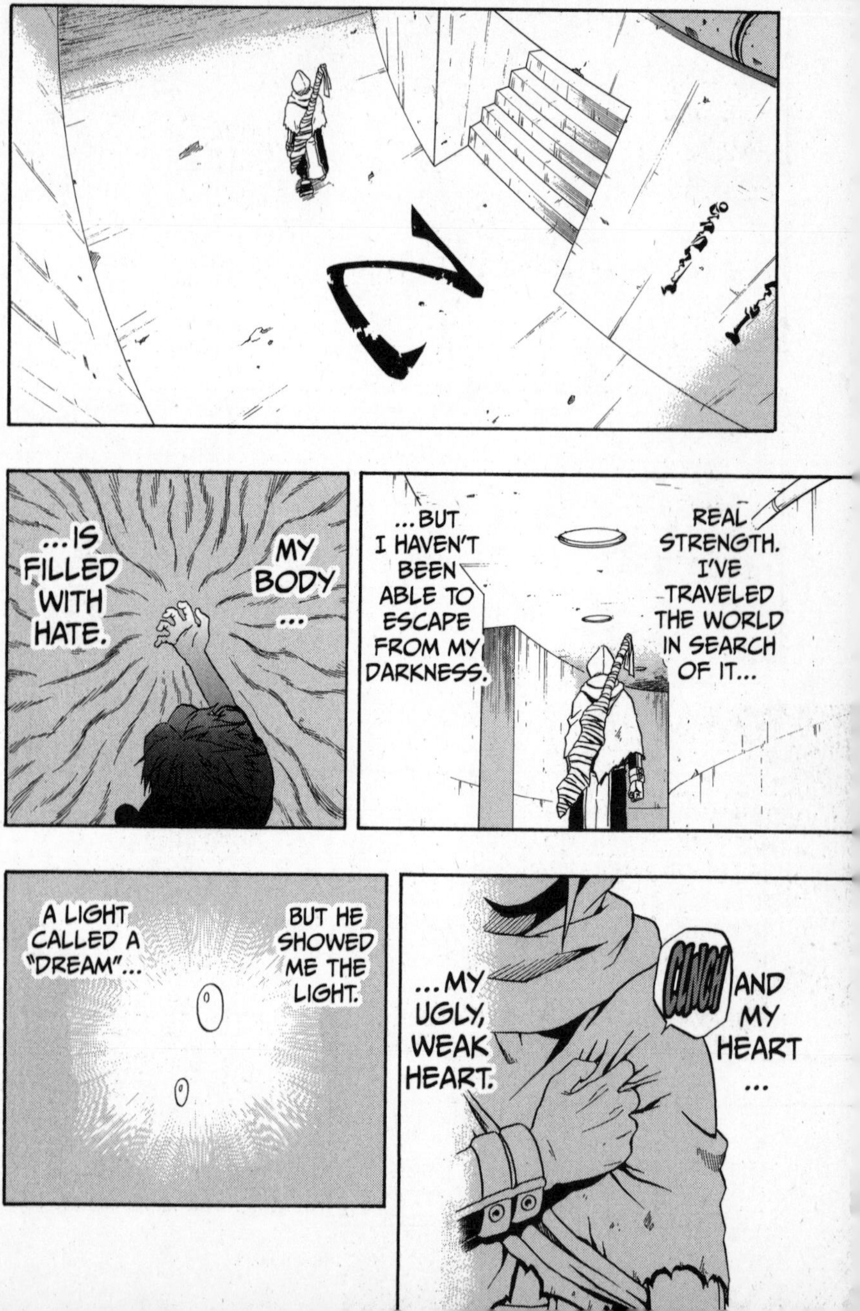
REAL STRENGTH. I'VE TRAVELED THE WORLD IN SEARCH OF IT...
...BUT I HAVEN'T BEEN ABLE TO ESCAPE FROM MY DARKNESS.
MY BODY...
...IS FILLED WITH HATE.
AND MY HEART...
CLINCH
...MY UGLY, WEAK HEART.
BUT HE SHOWED ME THE LIGHT.
A LIGHT CALLED A "DREAM"...

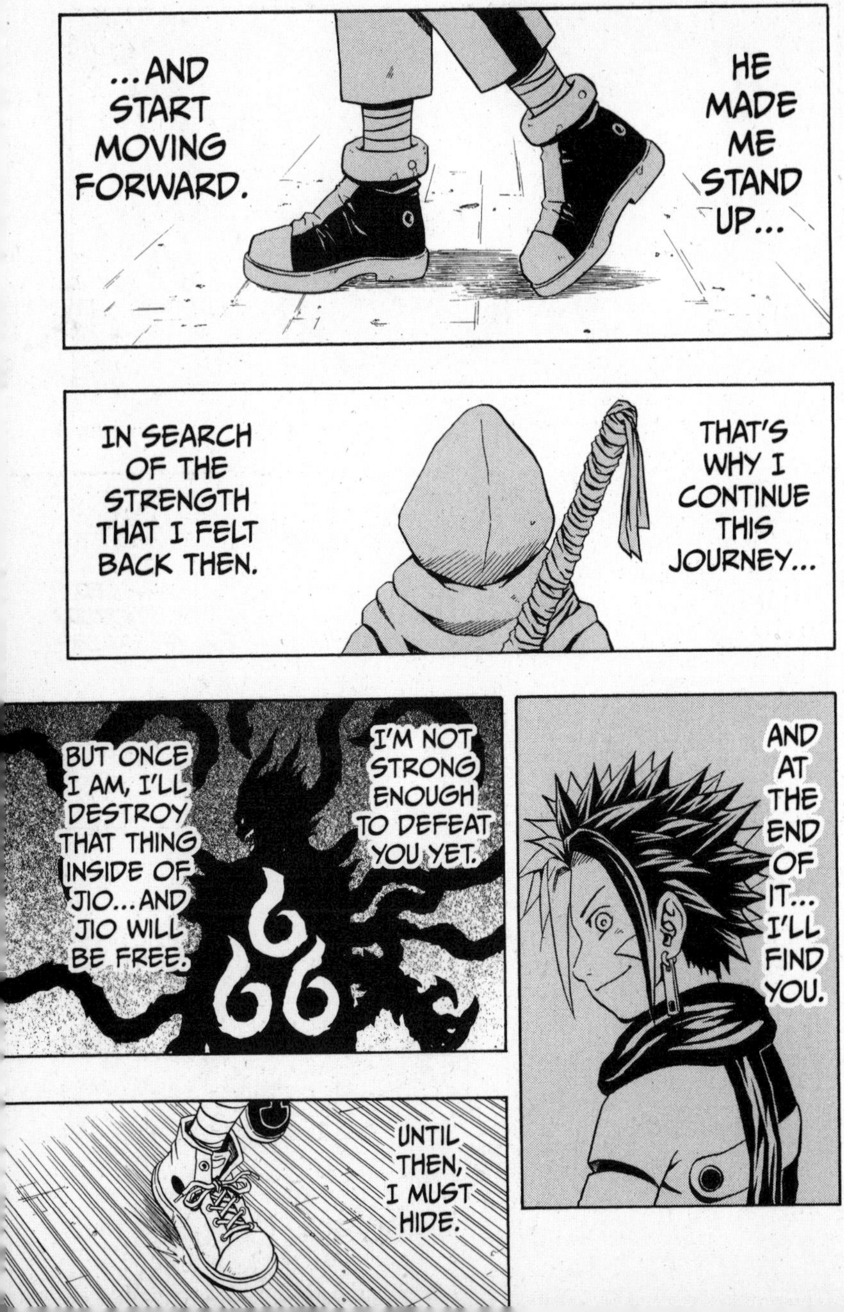
HE MADE ME STAND UP...
...AND START MOVING FORWARD.
THAT'S WHY I CONTINUE THIS JOURNEY...
IN SEARCH OF THE STRENGTH THAT I FELT BACK THEN.
AND AT THE END OF IT... I'LL FIND YOU.
I'M NOT STRONG ENOUGH TO DEFEAT YOU YET.
BUT ONCE I AM, I'LL DESTROY THAT THING INSIDE OF JIO... AND JIO WILL BE FREE.
666
UNTIL THEN, I MUST HIDE.

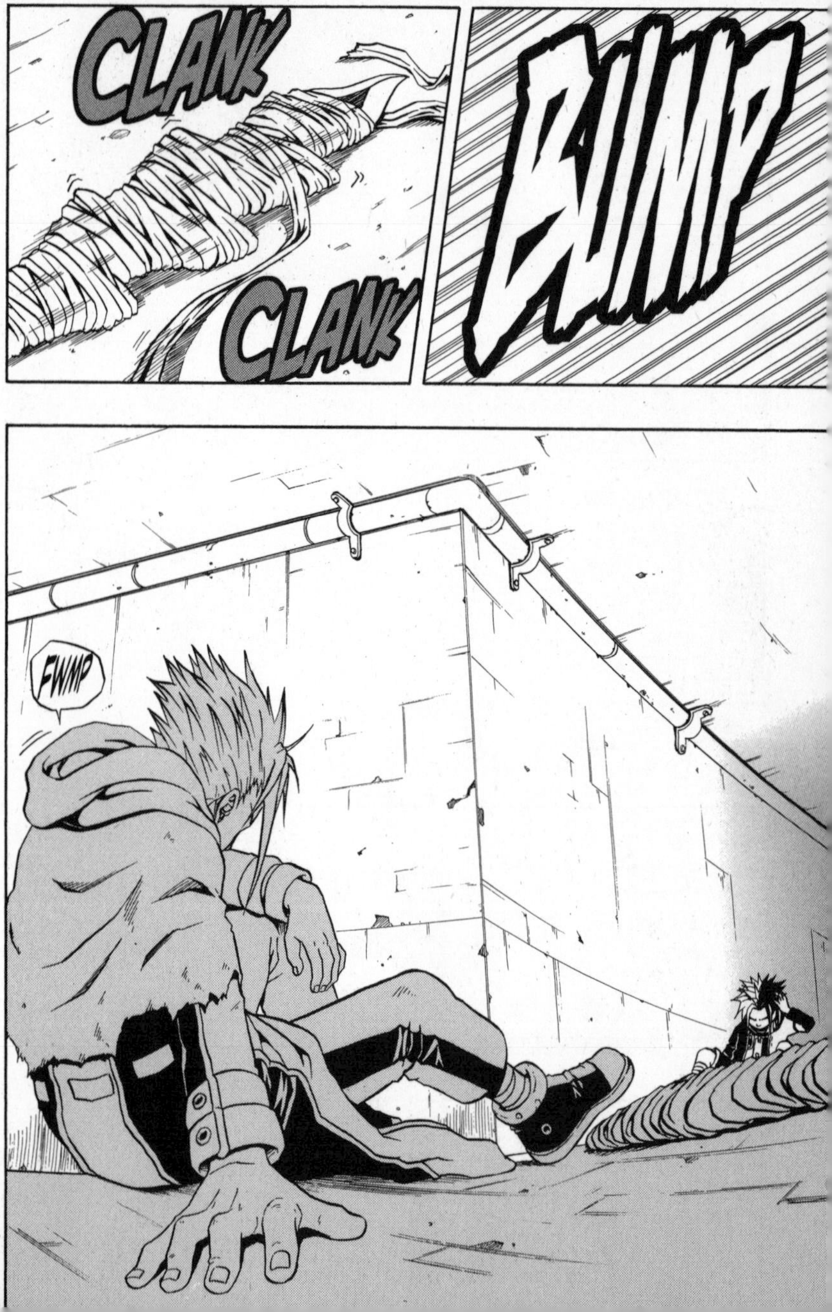
BUMP
CLANK
CLANK
FWMP

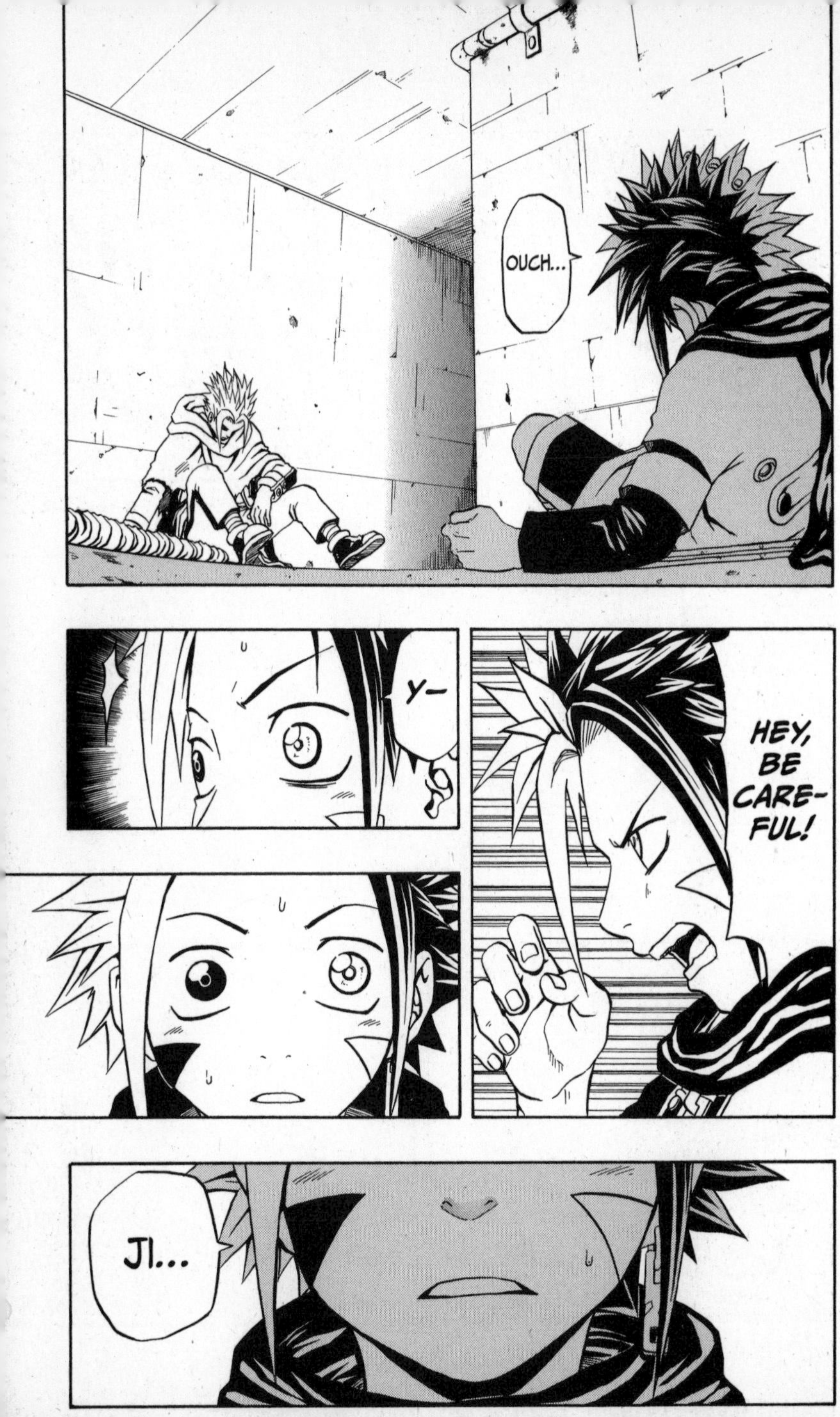
OUCH...
HEY, BE CARE-FUL!
Y--
JI...

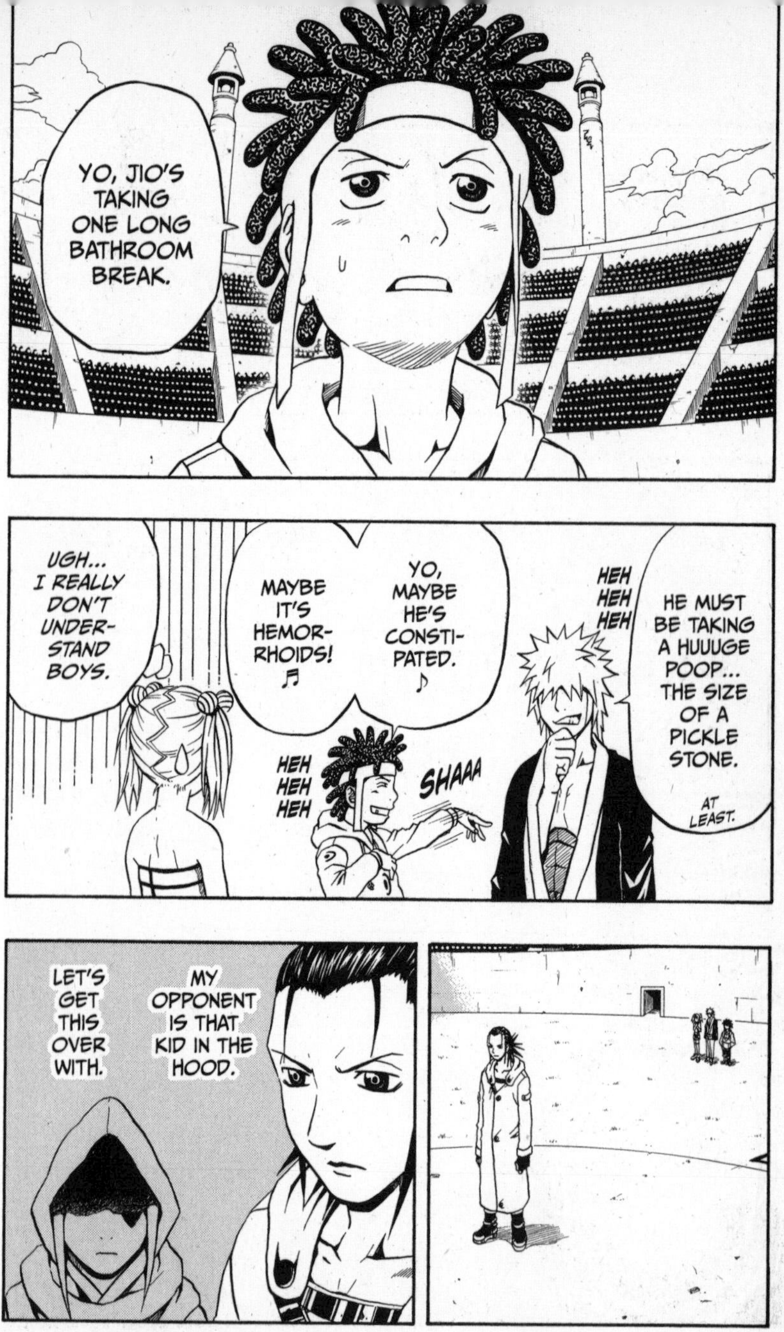
YO, JIO'S TAKING ONE LONG BATHROOM BREAK.
HE MUST BE TAKING A HUUUGE POOP... THE SIZE OF A PICKLE STONE.
HEH HEH HEH
AT LEAST.
YO, MAYBE HE'S CONSTI-PATED. ♪
MAYBE IT'S HEMOR-RHOIDS! ♬
SHAAA
HEH HEH HEH
UGH... I REALLY DON'T UNDER-STAND BOYS.
MY OPPONENT IS THAT KID IN THE HOOD.
LET'S GET THIS OVER WITH.

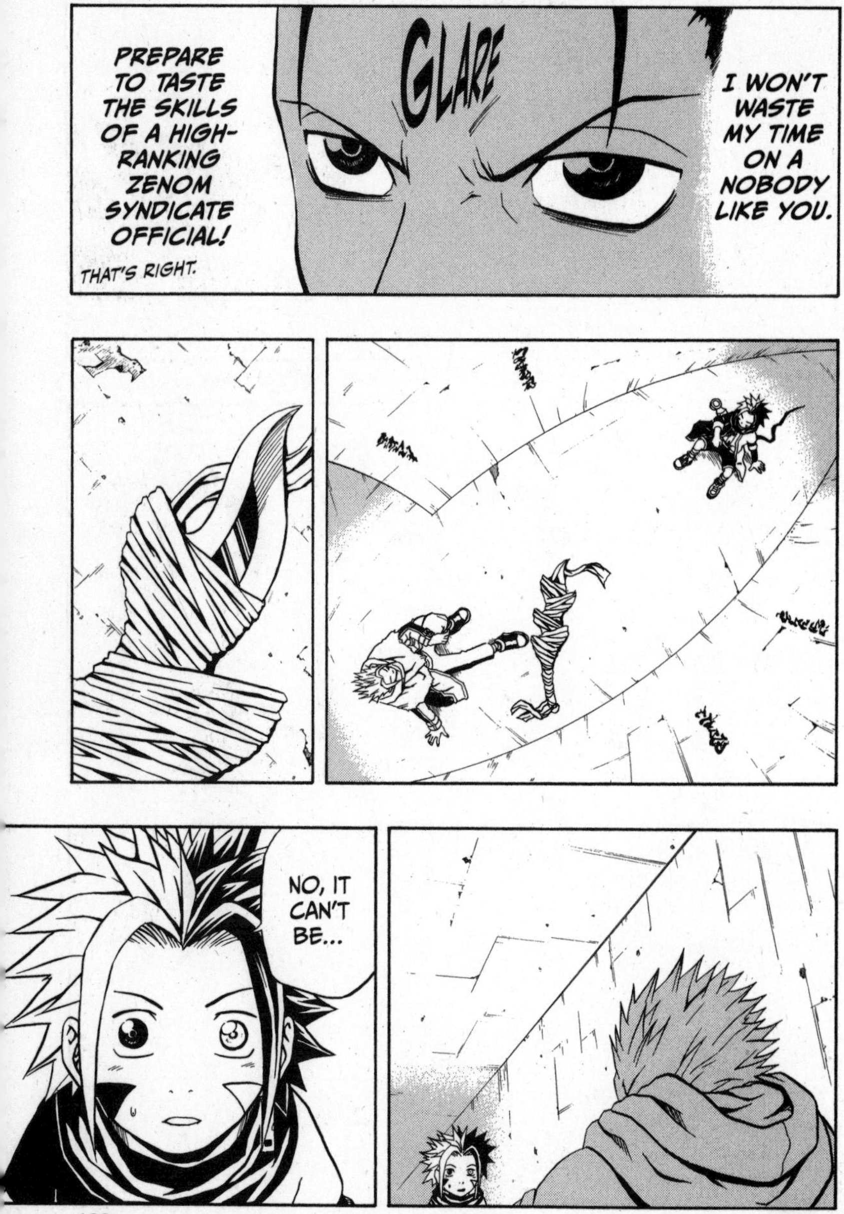
I WON'T WASTE MY TIME ON A NOBODY LIKE YOU.
GLARE
PREPARE TO TASTE THE SKILLS OF A HIGH-RANKING ZENOM SYNDICATE OFFICIAL!
THAT'S RIGHT.
NO, IT CAN'T BE...

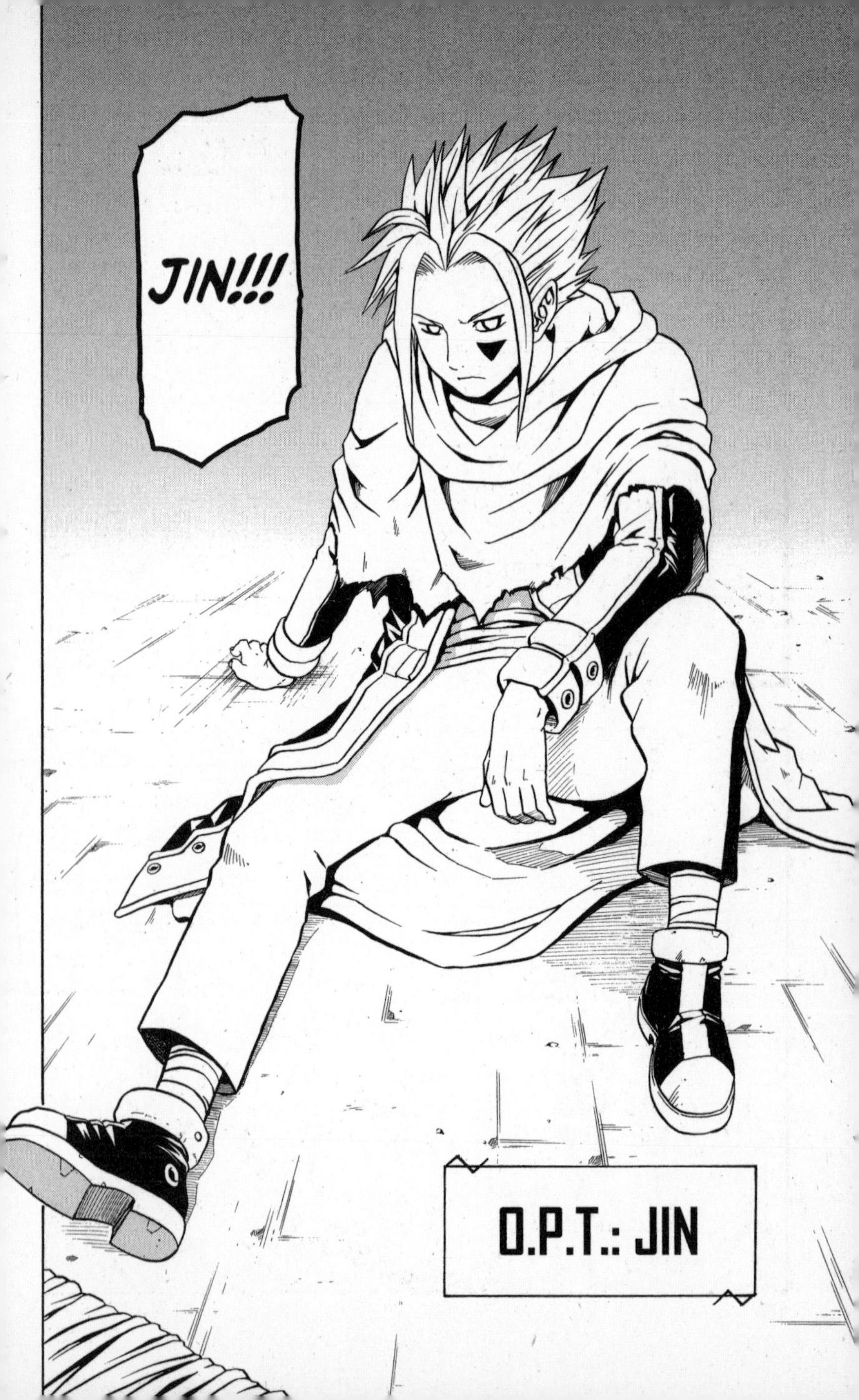
JIN!!!
O.P.T.: JIN

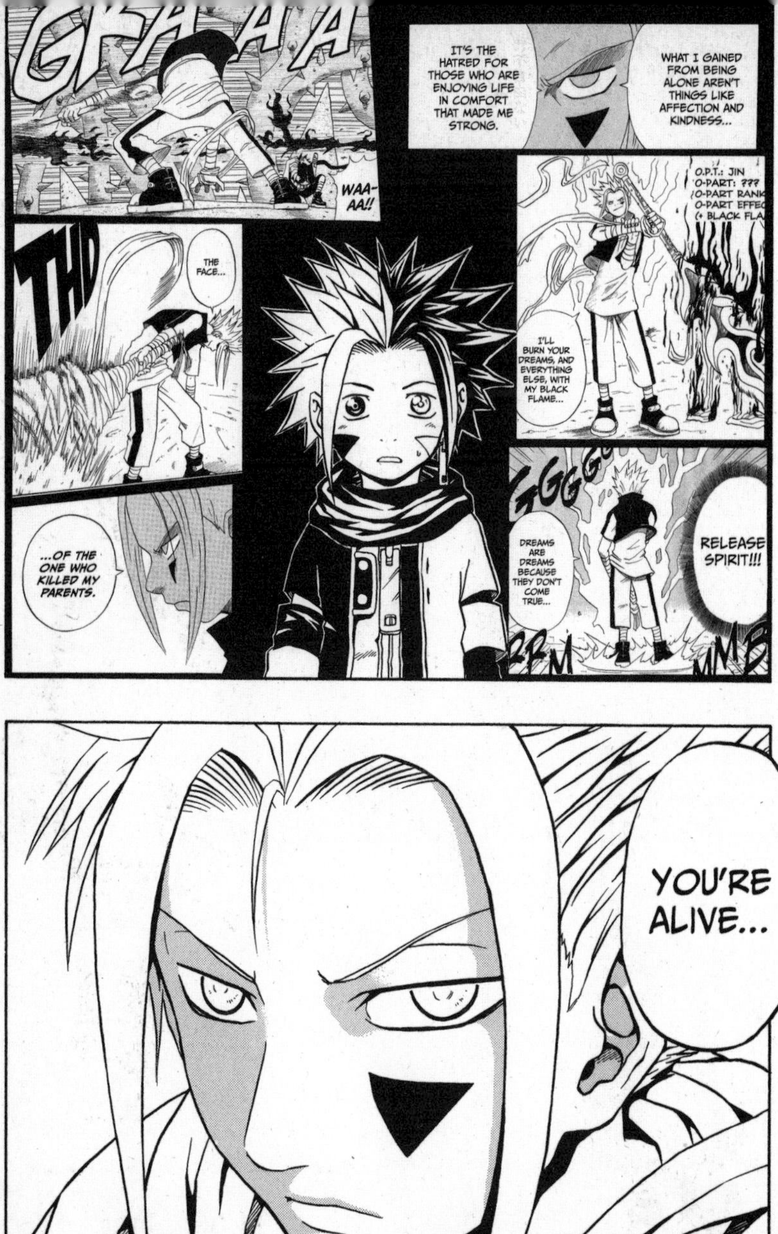
WHAT I GAINED FROM BEING ALONE AREN'T THINGS LIKE AFFECTION AND KINDNESS...
IT'S THE HATRED FOR THOSE WHO ARE ENJOYING LIFE IN COMFORT THAT MADE ME STRONG.
GRA-A-A
WAA-AA!!
O.P.T.: JIN
O-PART: ???
O-PART RANK
O-PART EFFEC
(+ BLACK FLA
I'LL BURN YOUR DREAMS, AND EVERYTHING ELSE, WITH MY BLACK FLAME...
GGGG
RELEASE SPIRIT!!!
DREAMS ARE DREAMS BECAUSE THEY DON'T COME TRUE...
ZRM
MMB
THD
THE FACE...
...OF THE ONE WHO KILLED MY PARENTS.
YOU'RE ALIVE...

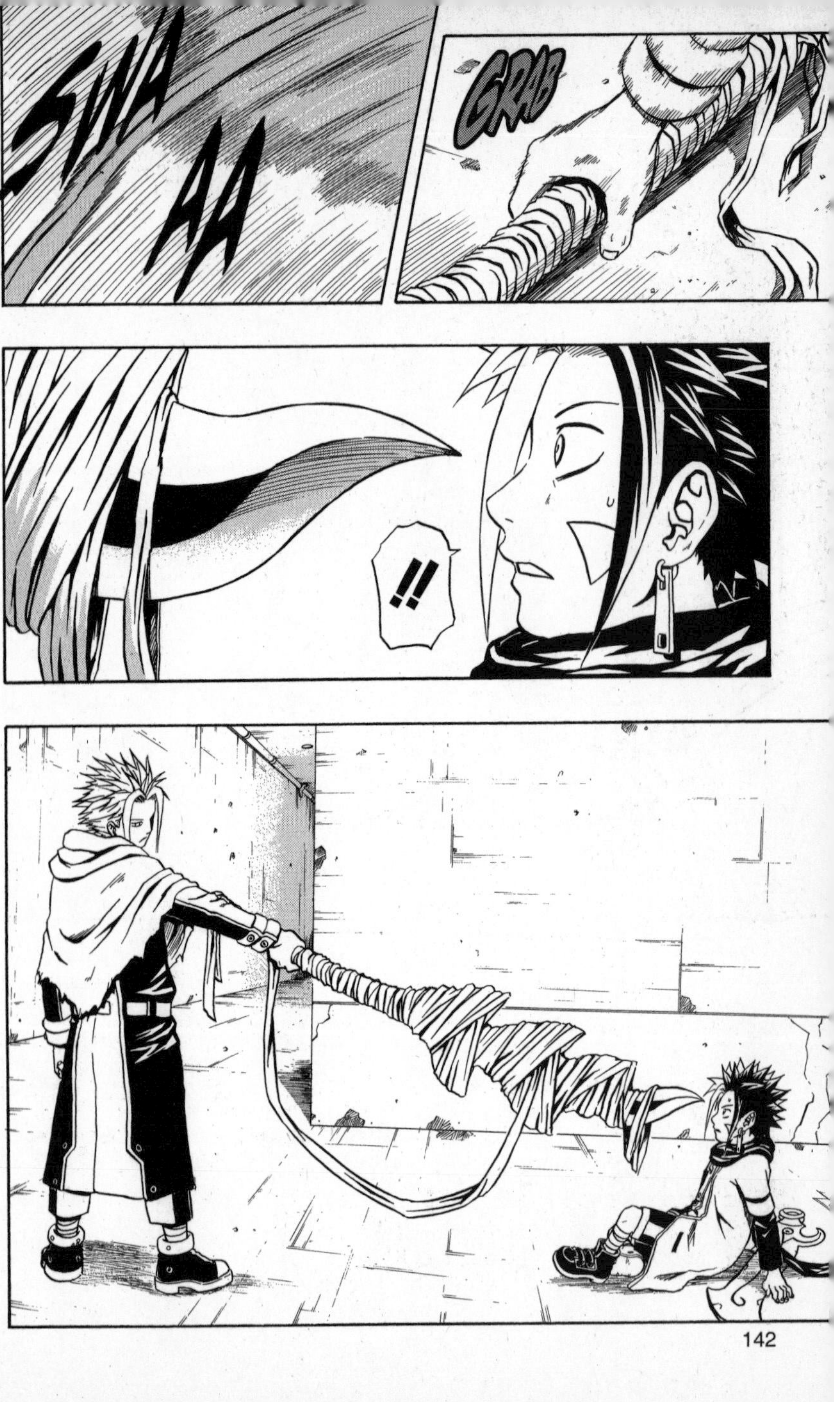
GRAB
SWAAAA
!!

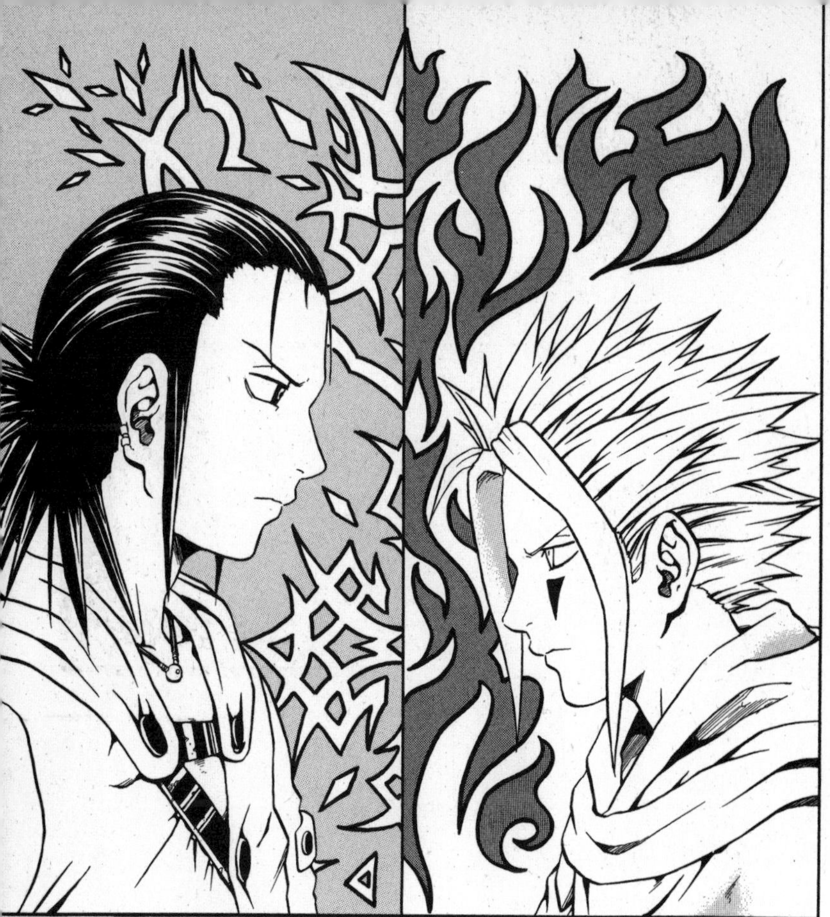

CHAPTER 40
THE SHAPE OF ONE'S HEART

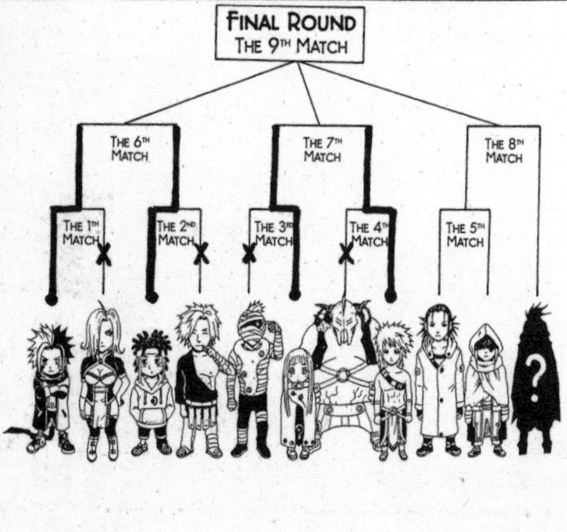

FINAL ROUND
THE 9TH MATCH
THE 6TH MATCH
THE 7TH MATCH
THE 8TH MATCH
THE 1TH MATCH
THE 2ND MATCH
THE 3RD MATCH
THE 4TH MATCH
THE 5TH MATCH
?

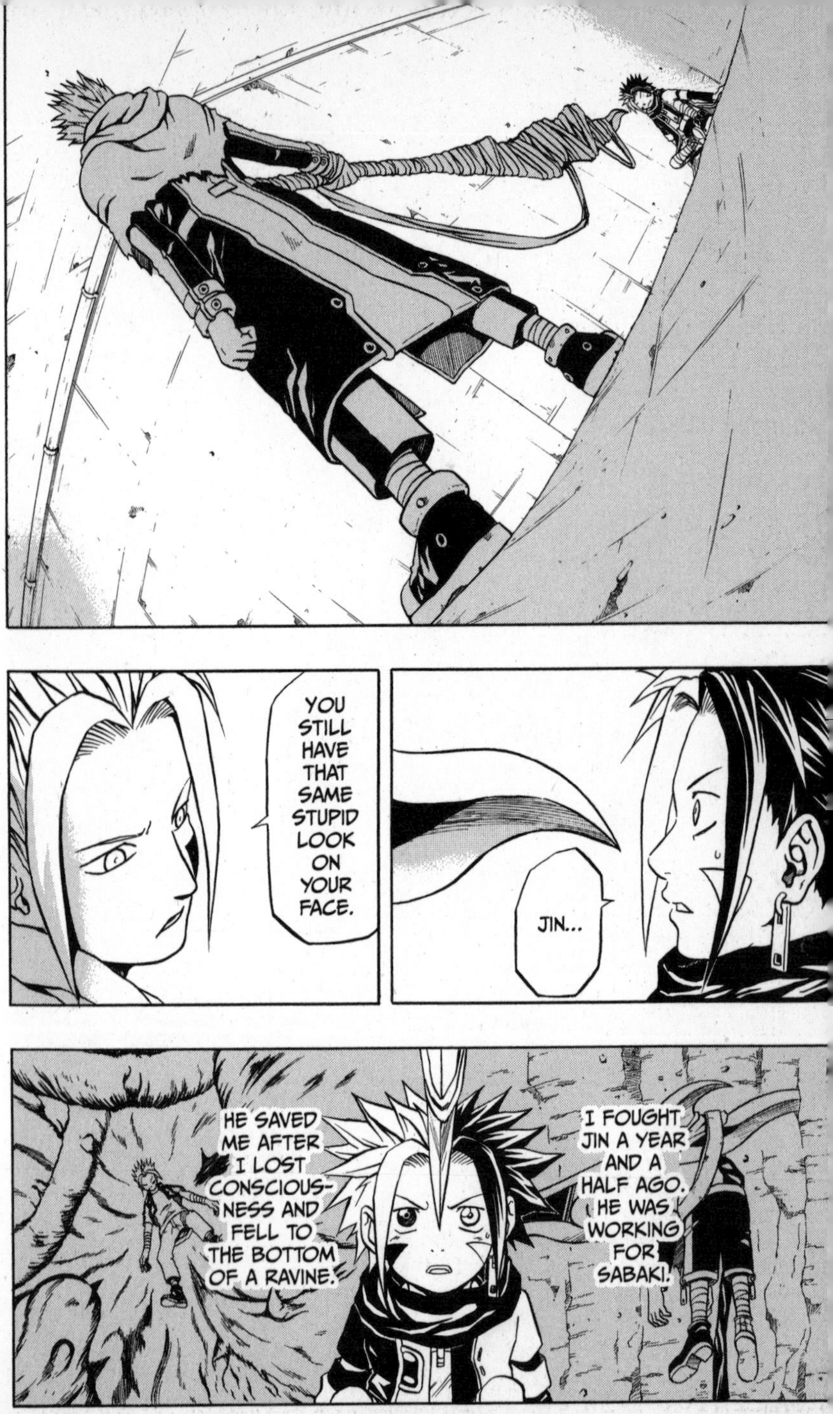
JIN...
YOU STILL HAVE THAT SAME STUPID LOOK ON YOUR FACE.
I FOUGHT JIN A YEAR AND A HALF AGO. HE WAS WORKING FOR SABAKI.
HE SAVED ME AFTER I LOST CONSCIOUS-NESS AND FELL TO THE BOTTOM OF A RAVINE.

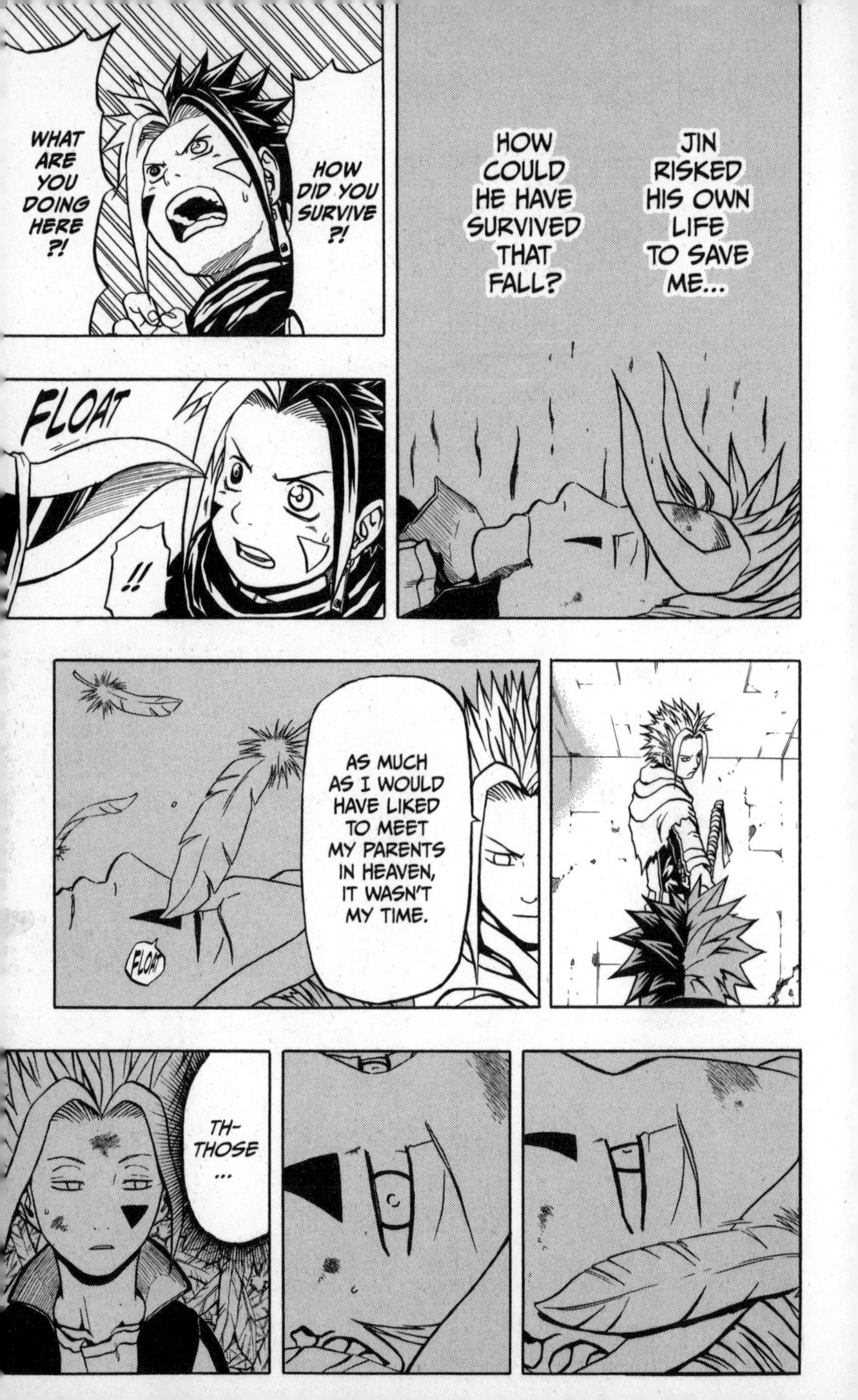
JIN RISKED HIS OWN LIFE TO SAVE ME...
HOW COULD HE HAVE SURVIVED THAT FALL?
HOW DID YOU SURVIVE ?!
WHAT ARE YOU DOING HERE ?!
FLOAT
!!
AS MUCH AS I WOULD HAVE LIKED TO MEET MY PARENTS IN HEAVEN, IT WASN'T MY TIME.
FLOAT
TH-THOSE ...

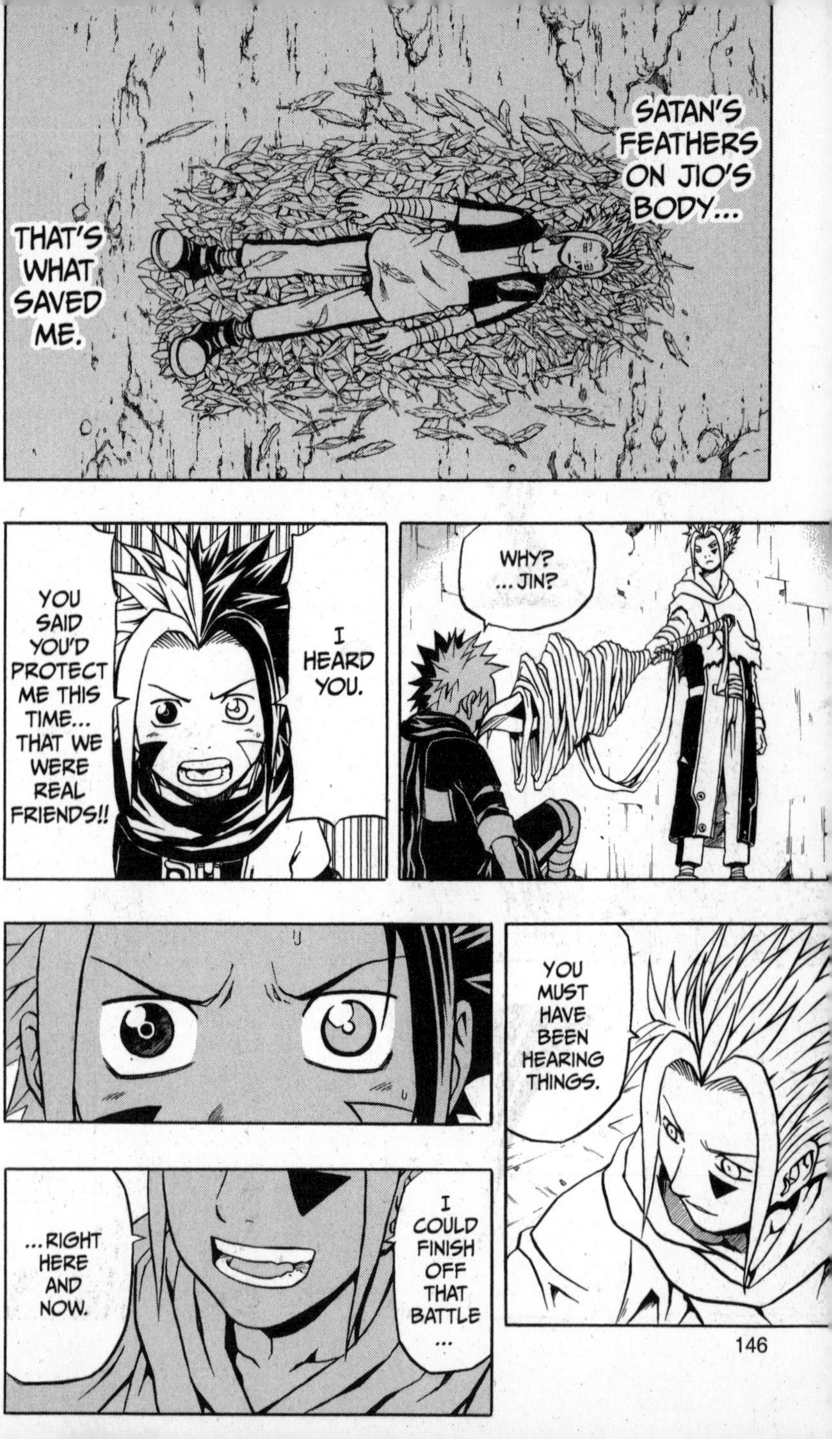
SATAN'S FEATHERS ON JIO'S BODY...
THAT'S WHAT SAVED ME.
WHY? ...JIN?
I HEARD YOU.
YOU SAID YOU'D PROTECT ME THIS TIME... THAT WE WERE REAL FRIENDS!!
YOU MUST HAVE BEEN HEARING THINGS.
I COULD FINISH OFF THAT BATTLE ...
...RIGHT HERE AND NOW.

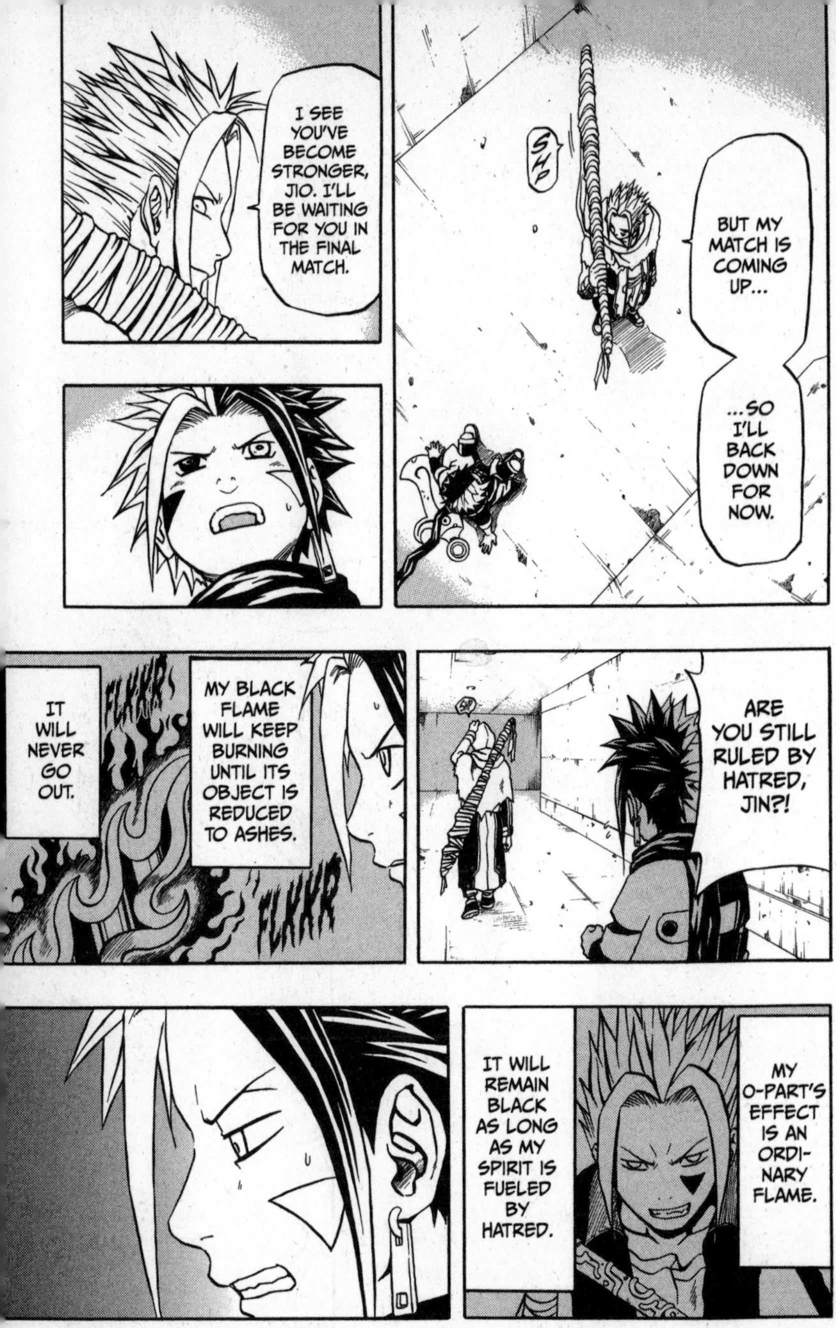
SHP
BUT MY MATCH IS COMING UP...
...SO I'LL BACK DOWN FOR NOW.
I SEE YOU'VE BECOME STRONGER, JIO. I'LL BE WAITING FOR YOU IN THE FINAL MATCH.
SHP
ARE YOU STILL RULED BY HATRED, JIN?!
FLKKR
MY BLACK FLAME WILL KEEP BURNING UNTIL ITS OBJECT IS REDUCED TO ASHES.
IT WILL NEVER GO OUT.
FLKKR
MY O-PART'S EFFECT IS AN ORDINARY FLAME.
IT WILL REMAIN BLACK AS LONG AS MY SPIRIT IS FUELED BY HATRED.

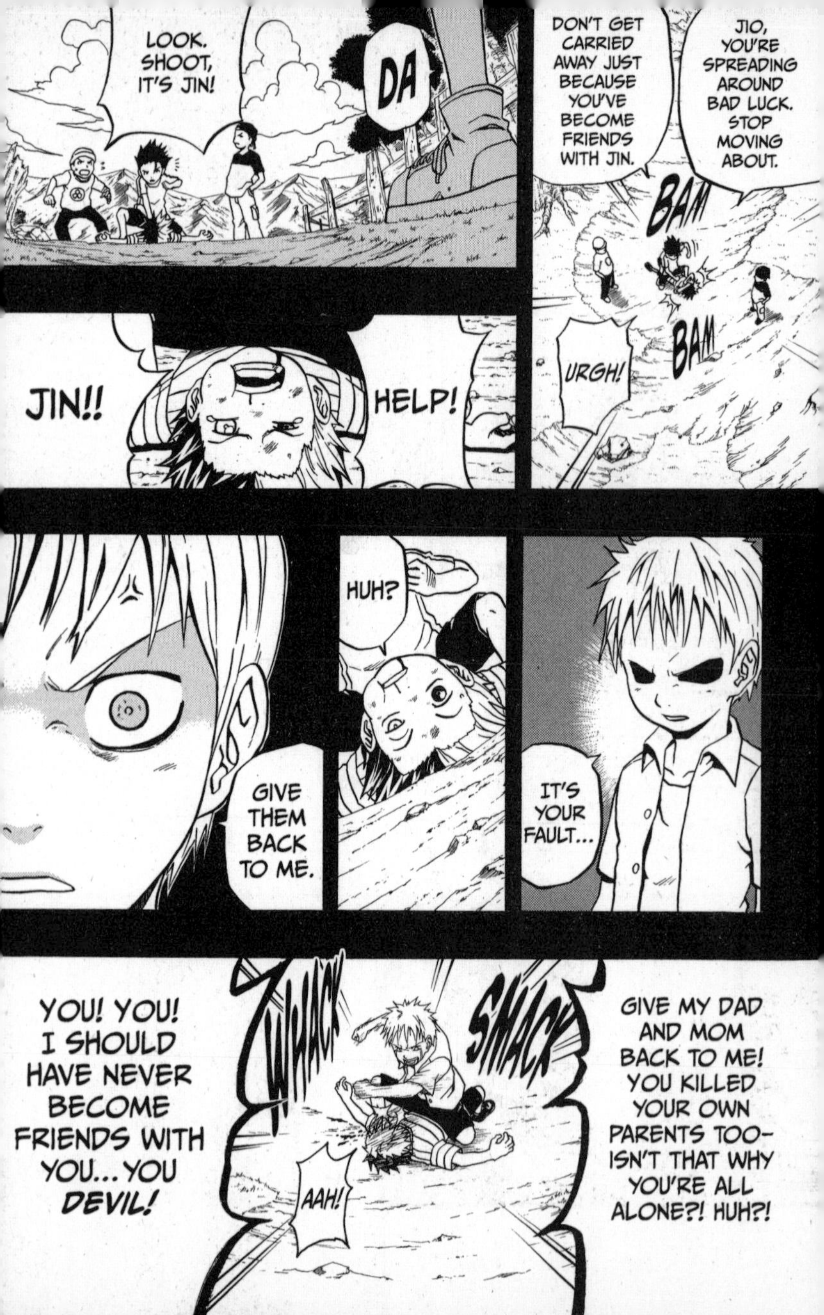
JIO, YOU'RE SPREADING AROUND BAD LUCK. STOP MOVING ABOUT.
DON'T GET CARRIED AWAY JUST BECAUSE YOU'VE BECOME FRIENDS WITH JIN.
BAM
BAM
URGH!
DA
LOOK. SHOOT, IT'S JIN!
HELP!
JIN!!
IT'S YOUR FAULT...
HUH?
GIVE THEM BACK TO ME.
GIVE MY DAD AND MOM BACK TO ME! YOU KILLED YOUR OWN PARENTS TOO–ISN'T THAT WHY YOU'RE ALL ALONE?! HUH?!
SMACK
WHACK
AAH!
YOU! YOU! I SHOULD HAVE NEVER BECOME FRIENDS WITH YOU... YOU *DEVIL!*

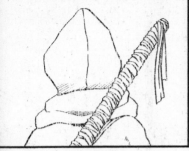

...JIN'S PARENTS ...

I KILLED ...

I'M THE ONE...

...WHO CHANGED JIN.

RAAAH

RAAAH

RAAAH

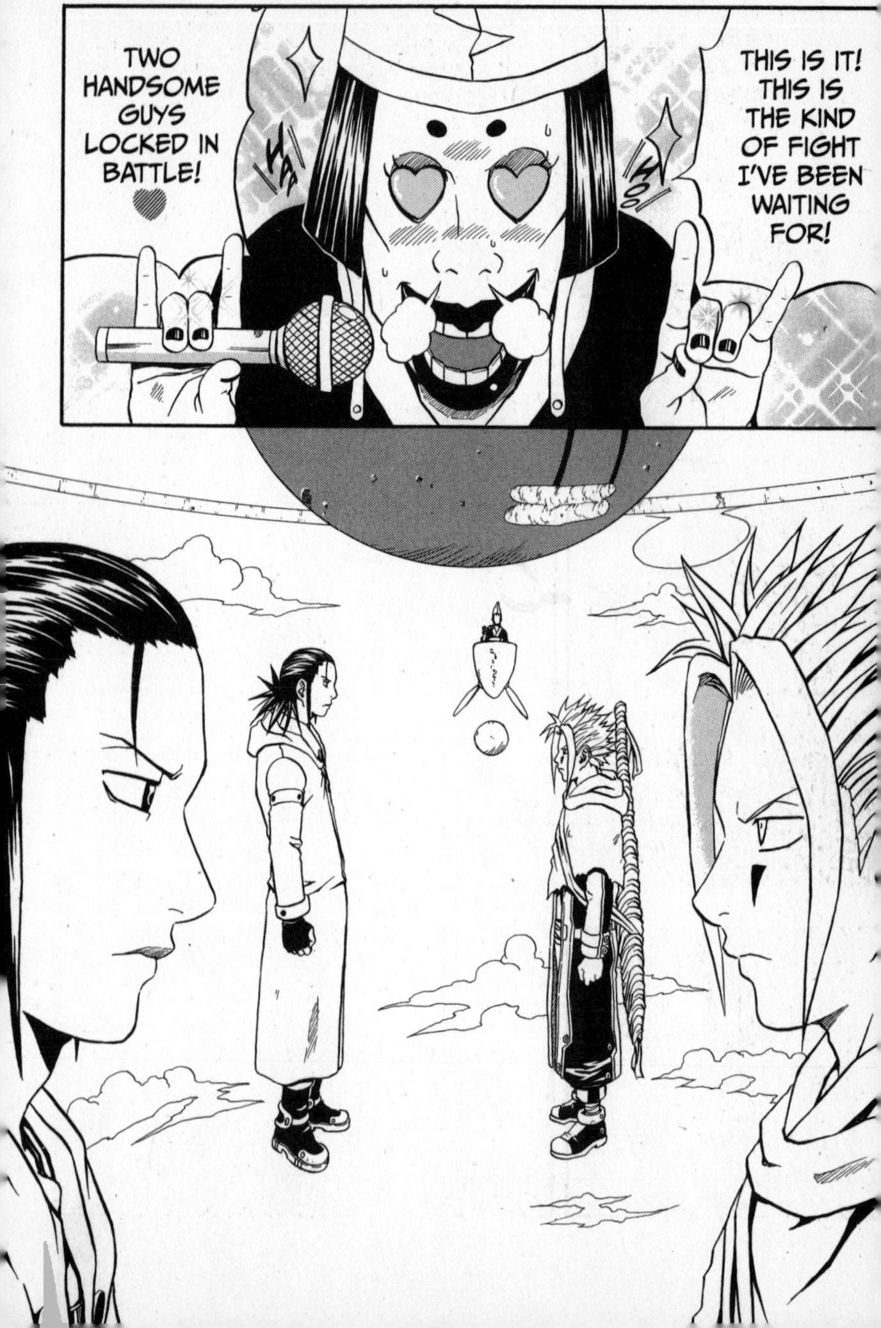
THIS IS IT! THIS IS THE KIND OF FIGHT I'VE BEEN WAITING FOR!
TWO HANDSOME GUYS LOCKED IN BATTLE! ♥

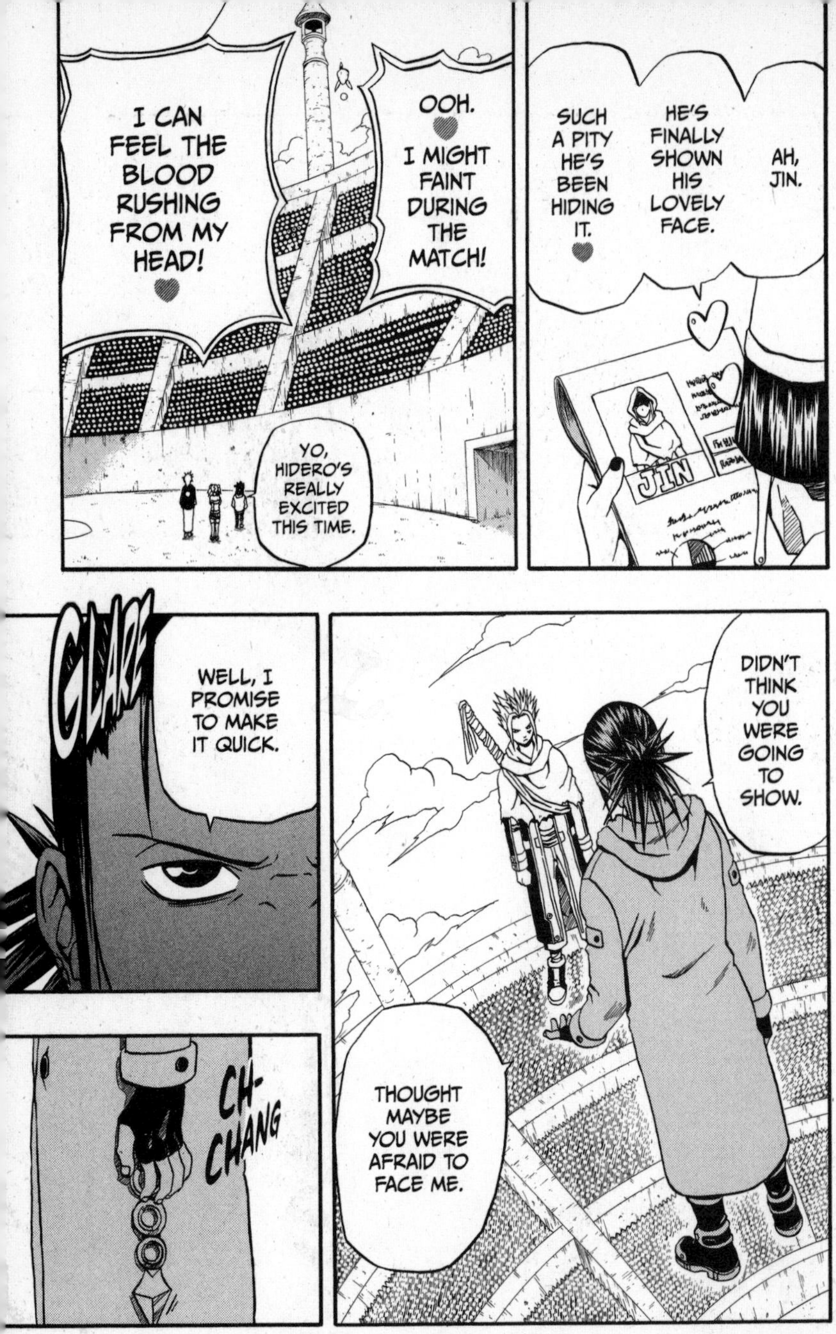
AH, JIN.
HE'S FINALLY SHOWN HIS LOVELY FACE.
SUCH A PITY HE'S BEEN HIDING IT.
JIN
OOH. I MIGHT FAINT DURING THE MATCH!
I CAN FEEL THE BLOOD RUSHING FROM MY HEAD!
YO, HIDERO'S REALLY EXCITED THIS TIME.
DIDN'T THINK YOU WERE GOING TO SHOW.
THOUGHT MAYBE YOU WERE AFRAID TO FACE ME.
CLARE
WELL, I PROMISE TO MAKE IT QUICK.
CH-CHANG

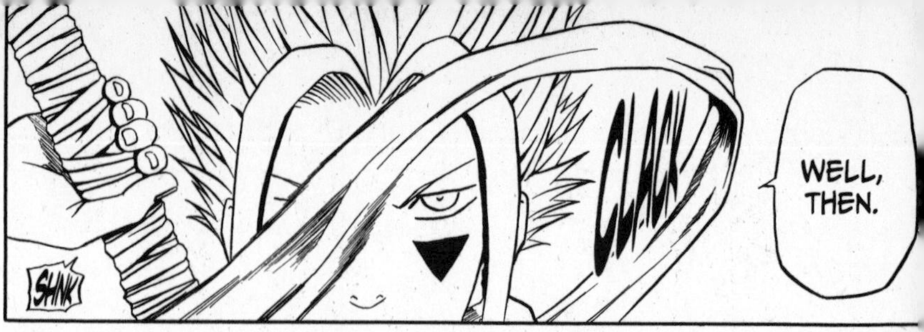
WELL, THEN.
CLACK
SHNK

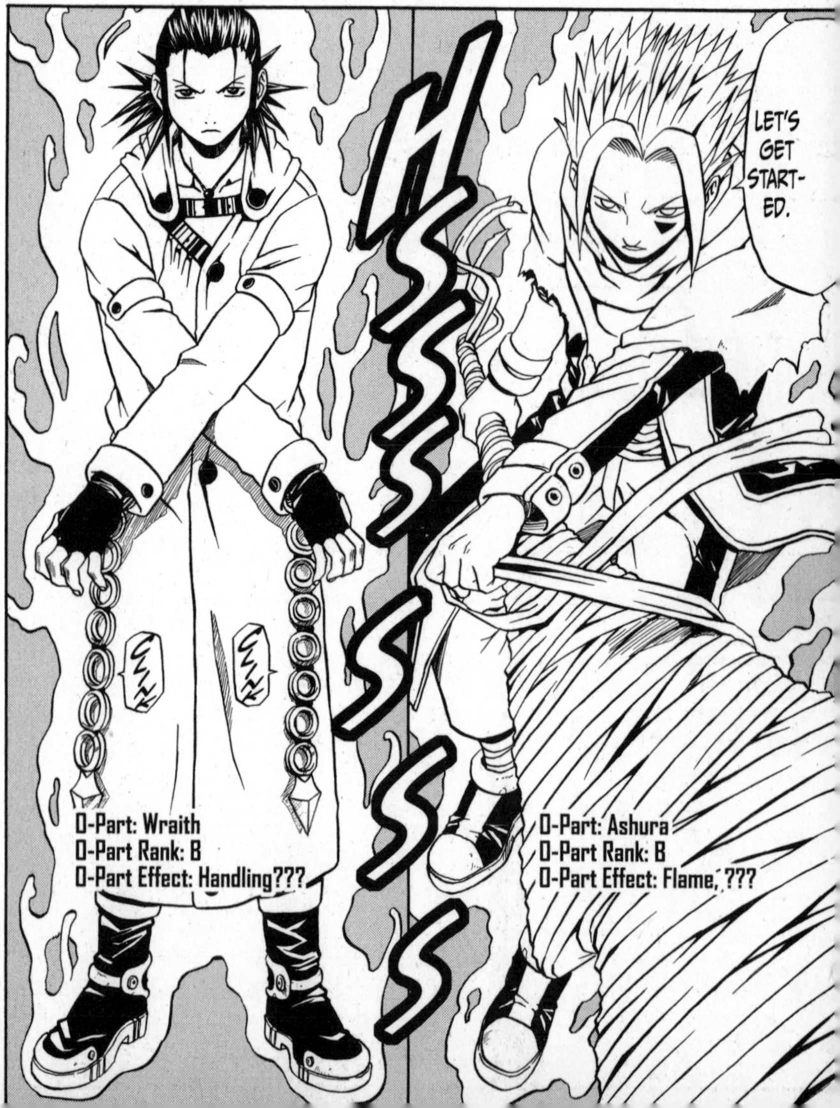
LET'S GET START-ED.
HSSSSSS
O-Part: Ashura
O-Part Rank: B
O-Part Effect: Flame, ???
O-Part: Wraith
O-Part Rank: B
O-Part Effect: Handling???
CLINK
CLINK

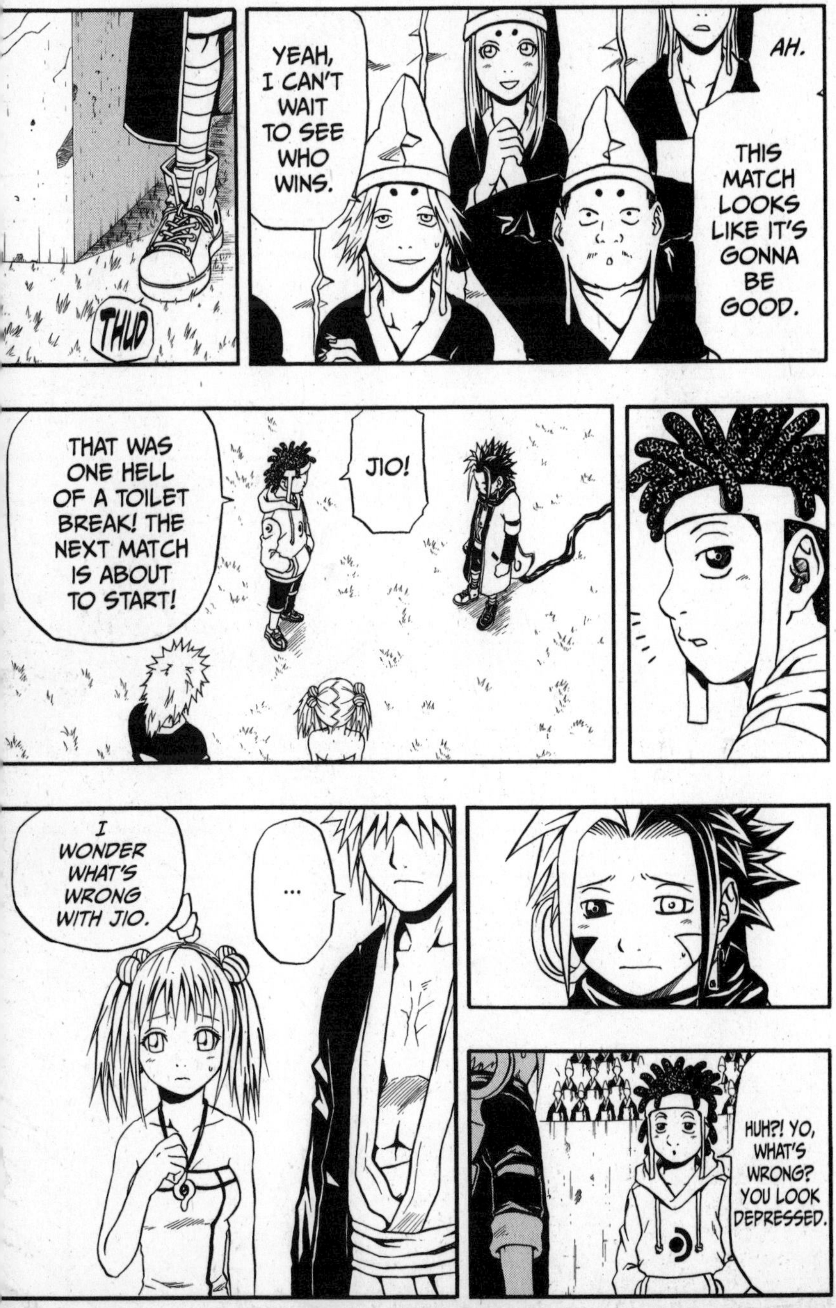
AH.
THIS MATCH LOOKS LIKE IT'S GONNA BE GOOD.
YEAH, I CAN'T WAIT TO SEE WHO WINS.
THUD
JIO!
THAT WAS ONE HELL OF A TOILET BREAK! THE NEXT MATCH IS ABOUT TO START!
HUH?! YO, WHAT'S WRONG? YOU LOOK DEPRESSED.
...
I WONDER WHAT'S WRONG WITH JIO.

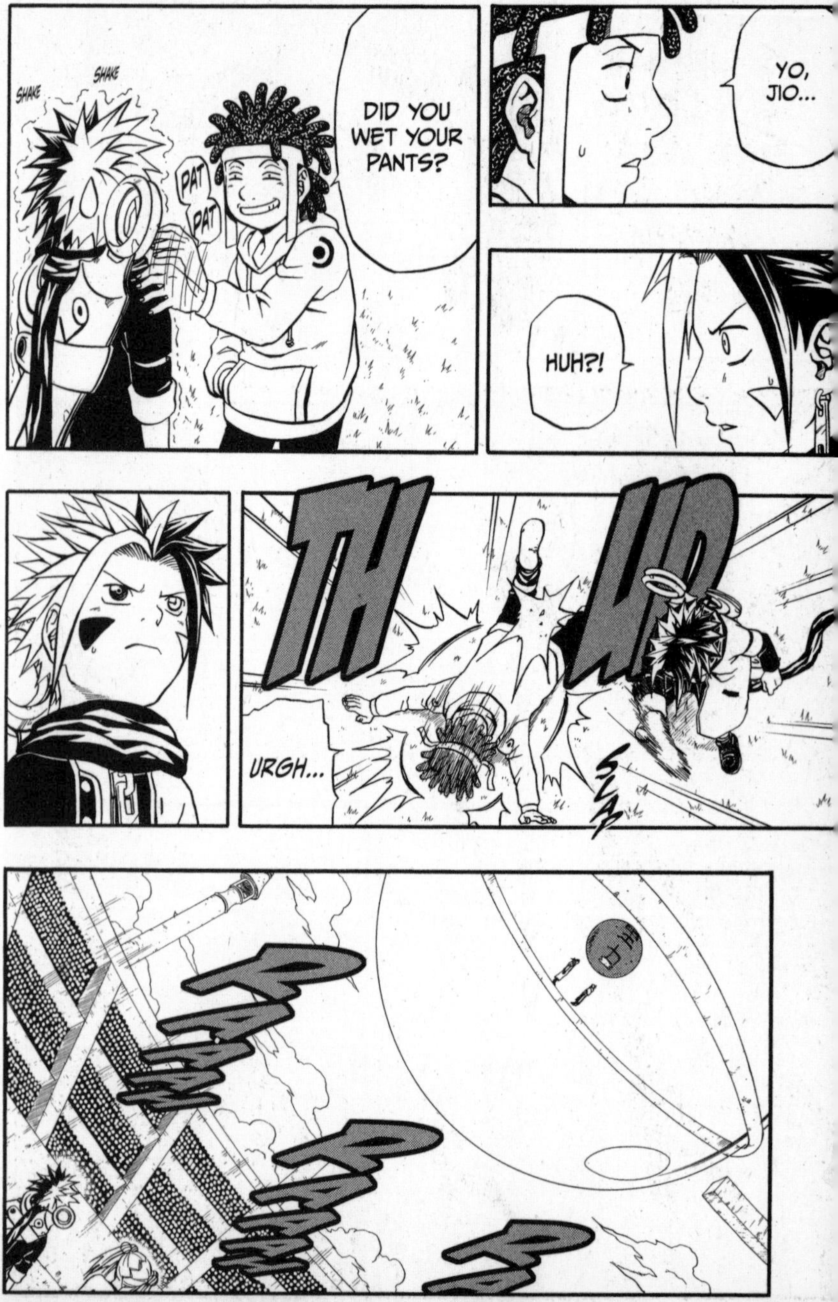
YO, JIO...
HUH?!
DID YOU WET YOUR PANTS?
SHAKE
SHAKE
PAT
PAT
THWIP
SLAM
URGH...

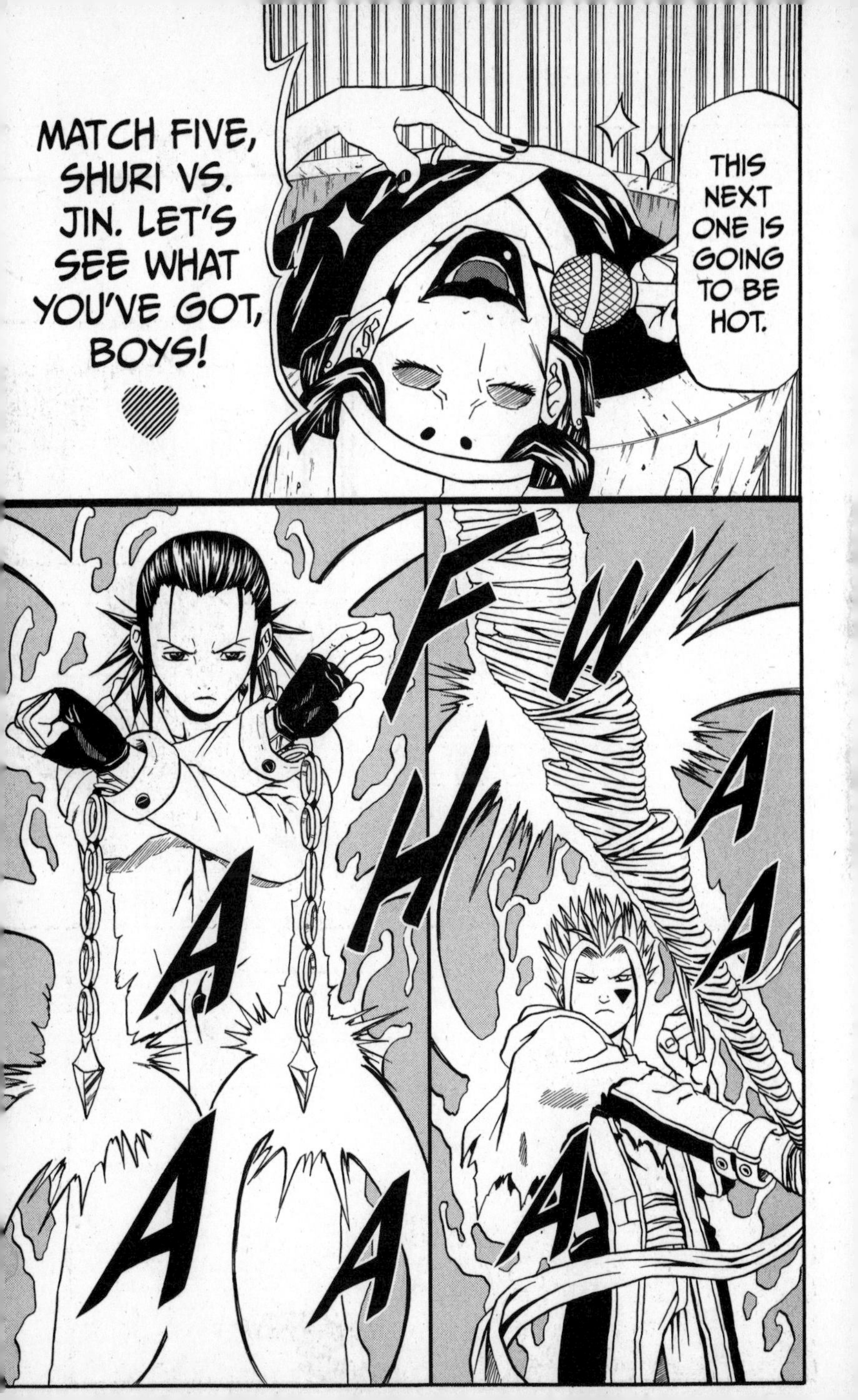
THIS NEXT ONE IS GOING TO BE HOT.
MATCH FIVE, SHURI VS. JIN. LET'S SEE WHAT YOU'VE GOT, BOYS!
FWHAAAAAAAA

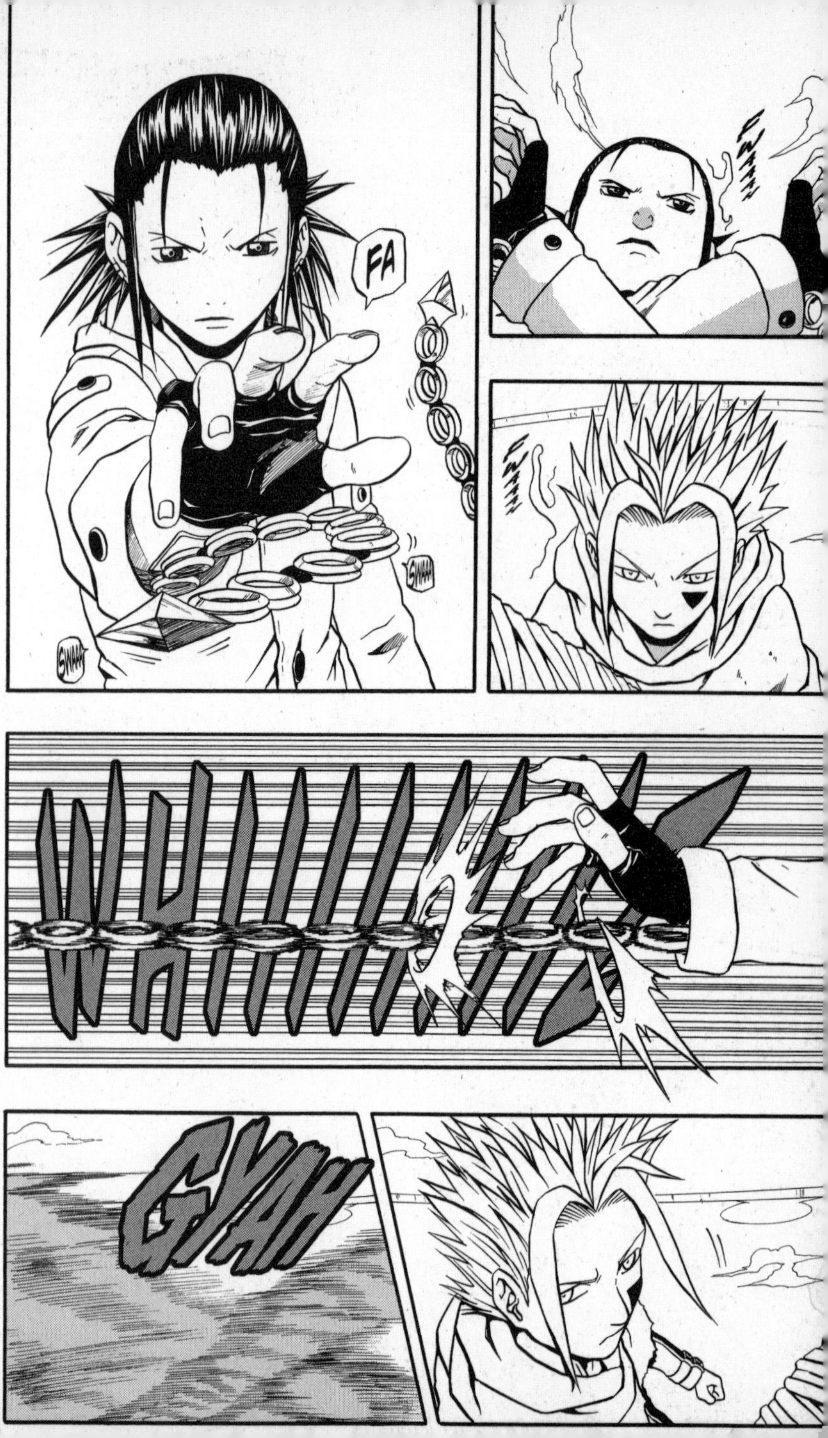
CWAAAN
CWAAAN
FA
SWAAA
SWAAA
GYAH

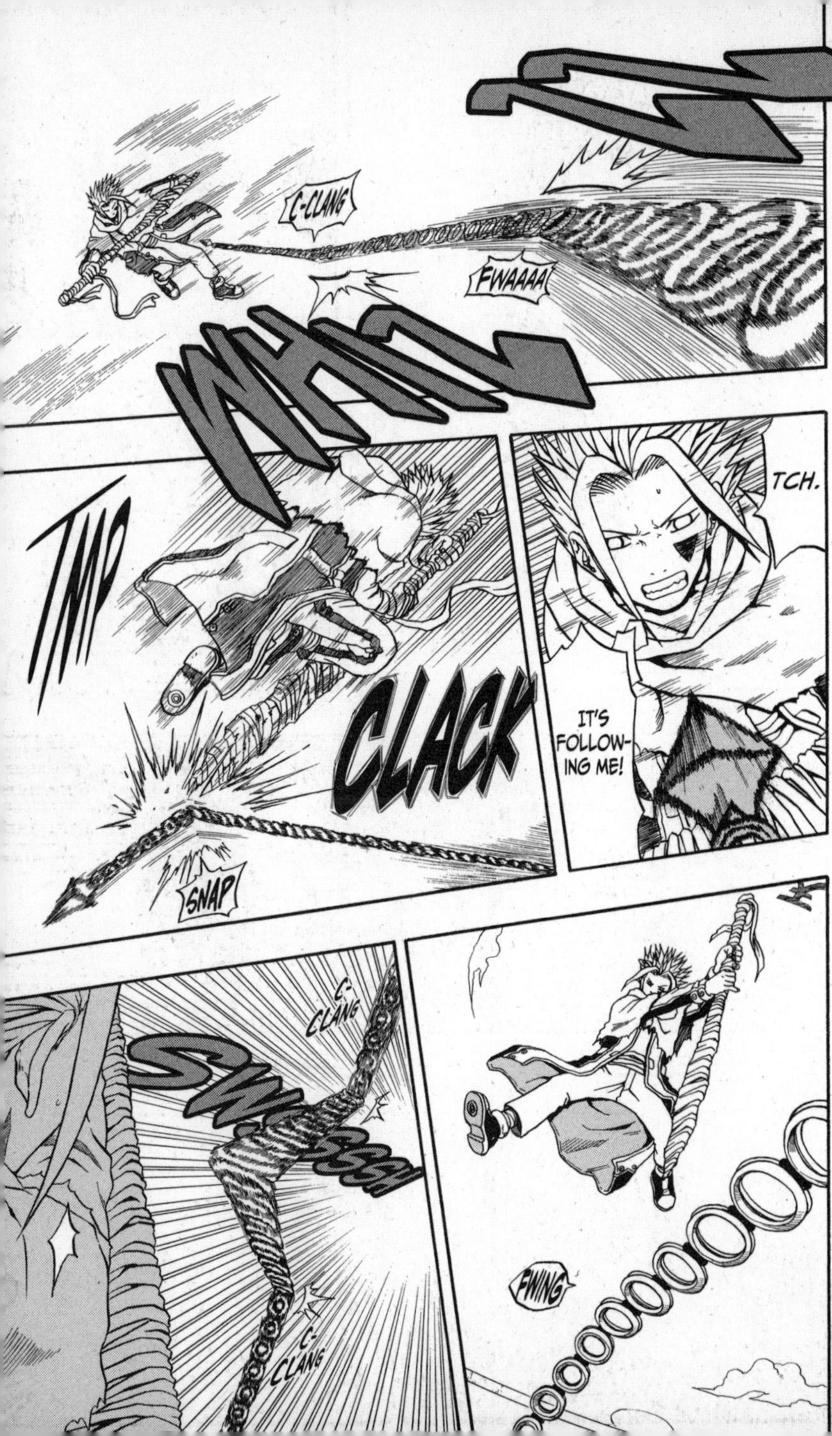
C-CLANG
FWAAAA
TCH.
IT'S FOLLOWING ME!
CLACK
SNAP
FWING
C-CLANG
C-CLANG

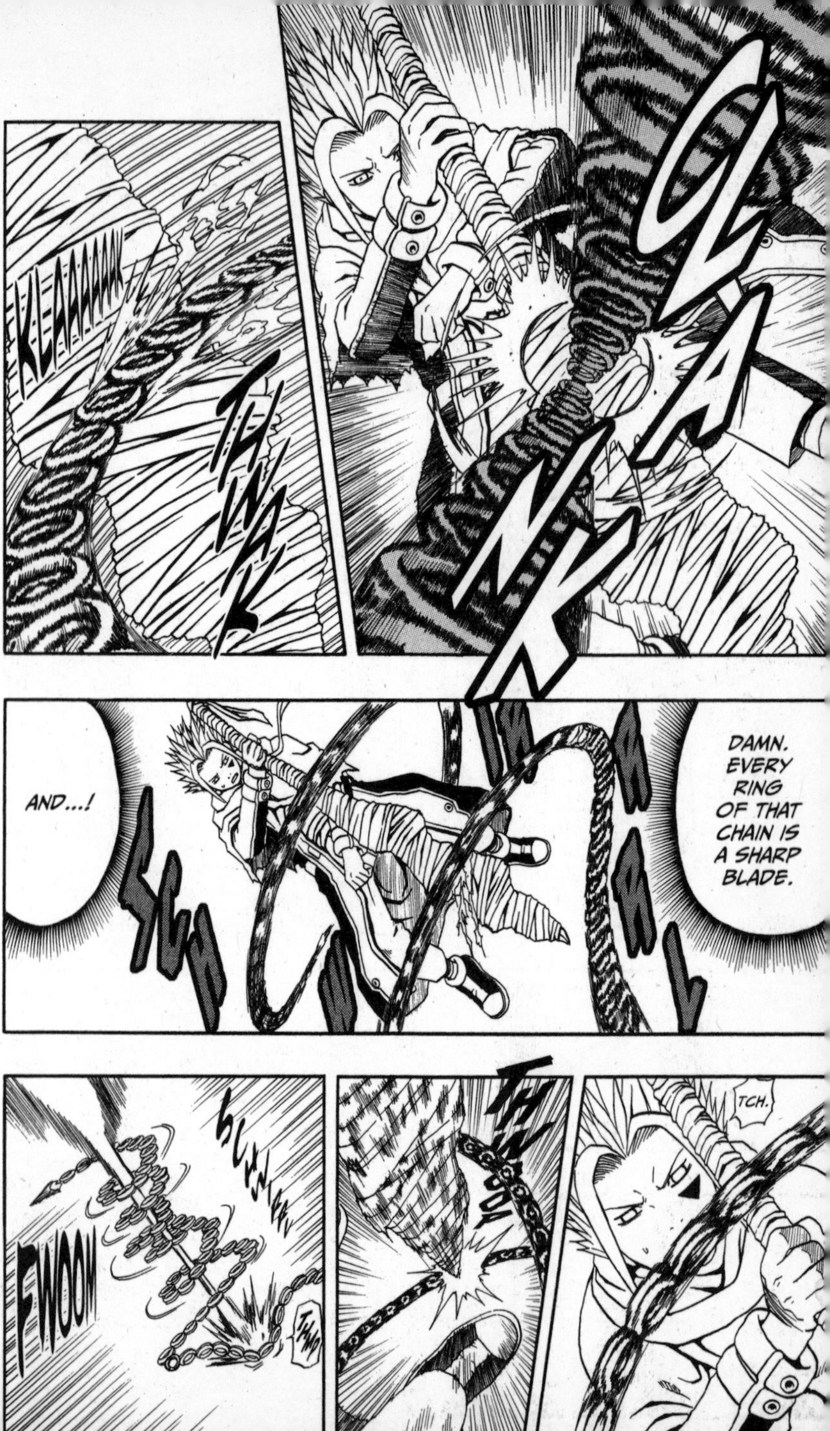
CLANK
DAMN. EVERY RING OF THAT CHAIN IS A SHARP BLADE.
AND...!
TCH.
FWOOM

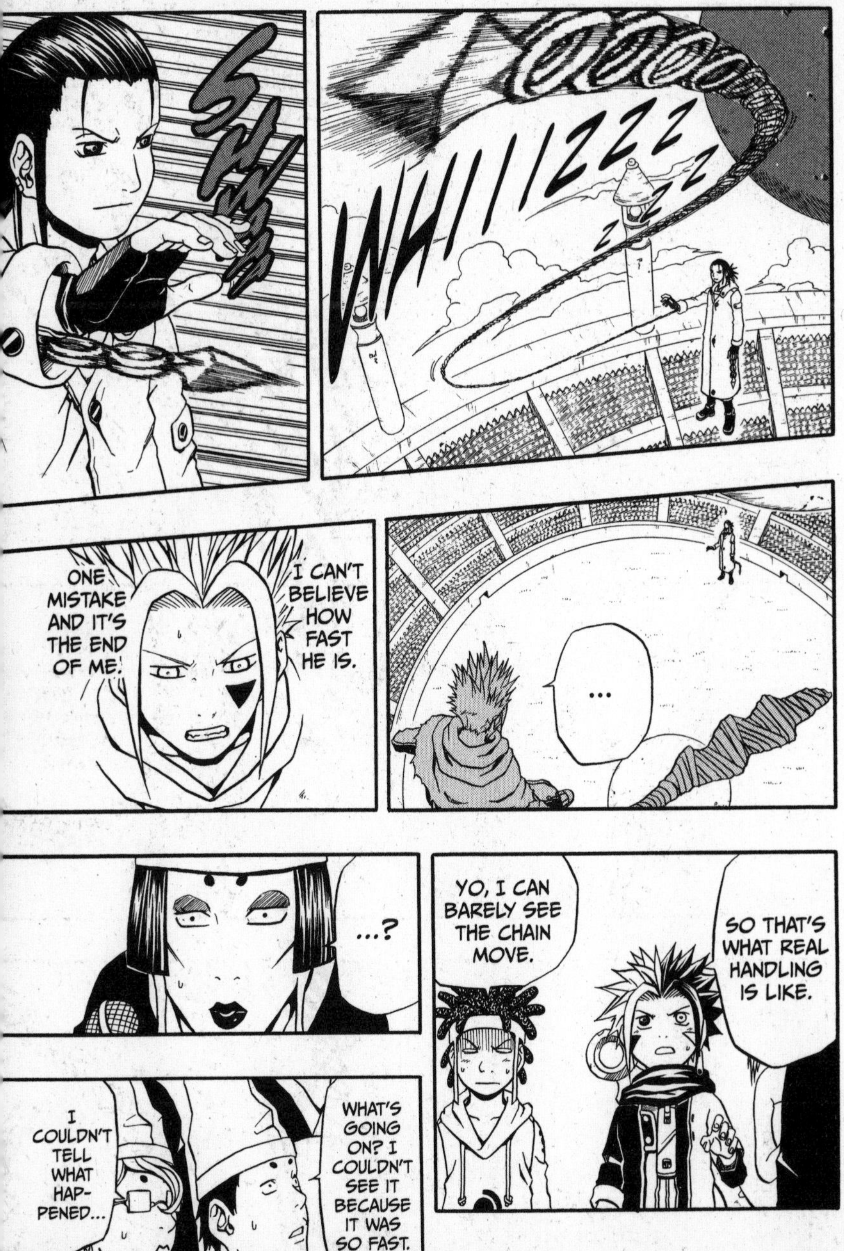
WHIIIIZZZZ
...
I CAN'T BELIEVE HOW FAST HE IS.
ONE MISTAKE AND IT'S THE END OF ME!
SO THAT'S WHAT REAL HANDLING IS LIKE.
YO, I CAN BARELY SEE THE CHAIN MOVE.
...?
WHAT'S GOING ON? I COULDN'T SEE IT BECAUSE IT WAS SO FAST.
I COULDN'T TELL WHAT HAP-PENED...

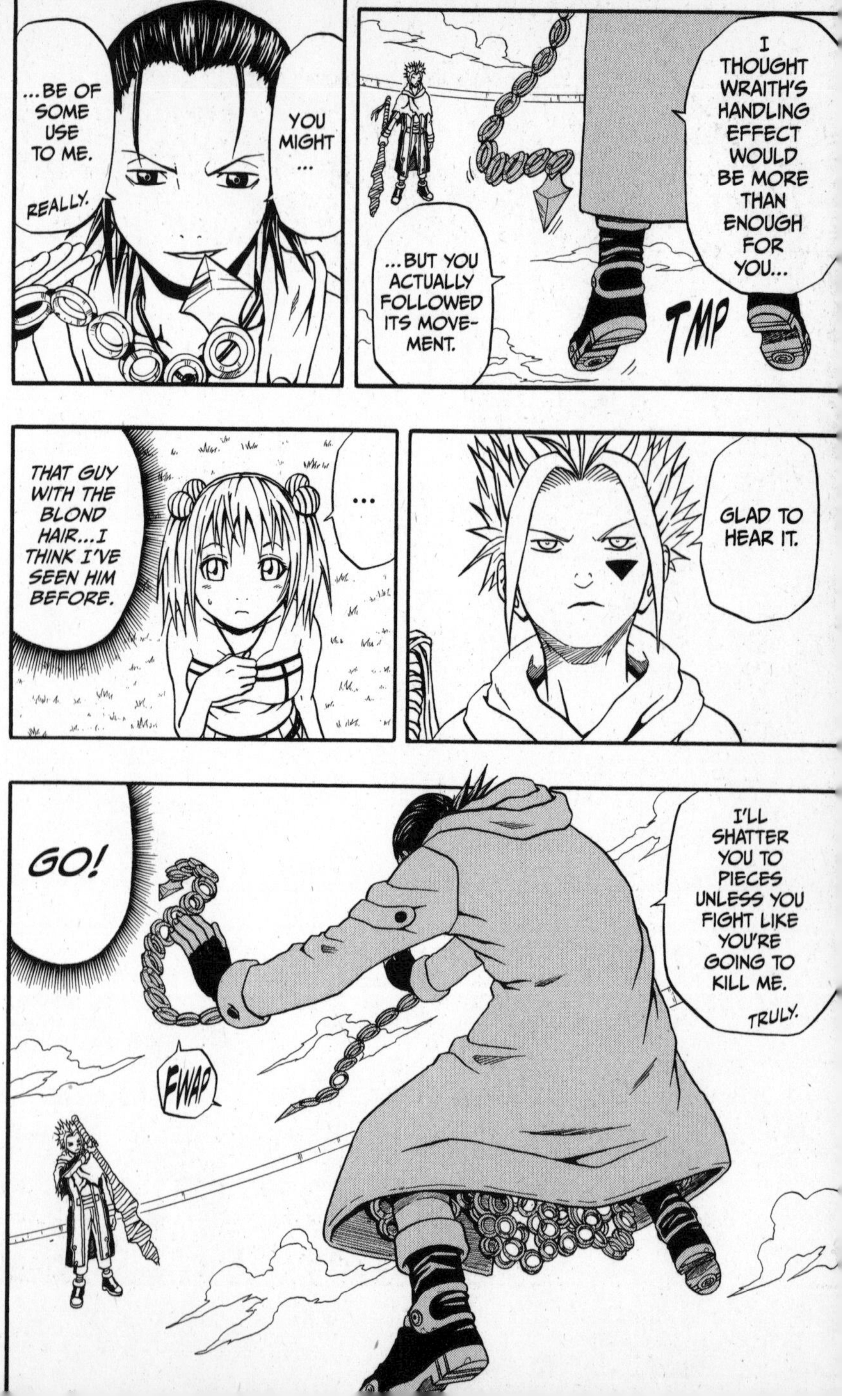
I THOUGHT WRAITH'S HANDLING EFFECT WOULD BE MORE THAN ENOUGH FOR YOU...
...BUT YOU ACTUALLY FOLLOWED ITS MOVE-MENT.
TMP
YOU MIGHT...
...BE OF SOME USE TO ME.
REALLY.
GLAD TO HEAR IT.
...
THAT GUY WITH THE BLOND HAIR...I THINK I'VE SEEN HIM BEFORE.
I'LL SHATTER YOU TO PIECES UNLESS YOU FIGHT LIKE YOU'RE GOING TO KILL ME.
TRULY.
GO!
FWAP

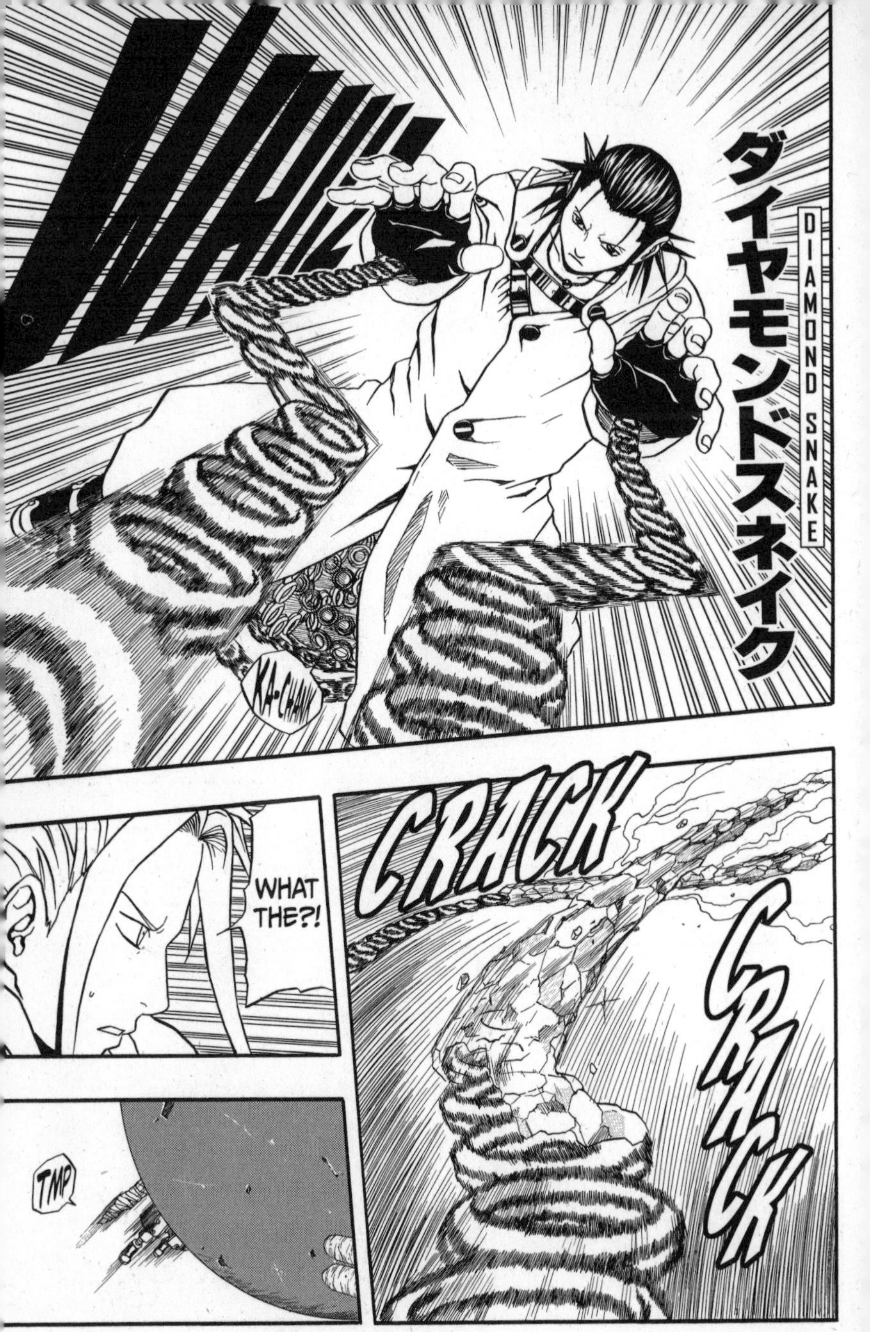
ダイヤモンドスネイク
DIAMOND SNAKE
KA-CHAN
CRACK
CRACK
WHAT THE?!
TMP

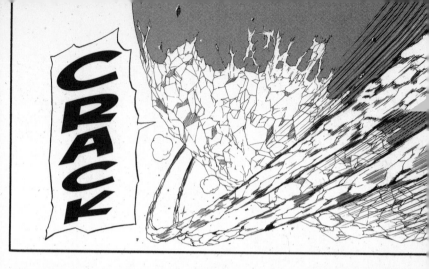

CRACK
WHOA, THE GRAVITY BALL FROZE EVEN THOUGH THAT THING DIDN'T TOUCH IT!
THAT CHAIN O-PART...
...I GUESS YOU COULD SAY IT'S LIKE ANNA'S O-PART.
IT CAN ATTACK AND DEFEND AT THE SAME TIME... BUT IT WORKS EVEN BETTER WITH THE FROST EFFECT.
CRACK
BECAUSE OF THAT EFFECT, YOU CAN'T DEFEND YOURSELF LIKE YOU DID WITH ANNA.
THE MOMENT YOU TOUCH THAT THING YOU'LL BE FROZEN TO THE BONE.
CRAAAAAAACK
TCH...

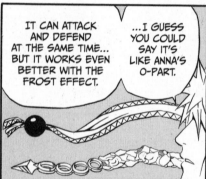

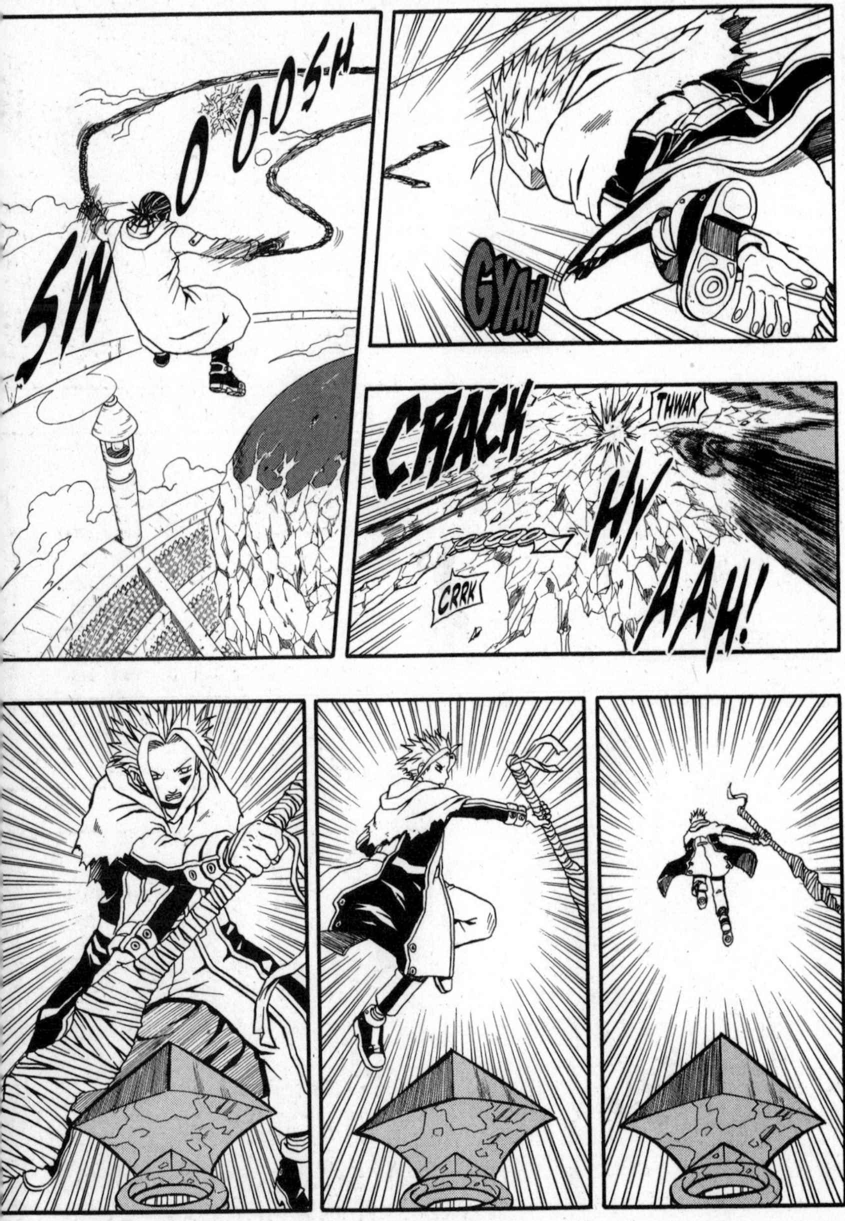
GYAH
THWAK
CRACK
HYAAH!
CRRK
SWOOOOSH

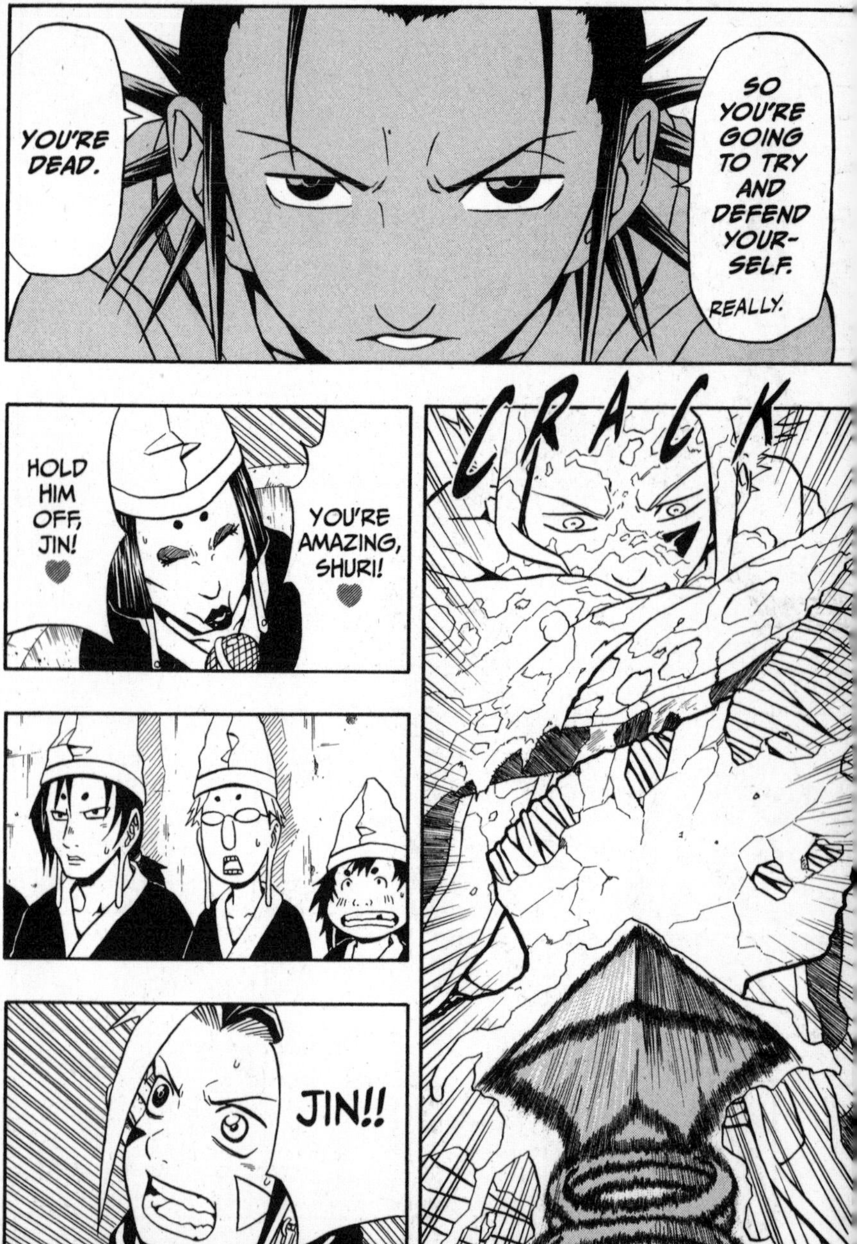
SO YOU'RE GOING TO TRY AND DEFEND YOUR-SELF.
REALLY.
YOU'RE DEAD.
CRACK
YOU'RE AMAZING, SHURI!
HOLD HIM OFF, JIN!
JIN!!

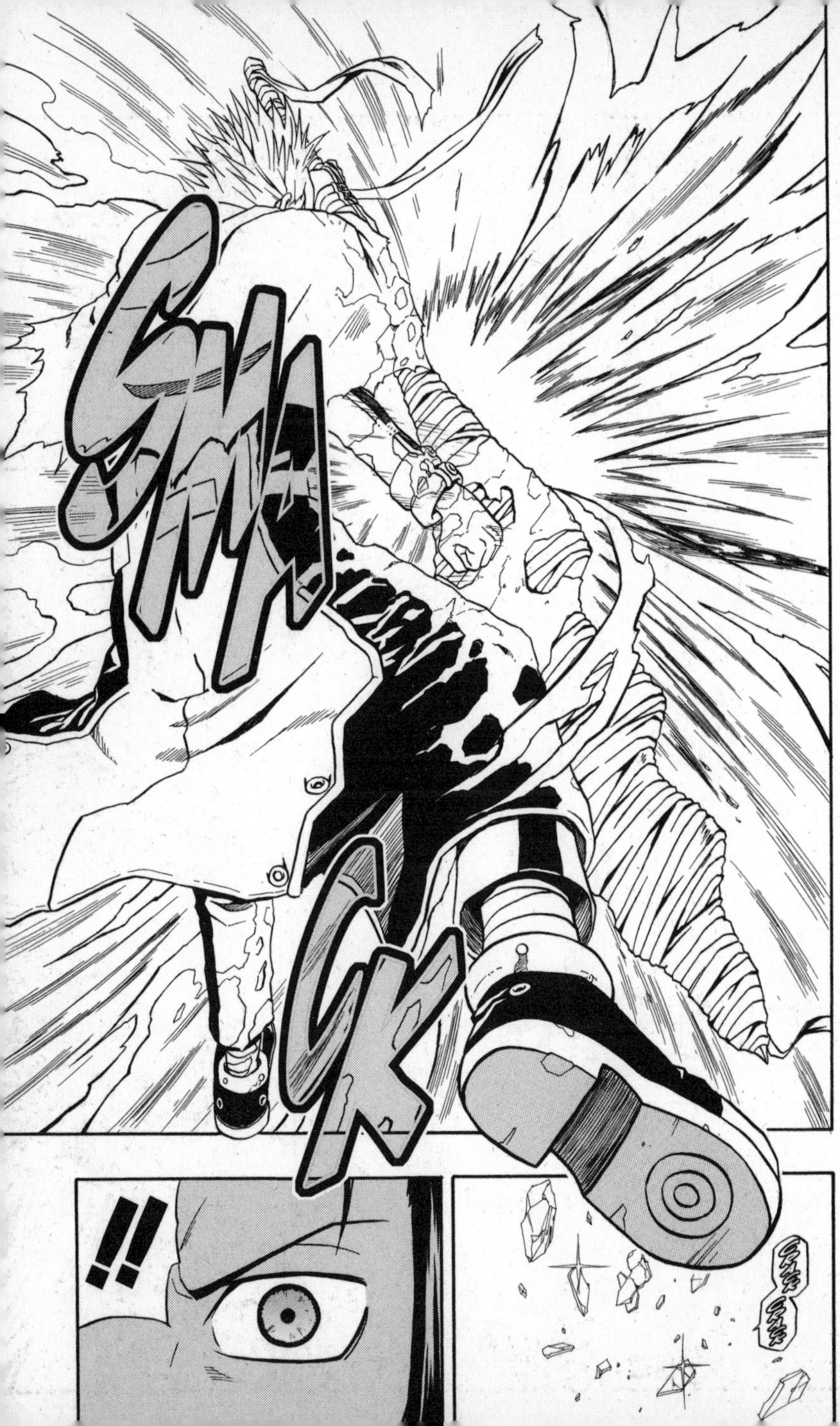
SMACK
CRAK CRAK
!!

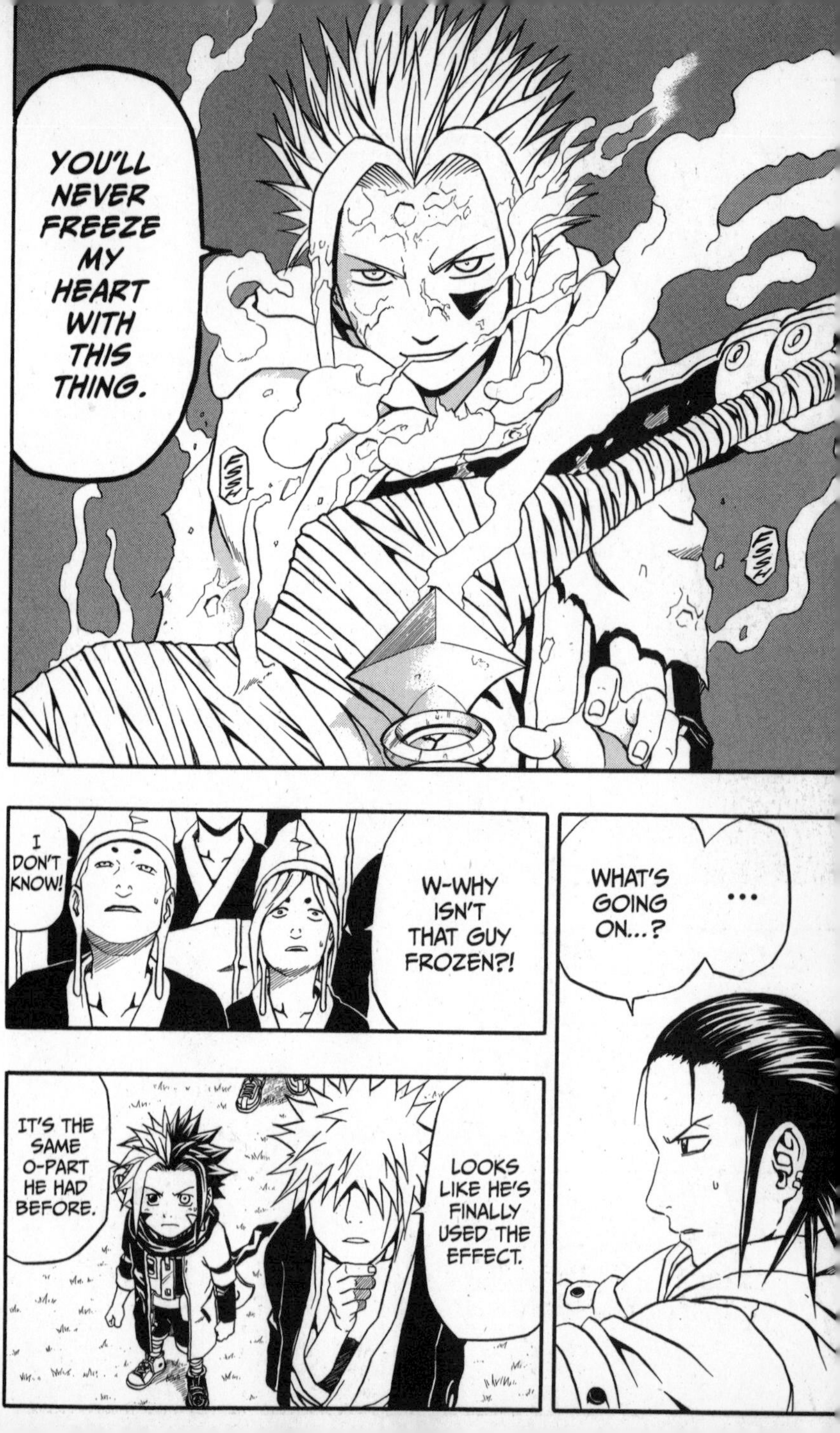
YOU'LL NEVER FREEZE MY HEART WITH THIS THING.
...
WHAT'S GOING ON...?
W-WHY ISN'T THAT GUY FROZEN?!
I DON'T KNOW!
LOOKS LIKE HE'S FINALLY USED THE EFFECT.
IT'S THE SAME O-PART HE HAD BEFORE.

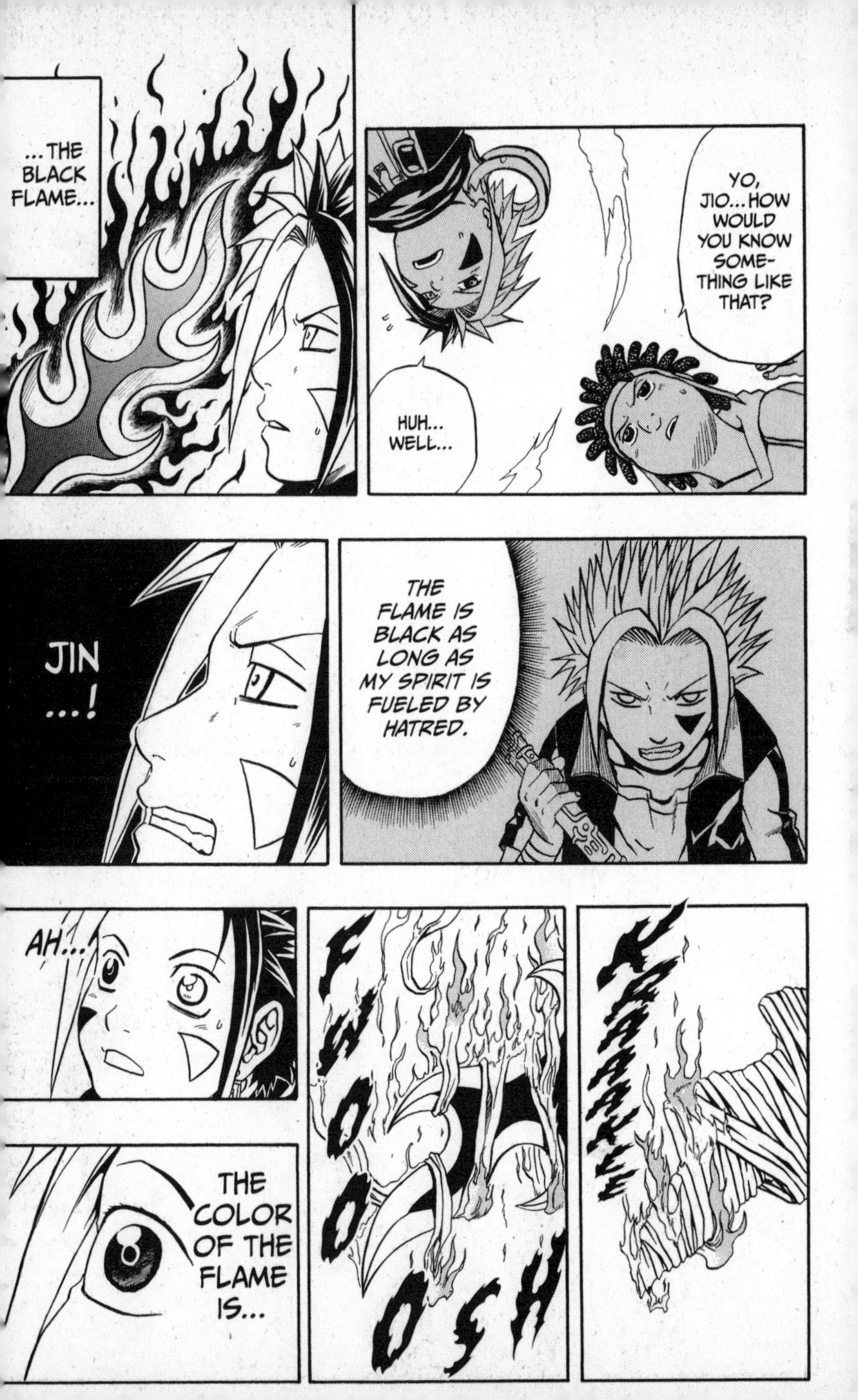
YO, JIO...HOW WOULD YOU KNOW SOME-THING LIKE THAT?
HUH... WELL...
...THE BLACK FLAME...
THE FLAME IS BLACK AS LONG AS MY SPIRIT IS FUELED BY HATRED.
JIN ...!
AH...
THE COLOR OF THE FLAME IS...

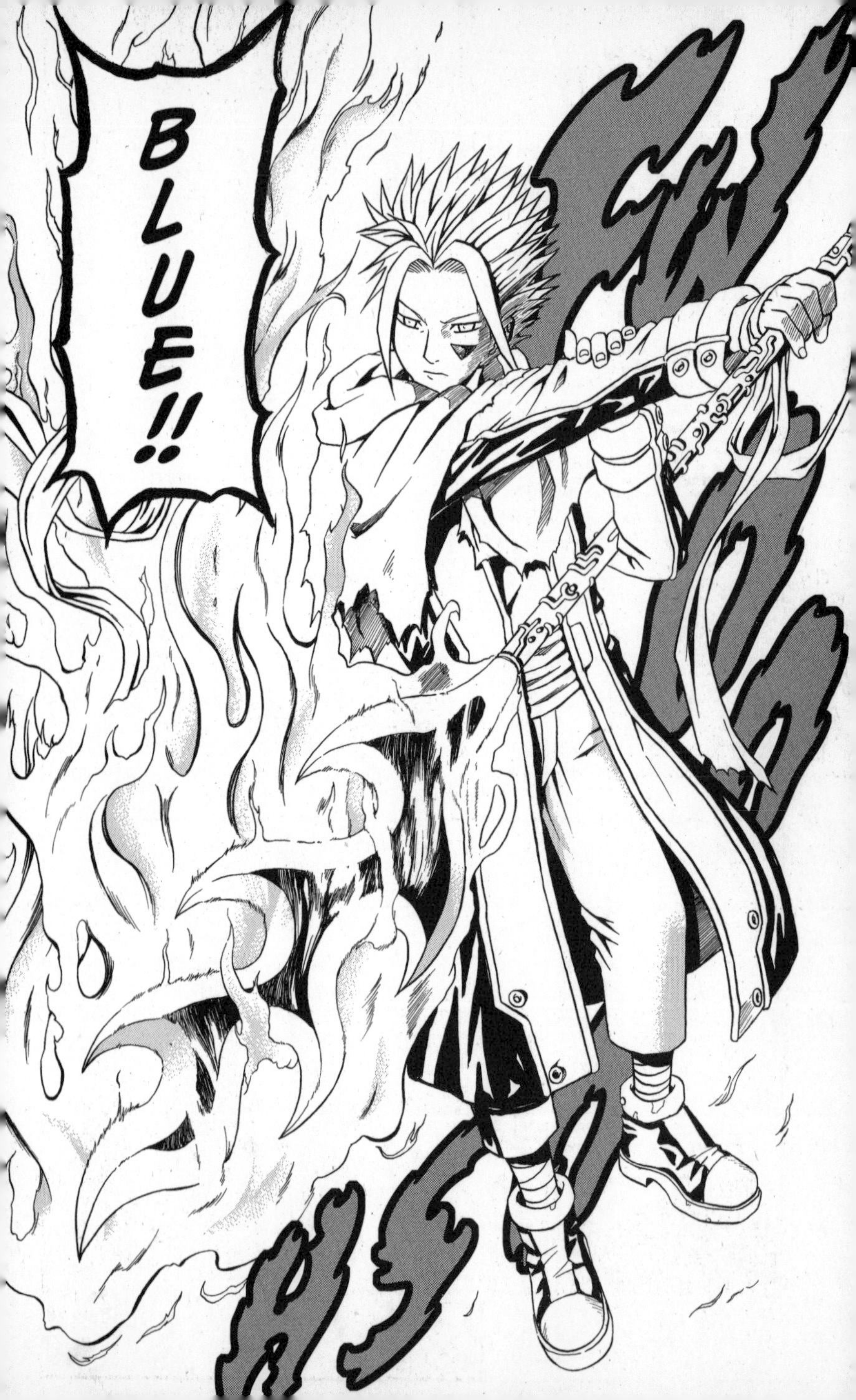
BLUE!!

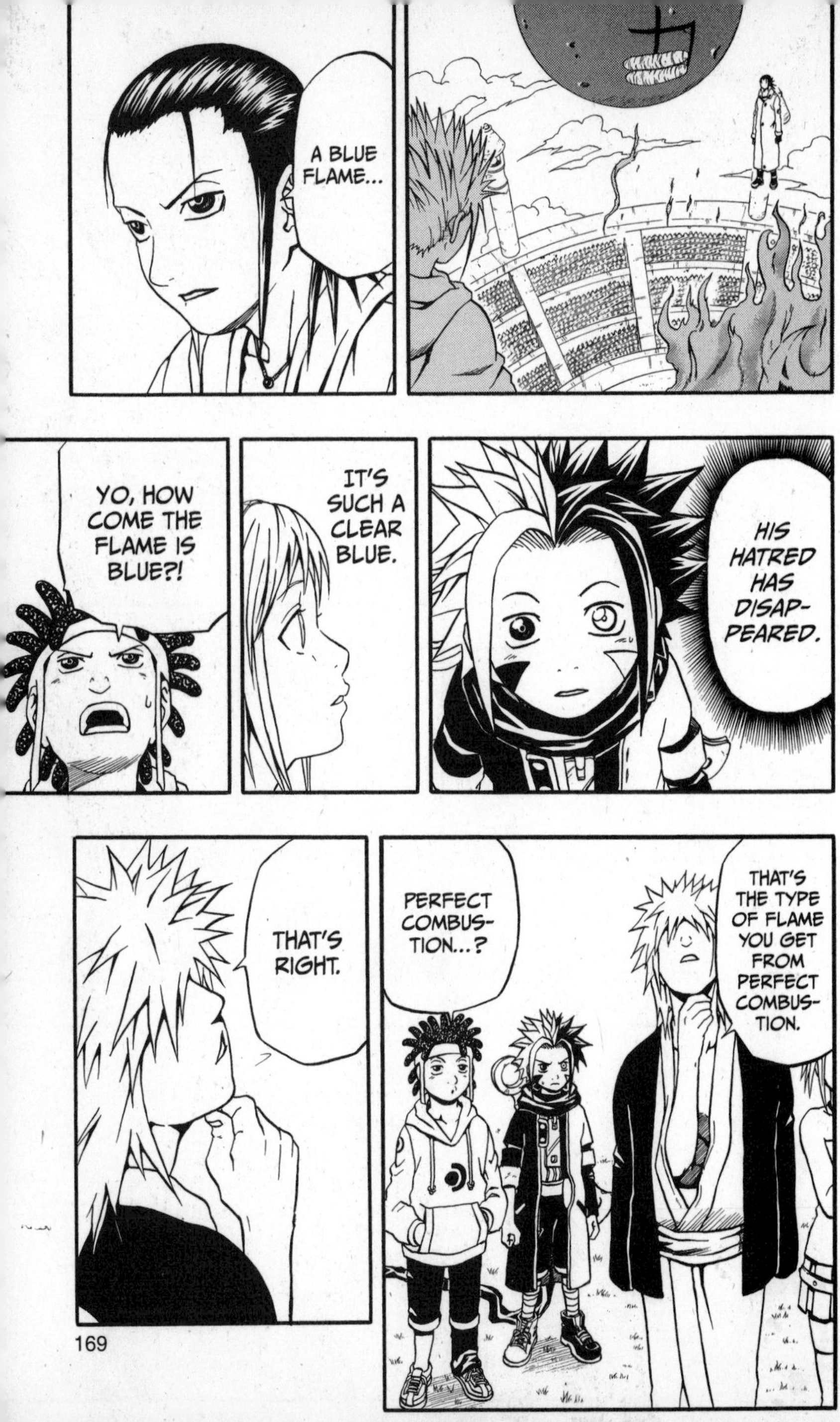
A BLUE FLAME...
HIS HATRED HAS DISAP-PEARED.
IT'S SUCH A CLEAR BLUE.
YO, HOW COME THE FLAME IS BLUE?!
THAT'S THE TYPE OF FLAME YOU GET FROM PERFECT COMBUS-TION.
PERFECT COMBUS-TION...?
THAT'S RIGHT.

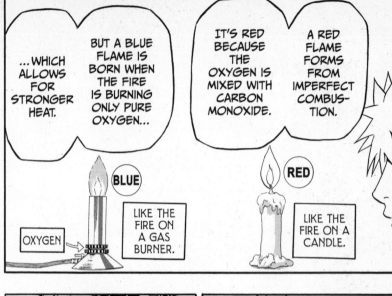

A RED FLAME FORMS FROM IMPERFECT COMBUSTION.
IT'S RED BECAUSE THE OXYGEN IS MIXED WITH CARBON MONOXIDE.
RED
LIKE THE FIRE ON A CANDLE.
BUT A BLUE FLAME IS BORN WHEN THE FIRE IS BURNING ONLY PURE OXYGEN...
...WHICH ALLOWS FOR STRONGER HEAT.
BLUE
LIKE THE FIRE ON A GAS BURNER.
OXYGEN
THE EFFECT OF THAT O-PART IS A NORMAL FLAME.
WHAT?
YO, YOU DO KNOW SOMETHING ABOUT THAT GUY, DON'T YOU?
HUH!
...
IF HE'S UPGRADING A NORMAL FLAME TO A BLUE FLAME...
...THEN HE'S AN EXTREMELY SKILLED O.P.T. THE QUALITY OF HIS SPIRIT MUST BE REALLY GOOD.

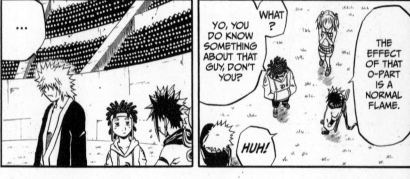

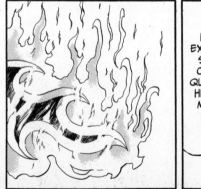

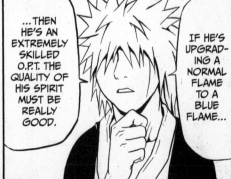

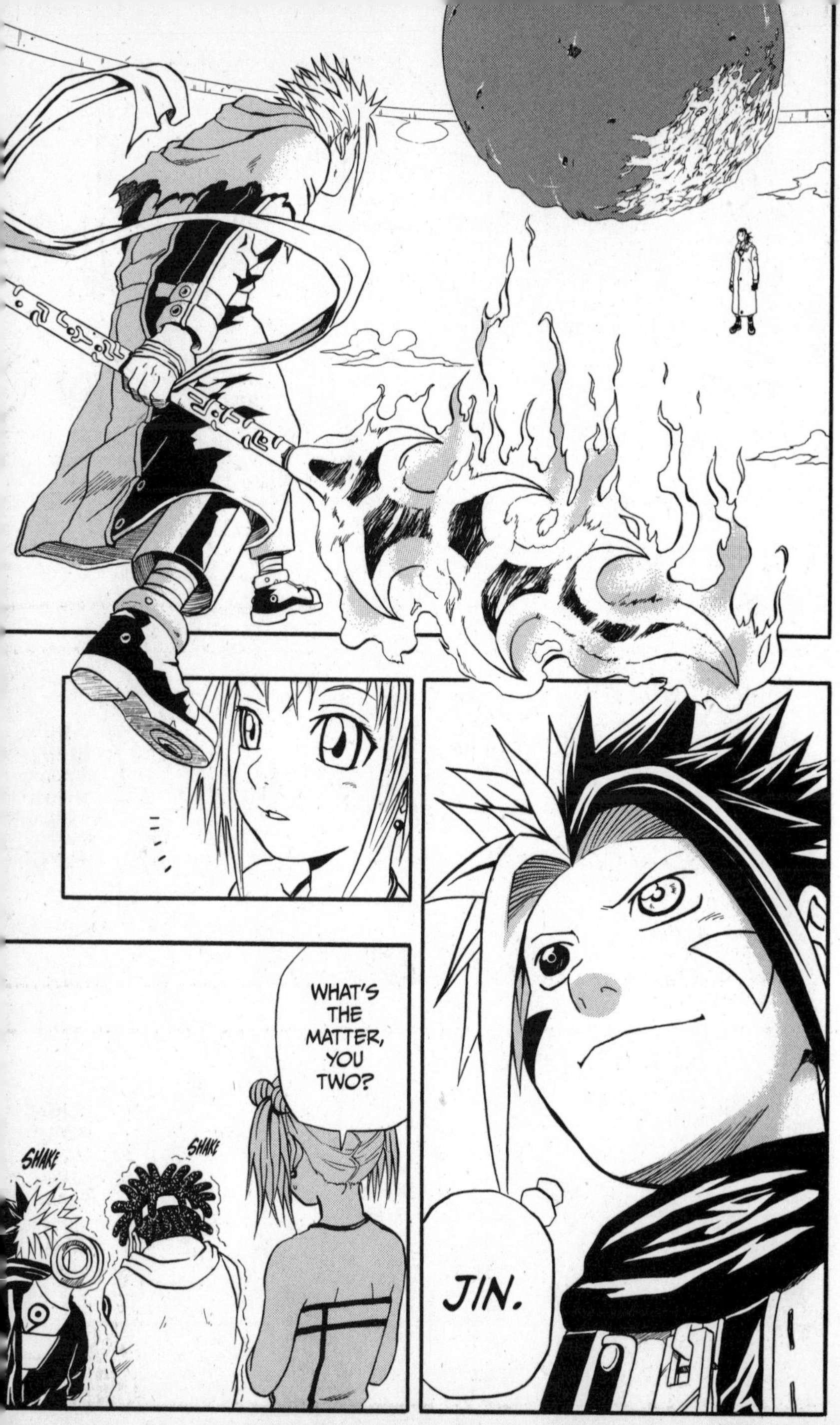
JIN.
WHAT'S THE MATTER, YOU TWO?
SHAKE
SHAKE

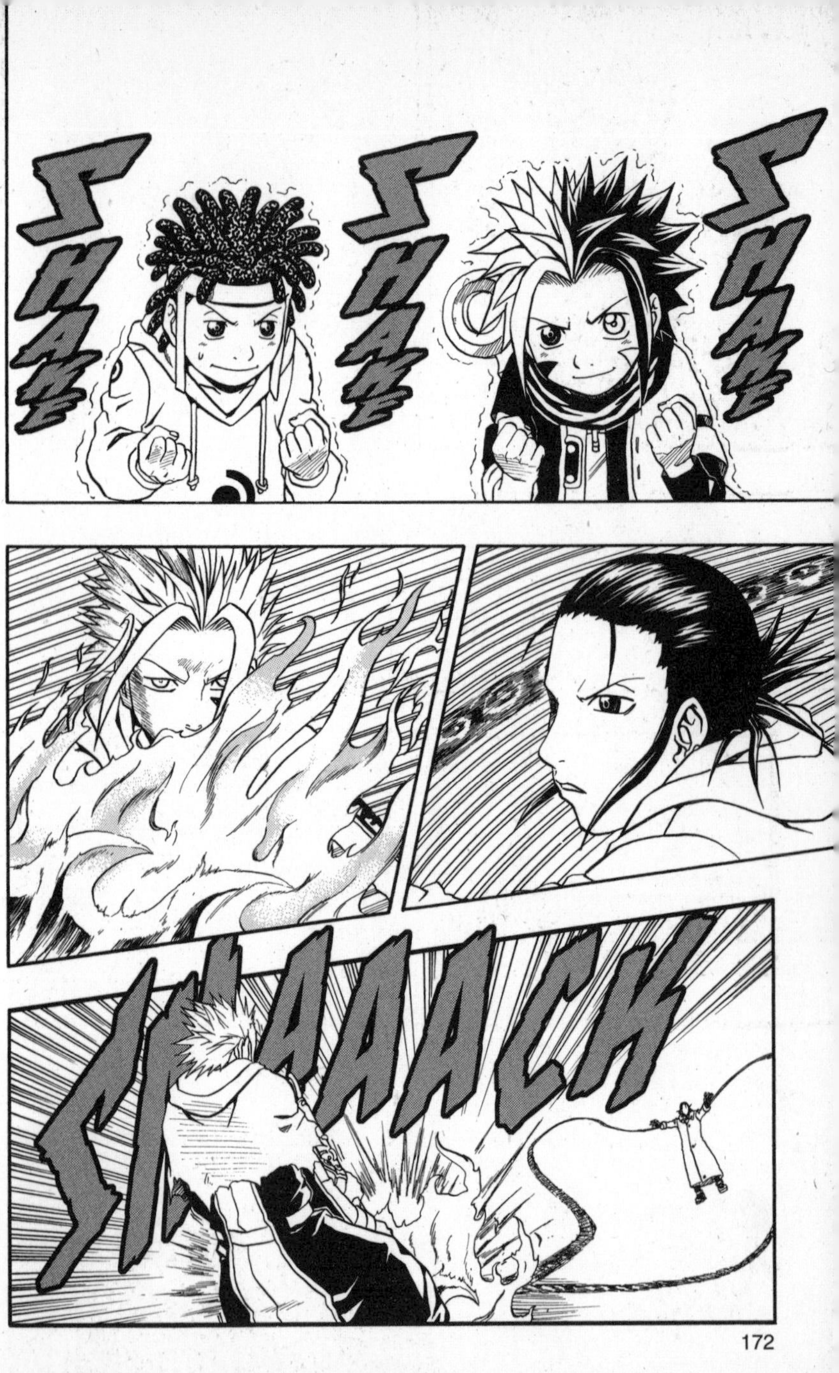
SHAKE
SHAKE
SHAKE
SHAAACH

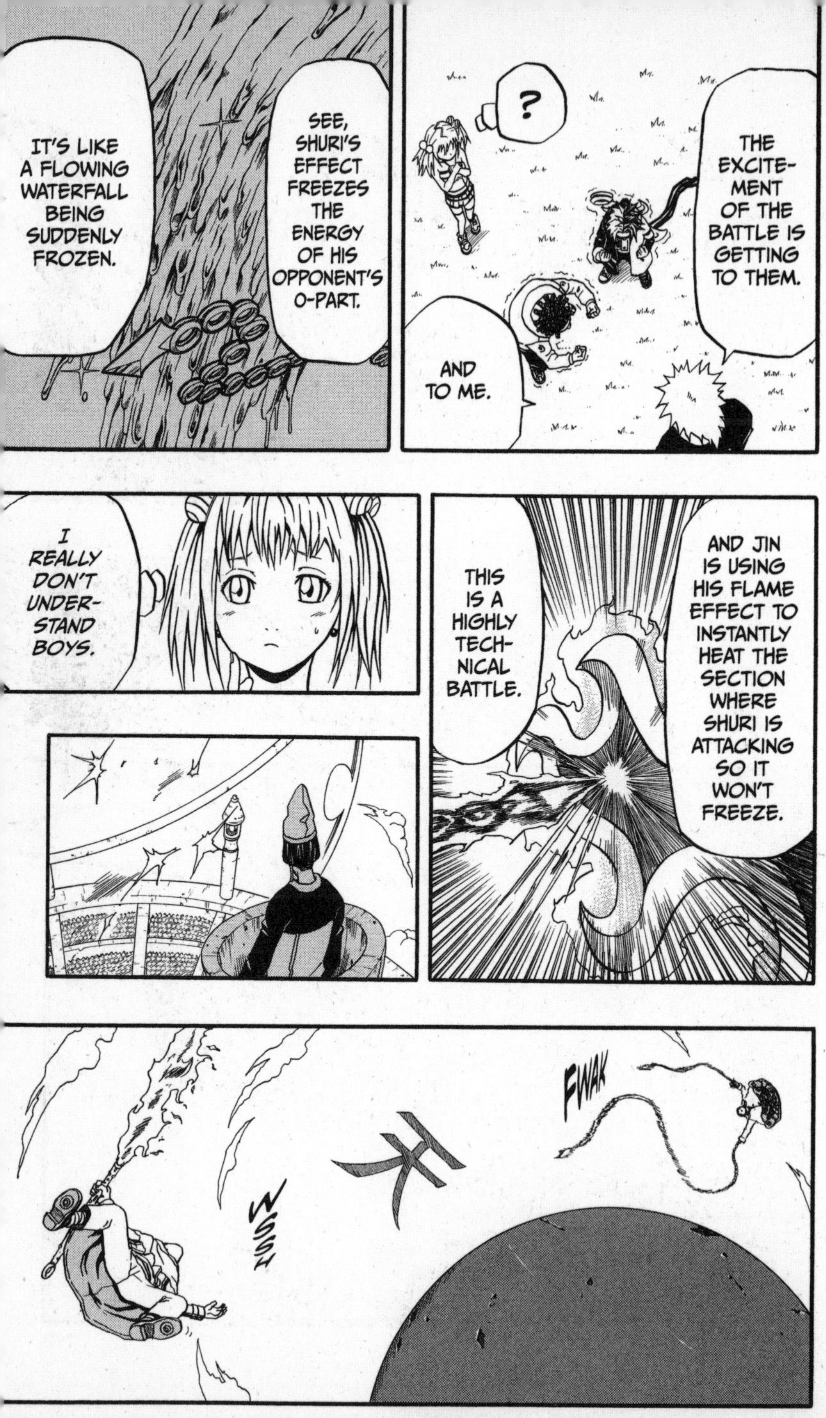
?
THE EXCITEMENT OF THE BATTLE IS GETTING TO THEM.
AND TO ME.
SEE, SHURI'S EFFECT FREEZES THE ENERGY OF HIS OPPONENT'S O-PART.
IT'S LIKE A FLOWING WATERFALL BEING SUDDENLY FROZEN.
AND JIN IS USING HIS FLAME EFFECT TO INSTANTLY HEAT THE SECTION WHERE SHURI IS ATTACKING SO IT WON'T FREEZE.
THIS IS A HIGHLY TECHNICAL BATTLE.
I REALLY DON'T UNDERSTAND BOYS.
FWAK
WSSH

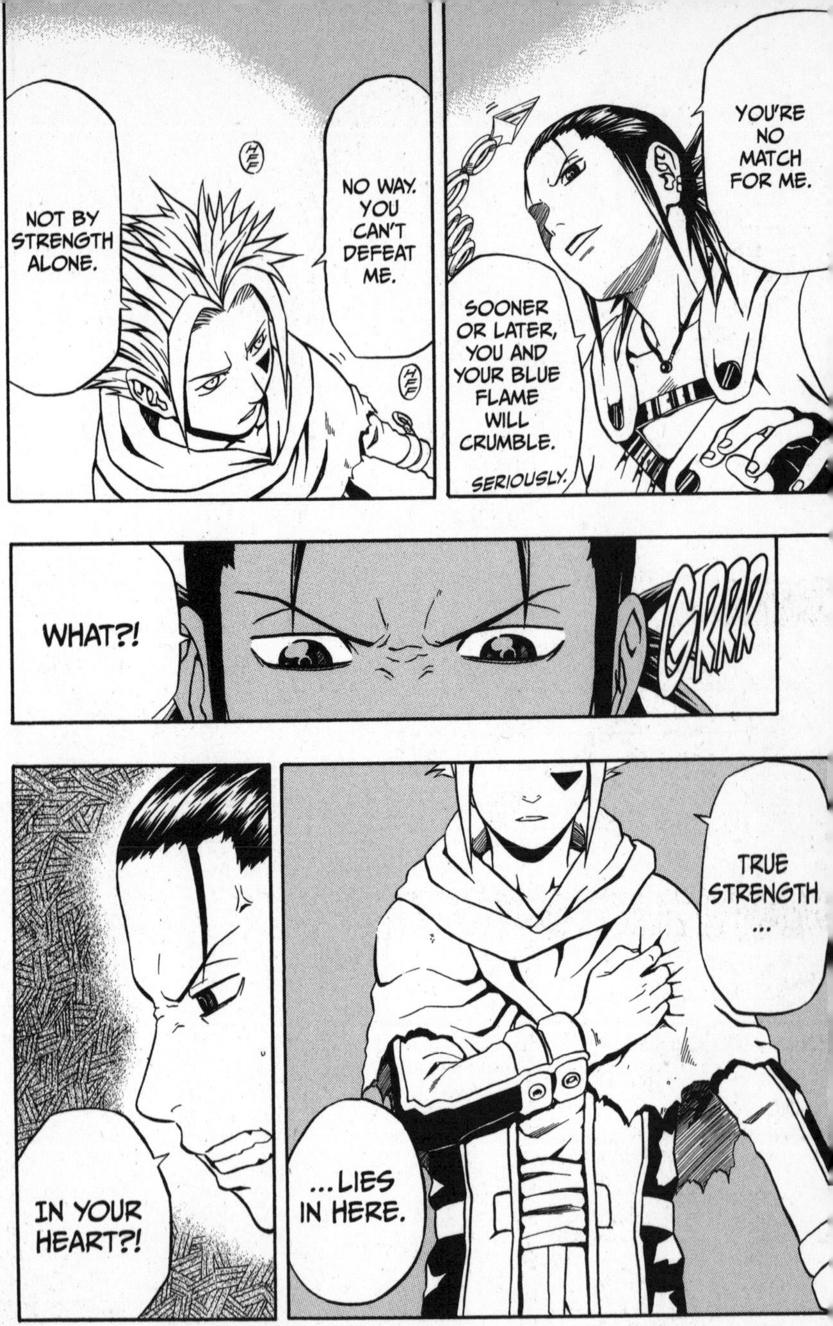
YOU'RE NO MATCH FOR ME.
SOONER OR LATER, YOU AND YOUR BLUE FLAME WILL CRUMBLE.
SERIOUSLY.
HEF
NO WAY. YOU CAN'T DEFEAT ME.
HEF
NOT BY STRENGTH ALONE.
GRRR
WHAT?!
TRUE STRENGTH ...
...LIES IN HERE.
IN YOUR HEART?!

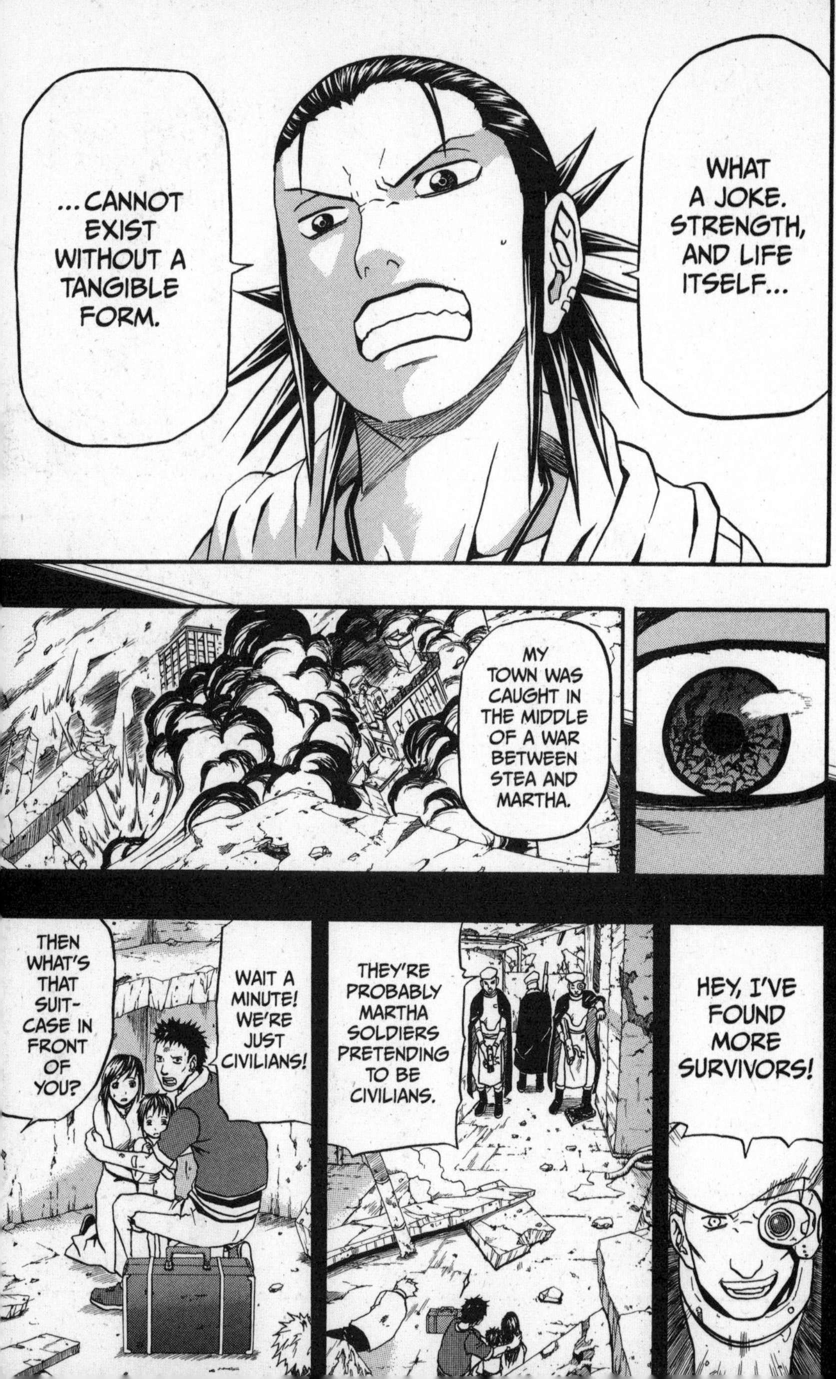
WHAT A JOKE. STRENGTH, AND LIFE ITSELF...
...CANNOT EXIST WITHOUT A TANGIBLE FORM.
MY TOWN WAS CAUGHT IN THE MIDDLE OF A WAR BETWEEN STEA AND MARTHA.
HEY, I'VE FOUND MORE SURVIVORS!
THEY'RE PROBABLY MARTHA SOLDIERS PRETENDING TO BE CIVILIANS.
WAIT A MINUTE! WE'RE JUST CIVILIANS!
THEN WHAT'S THAT SUIT-CASE IN FRONT OF YOU?

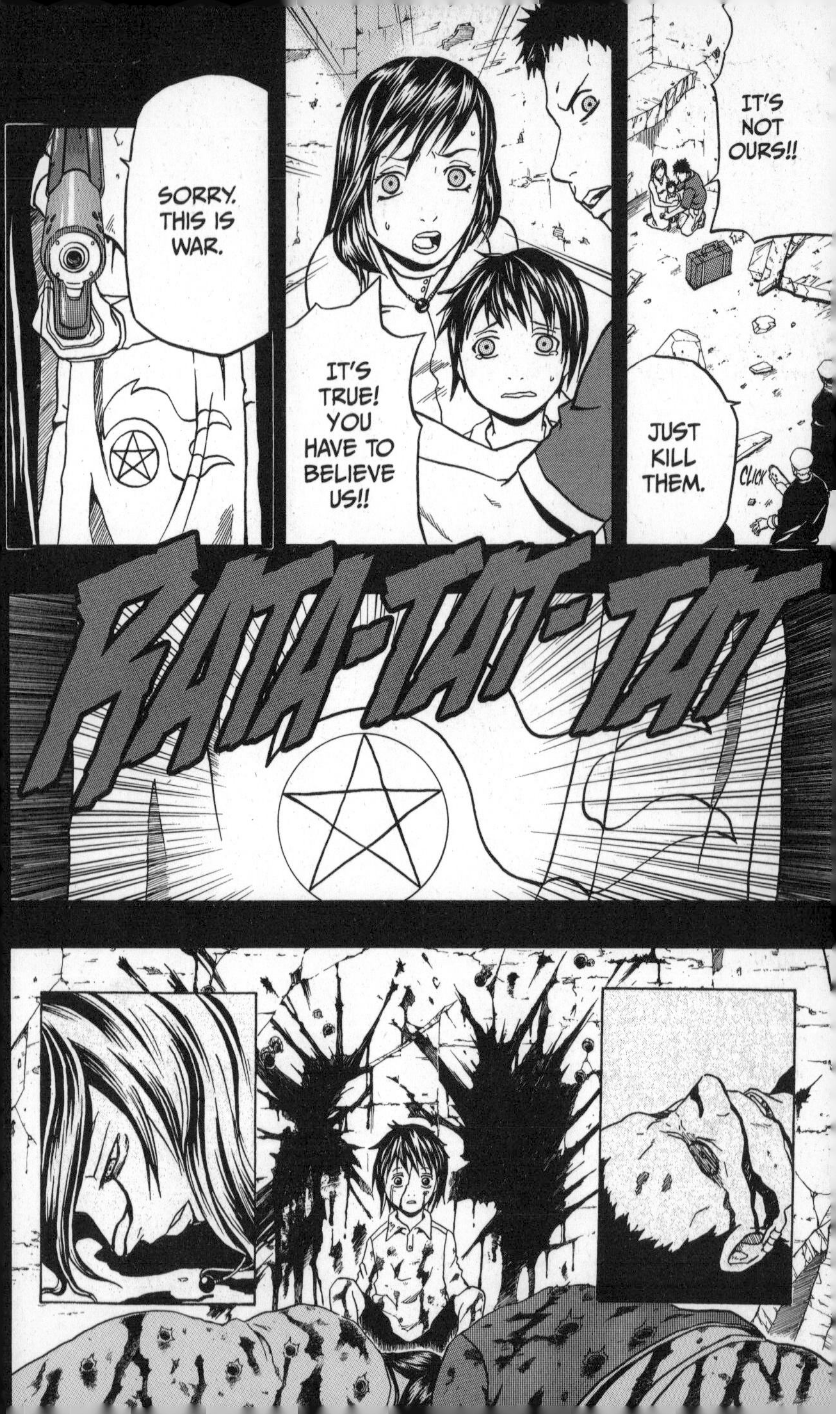
IT'S NOT OURS!!
JUST KILL THEM.
CLICK
IT'S TRUE! YOU HAVE TO BELIEVE US!!
SORRY. THIS IS WAR.
RATA-TAT-TAT

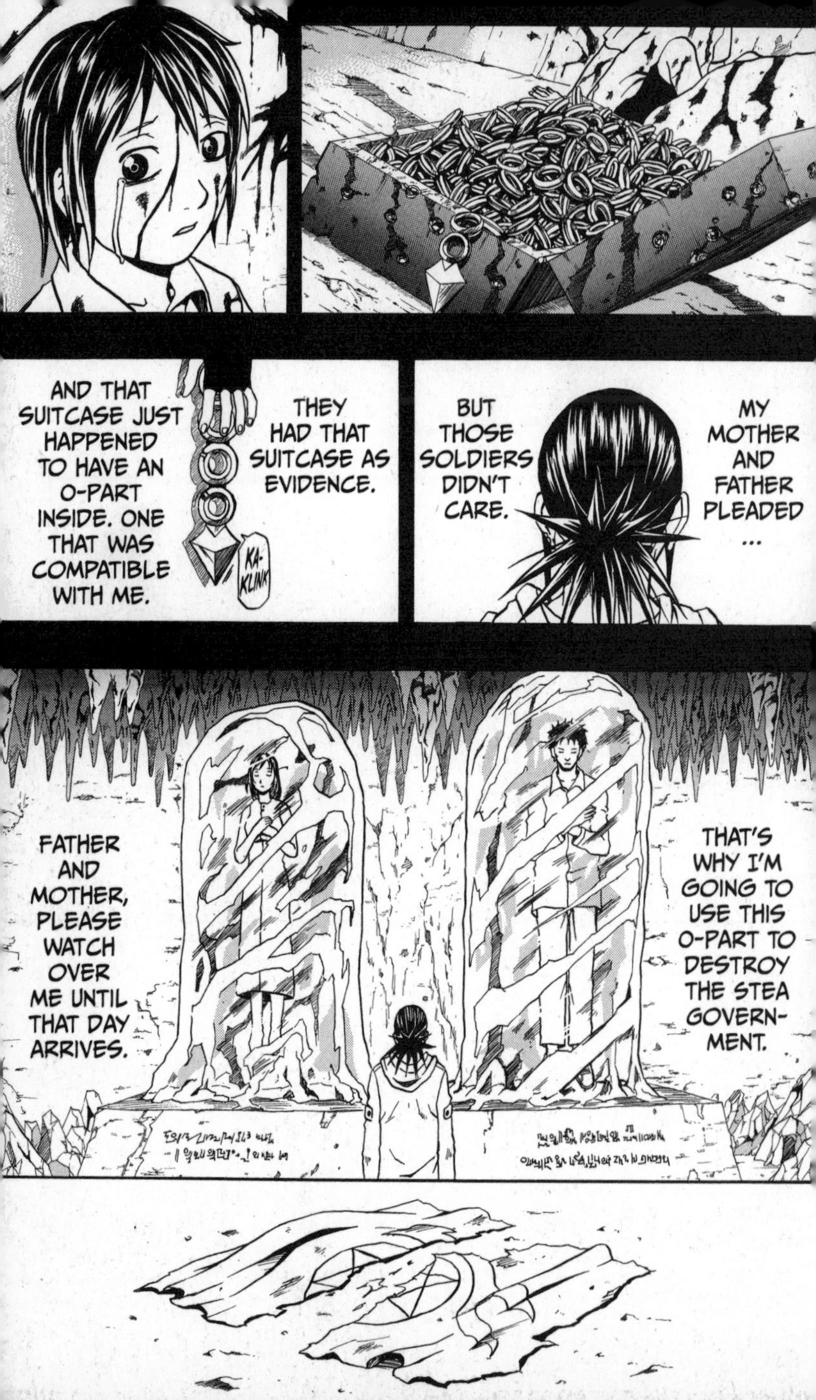
MY MOTHER AND FATHER PLEADED ...
BUT THOSE SOLDIERS DIDN'T CARE.
THEY HAD THAT SUITCASE AS EVIDENCE.
AND THAT SUITCASE JUST HAPPENED TO HAVE AN O-PART INSIDE. ONE THAT WAS COMPATIBLE WITH ME.
KA-KLINK
THAT'S WHY I'M GOING TO USE THIS O-PART TO DESTROY THE STEA GOVERN-MENT.
FATHER AND MOTHER, PLEASE WATCH OVER ME UNTIL THAT DAY ARRIVES.

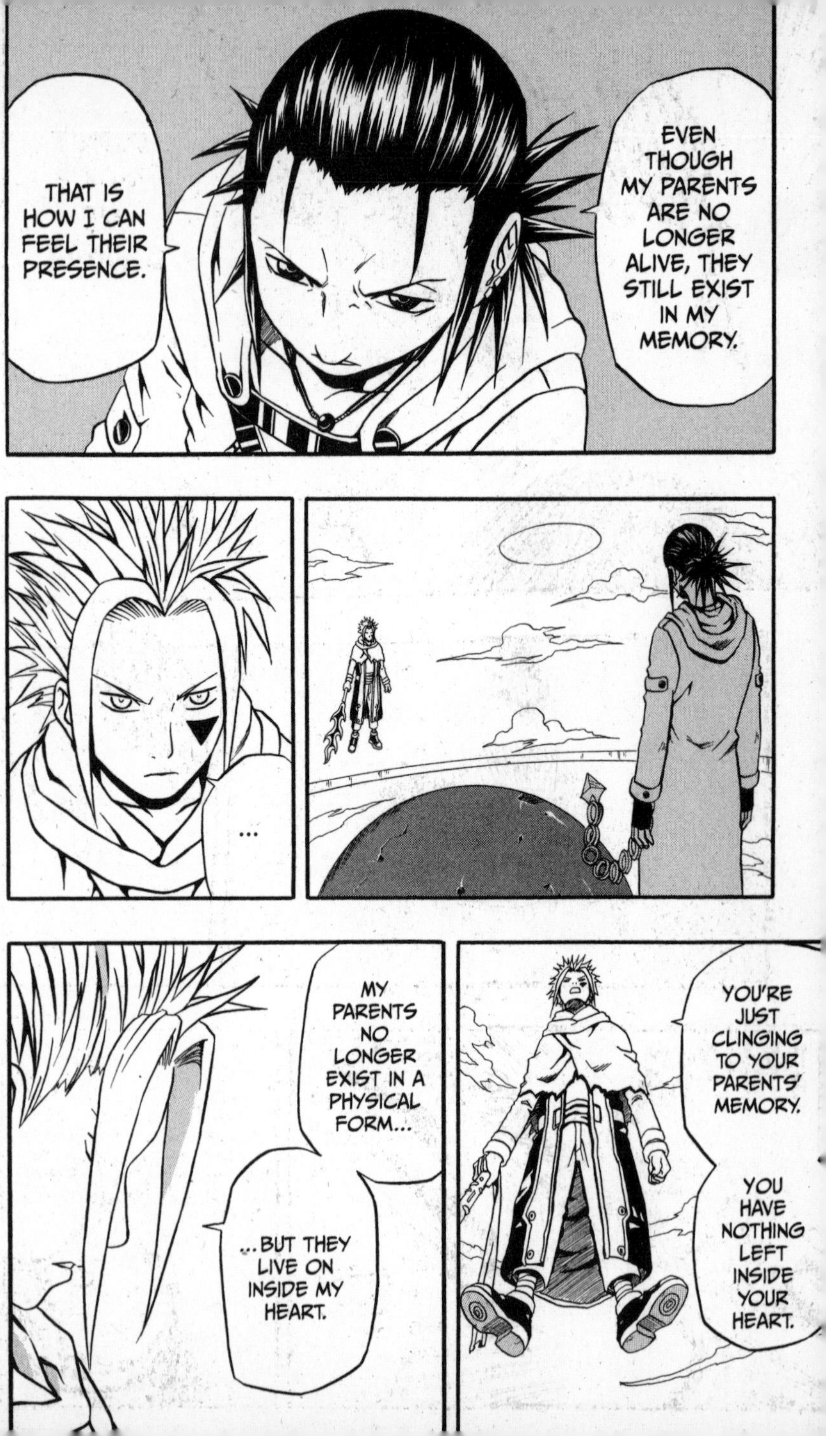
EVEN THOUGH MY PARENTS ARE NO LONGER ALIVE, THEY STILL EXIST IN MY MEMORY.
THAT IS HOW I CAN FEEL THEIR PRESENCE.
...
YOU'RE JUST CLINGING TO YOUR PARENTS' MEMORY.
YOU HAVE NOTHING LEFT INSIDE YOUR HEART.
MY PARENTS NO LONGER EXIST IN A PHYSICAL FORM...
...BUT THEY LIVE ON INSIDE MY HEART.

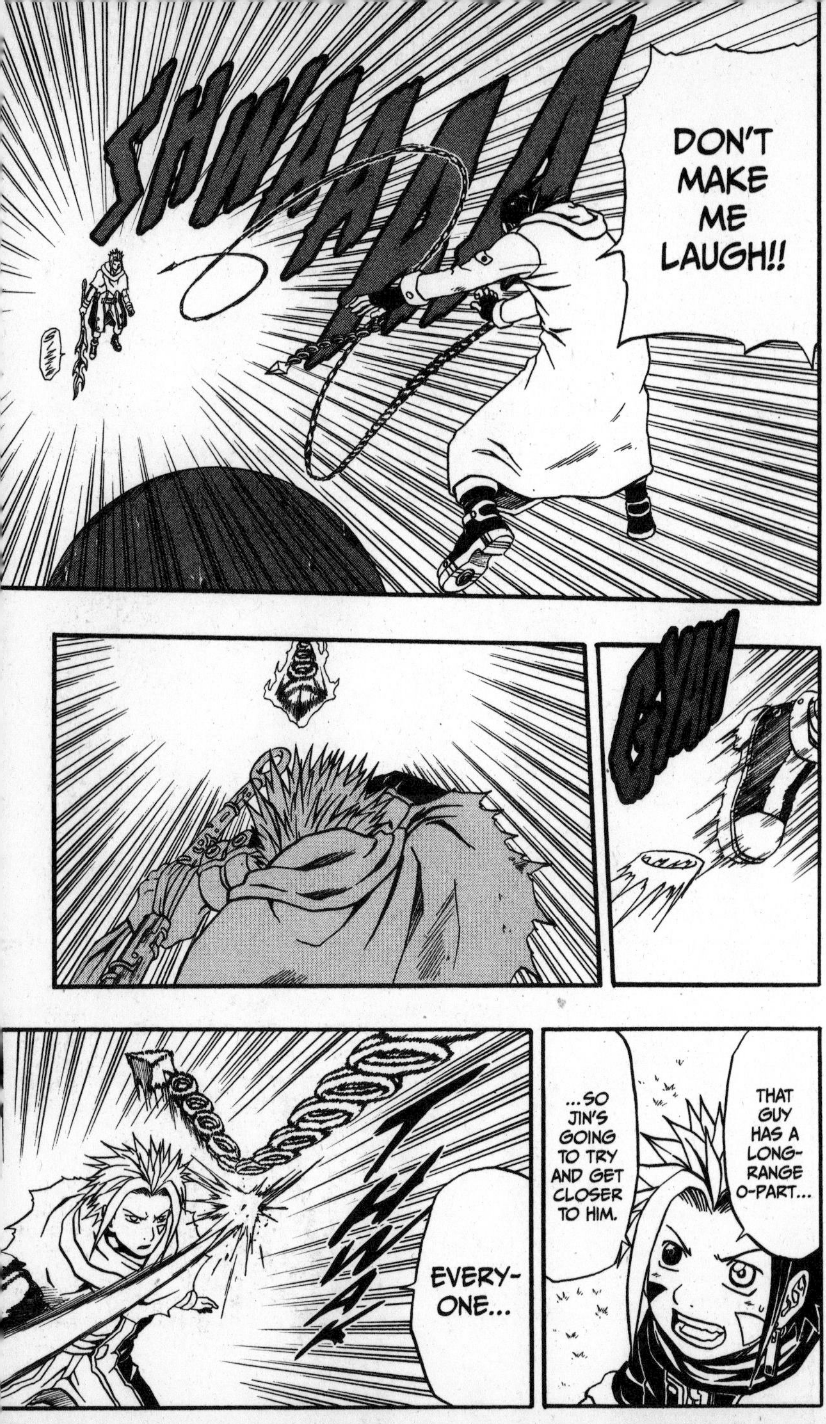
DON'T MAKE ME LAUGH!!
THAT GUY HAS A LONG-RANGE O-PART...
...SO JIN'S GOING TO TRY AND GET CLOSER TO HIM.
EVERY-ONE...

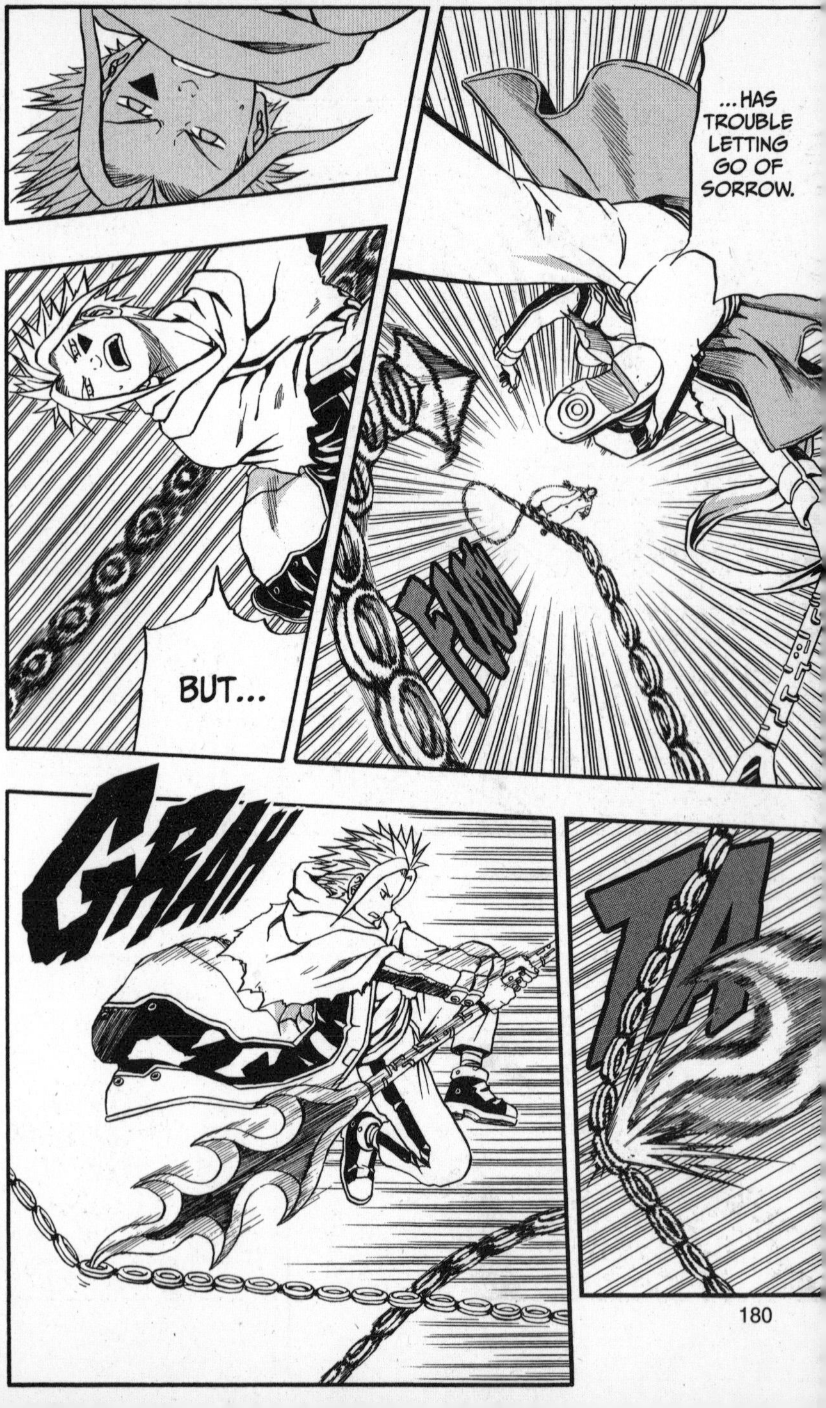
...HAS TROUBLE LETTING GO OF SORROW.
BUT...
GRAH

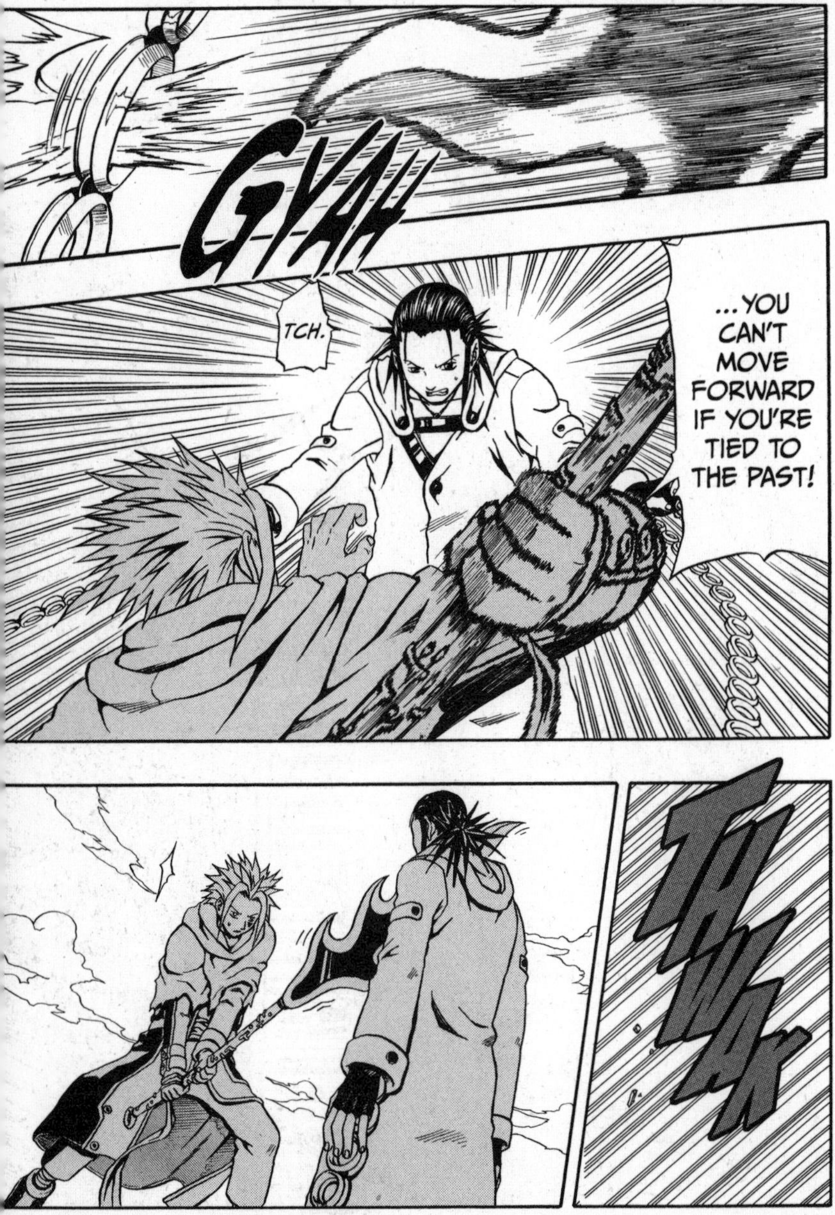
GYAH
...YOU CAN'T MOVE FORWARD IF YOU'RE TIED TO THE PAST!
TCH.
THWAK

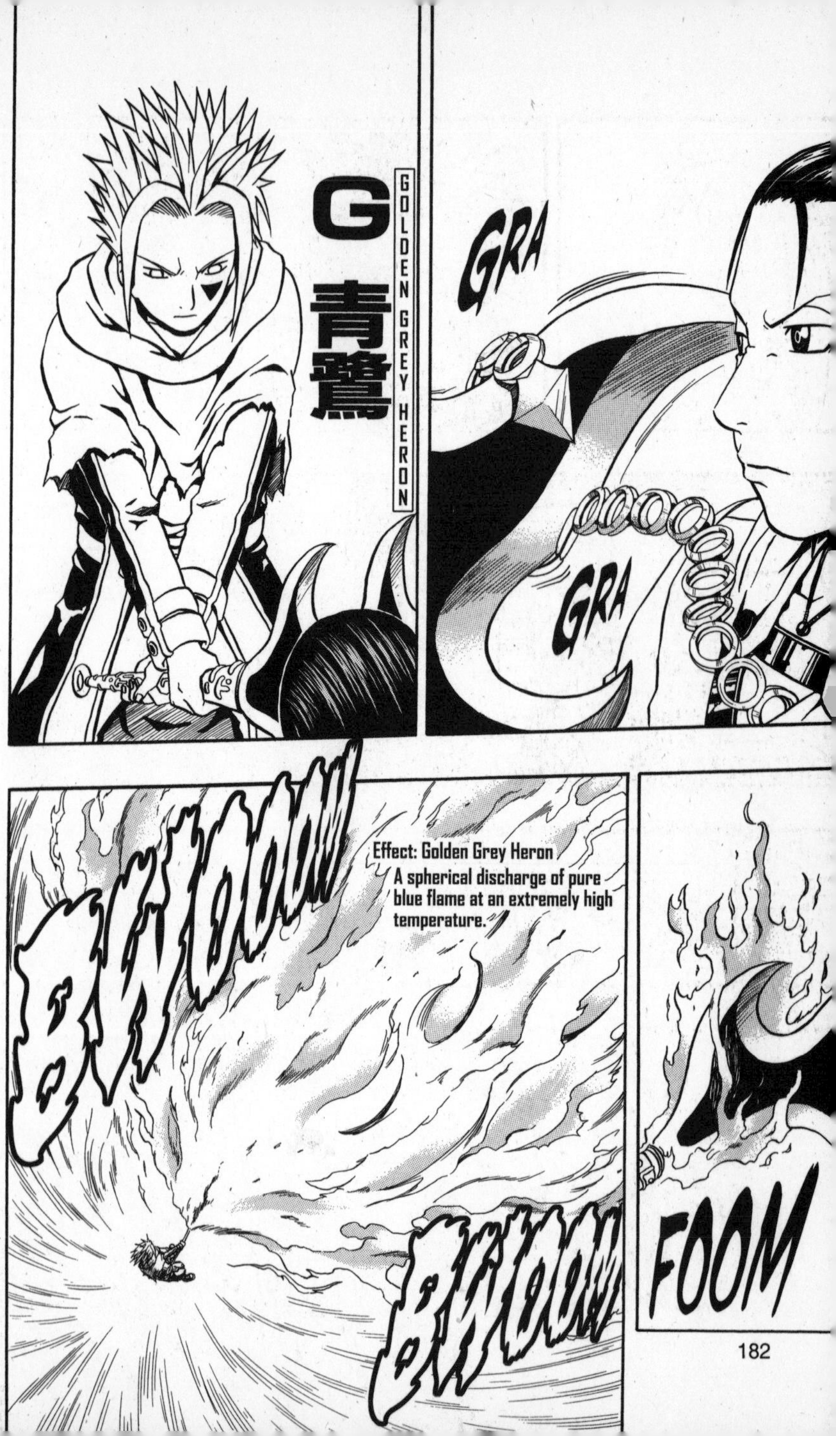
GRA
GRA
G 青鷺
GOLDEN GREY HERON
FOOM
Effect: Golden Grey Heron
A spherical discharge of pure blue flame at an extremely high temperature.

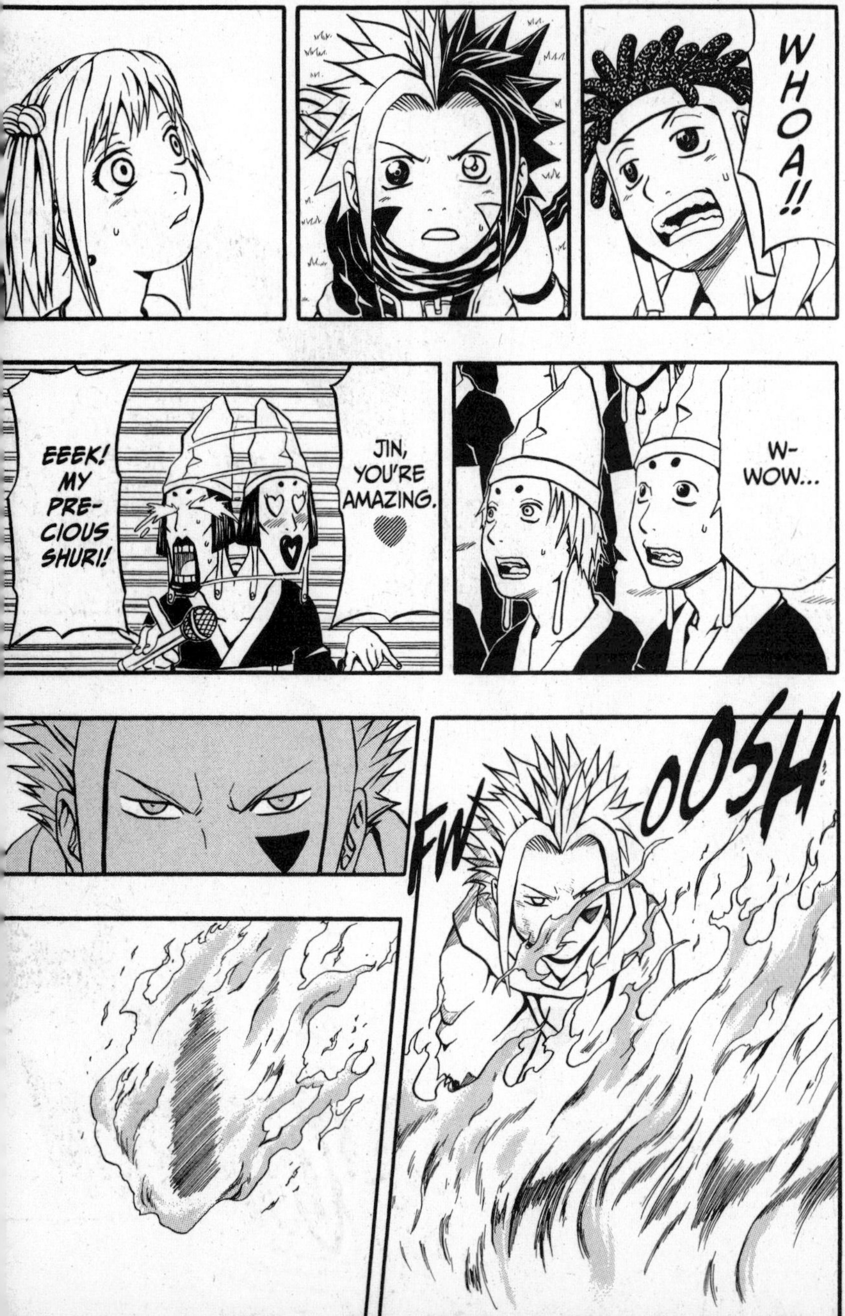
WHOA!!
W-WOW...
JIN, YOU'RE AMAZING.
EEEK! MY PRECIOUS SHURI!
FWOOSH

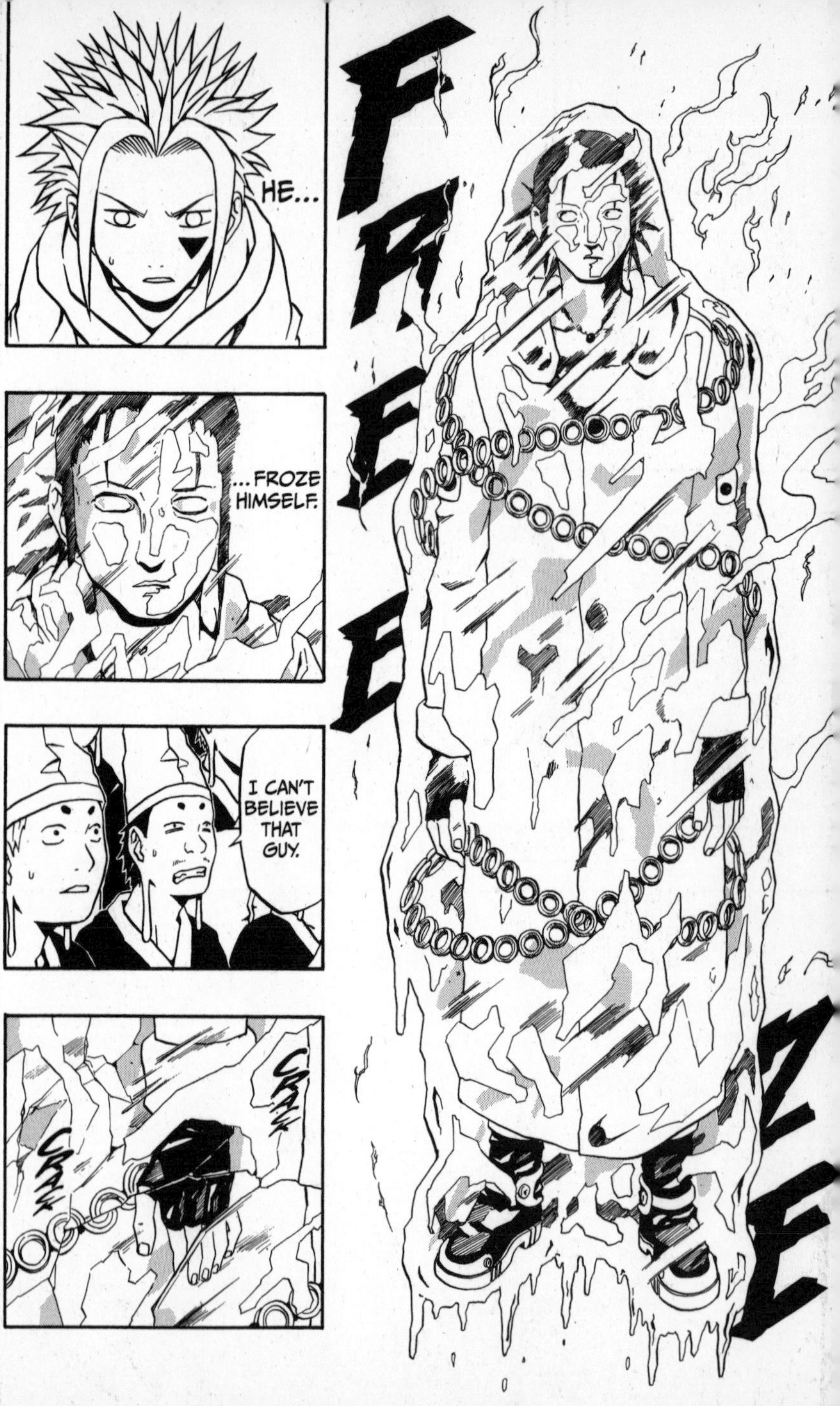
FREEZE
HE...
...FROZE HIMSELF.
I CAN'T BELIEVE THAT GUY.
CRAK
CRAK

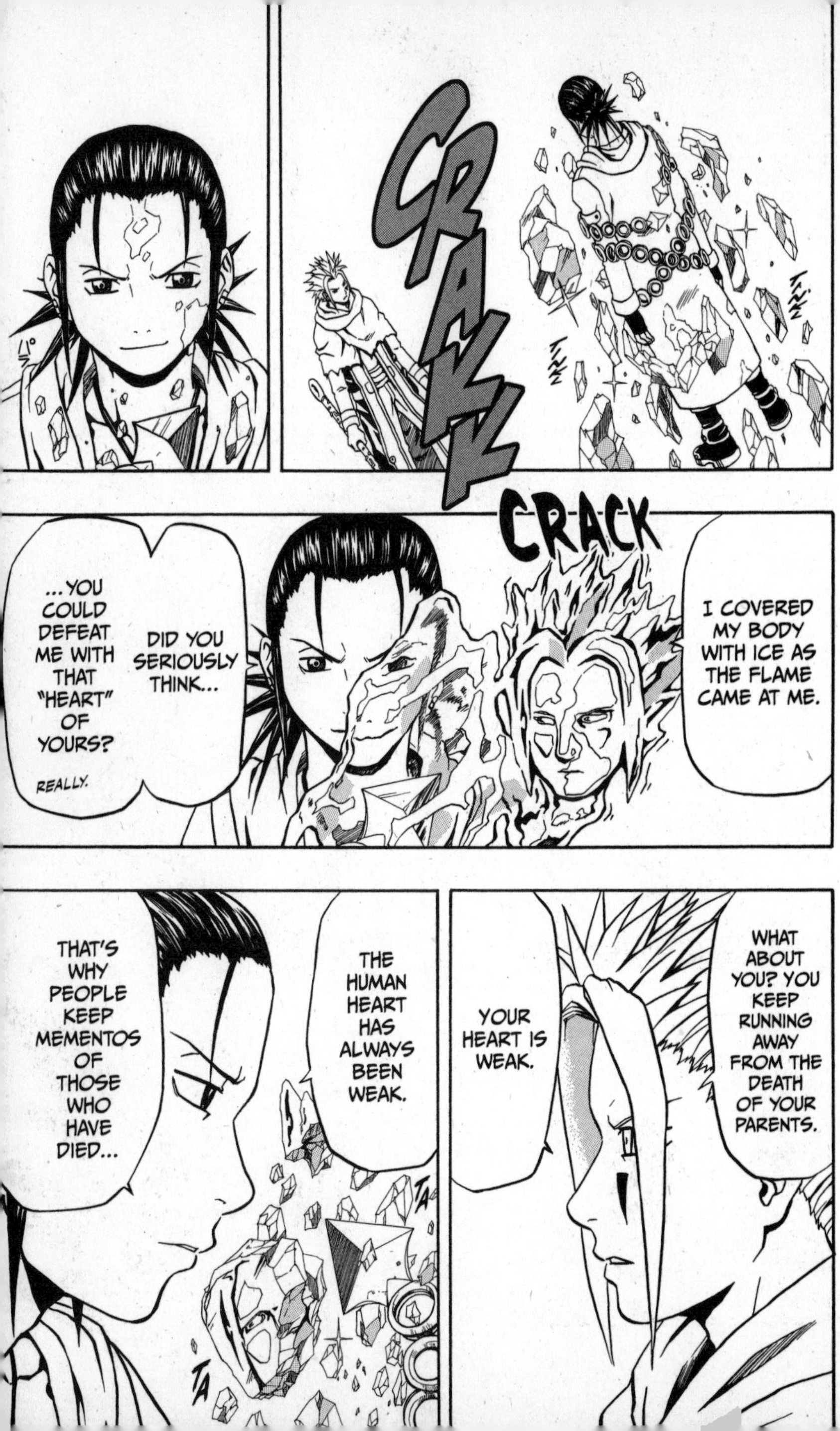
CRACK
I COVERED MY BODY WITH ICE AS THE FLAME CAME AT ME.
DID YOU SERIOUSLY THINK...
...YOU COULD DEFEAT ME WITH THAT "HEART" OF YOURS?
REALLY.
WHAT ABOUT YOU? YOU KEEP RUNNING AWAY FROM THE DEATH OF YOUR PARENTS.
YOUR HEART IS WEAK.
THE HUMAN HEART HAS ALWAYS BEEN WEAK.
THAT'S WHY PEOPLE KEEP MEMENTOS OF THOSE WHO HAVE DIED...
TA
TA

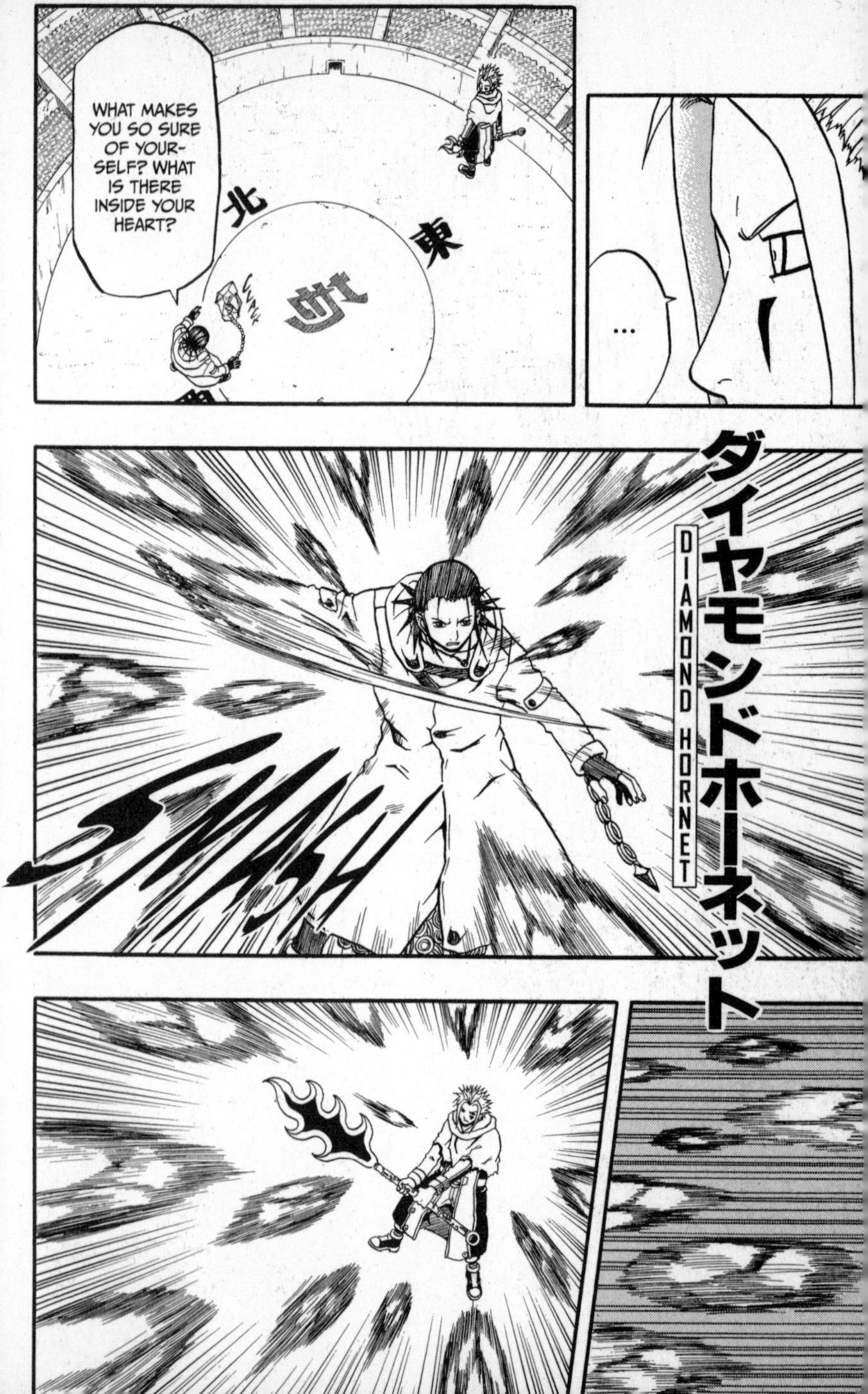
...
WHAT MAKES YOU SO SURE OF YOUR-SELF? WHAT IS THERE INSIDE YOUR HEART?
北
東
ダイヤモンドホーネット
DIAMOND HORNET
SMASH

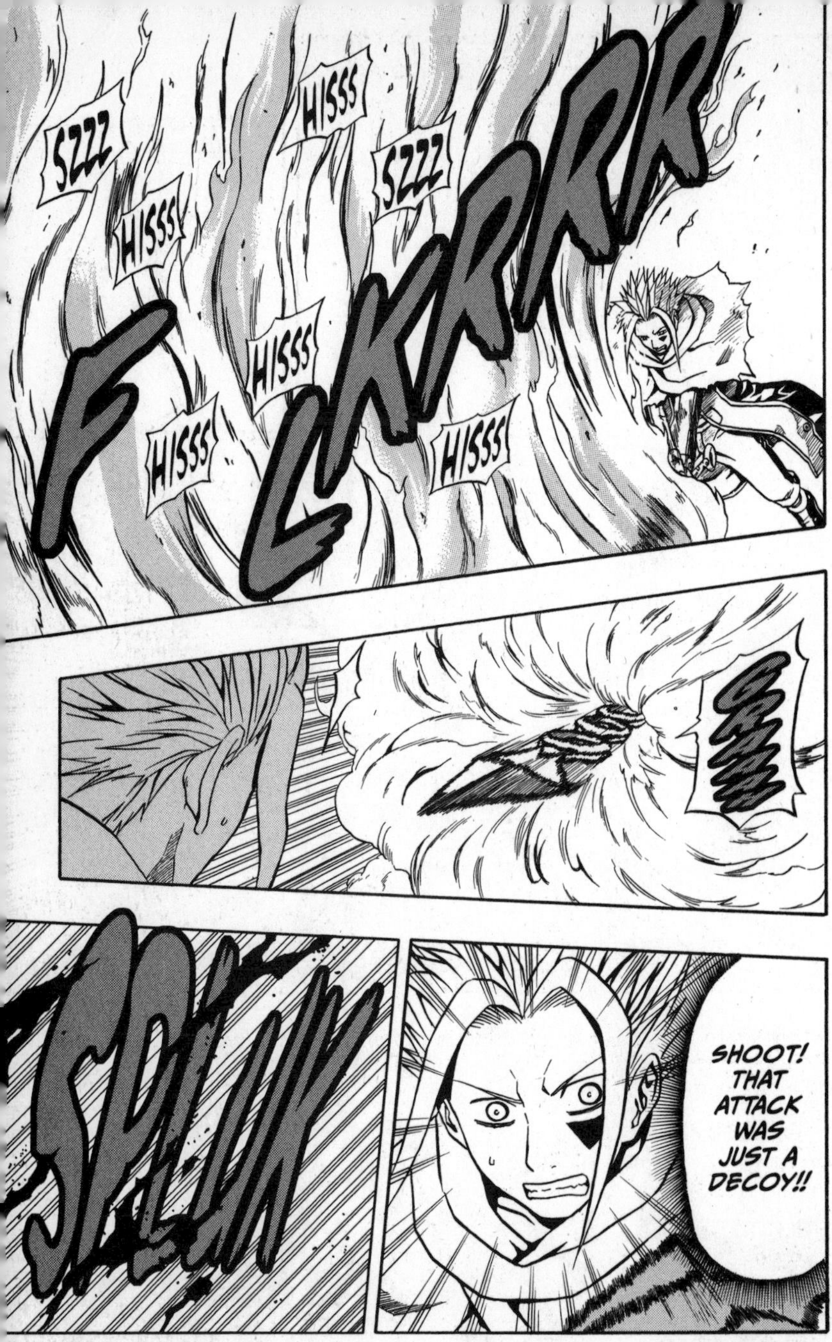
HISSS
SZZZ
SZZZ
HISSS
HISSS
HISSS
HISSS
SHOOT! THAT ATTACK WAS JUST A DECOY!!

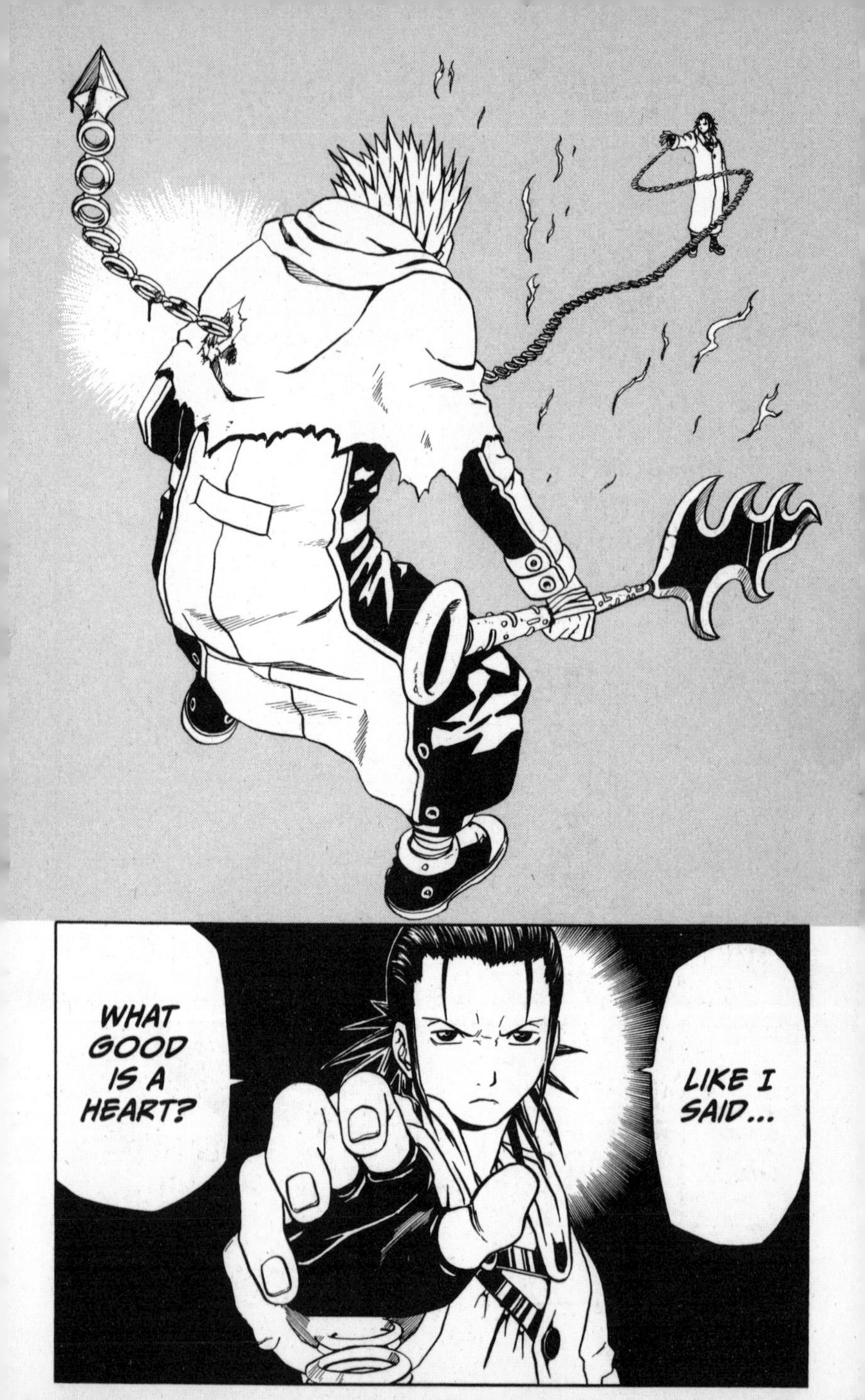
LIKE I SAID...
WHAT GOOD IS A HEART?

SEISHI AND THE GAS STATION

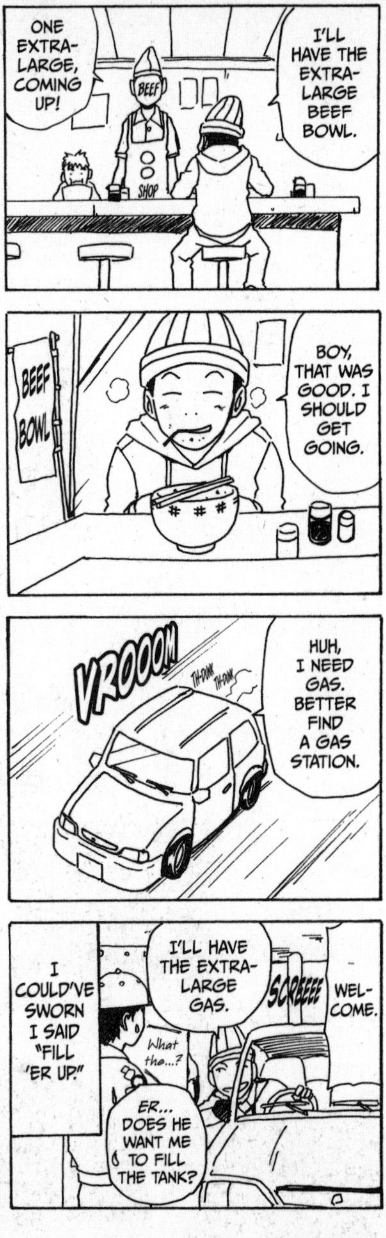
I'LL HAVE THE EXTRA-LARGE BEEF BOWL.
ONE EXTRA-LARGE, COMING UP!
BEEF
SHOP
BOY, THAT WAS GOOD. I SHOULD GET GOING.
BEEF BOWL
HUH, I NEED GAS. BETTER FIND A GAS STATION.
TH-DUNK TH-DUNK
VROOOM
WEL-COME.
SCREEEE
I'LL HAVE THE EXTRA-LARGE GAS.
What the...?
I COULD'VE SWORN I SAID "FILL 'ER UP."
ER... DOES HE WANT ME TO FILL THE TANK?

SEISHI AND THE FEMALE TEACHER

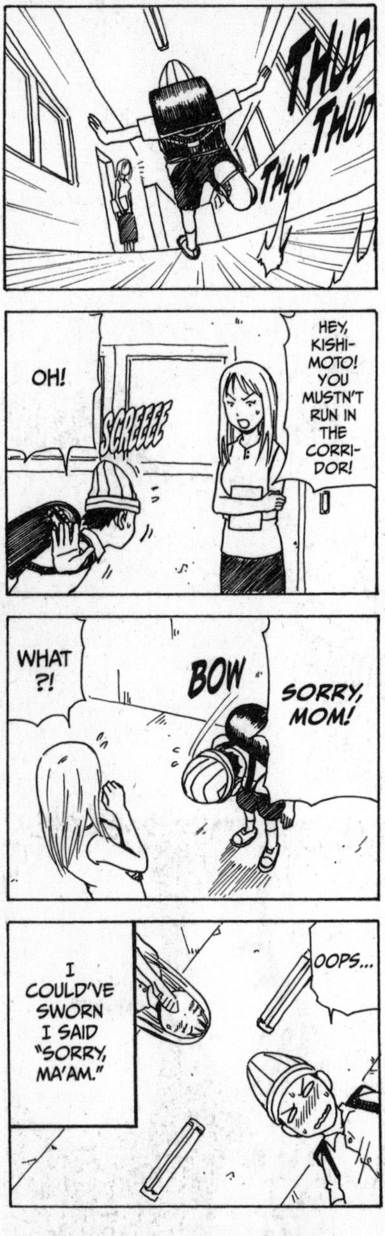
THUD THUD THUD
HEY, KISHI-MOTO! YOU MUSTN'T RUN IN THE CORRI-DOR!
SCREEEEE
OH!
SORRY, MOM!
BOW
WHAT ?!
OOPS...
I COULD'VE SWORN I SAID "SORRY, MA'AM."

O—Parts CATALOGUE⑩

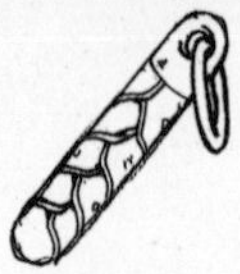

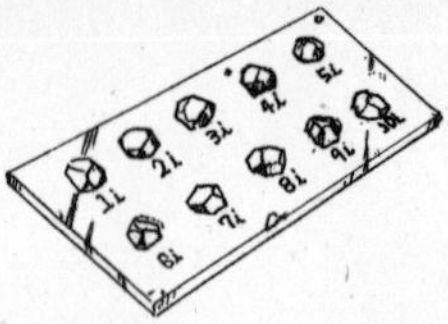

O-PART: SKULL
O-PART RANK: E
EFFECT: ?

A DEVIL DETECTOR CREATED FROM THE FRAGMENTS OF THE REVERSE KABBALAH.

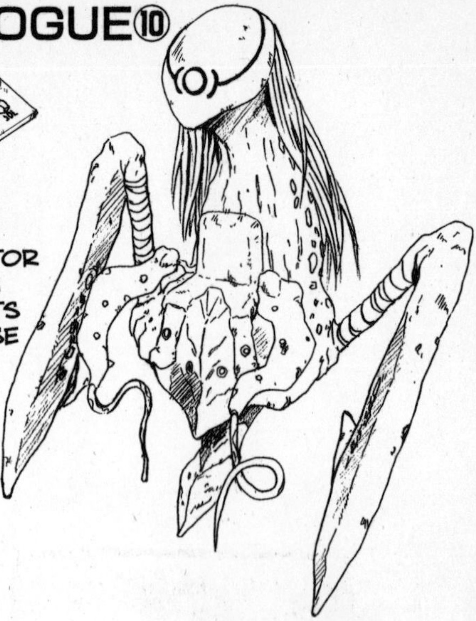

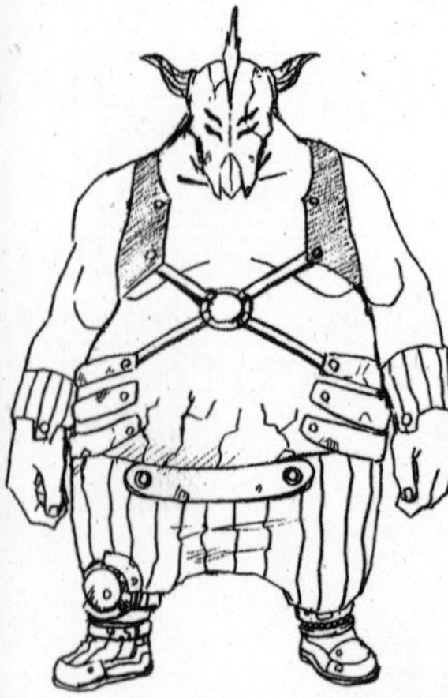

O-PART: MEE
O-PART RANK: B
EFFECT: POISONOUS GAS S.E.P.
HIS BODY IS AN O-PART. HE WEARS A BONE GAS MASK SO HE WON'T BREATHE IN HIS OWN POISONOUS GAS.

O-PART: VIRAIA
O-PART RANK: A
EFFECT: ① ACID
② HIGH-SPEED MOVEMENT.
NUMEROUS O.P.T.S HAVE BEEN EATEN BY VIRAIA WHILE TRYING TO USE IT.

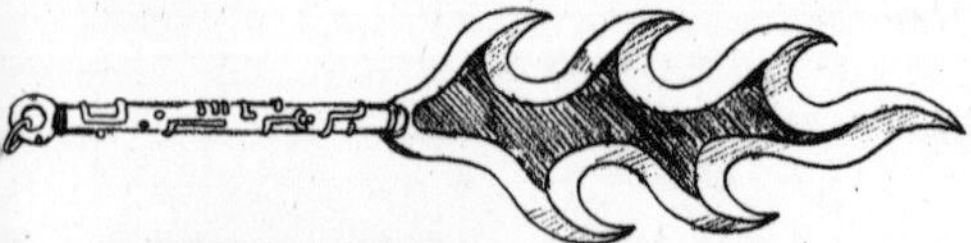

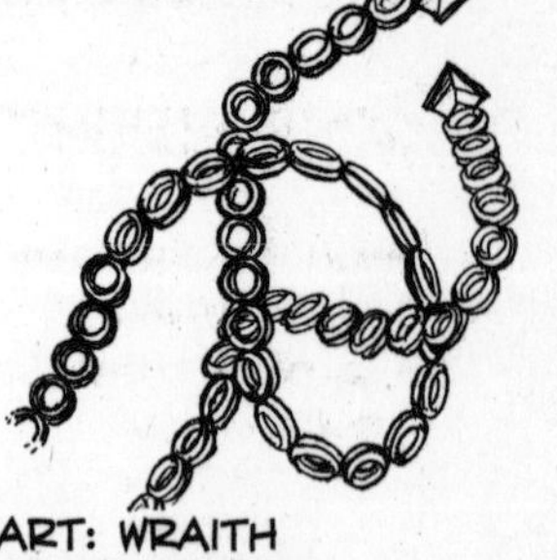

O-PART: ASHURA
O-PART RANK: B
EFFECT: FLAME
IT CHANGED AS JIN'S SPIRIT CLEARED, MAKING ITS EFFECT A SUPERIOR BLUE FLAME.

O-PART: WRAITH
O-PART RANK: B
EFFECT: ① FROST
② HANDLING (MANIPULATION)
AN EXTREMELY STRONG O-PART WITH SHARP BLADED CHAINS. THE FROST EFFECT IS ONLY USED IN EXTREME SITUATIONS.

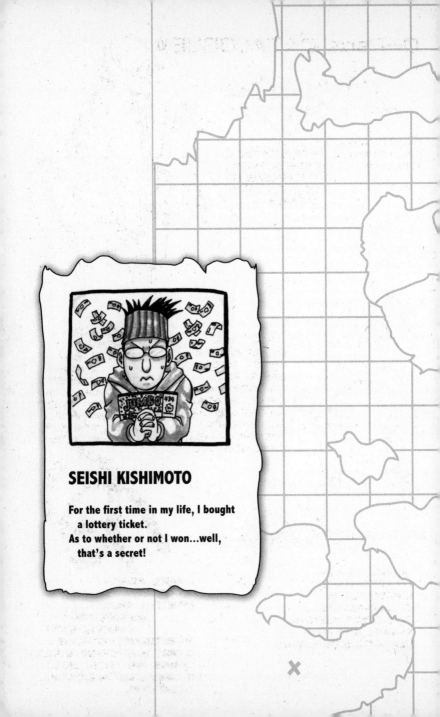

SEISHI KISHIMOTO

For the first time in my life, I bought
    a lottery ticket.
As to whether or not I won...well,
    that's a secret!

O-Parts HUNTER 10

VIZ Media Edition
STORY AND ART BY SEISHI KISHIMOTO

English Adaptation/Tetsuichiro Miyaki
Touch-up Art & Lettering/Gia Cam Luc
Design/Andrea Rice
Editor/Carol Fox

Editor in Chief, Books/Alvin Lu
Editor in Chief, Magazines/Marc Weidenbaum
VP of Publishing Licensing/Rika Inouye
VP of Sales/Gonzalo Ferreyra
Sr. VP of Marketing/Liza Coppola
Publisher/Hyoe Narita

© 2005 Seishi Kishimoto/SQUARE ENIX. All rights reserved. First published in Japan in 2005 by SQUARE ENIX CO., LTD. English translation rights arranged with SQUARE ENIX CO., LTD. and VIZ Media, LLC. The stories, characters and incidents mentioned in this publication are entirely fictional.

Printed in the U.S.A.

Published by VIZ Media, LLC
P.O. Box 77010
San Francisco, CA 94107

10 9 8 7 6 5 4 3 2 1
First printing, June 2008

www.viz.com   store.viz.com